15.00

St. John's

August 1983

WITHDRAWN

D1325418

R35117F0577

OXFORD STUDIES IN AFRICAN AFFAIRS

*General Editors*
JOHN D. HARGREAVES *and* GEORGE SHEPPERSON

# THE ADMINISTRATION OF NIGERIA 1900–1960

# THE ADMINISTRATION OF NIGERIA 1900–1960

*Men, Methods, and Myths*

BY
I. F. NICOLSON

CLARENDON PRESS · OXFORD

*Oxford University Press, Walton Street, Oxford OX2 6DP*

OXFORD LONDON GLASGOW
NEW YORK TORONTO MELBOURNE WELLINGTON
IBADAN NAIROBI DAR ES SALAAM LUSAKA CAPE TOWN
KUALA LUMPUR SINGAPORE JAKARTA HONG KONG TOKYO
DELHI BOMBAY CALCUTTA MADRAS KARACHI

ISBN 0 19 821652 1

© OXFORD UNIVERSITY PRESS 1969

*First published 1969*
*Reprinted 1977*

*Printed in Great Britain by*
*Lowe & Brydone Printers Limited, Thetford, Norfolk*

# PREFACE

THE idea of a book on the development of the public services and of public administration in Nigeria was first suggested to me by a friend and former administrative service colleague, not long before Nigerian independence. It was to be a fairly simple, straightforward and (necessarily) sanguine description, from the inside, by a serving administrator familiar with both the old colonial service machinery and with the then new machinery of federal and regional ministerial government, and with the process of transformation from the one to the other. It was to be a book of practical use to Nigerians and others in, or interested in, Nigerian government. At the same time, we both thought it might serve to put right some prevalent misconceptions about the past.

It proved impossible for me, while still in the federal public service, to do more than a few months of preliminary reading during vacation leaves in the United Kingdom; but even this was enough to show that there could be no simple account which would not also be superficial, or misleading, or both. So it was not until after retirement from Nigeria in 1962, and the award of a Simon Research Fellowship at the University of Manchester, that the opportunity came for full-time study and for reflection on some of the biggest puzzles demanding attention before adequate sense could be made of Nigerian administrative history. What had made the administrations of North and South so different from the beginning? What kept them so different, even half a century after their supposed amalgamation? What kind of men had the founders been, what had they been trying to do? Was it planned, or unplanned activity? How was the past still affecting the present?

There are many other intertwined puzzles. The attempt to unravel some of them offered in this book may make rather surprising and complicated reading, in particular, the parts which deal with the Lugard legend. But I think it has been possible to retain, in the rest of the book, a certain simplicity, by keeping to the theme of the administrators from 1900 to 1960 (who were never numerous) and to their most salient problems; by not attempting detailed description of the administered territories and peoples; and by looking towards the main centres of the changing administrative apparatus rather than towards the periphery of provincial and district administration.

The account is on the whole one of honest and straightforward stewardship of the estate. In recent years, the words 'administration' and 'administrator' have acquired new meanings and nuances of meaning. It is one of the original senses of the word 'administrator' which seems to fit best the British colonial service role in Nigeria: that is, the concept of men appointed as trustees or stewards of an estate during the minority or legal incapacity of its rightful owners, expected to do a good job and to give a regular and honest account. It is a simple enough theme that nearly all of Nigeria's colonial administrators did just this, according to their various lights; it becomes more complicated when Lugard has to be regarded as a major exception, in both ideas and actions.

I have also sought simplicity by avoiding detailed discussion of the growing theoretical literature on such themes as colonialism, decolonization, and patterns or processes of political socialization and mobilization. This book is not an analysis of government in terms of systems and sub-systems, or of structures and functions, nor does it deal with organization, administration, or development in a very scientific way. The interactions of persons and the unfolding of events in Nigerian government and politics, as seen partly from the inside and partly from archives and published sources for the earlier decades, do not seem to fit very well into any of the formal theoretical frameworks known to me. A failure either to make fact and theory fit, or to demonstrate fully their incompatibilities, may be my own fault, just as any other errors and omissions in the book are my own responsibility. But I think one main reason for this lack of 'fit' is that much of the literature about new states in general, including Nigeria, is not based on knowledge of the immediate colonial past, and of the men caught up in it. It has never been generally accepted, even in Britain, that British colonial administration was honest work, as good and as difficult as any in the world, and that on the whole it was done well (given the difficulties) by good and able men, not lacking in compassion, sensitivity, or understanding. This simple and I think true version (so far as it goes) is not accepted; instead, explanations are often preferred (consciously or unconsciously) which make the colonial past a story of exploitation, carried out by a special breed of men, characterized, with few exceptions, by an incredible blend of short-sighted stupidity, snobbery, hypocrisy, and cunning. In fact, it was the other way round, in Nigeria at any rate—mostly good, with a few bad patches.

Clearly, in the world as it has been so far in the twentieth century, it was not and still is not possible for even the most basic facts about colonial administration to gain general acceptance. A world in which matters involving politics, race, colour, class, nationality, religion, and ideology could be calmly considered and agreed would be one different in many ways from the one we inhabit. But even this world changes; perhaps, when it becomes possible to accept the plainer facts of the recent past, there will be deeper appreciation of the real problems of new countries like Nigeria, better predictions, more effective plans and policies; perhaps even new and better theory built on a broader and firmer factual base. Meanwhile, it seems a good thing to try to find out and to say what the men concerned did and tried to do.

The book is itself intended in part as a kind of acknowledgement to past generations of public servants in Nigeria, and also as something which may be of some use to their hard-pressed Nigerian successors. Published individual acknowledgement of all who have helped with information, comment, and advice is for various but sufficient reasons not possible. Out of many approached, none, British or Nigerian, serving or retired, was unhelpful or uninterested. Perhaps three men now beyond reach of praise or blame should be mentioned: Sir Abubakar Tafawa Balewa, the late Prime Minister, at heart an administrator rather than a politician, who took the trouble to give me his personal blessing for the project, and looked forward to seeing it in print; the late Sir Sydney Phillipson, whose immense contributions to Nigeria are not fully known, gave similar help and encouragement towards starting the book; the late Mr. L. C. Gwam, of the Nigerian National Archives, helped generously by tracing information and by discussing the records of the past in which he had himself delved with such enthusiasm.

For the original suggestion of the book, and for constant help and encouragement throughout its preparation, I am greatly indebted to Mr. Philip Harris, now Director-General of the Book Development Council. For much wise and tactful guidance, many kindnesses, and many fruitful suggestions, questions, and comment, I am deeply grateful to Professor W. J. M. Mackenzie. Acknowledgement is due to the Simon Research Fund trustees for the provision of financial means for research from 1962 to 1964; to the then Department of Technical Co-operation (now the Ministry of Overseas Development) for the provision of funds for a research visit to Nigeria in 1963 which permitted searches in the National Archives at Ibadan, Kaduna, and Enugu, interviews with public servants in regional headquarters and in Lagos, and contacts with university scholars at Ibadan and Zaria. Most of the documentary research, however, was necessarily done in England, Nigeria's 'memory bank' being still defective, despite remarkable changes in the last few years. For library facilities, my chief acknowledgements are to the libraries of the University of Cambridge, of the British Museum, of the Royal Commonwealth Society, of the Colonial Office and of the Commonwealth Relations Office, of the Universities of Manchester, Ibadan, and Queensland. Special thanks are due to the staff of the Public Record Office, both those in London and more particularly those at Ashridge, where many of the relevant Colonial Office records of old, turbulent, and difficult business in Africa could be studied in a setting of tranquil beauty, and where the staff gave more courteous and friendly help than one had any right to expect.

My cordial thanks are due also to Miss Gabrielle Chicoteau for her skill and patience in transforming much untidy manuscript into impeccable typescript in which the only errors were the author's own responsibility.

I. F. N.

*University of Queensland,*
*St. Lucia,*
*Brisbane*

# CONTENTS

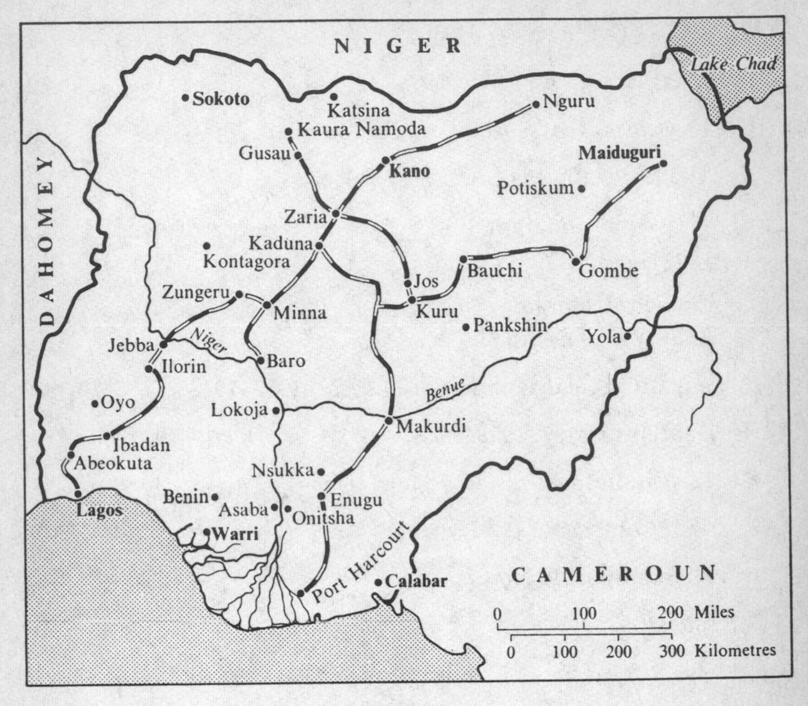


## NIGERIA

SHOWING PRINCIPAL TOWNS, AND THE PRESENT RAILWAYS

The towns *Lagos*, *Warri*, and *Calabar* were in 1912 the already established capitals of the three provinces of Egerton's Southern Nigeria. The three Northern towns, *Sokoto*, *Kano*, and *Maiduguri* were then, and have since remained, the capitals of three 'natural' provinces.

An amalgamation by a hand other than Lugard's would probably have left this pattern of six provinces undisturbed, on the whole—leaving for settlement only the problem of a suitable division of the middle belt into three or four comparable provinces. See Chapters 5 and 7.

# CHAPTER I

## 1900 – The Starting Point

Whatever we do in Africa today, a thousand years hence there will be Africans to thrive or suffer for it.

Mary Kingsley

To choose the first day of the twentieth century[1] as the best starting point for an account of the evolution of Nigerian administration does not imply that there was nothing before then worth calling 'administration'. On the contrary, there was in the colony of Lagos a well established career service of qualified officials, including Nigerian and other African doctors, lawyers, police officers, Customs and prison officials, printers, stenographers, and clerks. At Calabar, the Niger Coast Protectorate possessed the rudiments of administrative and clerical staffs, as did the Royal Niger Company in its stations on the river like Asaba and Lokoja. In the rest of what became Nigeria some of the more elaborate and complex societies included official hierarchies with duties of day-to-day government. But where these latter survived the British occupation, they did so in modified form as part of the limited and subordinate system of government later to be known, somewhat paradoxically, as indirect rule; their retention affected the size rather than the shape of the officialdom which for the first half of the twentieth century directly ruled Nigeria. It is with the evolution of this system of alien officialdom and with its transformation into indigenous Nigerian public services that this book is concerned. That process can be said to have begun on 1 January 1900, in something more than a purely arbitrary or purely symbolic way, because it was then that the word 'Nigeria' first came into official use to describe the new protectorates of Southern and Northern Nigeria formed by Orders in Council which became operative on that day.

This event was the culmination of a long process, the end of one administrative era and the beginning of a new and very different one. The obvious outward sign of change was the creation of the new pro-

[1] By this is meant 1 Jan. 1900; opinions differ as to when centuries begin, many authorities preferring to date them from a year later, i.e. 1 Jan. 1901. Letters to *The Times* in 1900 debated the point at length.

tectorates, under High Commissioners charged with responsibility for their development, by a Secretary of State for the Colonies, Joseph Chamberlain, then at the height of his power, 'the prophet of development' or 'Josephus Africanus', who regarded the Empire as a vast 'undeveloped estate' and was determined to develop it. The word 'development' was as much on officials' lips during his period of office as it was in the first years of Nigerian independence and of the United Nations 'Development Decade'.

Many of the problems of development in the 1960s, despite the immense difference between the Nigeria of 1960 and the Nigerian protectorates of 1900, were strikingly similar to the problems which confronted the early administrators. Then, too, there was a preoccupation with problems of capital for development, with possible new industries, with the improvement of communications and of agricultural production, with the cost of education and the forms it should take; and there were fears that the impact of Western ways might do more harm than good. Since the main instruments of the planned and directed part of this impact were the officials appointed to take over and develop the new protectorates, at a time when British confidence in national and apparently inherent ability to master world-wide problems was at its greatest, it was the officials who planned, directed, and imposed nearly all the measures of material development, on peoples powerless to affect the course of events to any great extent, whose greatest efforts had previously been absorbed in the struggle for survival and subsistence.

The remarkable transformation which came over the Nigerian scene as the result of the energetic imperial expansion of the Chamberlain era can only be explained in terms of the greater transformation of the whole world which had been taking place in the last three decades of the nineteenth century—the revolution in industry, communications, weapons, and international trade which had 'opened up' the whole world, except for tropical Africa and Oceania, and had made tropical Africa obviously 'ripe for development'. For an understanding of the changes which took place in the last decades of the nineteenth century and made the final act of expansion in Africa under Chamberlain politically practicable, and perhaps inevitable, it is necessary to look back as far as 1865—a point in time described by Lady Lugard as representing 'the lowest ebb of British sentiment in regard to the West African Colonies'.[1] It was in that year that the

[1] Flora Lugard, *A Tropical Dependency* (1905).

famous resolution[1] was passed in Parliament, in favour of halting, and then reversing, the insidious and politically unpopular (because unprofitably expensive and unhealthy) process of expansion in West Africa.

'Lowest ebb of sentiment' though it may have been, from the point of view of the imperially-minded Lady Lugard, it did represent the temporary ascendancy (over the contemporary advocates of expansion on humanitarian, anti-slavery grounds) of one continuing school of thought, the essence of which was the belief in the absolute minimum of government, and the firm conviction that colonies and empires were inconvenient and expensive millstones round the neck of the mother country. At that time, Britain was still the leading industrial power, feeling no need for further expansion, possessing, in Lord Lugard's words, 'great tracts in the temperate zone';[2] the turn of the last continent, tropical Africa, had not yet come.

Had the policy behind the resolution been carried through to its logical conclusion, there would have been no Nigeria as we know it, but in all probability a French-speaking West Africa with English and German-speaking enclaves on the coast. That the policy was not carried out was due to the rapid changes in the world between 1870 and 1900, more extensive changes than in any corresponding period in history. In the course of these changes, British policy towards West Africa was turned upside down; a mild desire to withdraw from West Africa was turned into the strong imperialist impulse which led to the occupation of Nigeria, and made efficient development of the territory seem more urgent than the policy of 'Africanization' and withdrawal foreshadowed in the 1865 Committee Resolution.

It is beyond the scope of this study to attempt an analysis of the growth of imperialism in the last three decades of the nineteenth century—except in so far as British experience affected the motivations and actions of the new officialdom called into existence at the end of the nineteenth century to develop one large part of the enormous tropical area parcelled out between the European powers in the period of diplomatic 'gamesmanship' of the 'scramble for Africa'.

[1] 'That all further extensions of territory or assumption of government or new treaties offering protection to native tribes would be inexpedient, and that the object of our policy should be to encourage in the natives the exercise of those qualities which may render it possible for us more and more to transfer to them the administration of all the governments, with a view to our ultimate withdrawal from all except probably Sierra Leone.' Parl. Papers, 1865, vol. i.

[2] F. D. Lugard, *The Dual Mandate in British Tropical Africa* (1922), p. 9. (Pagination as in 3rd ed., 1926.)

There have been several brilliant analyses of this period and phase of imperialism. There are the theoretical studies like J. A. Hobson's *Imperialism: a Study* published in 1902, a seminal work deeply influencing British, American, and Russian writings—including, for instance, Lenin's *Imperialism, the Highest Stage of Capitalism* (1916), Leonard Woolf's *Empire and Commerce in Africa* (1920) and *Economic Imperialism* (1921). These studies affected Lugard's own *The Dual Mandate* (1922), turning what might have been a more simple confession of an active imperialist into a blend of theory, apologia, and after-thought. Recent writings, like *Africa and the Victorians* by Ronald Robinson and John Gallagher (1961), *Imperialism: the story and significance of a Political Word* by R. Koebner and H. D. Schmidt (1964), and *The Imperial Idea and its Enemies* by A. P. Thornton (1959), illuminate other facets in the incredibly complex, refracted, and distorted reflection, in Africa, of the changes taking place in Britain's position in the world, and in the rapidly contracting world itself. Perhaps there can be no certainty about the motives and ambitions behind the last phase of expansion which under Chamberlain made Nigeria a new country, and no finally convincing theory; the ingredients in the mixture were so richly confused; the rationalizations were different from the irrational and less conscious impulses; and the effects of what was done were often quite different from what was intended.

Lugard's version of the stages by which Nigeria became caught up in the British Empire and in the great changes which were transforming the outside world is given in the opening chapters of *The Dual Mandate*, written in the years immediately following his retirement from Nigeria. His version is of the greatest importance for this study, since his was the dominant influence in two important periods of administration in Nigeria (the conquest of Northern Nigeria 1900–6 and the amalgamation of Nigeria 1912–18). He had also played a part in the earlier hectic scramble for Africa, and in the exertion of pressure for expansion on the reluctant home Government. Even after his retirement he continued to influence events and opinion by his writings, speeches, and personal contacts. It is worth giving the gist of his eyewitness account of the stages by which Nigeria came into being, bearing always in mind that the account in *The Dual Mandate* was written long after the events they describe, partly as an elderly man's vindication and defence of his own highly controversial part in one of the great controversies of the age.

Of the 1865 resolution, Lugard remarked that the British colonies in West Africa were not the result of a definite policy for which Britain was 'willing to risk war'[1] (a strange criterion for humanitarian policy), but were maintained to assist in ending the overseas slave trade. The value of tropical products had not been fully recognized. Britain had no need to seek an outlet for emigrants, the African interior was still unknown, economic pressure caused by expansion of population in Europe was still satisfied by outlets in India and America and by food and raw materials from those countries.

In Lugard's view the change in the economic background came when the continuing rapid increase of population in Europe and rising living standards built up pressure for materials and markets which America and India no longer satisfied, American industry beginning to absorb her raw materials in her own industries. The political change started when, after crippling defeat in the Franco-Prussian War of 1870, France looked to Greater France in Africa for rehabilitation, believing colonization of Africa by Frenchmen to be practicable. Germany, with her increasing industry and population, looked for raw materials, and the rivalries of France and Germany prompted the partition of Africa. Britain 'woke up' to discover after the Berlin Act that France and Germany, who did not adopt the British policy of the 'open door', were about to appropriate the 'hinterlands' of the British colonies—which would ruin British trade. There was then an 'irresistible' popular demand that Britain too should 'peg out claims' for the future.[2] The Berlin Conference had laid down a basis for determining the validity of sovereignty in coast lands by the test of 'effective occupation', but, in the absence of such a basis for the interior, the 'hinterland' theory was gradually accepted in practice, each power claiming the right to exercise influence for an indefinite distance inland. Hence, according to Lugard, the 'scramble', and its climax, in which France claimed Northern Nigeria as the 'hinterland' of the Mediterranean, while Britain claimed it as the 'hinterland' of the West African coast.

Lugard maintained that the rulers of Great Britain (i.e. those responsible for colonial and foreign policy) were strongly opposed to extension of territory in Africa, 'but the popular demand left the Foreign Office with no alternative. The Government viewed with alarm the great cost of effective occupation, as that phrase was translated in England. But the British public never considers the cost of its

[1] Lugard, op. cit., p. 9. [2] Lugard, p. 10.

demands, though it holds the Government to strict account for any disaster due to an inadequate staff and insufficient force to protect its officers.'[1]

Lugard's idea of a popular demand for expansion pressed upon a reluctant Government is somewhat at variance with Hobson's classic diagnosis, in which he traced the pressure for expansion to the selfish interests of the 'investing classes' and to something like a conspiracy between them and the professions (the army, the Church, the universities, the bureaucracy, and the schools) interested in finding overseas opportunities for themselves and their sons. No doubt what Lugard had in mind were incidents like the death of Gordon at Khartoum in 1885, and the relief of Mafeking, but there was no comparable situation in West Africa to arouse an outcry by the 'public' for vengeance upon their own Government as well as upon the Government's adversaries abroad. There is in fact no evidence of any popular or public demand for expansion in West Africa, however sympathetic public opinion might be to colonies of settlement in healthier climates. Lugard himself had tried hard, by writings and by speeches, to whip up public enthusiasm for the retention of Uganda in British hands, and must have been aware of the continuing attitude of indifference with which he and other advocates of imperial expansion in Africa had continually to contend. But wherever the real pressures developed, the Government of the day, once embroiled in imperial ventures (however reluctantly, like Gladstone's Government in Egypt), found it impracticable to retreat, in the face of European rivals, without such loss of face and prestige as might destroy their popularity, and with it the real power dependent on maintaining popularity.

The formation of the Royal Niger Company and the other charter companies in Africa Lugard explained as the Government's way out of its dilemma. Feeling itself compelled to expand but at the same time hating to spend money it adopted an expedient by which the companies (who 'were overwhelmed by volunteers eager for adventure') were allowed to undertake 'the responsibility which the Government shunned'[2] of financing expansion, and to make 'treaties' with African chiefs on which their title to land and other rights would rest. 'Treaties were produced by the cartload in all the approved forms of legal verbiage—impossible of translation by ill-educated interpreters.'[3] 'In some cases, it is said, the assent had been obtained by the

[1] Lugard, p. 13. [2] Lugard, p. 14. [3] Lugard, p. 15.

gift of a pair of boots or a few bottles of gin—the Kaiser sent a parcel of opera hats working with a spring.'[1]

Lugard, writing in retirement, expressed a clear preference for intervention by force, applied professionally and briskly, rather than 'naked deception', 'make-believe', and 'subterfuge'. For one thing, conquest established legitimacy of rule in international law. It also seemed, to him, to leave behind less misunderstanding, bitterness, and resentment than 'peaceful penetration' achieved by trickery. But it must be remembered that Lugard's past had included much treaty-making, as well as force; and that his condemnation of 'peaceful penetration' was part of a double-barrelled defence against accusations of using unnecessary force—first a denial that he had, second a claim that force was better anyway.

Lugard's outline distinguished three main stages—first, the reluctantly held and undervalued colony on the coast; next, under the pressure of competition from other European powers, economic circumstances, and popular demand, the stage of vaguely defined 'hinterland' and 'sphere of influence', and the expedient of letting merchant adventurers and investors have their way, in an atmosphere of growing optimism about the value and wealth of tropical Africa, to the point where the British Government could no longer escape responsibility for the risks, dangers, and abuses inherent in chartered company rule; and finally, the decision to take over the country effectively, by conquest if necessary, to accept fully the obligations of administration and development, and to raise men and money to carry out these tasks.

The importance of this account by Lugard lies in the things which he omits, rather than in the simplified economic and strategic view of events. The important omission is repaired in the closing peroration of *The Dual Mandate* where he lets the real, the true imperialist cat out of the bag:

> We hold these countries because it is the genius of our race to colonise, to trade, and to govern. The task in which England is engaged in the tropics—alike in Africa and in the East—has become part of her tradition, and she has ever given her best in the cause of liberty and civilization. There will always be those who cry aloud that the task is being badly done, that it does not need doing, that we can get more profit by leaving others to do it, that it brings evil to subject races and breeds profiteers at home. These were not the principles which prompted our forefathers, and secured for

[1] Lugard, p. 16.

us the place we hold in the world today in trust for those who shall come after us.[1]

This conviction of a kind of divine right, and indeed a duty, to govern the world, vested in the British people, seems now as quaint, after only half a century, as the centuries-old Stuart belief in the divine right of kings. Compared with the driving force of such a conviction, the rational arguments about strategic and economic considerations seem pale shadows of 'reasons' for imperial expansion—but they were used by convinced imperialists like Lugard to convince others who did not share their intoxicating faith in 'the genius of the race'. There were many of these sceptics in the colonial service itself: indeed Lugard is the only one of the Nigerian proconsuls to go beyond a cautious claim that, on the whole, the peoples of Nigeria had derived more good than harm from British rule. He was also the only one who prior to appointment had been an imperialist adventurer and campaigner for extension of Empire, and the only one who after retirement was active in defending and publicizing the achievements of British imperialism.[2]

Since *The Dual Mandate* was written, not long after the first World War, events have put the economic and political background into clearer perspective. In particular, the great depression of the early thirties marked the collapse of efforts to re-establish prosperity by international trade on the pre-war pattern, and showed that the phenomenal expansion of the last decades of the nineteenth century by the simple formula of free trade and 'the open door' had been greatly assisted by specially favourable but impermanent circumstances. Of these, one of the most important was the continual process of 'opening up' new agricultural countries—a process in which Britain had led the way for so long that it seemed to prove some inherent superiority in the 'Anglo-Saxon' peoples; a process which ended, inevitably, when there were no more 'wide open spaces' in the 'newer' continents to bring under cultivation and when Europe's population ceased its dramatic expansion (30 per cent increase, or one hundred million, between 1870 and 1900). Other factors had included the world-wide acceptance of British sterling as a stable currency for international trade, and the maintenance of open trade routes in the long period of peace between the great powers from

[1] Lugard, p. 619.

[2] See Perham, *Lugard, the Years of Adventure* (1956) for his earlier life, and *Lugard, The Years of Authority* (1960) at pp. 719–27 for an (admittedly incomplete) list of nearly 200 publications by Lugard from 1893 to 1945.

1870 to 1914, during which the spate of technical innovation in Europe first made international trade on a large scale practicable.

Before these innovations, Britain was the only industrial power of importance, accounting, about 1870, for one-third of total world production; she was a maritime power carrying her products, and her emigrants, slowly around the world in sailing ships on trade routes effectively policed by the Royal Navy. Already London had become the financial centre of the world, just as Greenwich had become the centre for calculating the world's time and the position in the world of ships and countries. It was clearly in Britain's trading interests that trade should remain free, that all countries should open their doors to trade, and that the seemingly perfect and elegant laws of classical economics should be allowed full beneficent sway, without interference by pirates or by tariffs, tolls, and taxes; these latter seemed to merchants and to sea-captains little different from piracy in their economic effects. At that period the untapped resources of the world, even excluding tropical Africa, must have seemed large enough for everyone for all foreseeable time, and there was, as Lugard said, no immediate need of further territory.

But rapid and sweeping changes were on the way, by which, between 1865 when withdrawal from West Africa was contemplated and 1900 when the planned acquisition of Nigeria took place, the whole world situation had been transformed, and new attitudes, hopes, and fears had come to dominate men's minds. By 1900 Britain was only one of many industrial powers, including the United States, most of Western Europe, and Japan. Britain's industrial production had doubled, but world production had increased fourfold. Shipping tonnage had doubled, and by the 1890s steam tonnage equalled the tonnage of ships under sail. The volume of world trade had doubled. As other countries set up industries, they became a potential or actual threat to British trade, raising tariffs against British goods, changing what had been private competition between individual enterprises into something more like competition between states, nations, and governments, giving an impetus to nationalistic, militaristic feeling. As Britain's new territories in the temperate zone developed, they produced wheat, meat, and other foodstuffs in increasing quantities. Material output thus tended to go ahead of demand, prices fell (by about 40 per cent generally between 1873 and the early 1890s), and profits fell with them. New consumer industries grew up (soap, chocolate, cheap newsprint, ready-made clothing, and shoes) as the result of applied science and technology and of the cheap transportation and large-scale production which they made possible. Specialization in industry increased with the increase in scale of production; new industries were born, like the chemical industry, and electrical, mechanical, and marine engineering, soon to prove so vital in 'opening up' Africa. Firms became bigger, cartels were formed, capital investment increased greatly with the new device of limited liability companies. Banks and other financial institutions grew enormously. Many of these developments can be traced directly back to the introduction of cheap steel-making by the Bessemer process, which revolutionized transportation, making possible lighter, stronger, more economical ships and railways, so that goods could be transported without prohibitive cost from one end of the world to the other.[1] It was in this period that men who were to play an important part in influencing events in Nigeria at a later date were building up their industrial empires in industrial Lancashire—men like Sir Alfred Jones taking over the Elder Dempster lines, amalgamating other shipping companies, and acquiring Welsh anthracite mines to supply his new steel ships;[2] men like William Lever, later Lord Leverhulme, building up what was to prove one of the world's largest industrial empires from the family grocery business in Bolton.[3] It was in this period that Nigeria's commerce became firmly linked with Liverpool and the industrial north, while the Nigerian official links were forged with the different world of London. Even now, it is customary to talk of the two nations in England, the north and the south; in the nineteenth century, apart from Disraeli's distinction of the two nations, rich and poor, the differences between London and Lancashire were even wider and deeper. Manchester and Liverpool were strongly linked by trading interests with the West African coast, and not so much with the hinterland. There official and military influence was stronger, one reason for the different faces which Northern and Southern Nigeria and their people show to the world today.

In the same period, the necessity to govern growing cities (and to put right by Government intervention some of the glaring evils of industrial exploitation and *laissez-faire* in those cities) led to a rapid increase in the domestic powers and functions of the state. Each new

[1] See *New Cambridge Modern History*, 1870–1898, vol. xi, for a statistical survey of industrial change in this period.

[2] See A. H. Milne, *Sir Alfred Lewis Jones: a Story of Energy and Success* (1914).

[3] See 2nd Viscount Leverhulme, *Viscount Leverhulme; by his Son* (1927), and W. S. Adams, *Edwardian Portraits* (1957).

scientific and industrial innovation led to new powers of control, regulation, and inspection by new bureaucratic agencies. Factories, mines, schools, ships, docks, farms, railways, and even private houses—all became subject in the interests of human health, safety, and education to inspection by Government officials. Such developments struck repeated blows at the old doctrines of individual freedom and free trade, and severely weakened the traditional resistance to interference by the Government in the private citizen's concerns. Taxation increased to pay for all the new functions and services. Paradoxically, it was often on liberal initiative and as a result of sustained pressure by liberal, humanitarian groups that those steps were taken which increased the powers of the state and encroached on the older liberal principles. Often, like the abolition of the slave trade, and the succession of Factory Acts, they were measures, designed to end or restrict oppression and cruelty by individuals, which had far-reaching and unintended effects. The acquisition of Lagos can be seen as an early example of an action designed to end the activities of slave-trading individuals, which had the eventual and unplanned effect of extending the power of the British state into a new sphere where it had not before been exercised.

The world shrank, with the advent of railways, steamships, telegraphs, telephones, wireless, the internal combustion engine, cheap paper, international postal facilities. Some of these from the start were operated directly by governments—particularly services from which no direct profit could be expected—adding to the numbers of professional bureaucrats. Other services, even when their management was left in private hands, involved legislation and regulation by governments, and more bureaucratic work in consequence. To meet the growing demands for educated and professionally trained men the old universities were revitalized and new ones were built. New public schools were opened in England to educate new middle classes as potential leaders of society, disciplined to take their place in a social hierarchy where they would be required both to command and lead and to obey and conform. Armies and navies too became more professional, weapons of war being transformed by science and by industry; in 1898 their range was about forty times greater than in 1870. The Maxim gun, with which Lugard's troops first in Uganda and then in Nigeria were armed, was invented in 1889, a weapon no army without modern weapons could withstand, however great their numerical strength or their courage.

From 1870 to 1914 the fear of these new weapons served as one of the deterrents to war between the great industrial powers. Although they were brought to the edge of armed conflict several times during the period of peace in Europe and diplomatic war games in Africa, played out by professionals as part of the game of balance of power and of 'prestige' in Europe, the apportionment of Africa was achieved without open warfare between them.

When, therefore, Chamberlain set out to develop Nigeria at the end of the century he had available to him not only a reservoir of scientific and industrial techniques and of economic and military power such as had never before been seen, but he had also available a choice of men educated for leadership and trained for the professions, confident in their country's mission, and in their own ability to meet any difficulties. In particular, the public schools and the older universities had been producing over the years a new class of gentlemen trained for responsibility and leadership, for danger and physical hardship, prepared for exile and separation from families as a matter of course, and imbued with patriotism and a strong sense of duty. It was not only in the public schools that these qualities could be found, but they provided a rich and convenient source, and there was little need to look further than the largely self-selected class of men who applied to the Patronage Private Secretary of the Secretary of State, supplemented by those whom Colonial Governors and the Crown Agents found for subordinate and technical posts.

Britain's recent achievement of rapid development in other parts of the world—India, Canada, Australia, New Zealand, South Africa, Ceylon, and Malaya—gave confidence and conviction that the wealth of tropical Africa could be quickly 'unlocked' or 'opened up' for the benefit of the world. Chamberlain gave frequent expression to his sense of the urgency of finding new markets for British products and new sources of foodstuffs and raw materials for the industrial millions of Great Britain—as befitted the first industrialist Secretary of State for the Colonies, after a long line of aristocratic predecessors with rural and courtly backgrounds.

Nigeria's great forests and indications of unused agricultural wealth (e.g. the 'ungarned fruits of the oil palm') were taken as proof of enormous potential wealth which could soon be made to flow into the stream of international trade. On the face of it, there seemed little reason why modern geological surveys should not bring rich mineral rewards comparable with those of contemporary South Africa,

Canada, and Australia. There was reason to hope that new medical discoveries and techniques of public health would put a speedy end to the heavy toll of lives in the West African colonies. For most of the period when the rest of the world was being transformed and brought into the system of international trade, these colonies had been becalmed by lack of capital for development and by uncertainty as to their future, suspended awkwardly between the old era and the new. The old palm-oil ruffians, slave traders, missionaries, independent explorers and adventurers (and even the official consular representatives) had not worried too much about the colour of the flag which flew over their activities, and had no sense of the full resources of a modern state behind them. The immediate contribution of Chamberlain and that of his imperial officials on the new pattern was to ensure that the impact of Britain and Europe on Nigeria was at last under the direct control of the officials of the modern state, a control exercised with a sense of responsibility 'higher' and more impartial than the motives which they attributed to the traders, miners, and missionaries. Lugard's defence of his forceful conquest of the North was based on the same conception of duty. The diplomats having agreed that this part of Africa was Britain's responsibility, it was his high duty, as High Commissioner, to make what would otherwise be a hypocritical pretence of responsibility into something much more positive, and that quickly.

In the prosperous but competitive closing years of Queen Victoria's reign there was great and natural pride in Britain's achievements, brimming over at times and in places into complacency and a kind of narcissicism, fed by prolonged success, prolonged peace, and by the tendency—the result of popularizing Darwin's theory of evolution and Mendel's discoveries in genetics—to transfer to the race and the state the feelings of awe, reverence, and worship which religion could no longer fully command. Confidence and pride of race were reinforced by determination not to be outdone by the rival 'nations' of France and Germany in what seemed inevitably a struggle for the survival of the fittest rather than an opportunity for co-operation and peaceful progress. At this time, the expansion of Empire found few powerful opponents. There were imperialists of all kinds, proud to call themselves by that name—Tory imperialists, Fabian imperialists, Liberal imperialists, imperialists for the sake of Christian evangelism, imperialists in purple prose, and imperialists in more popular prose and verse like Kipling, academic and professional imperialists and imperialists in action who were the heroes of the day—Rhodes, Milner, Roberts, Lugard. Rhodes wrote, in 1899:

They are tumbling over each other, Liberals and Conservatives, to show which side are the greatest and most enthusiastic Imperialists. . . . The people have found that England is small, and her trade is large, and they have also found that other people are taking their share of the world, and enforcing hostile tariffs. The people of England are finding out that 'trade follows the flag' and they have all become Imperialists. They are not going to part with any territory. . . . The English people intend to retain every inch of land they have got, and perhaps they intend to secure a few more inches.[1]

This certainly agrees with Lugard's version of a popular demand for expansion; but by that time the physical process of expansion was complete—the earth was apportioned, more or less, and the turn of the moon had not yet come. So it is not the least of the difficulties in a study of imperial motives to know what this popular mood portended. There was pride in past achievement and present magnificence, adequately conveyed in the words and music of 'Land of Hope and Glory', but there was fear compounded in it too, a fear which Chamberlain's speeches and imperialist propaganda for more than a decade had helped to build up—the following, for instance, from 1888:

Is there any man in his senses who believes that the crowded population of these islands could exist for a single day if we were to cut adrift from us the great dependencies which now look to us for protection and for assistance, and which are the natural markets for our trade? If tomorrow it were possible, as some people apparently desire, to reduce by a stroke of the pen the British Empire to the dimensions of the United Kingdom, half, at least, of our population would be starved.[2]

No such dire consequences have so far befallen the people of the United Kingdom, whose diet has improved with each contraction of Empire; but the fears were real enough and felt most acutely in those industrial parts of the country most dependent on markets and raw materials abroad (and yet by tradition most opposed to extensions of Government interference at home and of officialdom abroad). The fears thus raised reinforced determination not to be beaten by foreign entrepreneurs in the search for assured markets, and further weakened opposition to governmental intervention in matters of trade and

[1] Quoted in Semmel, *Imperialism and Social Reform* (London, 1960), p. 53.
[2] Semmel, op. cit., p. 85.

economics. In 1897, in a speech before the Birmingham Chamber of Commerce, Chamberlain stressed the importance of commerce, and in so doing implicitly admitted the new powers which the Government was assuming:

All the great offices of state are occupied with commercial affairs. The Foreign Office and the Colonial Office are chiefly engaged in finding new markets and in defending old ones. The War Office and Admiralty are mostly occupied in preparation for the defence of these markets and for the protection of our commerce. The Boards of Agriculture and of Trade are entirely concerned with these two great branches of industry. It is not too much to say that commerce is the greatest of all political interests, and that the Government deserves most the popular approval which does most to increase our trade and settle it on a firm foundation.

Chamberlain's great dream was of a federal Empire which would be a complete commercial and political entity in itself, or, as he put it, 'an Empire which with decent organisation and consolidation might be absolutely self-sustaining'. He resigned office in 1903 to devote himself to the advocacy of this cause. Although he did not succeed, his campaign kept his concept of Empire somewhere near the forefront of the public mind for many months.

The new mass-circulation newspapers made possible by the spread of education and by cheaper, more plentiful newsprint were marked by fervent nationalism (e.g. the *Daily Mail*, launched in 1896, and the *Daily Express*, which launched itself in 1900 with the slogan 'Our policy is simple: our policy is the British Empire'[1]).

To return from imperial London to the Lagos of 1895, we find that Chamberlain's appointment rejoiced the heart of one of the most unusual imperialists of them all, Mary Kingsley, one of a succession of British women whose studies of West Africa have been marked by perceptive sympathy with 'the African personality' in its struggles for freedom and self-expression, but one who was convinced that energetic and consistent British rule was the best thing that could happen for the African. She was fascinated by West Africa, liked the people, got on well with the traders, and was exasperated by the languid official policy which preceded the Chamberlain regime.[2] She quoted, as the only description of the previous policy which seemed to do it justice, the comment of a medical friend of hers who said it was 'a coma accompanied by fits'. Writing to Chamberlain on his appoint-

[1] Leading article of 24 Apr. 1900.
[2] See bibliography for works by and about Mary Kingsley.

ment she described its effect in Lagos: 'The news went round that things had got to be done . . . conversation became stiff with railways, drains, hospitals and coinage.'[1]

Her success as a writer and as a speaker was great, and used frankly in the cause of the intensification of British efforts—her utterances were a call to action, to an awakening from the unhealthy drowsiness of the little coastal colonies. Typical of her is the following quotation, striking a very different note from the complacent political utterances of the time (e.g. Rosebery's phrase that the British Empire was 'the greatest secular agency for good that the world had ever seen'):

If you will try Science, all the evils of the clash between the two culture periods could be avoided, and you could assist these West Africans in their Thirteenth Century state to rise into their Nineteenth Century state without their having the hard fight for it that you yourself had. This would be a grand humanitarian bit of work: by doing it you would raise a monument before God to the honour of England such as no nation has ever yet raised to Him on Earth.

This was humanitarian imperialism; there can be no doubt about Mary Kingsley's sincerity, since her life (and her death in 1900 nursing the sick) bears very adequate witness to it, even if it did not shine out so clearly from all that she wrote. But it is very difficult to assess the strength of humanitarian motives in some other cases, or in the general expansionism of the time. Very often those in whom the desire to be of selfless help to their fellow men was strong would either keep silence or would use arguments of economic advantage, or national interest, or enlightened self-interest, to persuade others towards intervention; while those in whom the drive to power and wealth was uppermost were often the readiest to preach the humanitarian case for intervention. So, within the imperialist fold there was many a wolf in sheep's clothing, and more than one sheep in wolves' clothing, as well as some remarkable hybrids—but by the end of the century the *Zeitgeist* was moving them all towards the new pastures.

Another woman imperialist, Lady Lugard, was able later to inform J. L. Garvin, Chamberlain's biographer, of the effect upon the Colonial Office of his appointment in 1895—literally an electrifying effect, one of his first acts being to replace by electric light the 'antique candles' by which the clerks' work was dimly lit. But there was immediately a more fundamental change—for the first time the Colonial Office, which had been a sleepy and leisurely place, had a Secretary

[1] Quoted in J. L. Garvin, *The Life of Joseph Chamberlain*, vol. iii, p. 206.

of State prepared to stand up to his Cabinet colleagues and to the Prime Minister in the interests of his department, and also prepared, once he had chosen his Governors, to give them their heads.[1] Lugard wrote, 'Though I was one of the youngest of them, he spoke with such entire frankness and freedom from official reticence as to make one feel how entirely he trusted one's discretion.'[2]

Chamberlain assumed office in late June 1895; as early as August he was addressing the House of Commons in these forceful terms:[3]

I regard many of our Colonies as being in the condition of undeveloped estates which can never be developed without Imperial assistance. It appears to me to be absurd to apply to savage countries the same rules which apply to civilized portions of the United Kingdom. Cases have already come to my knowledge of Colonies which have been British Colonies perhaps for more than 100 years in which up to the present British Rule has done absolutely nothing, and if we left them today we should leave them in the same condition as that in which we found them. How can we expect, therefore, either with advantage to them or ourselves, that trade with such places can be developed? I shall be prepared to consider very carefully myself and then, if I am satisfied, to confidently submit to this House any case which may occur in which, by the judicious investment of British money, those estates which belong to the British Crown may be developed for the benefit of their populations and for the benefit of the greater population which is outside.

The last sentence is one of the earlier expressions of the theme elaborated by Lugard's *Dual Mandate*—neither exploitation in the selfish interest of the conqueror, nor a pure humanitarian civilizing mission, but a kind of symbiosis for the benefit of both—in Lugard's words the 'dual mandate' to develop 'the abounding wealth of the tropical regions of the earth' for the benefit of mankind and at the same time 'to safeguard the material rights of the natives' and 'to promote their material and moral progress'. In this Lugard was stating a policy normatively, rather than describing the facts as they were. In practice, there was a good deal of selfish exploitation at one extreme and a good deal of selfless service at the other, rather than the perfected system of mutually profitable, nicely balanced advantage which the idea of *The Dual Mandate* suggested.

There were however practical proofs, even before 1900, that Chamberlain meant business when he spoke of development. One early sign was the raising of a loan of £255,000, in 1896, through the Crown Agents, to begin railway bridges between Lagos Island and

[1] Garvin, op. cit., p. 11. [2] Lugard, op. cit., pp. 185–6. [3] 22 Aug. 1895.

Ebute Metta. The previous financial doctrine had been the crippling one that expenditure must be met from revenue, a vicious circle when the lack of local revenue was chiefly due to lack of development capital. Later the Colonial Loans Act of 1899 permitted the British Treasury to raise funds for lending to the colonies. By this means, before the end of the century, Lagos borrowed £792,500 for public works—not vast sums, but a new departure and sufficient to make a real beginning in railway construction. Chamberlain also took immediate steps to lay the bogy of the White Man's Grave by encouraging the establishment of two new Schools of Tropical Medicine, at London and Liverpool, and by the appointment to the colony of Lagos of a Governor, Sir William MacGregor, who was not only a successful administrator but also a medical man with an impressive public health record and scientific interests. With this appointment, the appointment of a former police officer, Moor, as High Commissioner for the 'unruly' Southern Nigeria, and the appointment of an exceptionally ambitious and energetic frontier soldier, Lugard, to the 'unpacified' Northern Nigeria, Chamberlain had clearly taken good care to get Nigeria off to a flying start in the twentieth century.

So, by January 1900, the will and the means to develop Nigeria were there, for the first time. For the first time, the various British agencies came under one controlling Minister, instead of a combination of Colonial Office, Foreign Office, and chartered company. Chamberlain had men, money, and weapons of science and of war sufficient to unlock the wealth of Nigeria.

The plan of development—and there was such a plan, since economic development was to precede and to finance an extension of law and order—required no public debate or exhaustive reports by experts and commissions; experienced British administrators and engineers knew well the formula applied already with success practically everywhere in the world—railways to open up the country, telegraphs, roads, the introduction of currency, the marketing of existing crops and the development of new ones, rapid reconnaissance of mineral resources (and 'fair play' for the native peoples). It was clear that slavery in the country was not a simple evil, but a system of transport, labour, currency, and commerce. Slavery must cease, so there was a special urgency about railways, currency, and 'legitimate trade' to replace slavery. There were pressures from special interests at home, and there were susceptibilities, parliamentary and other, which must influence the speed and direction of the advance. But Chamberlain's officials faced their immense task with a confidence and a sense of duty which made them formidable, despite the paucity of their numbers and the vast problems, known and unknown, which they faced. Mary Kingsley, for one, was well pleased with the prospect, observing with satisfaction, on the appointment of the three men to whom the development of Nigeria was entrusted, MacGregor in Lagos, Moor in the South, and Lugard in the North:

> Three such men ought to give us success, particularly when they have at home in England so ardent an Imperialist as Mr. Chamberlain in the position of Her Majesty's Secretary of State for the Colonies; but whether they will be able to make the British Empire in West Africa a success remains to be seen.[1]

[1] See Stephen Gwynn, *The Life of Mary Kingsley* (1933), p. 231.

## CHAPTER II

# The Planners and the Plan

Our rule can only be justified if we can show that it adds to the happiness and prosperity of the people.

Joseph Chamberlain

THE high tide of expansionist confidence described in the previous chapter made Chamberlain's forward policy practicable, and lasted into the new century just long enough to carry British rule into the far corners of Nigeria. The plans were prepared and the men chosen in the days of confidence in Britain's power and destiny to manage and to develop the world. But even before the chosen proconsuls took up their new tasks the ebb-tide had begun, laying bare over the following decades the old difficulty of indifference, of lack of financial and moral support from home—the perennial unfitness of one country to govern another, of one man to be another man's master. The change from passing enthusiasm for Empire back first to doubt and indifference and then to something more actively hostile was a slow process; changes in climate do not happen overnight. As early as 1898, the year in which the first serious official planning for the new Nigeria began, the first cracks in the grand façade of imperial pomp and pride were visible, and there were expressions of doubt and misgiving amidst the drum-beatings and lusty shouts of the Jingoes. The Prime Minister himself, Lord Salisbury, repeatedly prophesied disaster if Britain continued to take on new commitments. One example is this quotation from a speech in the Commons on 8 February 1898: 'However strong you may be, whether you are a man or a nation, there is a point beyond which your strength will not go. It is madness: it ends in ruin, if you allow yourselves to pass beyond it.'

The first real demonstration that Britain had taken on too much was the South African War. The outbreak of the war in October 1899 was not sufficient of a shock to prevent the return to power of the Conservatives, with their Liberal Unionist allies, on a new wave of patriotic excitement in the Khaki election of 1900; but early defeats by the Boers proved beyond doubt the weakness of the whole imperial edifice. If it took, as it did, 400,000 troops and £250,000,000 to conquer a mere handful of Boers in South Africa, in a war caused by Chamberlain's imperialism, how would Britain deal with the powerful and envious European powers whose enmity for Britain had the same cause, and who were now both angry at Britain's bullying war against the tiny Boer republics and contemptuous of the military inefficiency the British army had displayed? The course of the war, the humiliation of the failure to dispose of a numerically feeble enemy, and the embarrassment of such a war to a nation which had long prided itself on its friendship and support for small nations struggling against tyranny—all these things strengthened the enemies of the imperial idea at home and helped their return to power in 1905. The subsequent election of 1906 confirmed in office a Liberal Government with a large majority, interested more in 'the condition of England' than in the Empire, in 'Darkest England' rather than 'Darkest Africa'. Their priority tasks were not the development of Chamberlain's remote new estates, but the remedying of poverty and desperate social evils at home, and the reform of the armed forces to meet the danger of war in Europe.

From that time on, although British proconsuls and Governors abroad had to do what they could in the tasks assigned them, they could no longer reckon on ready financial or moral support from home. The very best they could hope for was quiet, uneventful progress. There would be occasional assistance, for some desirable project, from some sectional interest at home, like the sustained pressure for railways, public health measures, and cotton growing in West Africa exerted by the Manchester and Liverpool Chambers of Commerce, concerned for the safety of both supplies of raw cotton and markets for Lancashire's cotton manufactures. This was the most consistent single source of economic pressure for Nigerian development, lasting from the time of the American Civil War (when Lancashire Quaker cotton manufacturers imported cotton from Abeokuta, in preference to relying on American slave owners' plantations[1]) until after the first World War, when the Lancashire cotton industry began to shrink in size and national importance. But no Governor could afford to rely for unquestioning support on these interests; the merchants and traders were just as eager to condemn officials for expenditure on anything not directly helpful to trade as they were to press for improvements which did benefit them. And

[1] See E. D. Morel, *Affairs of West Africa* (London, 1902), p. 170.

there were other critics, for the most part without first-hand knowledge, ready to pounce upon anything which outraged the susceptibilities and moral convictions of the unenthusiastic absentee landlords of the undeveloped estates. There was a wide range of such things: slavery, and the suppression of slavery by force; interference with native ways, and interference with those who did interfere with native ways, like the missionaries; direct taxation and the only possible alternative, indirect taxation; expenditure on troops, police, officials, and armed expeditions on the one hand and any failure of the forces of law and order, on the other hand, to maintain the peace and order necessary for trade. Indeed, from the time of Chamberlain's departure from office in 1903 colonial administrators were felt by the Government at home as well as by the people to be doing a job which it had been a mistake, if not a sin, to undertake; one therefore which it was better to put out of one's mind if possible—rather like other necessary evils of the state, like prisons and gallows, warders and public hangmen. This is of course an exaggeration, but the essential point is that almost from the beginning of the new Nigeria there was indifference, if not hostility, to the commitments entered into by Chamberlain at a time of overconfidence in Britain's ability and destiny to rule and manage the world. This indifference was sharpened into dislike by a growing feeling that the tropical Empire was a preserve of the upper classes, and not the concern of the ordinary man, the 'working man' or 'man in the street'. Since it was the ordinary man's voice which was increasingly heard in politics, and since all parties were increasingly obliged to seek his support and model their policies on his tastes, this feeling that the colonial Empire was an upper-class concern led to greater indifference to the interests of the newly acquired territories.

There had also been, even when imperialism was at its height as a general sentiment, a particular indifference to West African expansion, outside the sectional interests directly concerned. These interests were, firstly, the active, committed expansionists like Chamberlain, Goldie, and Lugard (to all of whom the expansion of Empire was like a religion), and the 'service interests' associated with them; secondly, the missions and the humanitarians with whom they had contacts; and thirdly, the traders, centred on the Liverpool shipowners and 'soap-boilers' and the Manchester cotton manufacturers and merchants. Some, like Goldie himself, ex-officer as well as trader, and Churchill, ex-officer and M.P. for Oldham, and Sir Alfred Jones, philanthropist and millionaire shipowner, had connections with more than one of these interests simultaneously, and helped to bring them together in important matters. So too, Chamberlain, Radical turned Conservative, Birmingham industrialist, half-way between London and Lancashire, was able to serve as a bridge between the various sectional interests and the officials over whom he presided as Secretary of State. In the last decade of the nineteenth century Birmingham manufacturers, faced by contracting markets and intensifying competition, had shown intense interest in the new tropical markets, but two developments made their interest short-lived, by comparison with that shown in Lancashire. The first development was a great recovery and expansion in other markets after about 1900; the second was the fact that West African imports of Birmingham goods remained disappointingly small.

For the mass of the British people, the 'Empire' and the 'colonies' meant the areas of British settlement and to a lesser extent, India, an Empire on its own, of a size which even the most ignorant could not ignore. But Australia, Canada, and New Zealand were the countries of the British Empire with which ordinary people might have ties of friendship, from which they might have letters and news from settler friends and relations, and to which they might turn their eyes if they wished to emigrate within the Empire rather than to the United States. Of the stranger, more remote Empire full of people of different race and colour, only India was known to any extent at all—and that perhaps chiefly through the work of Rudyard Kipling. On Africa, apart from the missionaries and explorers, only a few men like Rider Haggard[1] had written in a style to excite wide interest—a romantic excitement rather than a practical interest.

Such information as came from West Africa must have seemed very sinister and incomprehensible—*The White Man's Grave*, *Benin, City of Blood*,[2] disease, cannibalism, slave-raiding, twin-murder, and other horrors. The chief single source of information at first, at the turn of the century, was mission propaganda; the army of missionaries in Africa, in good faith and zeal to obtain support for their work, stressed the evils of the old Africa they strove to transform, not sparing criticism of the morals and motives of the administrators who sometimes stood in their way, or failed to give them

[1] Haggard—like his famous successor John Buchan—had a colonial civil service background before becoming a professional writer.

[2] Book titles which were apt to evoke a conditioned response of distaste.

the support they thought their due from fellow Christians. Memoirs and biographies of missionary heroes were Sunday school prizes and prescribed Sabbath reading in many homes—some were best-sellers running into many editions, like the lives of Livingstone, and later, of Mary Slessor. This was not the side of Africa which a modern public relations consultant would have chosen to present to the world; usually it was the less attractive profile which was presented.

Many proofs could be given of this combination of ignorance of West Africa with distaste for the little that was known. There is, of course, the weight of negative evidence—the lack of books published, of mention in the newspapers, of parliamentary question and debate. Those who did write, like Mary Kingsley and E. D. Morel, commented on the degree of ignorance displayed in Britain, outside Liverpool. There are even long histories of the British Empire, published up to the time of the first World War, without a single reference to Nigeria. An example of the prevalent attitude comes from a rare and almost apologetic mention of West Africa in a leading article in *The Economist* of 16 June 1900:

We have a very big and costly war still on hand, we are confronted with one of the most formidable of problems in the case of China, the terrible famine and pestilence in India may well cause disquiet as well as sorrow, and now comes the Ashanti rising to remind us of the responsibilities we have undertaken in that unhealthy quarter of the world. Under ordinary circumstances we should probably pay little heed to the Ashanti difficulties: for, outside a limited commercial circle, few persons can be reasonably expected to pay much attention to that swampy and savage region.

and again:

It is one thing to annex a fine healthy country like New Zealand, as our Government did over half a century ago, and quite another to annex a malarious swamp[1] to keep which will cost several times the actual worth of its products.

These extracts illustrate how even educated men were surprised and puzzled by the insidious extension of Empire in Africa, and how little was known, in London, of West Africa. It was in this spirit of surprised inquiry that J. A. Hobson approached his famous study of imperialism. His diagnosis was that imperialism was 'a depraved choice of national life, imposed by self-seeking interests', a kind of

[1] cf. the 1897 comment by Salisbury, then Prime Minister, on the Niger area: 'a malarious African desert'. Quoted in Grenville, *Lord Salisbury and Foreign Policy* (1964), p. 97.

conspiracy between the investing classes and the professional classes interested in official employment, domination, and adventure overseas. The cure he proposed (apart from refusing official support to people venturing lives and capital in undeveloped lands) was internationally organized development of the backward countries which would otherwise fall an easy prey to nationalistic imperialism.

Whether Hobson's diagnosis was fully accurate or not, his study became a classic, and had a great seminal influence in strengthening reasoned opposition to empire-building. The work had a particular influence on both Russian and American political thought, and helped in the preparation of the indictment of British imperialism and of 'economic imperialism' which since the time of Lenin has divided and darkened the world's counsels. The pity of it was that the process of expansion was complete before Hobson wrote; the responsibilities had been assumed, and it was too late to alter course. It is possible that Hobson did not take into full account the influence of what *The Economist* had perhaps underrated as 'limited commercial circles', and for the same reason—the centres of these circles were not in London but in Liverpool and Manchester.[1] Nineteenth-century Liverpool had grown and flourished during the period of the slave trade, rivalling Bristol. Later, turning to legitimate trade, Liverpool became the centre of such industries as soap manufacture (helped by the salt fields and chemical industry of Cheshire) and the processing of raw materials; many of them, like palm oil, timber, cotton, and rubber, were imports from West Africa. The prosperity of the populous, rapidly industrialized area around Liverpool and Manchester depended very heavily and very precariously on the cotton trade and cotton manufacture. Shortage of raw cotton and the vagaries of the speculative American market meant constant anxiety; shortage of markets for cotton piece-goods spelled ruin to manufacturers, merchants, and shipowners, and hardship to the millions of people dependent on King Cotton for their livelihood. For Lancashire, which then had half the world's cotton spindles and supplied one-quarter of all Britain's exports, the encouragement of cotton growing in the tropical Empire and the finding of new markets there seemed matters of great urgency, matters almost of life or death. The men who formed the Liverpool and Manchester Chambers of Commerce were not

[1] Although Hobson went to Africa on behalf of the *Manchester Guardian*, it was to South Africa, at the time of the war, and there is no evidence that Hobson paid any detailed attention to West African affairs and personalities.

members of the hereditary ruling class, any more than was Chamberlain himself. For the most part they were free traders, radicals, dissenters (although one of those most interested in West Africa, the shipowner Sir Alfred Jones, was an Anglican, and also a Conservative, which helped him in his relations with Chamberlain). The social consciences of these men had long been at war with their tenets of *laissez-faire*, as evidence grew in the northern industrial cities of the precariousness of the prosperity which free trade had brought, and of the crying need to remedy the social evils industrialization had brought in its train. These men saw in West Africa, and in countries such as the Sudan, at once potential sources of raw cotton and potential mass markets, and set up the British Cotton Growing Association, in 1902, for the scientific pursuit of these aims. What they wanted, with an intensity shown by constant deputations and representations to the Colonial Office, was to satisfy the urgent needs of a complex industrial society in fierce competition with others, and the prescription of international co-operation which appealed to more detached observers like Hobson would have seemed to them irrelevant and unrealistic. In their anxiety to feed their hungry machines with palm oil and cotton (and to provide work and food for their own people) the steady pressure they maintained on the Colonial Office was for the development of communications and the improvement of health conditions in West Africa—things essential for the development of two-way trade, but beyond the scope of private enterprise to supply.

It was Lancashire's needs which were at the bottom of the mixed humanitarian and business interest shown by Liverpool shipowners like Sir Alfred Jones in the shipment of Nigerian cotton free of charge, in the setting up of the Liverpool School of Tropical Medicine and of the Liverpool University Institute of Commercial Research in the Tropics, in the formation of the British Cotton Growing Association, in the deputations to the Colonial Office from the Lancashire Chambers of Commerce, and in the invitations to West African Governors to attend and address luncheons and dinners in Liverpool and Manchester. It was their pressure, recorded in the *Monthly Journal* of the Manchester Chamber of Commerce for the years 1890–1910, which gave such emphasis to communications and health measures and the development of trade in the official plans for West Africa, and prompted the appointment as Governors of men with qualifications in port construction, public health, and railway construction. These were not the fortuitous appointments of specialists, leading to idiosyncratic emphasis on their own special interests—they were careful, clear-sighted selections for the work in hand, from within an already experienced cadre of colonial administrators.

Against the general background of apathy and indifference, the views of the special interests may have been given by the permanent officials in the Colonial Office a prominence and importance they would not have enjoyed if there had been more widespread interest and knowledge; but at least the varied pressures of merchants, of missionaries, and of service interests, the influence of critics like Hobson, and the strong pressures exerted on London by Governors like Lugard, MacGregor, and Moor did not permit the permanent officials of the Colonial Office to relapse into their earlier indifference. They were not only kept awake, but permitted, by the small number of the special interests exerting pressure upon them, to steer an expert course between the dangers of giving too much satisfaction or too much offence to any one interest. The skilled exponents of the art of compromise in the Colonial Office were able to prepare plans for Chamberlain's forward policy in Nigeria which met with the approval of the supporting interests and yet left the potential enemies, in the Treasury, in Parliament, and in the country, relatively undisturbed.

There were two kinds of compromise or balancing act going on continually—one the reconciliation so far as possible of the conflicting aims of the humanitarian, mercantile, and military advocates of expansion, and the other the larger compromise, which dominated colonial policy, the balance between the two impossible extremes of high-minded imperialist expansion given lavish financial, diplomatic, and moral support on the one hand, and, on the other, the disgraceful anarchy which complete abstention from official imperial intervention in West Africa would have guaranteed.

At the same time as the British Government was planning Nigeria the United States Government launched itself upon a career of empire-building in the Philippines. The American planners sought the assistance of the universities and of learned commissions, which made published recommendations. The approach of the British Government to the planning of Nigeria was much less open, less formal, and more practised. There were a few suggestions publicly canvassed, notably Mary Kingsley's idea that her allies the Liverpool and Manchester traders should form a kind of traders' government for West

Africa, a council of traders headed by Goldie 'to fight red tape and foreigners'. This would indeed have been the finest flower of free trade—a dislike of government, bureaucracy, and taxation so strong that the traders themselves must govern and legislate. According to one source, the offer of a Governor-Generalship of West Africa was made to Sir George Goldie and refused by him; it is more certain that he refused the offer of a Governorship of or in the new domain being planned.[1]

Whether he was ever intended to play a commanding role or not, Goldie was one of the planners, the only non-official in the official committee under the chairmanship of Lord Selborne, the Parliamentary Under-Secretary of State for the Colonies, which was appointed in 1898 to do the first concerted planning and to report to Chamberlain. Even Goldie, as effective head of the Royal Niger Company, was a 'quasi-official'. The other members were administrators of long experience—the Governor of Lagos (McCallum, replaced the following year, when ill-health prevented his return to Lagos, by MacGregor) and the Commissioner for the Niger Coast Protectorate (Moor)—and the senior clerks or permanent officials in the Colonial Office and Foreign Office departments concerned (Antrobus and Hill). A committee of this kind was hardly likely to produce such unorthodox solutions as Mary Kingsley's idea of government by the traders. Their job was to supply practical answers to two groups of related questions put to them.

Their answers were 'practical' only if one is ready to accept, as they did, that there were few dangers, discomforts, and difficulties which could deter selected British officers from their task, given reasonable time and good leadership. It is one of the myths which have grown up around the story of British administration in tropical Africa that the administrators of this period were ignorant of the problems they tackled. In an absolute sense, these men may have been ignorant—witness the wild guesses current as to the extent and population of Nigeria, ranging from half a million square miles to one million square miles, and from twenty to thirty-five million in population. But in so far as there was knowledge, these planners were the men who had it, acquired at first hand by experience in Africa, or in the form of long experience in office of the ways and means of administration at home and abroad. Goldie, McCallum, and Moor were acknowledged authorities on their own parts of the new country. Hill

[1] J. E. Flint, *Sir George Goldie and the Making of Nigeria* (1960), pp. 303–5.

of the Foreign Office had served long in Africa and in the African Department in London, throughout the period of the 'scramble'. Antrobus, head of the West African Department of the Colonial Office, who had acted as Governor of St. Helena, was an acknowledged authority on West African history; he compiled 'a great part of the historical matter' for the West African volume of the authoritative *Historical Geography of the British Colonies* (1894) by Sir Charles Lucas 'of Balliol College, Oxford, and the Colonial Office London'. These men were steeped in the knowledge to be gained by daily reading of the reports and dispatches of Governors and the representations and arguments of the various sectional interests. They knew what administration cost in terms of men, iron, and money, and were aware how steadily and softly they must go, particularly under a dynamic Minister trying to force his colleagues on, if they were not to overreach themselves and build up overwhelming opposition both at home and on the spot. Their report, though absolutely confident of success, sounds some of the first notes of caution and of compromise.

In the first group of questions were those of organization. Should the administration be 'united under one hand' or divided? If divided, how many administrations? What arrangements for military forces? What Customs duties? Should there be a Customs union? What other forms of taxation were practicable? What revenue could be expected and what was the expected cost of administration? This was indeed a brisk and business-like approach to Empire. Had the committee's deliberations been made public they would certainly have been much admired in France, where those interested in French expansion abroad were already comparing Britain's successful business-like methods with the French difficulties over expansion. The French difficulties were due partly to the ideological and theoretical disputes over the constitutional status of France overseas, the legacy of changes in France herself from kingdom to republic, from republic to Empire and back again twice, each change altering the whole concept of overseas rule. To their French contemporaries the Selborne Committee's questions and answers would have seemed very practical indeed and very 'British'.

The second group of questions centred round policy in regard to the Northern Emirates. What policy should be adopted towards Sokoto, Bornu, and Rabah? Should a Resident be placed at Sokoto? What about railways in the North?

The report,[1] which occupies less than twenty pages of typescript, is a fascinating document. There is no hint that the committee found the ends and the means disproportionate, or the prospect defeating. It seems rather as if they regarded their immense undertaking simply as one of the last necessary finishing touches to an already successful world-wide programme of development, a sizeable operation but one well within the compass of their nation. Even so, however, their emphasis was on 'not forcing the pace', on economy, and on self-financing growth.

They agreed that the object to be aimed at was the eventual establishment of a resident Governor-General for the whole of the territories; but this was undesirable for the present. Only a young man could do the job, and even a young, vigorous man must be absent recuperating on leave for one-third of the time—so any potential gain in continuity of policy would forthwith be lost. A suggestion by Goldie that this difficulty might be removed in time by making a 'Simla' in the Bauchi highlands is one of the few glimpses in the committee's report of romantic imperialist dreams. Another reason for not having a Governor-General at the outset was the absence of telegraphs and roads, which made internal communications more difficult, for the time being at least, than communication between Nigeria and Downing Street.

So they proposed 'provincial Governors under the direct superintendence of the Colonial Office'. The idea that the Niger would be a good dividing-line between administrations was discarded; international navigation commitments and the administrative difficulties which would arise from different systems of civil and criminal law on opposite banks made it preferable for both banks to come under one administration.

The split proposed was into two: 'a Maritime Province and a Soudan Province, between the Soudan regions governed by Mohammedans and the Pagan regions of the Niger Delta'. Although 'the Mohammedan Yorubas' were to be in the Maritime Province, Ilorin would be in the Soudan Province. The seats of government might be Lokoja and Asaba (the Niger Company's main military and commercial stations on the Niger). This was an indication of Goldie's influence, no doubt, and of the dominance so long exercised over men's minds by the idea of the Niger as a great potential highway, from the time of Mungo Park onwards; even now the idea has not

[1] C.O. 446/3.

ceased to fascinate the planners. Lagos, at the time, was literally in bad odour; the sanitation problem seemed insoluble, and in despair a move of the capital (to Olokomeji near Ibadan) had been contemplated.

Each province would be divided into divisions, each division into districts. Here McCallum suggested that the chiefs should be organized as village and district councils. McCallum's service in the Malay states led him to favour the gradual introduction of the Residential system as practised in Perak and Selangor. He had reported, soon after his arrival in Lagos in 1897, that he found things there about twenty-five years behind the Malay states.[1] The clear implication of this was that the colony of Lagos belonged still to the pre-1870 world, the outmoded world of sail and wooden ships.

Military forces, the committee proposed, should be under one command, with the idea of making units interchangeable as required between the provinces. Customs union was proposed, on the basis of the Lagos tariff.

The committee next considered what now seem to be absurdly small financial resources—less, in real terms, for the whole annual budget, civil and military, of the whole country, than would now be considered the absolute minimum for the purpose of preparing on paper a plan of development. Prudently, they declined to take account of either possible savings through common services or possible increased costs due to future improvements on the existing level of administration. They worked out roughly that revenue for the whole of Nigeria would be about £400,000 per annum. Civil expenditure would be about £348,000, military about the same, £351,000 (including the cost of Lugard's newly formed West African Frontier Force at £250,000). This would leave a deficit, for the first year's operations, of almost £300,000, nearly half the estimated minimum expenditure.

The expenditure figures were arrived at by the process of adding up the actual current costs of the three existing administrations. Total revenues were calculated by adding up each administration's revenue and then rounding off to £400,000 to allow for loss of revenue from the Niger Company's territories on the adoption of the Lagos Customs tariff. Before this adjustment was made the revenue figures were: Lagos £175,000, Niger Coast £144,000, Niger Company £110,000.

[1] Newbury, *The Western Slave Coast and its Rulers* (1961), p. 175.

The extent of the committee's radical departure from the tradition of making a dependency's ends meet is shown in this simple sum:

| | |
|---|---|
| Lagos | £175,000 |
| Niger Coast territories | £144,000 |
| Niger Company territories | £130,000 |
| West African Frontier Force | £250,000 |
| | £699,000 |
| Deduct Revenue | £400,000 |
| Deficit | £299,000 |

The committee then turned their attention to other possible taxation—as well they might, for the Treasury was soon to be faced with a bill for buying out the Niger Company, as well as this 'open-ended' annual commitment of nearly one-half of the minimum cost of running the new country, and would expect to be convinced first that all practicable sources of local revenue had been tapped. The committee found it possible to agree, but about the immediate future only:

We are unanimously of the opinion that it would not be prudent at the present time to attempt to impose any form of direct taxation on the natives, but with the exception of Sir George Goldie we think that a village tax in some form or other may be gradually imposed in the future.

McCallum, with the idea of conciliar administration in mind, and, as he put it on another occasion, the need to 'engage the Chiefs in Administration and make them happy,'[1] suggested some tax might be devised as revenue for chiefs deprived, as the result of British intervention, of their chief source of income—slaves and slave-raiding. Perhaps duties on spirits would do, or a salt duty farmed out to the chiefs themselves. Local taxation was to prove one of the most intractable practical problems of Nigerian administration.

In the replies to the second group of questions—policy in the North—the officials present were content to confess their ignorance, gracefully acknowledging Sir George Goldie as the only authority on the subject. He was very firm about not sending a Resident to Sokoto 'until the Fulah power is crushed'. No attempt should be made to do this by a general '*coup de main*'. It should be done gradually, each Emir being taken by turn. Now that agreement had been reached

[1] N.R.O. Misc., ADM/91373, quoted in Newbury, p. 189.

with the French, there was not such urgency—let the new Governor arrive, study the situation, and advise as to timing.

There was unanimous support for a trunk line from Kano down the valley of the Kaduna to the Niger, with access to some port for ocean-going ships—Lagos, Warri, or Asaba. When it came to the question of choosing between these possibilities, agreement ended. The Governor of Lagos predictably thought Lagos when dredged would be best, and that the Lagos–Abeokuta line should go on to the Niger to meet the line from Kano. Goldie and Moor thought the natural line from Kano would be to Warri or to Sapele, both of which, they said, were readily available for 'ocean-going steamers of the largest size'. McCallum questioned this. It is possible that some heat may have been generated in this discussion, for Lord Selborne's report picks its way very carefully:

So far as the very limited information at our disposal enables us to form an opinion, which must however be considered as purely provisional and subject to further knowledge and experience, Sir Clement Hill and I are inclined to agree with Sir Ralph Moor and Sir George Goldie.

The remaining member, Antrobus, as befitted the only real Home civil servant present, was even more cautious when faced with this invitation to reach a conclusion on inadequate data; the report reads: 'Mr. Antrobus holds his opinion in suspense.'

With one major change, and a few minor ones, the Selborne Report seems to have formed the basis of the subsequent preparations. The major change was Chamberlain's decision that for the time being there should continue to be three administrations, instead of the reduction to two proposed by the committee. Goldie busied himself with the preparations for the 'nationalization' of the Niger Company; there were to be protracted negotiations over compensation to the company during the handing over to the Crown of the company's administrative responsibilities.

The Colonial Office was by no means so keen to take over as the Foreign Office was to hand over, and the effective date was put off to January 1900. One of the Colonial Office's preoccupations was the need to get an extra body or two into its four-man West African Department to help with the extra work being 'thrown upon' the office, which would be 'very heavy and complicated'; they estimated that correspondence would increase from the 8,865 letters of 1895 to nearly 22,000 in 1900—and most of the outgoing letters were handwritten fair copies of manuscript drafts, the original drafts then being retained in the files. Typewriter and carbon paper had not yet conquered in Downing Street, although beginning to be used for documents like the Selborne Committee Report itself.

A telegram (the commercial rate at the time was 6*s*. 8*d*. per word!) was sent to Lagos to bring back Lugard from Nigeria to take part in the negotiations and discussions with Goldie, and to be offered the post of High Commissioner for Northern Nigeria, which he accepted. Moor was released by the Foreign Office to continue in charge of the Southern Protectorate. After discussion with Lugard and Goldie, Antrobus had the idea of making the two new protectorates into two small colonies with large protectorates attached to them—apparently with the object of making the new appointments Governorships while avoiding breach of precedent. This idea was dropped, however, and the legal drafting went ahead on the basis of the Foreign Jurisdiction Acts. This ingenious legislation, originally devised for the quite different work of legitimizing British consular courts for British subjects in the decaying dominions of the Sultan of Turkey, lent itself well enough for the different purpose of legitimizing expansion in Africa. Its use involved the issue of Orders in Council under the Act, on the legal fiction that what was planned was for the purpose of a special jurisdiction conferred upon the Crown by the existing rulers of the country. It had been the same fiction which had made the Niger Coast and Oil Rivers Protectorates the concern of the Foreign Office rather than the Colonial Office.

By 1900 the original distinction between colony and protectorate had become so blurred that the Colonial Office was able to take on responsibility for both, making little practical differentiation between them except in the fundamental legal instrument giving them their constitutional nucleus—an Order in Council for a protectorate, Letters Patent and Royal Instructions to the Governor for a colony. Nevertheless, some vestige of the original distinction remained in the minds of conscientious administrators and their legal advisers, influencing them in their conduct of business. In one sense Lugard's system of rule had its basis in the idea of protectorate (jurisdiction exercised, through Residents, by the High Commissioner), as opposed to the Crown colony system where the Governor presided over Executive and Legislative Council, and the law once made was the business of the Supreme Court and District Commissioners of the Supreme Court. The Crown colony was a development of the original colonies of British settlement in America. In the separation of administrative and judicial powers, in the ideas of the common law, and of the rule of law, and in the old tenaciously held principle of a representative body to deliberate on taxation, there were in the constitution of the Crown colony the essentials of the British constitution, points which with the right soil and attention could become growing points for sturdy, independent life. The protectorate, on the other hand, a newer device, did not possess the same warnings and safeguards against absolute, authoritarian rule.

Once the decision was taken by Chamberlain to preserve Lagos as a separate administration and to have two new protectorates (for the time being), further thought was given to naming them. The original suggestion by the Selborne Committee had been a Maritime Province and a Soudan Province; later, in a minute of 13 November 1898, Antrobus suggested Niger Soudan and Niger Coast. This submission was mislaid on its way: before it was found again Antrobus had a change of mind, minuting in April 1899:

> . . . as Nigeria has become a familiar term (although strictly speaking it should be 'Nigritia') I would suggest 'Southern' and 'Northern', or 'Lower' and 'Upper' Nigeria. The term 'British Soudan' will probably be wanted some day for the country to the East of the line settled with France, as the French already call the country to the West of it the 'French Soudan'.

After Selborne had expressed his preference for 'Northern' and 'Southern' Chamberlain himself decided, writing in the file rather illegibly on 10 April 1899, 'It must be Nigeria—and not Soudan', commenting that 'Northern' and 'Southern' were more descriptive, while 'Upper' and 'Lower' were more euphonious to his ear—but he didn't care which was adopted.[1]

So Nigeria it was, divided into three parts. There was the colony of Lagos with its own Yorubaland Protectorate, there was the large Southern Nigeria Protectorate, and the immense Northern Protectorate. Both the latter were still largely 'paper protectorates' under High Commissioners with autocratic legal powers, but not so much power over men, and even less power over money. They were subject to *Colonial Regulations* and to rigid control of expenditure, particularly where such expenditure was an actual or potential drain on the Treasury at home. In the short period between 1900 and the beginning of amalgamation under Lugard in 1912 the administrations of

[1] C.O. 446/3. He wrote: 'But I really do not care a shard [?] which it is.'

North and South managed to develop in strikingly different patterns—so different that they seemed more like the products of the influence of different ruling powers than the offspring of the same Secretary of State, brought up by the same Ministry, the Colonial Office.

Part of the explanation for the contrast in development between 1900 and 1912 lies in the history of North and South, and part in the existing differences between them—the differences of soil and climate, as it were, in which the seeds were sown. But the greater difference was in the seed itself, and in the sowers—unplanned differences, for which the explanation must be sought, not in the detailed official planning, which gives no hint of 'divide and rule' or deliberate choice of different methods, but in the general complex of changing assumptions, pressures, events, and personalities in which the planners and those who put the plans into operation had to work. And, in particular, there was the personality of the man chosen to administer the Northern Protectorate, Lugard.

It would of course have been impracticable for the Selborne Committee to introduce anything like a unitary system of administration at one blow for the whole country. Even setting aside the difficulties of distance and bad communications, and the effects of climate and terrain, in themselves sufficient to preclude the idea of one unitary administration, there were immense differences between the many peoples of the country.

At one extreme, in the urban part of the Crown colony of Lagos, there was an outpost of European, occidental, Atlantic culture, already of several decades standing, with Government departments, churches, schools—even Moslem schools teaching Western subjects (a bizarre instance of outside influence from an unexpected source, because it was the West Indian black man, Dr. Blyden, and a white, English Moslem[1] who joined forces to persuade the Lagos Moslems to take up education, getting the written blessing of the Sultan of Turkey to help them). The hospital was described by Lagos's medically qualified Governor as bearing comparison in nursing with the best in Europe. There were harbour works, a railway, a racecourse which was also a recreation ground held in trust for public use, a Palladian Government House open to the Lagos public—more open than it was later to become—where Legislative Council meetings and agricultural shows were held, as well as 'multi-racial' ladies' champagne lunches in aid of charitable public health efforts in the town.

[1] Abdullah Quilliam, 'Sheikh al Islam of the British Isles'.

There was electric light in the streets, there were telephones, printing-presses, newspapers. Amidst the white officials, and not segregated from them by separate residential areas and hospital facilities, there was an educated élite of 'Black Englishmen'—doctors (four out of the Government establishment of sixteen), clergy, pastors, teachers, lawyers, police officers, journalists, senior clerks (when 'clerk' corresponded nearly in the civil service with what is now administrative status, and the Governor's confidential clerk, for instance, an African, was also clerk to the Legislative Council). And, of course, there were substantial business men, traders, middle-men, some of them frequent visitors to Liverpool, some with sons and daughters being educated overseas.

At the other geographical extreme, in the North, was the south-western edge of the Moslem Empire. There Emirs and their Viziers ruled large and populous states whose orientation, in prayer, in trade, and in culture, was to the north and east, across the desert; their authority, laws, and taxes derived ultimately from the Caliphate, however much they had changed on the long journey across Africa.

Between these extremes were hundreds of communities, large and small, some without contact with either outside world, some in contact with both the Atlantic and the Moslem worlds, but mostly isolated one from the other; some seeking refuge in remote hill country from the slave raids of their neighbours, others separated by swamps, rivers, thick forest, and mutual fear and distrust. Where terrain and communications did permit there was a quite bewildering intermingling of creeds, crops, trade, blood, and language. And, naturally, there was incessant conflict between town and town, people and people. Any form of power reaching out in these conditions beyond the confines of acknowledged kinship and obligation tended towards naked power, tyranny, and slave-raiding; human sympathies and compassion stopped short at the confines of kinship.

But these confusions and distinctions were widespread throughout Nigeria, and do little in themselves to account for differences in the administrative methods applied, once the plan was put into operation, by the British in the North and the British in the South.

The formal, planned framework of the two new protectorates provided no evidence of different intentions towards North and South. The Orders in Council setting them up are almost identical in material wording. They enabled the High Commissioners to provide by proclamation (i.e. without the Crown colony provision for Legislative and Executive Councils) for the administration of justice, the raising of revenue, and generally for the peace, order, and good government of their protectorates. They were ordered to respect any native laws by which the civil relations of any chiefs, tribes, or populations under Her Majesty's Government were regulated, except so far as they were 'incompatible with the due exercise of Her Majesty's power and jurisdiction' or 'clearly injurious to the welfare of the natives'. There is only one significant difference in the two Orders which gave such sweeping autocratic powers: in the Northern Order there was provision for the senior military officer to take over the administration in the event of the High Commissioner's absence, incapacity, or death when no other specific successor had been appointed. In the South, in like circumstances, it was a civilian, the Senior Divisional Commissioner, who would have taken over. This, together with the appointment of a soldier as the first High Commissioner in the North, was the sole indication of any relative preponderance of military considerations in that protectorate.

Perhaps the most significant aspects of this first outline plan for the development of Nigeria, as revealed in the Selborne Committee's report, in the subsequent preparations, and in the legal drafting—apart from the planners' confidence—are, first and foremost, the overriding concern with economic development, in particular the improvement of communications (with a good deal of optimism about the navigability of the Niger); second, the emphasis on 'indirect rule', on associating the chiefs with the administration, and on avoiding direct taxation; third, the unanimous acceptance of the 'inevitability of gradualness' in the sense that improvements in trade and wealth must come first; fourth, the need for imperial financial assistance on the unprecedented scale of nearly half the recurrent costs of administration, bringing in its train the inescapable need for stringent financial economy, to begin with at least; and fifth, the desirability of amalgamation, when practicable.

There is nothing in either the words or the figures of the planners to suggest they envisaged anything other than a continuation of the current orthodoxy of 'peaceful penetration'. What was new—brand new—was the impetus which Chamberlain's drive and energy gave to the forward movement he had so long advocated. There was clearly no idea of rapid conquest and pacification of immense areas over which a 'steel grid' of administration would be imposed. Such a concept does not square with the money available. No experienced men, however confident, could really have expected to pacify and administer uniformly this immense, populous, unhealthy, undeveloped, complex, and disturbed territory at the rate of 14*s*. per square mile per annum, or something like 4*d*. per head of the estimated population. For this was what they expected to have—revenue, including help from the imperial Treasury, £700,000, population 'guesstimated' 35,000,000, territory anything up to 1,000,000 square miles—and no direct taxation in contemplation. And, of the £700,000 expenditure, the half which represented civil expenditure was almost entirely committed to the maintenance of the established settlements and installations of government at Lagos, Calabar, and Lokoja with their essential services and communications.

It becomes obvious that the experienced officials who did the planning were not departing from the tried and successful policy of 'peaceful penetration' along improving lines of communication which would serve as a cornucopia of wealth through civilizing trade, and also as the principal means for extending the activities and services of the modern state. With the revenue to be derived from indirect taxation on trade—limited in amount by the vigilant opposition to tax of both the populace and the British trader—would come more and better administration, health, education, more communications, more trade, more revenue, in a self-financing and accelerating spiral which would soon make it possible to dispense with imperial grants-in-aid. God and Mammon would co-operate: mission endeavours to convert, to educate, to civilize, and to heal the sick would supplement the efforts of traders and administrators to bring the country into the health and wealth-giving stream of world trade. In the conditions of the time, this was a sane, healthy, practical programme, capable of doing enormous good to an enormous number of people. It lacked the romance of military conquest, but there was nothing in it necessarily ignoble, or evil, or narrowly materialistic.

A prerequisite of imperial assistance at the outset, given the strength and unsentimentality of the 'Gladstonian garrison' of the Treasury[1] in the British system of government, the strength of the tradition that colonies worth acquiring could support themselves, and the political strength of other claims on financial resources, was that the new protectorates should trim their money costs to the very minimum, and raise themselves as much and as soon as possible by their own bootstraps. But there seems to have been no thought of

[1] Salisbury's phrase, used to Chamberlain, in 1896—see Garvin, op. cit., p. 177.

shirking the investment of British lives in unhealthy and sometimes fatal discomfort. It was taken for granted (in the age of self-help, of muscular Christianity, of imperialism, of belief in 'the survival of the fittest', and of the supremacy of the British gentleman) that men of 'the right sort' would be found more easily than money, gentlemen ready if necessary to sacrifice life and health and the society of friends and families in order to fulfil the ideal of public service, without great material reward, and at the same time to play a patriotic and adventurous part in the expansion of the British Empire. No imperial Treasury watched jealously over the expenditure of lives.

These considerations did not have to be explicitly stated by the planners, who were not producing material for public consumption, and had a tacit, shared awareness of the limitations, financial and other, within which they worked; the public statements came later, from the politicians, in the parliamentary debate on buying out the Royal Niger Company. The planners knew that a powerful Minister such as Chamberlain interested actively in West African development was a rare and transient phenomenon, and that there were limits to even his power to prise open the Treasury purse strings, when there were urgent demands for expenditure in 'Darkest England'. It was, for instance, in 1899 that the first scheme for old-age pensions was rejected as too costly, at about £20 millions, and imperial war was soon to cost more and leave less for the 'vast undeveloped estate' overseas. They were aware too of the attitudes of the Liverpool and Manchester traders, on whose continued interest and enterprise the development of Nigeria depended. Mary Kingsley, E. D. Morel, and the Chambers of Commerce themselves had made the traders' views quite well known, to those interested.

Briefly, the merchants and shipowners believed commerce to be the real and only valid reason why Britain should be in West Africa, not only because it was profitable, but because it was the source of the blessings of civilization. The building of bureaucratic governments and armed forces was anathema to them, especially when done at the expense of their trade. They were therefore ready to quarrel with any sign of extravagance in official expenditure, on the ground that government and taxation were only too liable to interfere with commerce; that commerce was the greatest civilizing agent; that government should therefore be limited to the creation and maintenance of the means and the services whereby commerce could be extended. If there had to be soldiers and police, they should be kept to the minimum, and well in the background; their activities disrupted trade, cost a fortune, and scared off or antagonized customers. So far as methods of administration were concerned, the traders were all for gradualism and organic growth—'tact, rather than the sword'—no officious meddling with native rule and institutions, co-operation rather than rigid control. The voices of the humanitarian and mission interests usually joined with those of the traders in preaching against the use of the sword, and in favour of tact and sympathetic treatment. The missions, Catholic and Protestant, shared the traders' belief in the beneficence of legitimate trade, and did much to stimulate it, although they were on the whole somewhat less inclined than the traders to leave native rule and institutions undisturbed—they had come to convert, to change men, not to leave them as they were.

There was however a rival school of thought among the British interested in Nigeria which corresponded (more closely than either the mercantile or the evangelical interests) to Hobson's concept of upper-class conspirators fostering imperial expansion. Until the Boer War ended half a century of 'major' peace, broken only by small 'subalterns' wars' on remote frontiers, waged against badly-armed tribesmen, there had been relatively little outlet for the energies and the craving for active adventure of some of the ablest and boldest professional soldiers. In the Navy, things were rather different; their peacetime role of policing the world was occupation and adventure enough, and the naval officer had constantly to acquire new skills and techniques as the Navy changed from sail to steam and gunnery developed. A certain diplomatic skill and tact were required too in the work of policing the seas and in formal ceremonial visits to foreign and colonial governments. But peacetime soldiering in the late nineteenth century was by no means a full-time job for intelligent and energetic young men. Hence the phenomenon of so many subalterns on half-pay roaming over Africa and all the remote places of the world looking for glorious deeds (or at least interesting things) to do.

Lugard himself had been one of these; at the turn of the century Winston Churchill was such another, with a similar restless desire for adventure and fame. A good number of these men found their way into the service of the colonies and protectorates, the colonial and consular services of the time, usually in the rougher, pioneering outposts which did not appeal to the professional civil servant and diplomat. Goldie was one of this imperial school; he was originally a

Royal Engineer, like many of the other empire builders.[1] For men like these, the plans made for Nigeria could offer adventure, employment, and fulfilment of a patriotic kind. Although peaceful penetration was what was proposed, the military preparations showed that no one expected the process of penetration to be peaceful from beginning to end. It is worth mentioning that the class which provided the army officers of the day, came, by and large, from different parts of Britain, and from an educational and social background subtly different from the Britain which provided the economic drive towards expansion and the religious and evangelical drive. The administrative and military officials appointed direct to Nigeria through the Patronage Private Secretary to the Colonial Secretary were for the most part public-school, 'officer class', conforming to the ideals of '*l'Angleterre chevaleresque*'. They were Matthew Arnold's 'Barbarians', in contrast to the traders, the missionaries, the sea-captains, and the specialist officials, who were more like Arnold's 'Philistines' from the industrial north, from Scotland, Wales, and Ireland, some of them dissenters in religion, with radical sympathies in politics. This added a variety of flavourings to the ingredients of British intervention in Nigeria—ingredients which did not always blend harmoniously, but tended to separate out, 'Barbarians' to the North, 'Philistines' to the South, where missions, the law, and commerce were the main influences on the Government.[2]

How the plan worked out in practice is the theme of the following chapters on the period of separate development. So far as the planners of the Selborne Committee were concerned, the Colonial Office, and Chamberlain himself, they could legitimately have congratulated themselves on the new ship of state which they had designed and launched—they had avoided the various dangers of too quick and too slow, too much and too little; they had responded to the pressures put on them adequately, and had prepared a plan for action which took full account of the pressures it would have to withstand. Except for the bargain with the Royal Niger Company which had to be presented by a reluctant Chancellor of the Exchequer to an unenthusiastic Parliament, the launching was done quietly, with no public fan-

[1] e.g. McCallum of Lagos, Gordon and Kitchener of the Sudan, Girouard of Northern Nigeria, Nathan and Guggisberg of the Gold Coast.

[2] Even a cursory examination of the staff lists reveals this—the few 'Hons.' who served in Nigeria (in the early years) served in the North, where too there were far more 'double-barrelled' surnames, and a more marked disposition to retain military ranks in civil life.

fare—no mention, for instance, in the Speech from the Throne for the session. It was put to Parliament that the taking over of Nigeria was both inevitable and also a sound investment. As Dame Margery Perham says of the debate in her biography of Lugard, 'There was a gloomy feeling that the country was being let in for a bad bargain.'[1] Chamberlain himself did nothing to arouse emotion for or against the project, and the House accepted the Bill without any of the welter of conflicting moral, strategic, economic, and humanitarian argument which inferior tactical skill might have caused. By tactical skill, and by accepting the 'inevitability of gradualness', Chamberlain and his planners seemed to have avoided all the obvious and immediate dangers, and not to have overreached themselves.

In all this, however, and particularly in the Selborne Committee's concept of peaceful penetration, self-financing, gradual, and relying upon commerce as the principal agency for good and for progress, the planners had reckoned without the most conspicuous absentee from the committee's deliberations, Lugard, the frontier soldier selected first as High Commissioner for Northern Nigeria (1900–6) and later as the first Governor-General and amalgamator of the two Nigerias (1912–18).

The choice of Lugard as the first High Commissioner in the North, despite his lack of civil experience, was in some ways an obvious one, if Goldie was out of the running, and if Chamberlain as patron chose to look outside the ranks of the as yet unorganized colonial service itself. Lugard's claims as a worker for the Empire in the field were strong, his supporters and friends influential, and perhaps there was no intense competition from serving officials for this enormous, new, uncomfortable pioneering assignment. His biographer has described Lugard's personal qualifications vividly:

> For the task set him, Lugard was so exactly fitted that his life up to this moment might have been a training especially designed by Providence. He was experienced in every activity that the newly annexed country demanded; in transport and supply; in survey work; in prospecting for minerals; in dealing with Africans, whether potentates, raw tribesmen or wage labourers. He knew Africa and Africans as did few men of his time. He was a soldier, and a jungle soldier, in a job that was still half military and he had himself created the Regiment he employed. He knew his region, having worked around the middle Niger for six years, helping to win its western frontiers. He had been in contact with Islam and he was

[1] Perham, *Lugard, The Years of Authority*, p. 13.

an expert on slavery in a region where it was a major problem. His physique allowed him to do two men's work in a climate and conditions which halved the capacities of most men. But no list of qualities, however long, would have met the needs of the work if they had not been fused within an ardent temperament and directed by a will of exceptional strength. He entered upon his work with complete confidence.[1]

But what was this work? What was the task set him? We have seen what the Colonial Office planners including McCallum of Lagos and Moor of Southern Nigeria understood it to be. It was the process of peaceful penetration, gradual, diplomatic, not forcing the pace. In fact, it was not a soldier's job at all, unless the soldier happened to be a man of exceptional tact and patience, prepared not to behave like a commander in the field, prepared indeed to unlearn all 'the principles of war'—speed, surprise, concentration of force, etc. It was not necessarily a task for epic heroes; there had to be economy in money, which meant hardship and spartan conditions, but if Lugard himself had so chosen there could have been a matching economy in armed force.

The elements of the task were that the man on the spot should subordinate himself to the policy of the home Government as expressed through the Colonial Office; that he would work to the limitations of Treasury control, using the funds granted to him economically, and for the purposes for which they were intended. The rewards for doing such a job were not fame and fortune and a position of greater power, but more probably promotion to a better-paid Governorship in a more advanced, more comfortable, wealthier, and no doubt smaller colony, after a stint in West Africa. McCallum and MacGregor, for instance, leaving Lagos with health impaired, went each in turn to Newfoundland. Lugard himself joined briefly in this stately dance from one Governorship to another, when he accepted promotion from Northern Nigeria to Hong Kong—but he did so with misgivings, uncomfortably, recognizing that his qualities were not those required in the senior civil official presiding over a complex civil administration.[2]

For the carrying out of the Selborne Committee's plan, therefore, Lugard was far from exactly fitted. Indeed, his temperament and his military training might have been especially designed to make it hard for him to understand the task or to accept its limitations and its implications. He had the born soldier's love of fame and glory, but

[1] Perham, op. cit., p. 139. [2] See Perham, op. cit., p. 287.

here the plan was for peaceful development, not for glory. He had the soldier's love of discipline and of ranks, each rank obedient through the official hierarchy to its head; for him law and authority proceeded downwards; they were not working arrangements evolved through discussion and democratic process. Even before his appointment Lugard was influentially connected, and well known both as a man of action and as a writer, speaker, and publicist. He had been arraigned for inhumanity in East Africa, and involved as a result in fierce public controversy. His military pride, and connections with men like Goldie and Chamberlain, made it all the more difficult for him to accept directions from those whom he called at various times the 'mandarins', the 'office clerks', and 'hostile microbes' of the Colonial Office and the Treasury. His marriage with Flora Shaw, Colonial Editor of *The Times*, opened up a new and important sphere of influence which neither he nor she hesitated to use to advance his views and ambitions. He regarded himself, as army officers are apt to do, as 'the servant of the King and Nation', not as the servant of the Secretary of State.[1]

A more detailed comparison of the Northern pattern of administration with the more orthodox working out of the official plan brings out the validity of the thesis that Lugard's administration was conceived in classic militaristic and authoritarian terms. But, since the Southern administrations were both older and more orthodox, it seems appropriate to give an account first of the developing public services in the South, during the period of separate development from 1900 to 1912.

[1] Perham, op. cit., p. 196.

# CHAPTER III

# Lagos and the Yorubaland Protectorate 1900–1904

Soundness on Railway extension, on provincial government by the chiefs, and on Sanitation should be the great political tests applied to the public men of this country.

Sir William MacGregor.

LAGOS and its Yorubaland Protectorate remained a state apart from the new protectorate of Southern Nigeria until impaired health led to the departures of Governor MacGregor from Lagos and High Commissioner Moor from Calabar. The two territories were then joined, by the expedient of appointing one man, Walter Egerton, to replace them both and to fuse the two administrations together. That process began in 1904, and Egerton stayed in Southern Nigeria until Lugard was appointed, in 1912, to govern the two remaining administrations, North and South, and to do the same work of fusing two into one. This chapter is concerned with the brief twentieth-century duration of Lagos and its hinterland, as a separate administrative entity, up to 1904.

From what has been written in the preceding pages about Chamberlain's policy of development, about peaceful penetration, and about the commercial pressure for better communications and sanitation; and from the fact that Lagos was already under the Colonial Office in 1895 when Chamberlain took office, one would expect the changes wrought in Lagos in the decade between 1895 and Egerton's arrival to reflect the five years' start of Lagos over the rest of the country, and to illustrate the current ideas of development—if the officials to whom Chamberlain entrusted the task of governing Lagos were able men faithfully carrying out their duty. In fact, his policy of energetic development in trade, communications, and health conditions was ably and faithfully carried out by both the Governors whom he selected for Lagos, until each in turn was invalided—first by McCallum, until his premature departure in 1899, and then by MacGregor, from 1899 to 1904.

Each of these men, in his own way, is an interesting example of the comparative ease with which an able specialist officer, in those days before a special corps of generalist colonial administrators was formed, could move from special to general duties and so gain the experience and reputation which led to high administrative office. They were not, like Lugard, thrown in at the deep end from military command to high civil office, but acquired administrative experience more gradually, within the colonial service. McCallum's road to Governorship had first taken him through the Royal Military Academy at Woolwich, where in 1874 he passed out first of his year into the Royal Engineers. His first appointment overseas was as a Royal Engineer officer, superintendent of telegraphs in the Straits Settlements, and later working on the Singapore fortifications. This was followed by a spell as Private Secretary to the Governor of the Straits Settlements, and then by assignments as various as the preparation of a defence project for Singapore, a commission of inquiry into disturbances in Perak, and the superintendence of admiralty engineering works in Hong Kong. In 1880 he became Deputy Colonial Engineer, Straits Settlements, in 1884 Colonial Engineer and Surveyor General. From 1881 to 1886 he was president of the Singapore municipality, and also served as a member of the Executive and Legislative Councils. He was a Special Commissioner in Pahang during disturbances there in 1891. He was an Associate of the Institute of Civil Engineers, as well as a Royal Engineer, and for some of his years in Singapore his chief task had been the construction of the harbour and its fortification. These were exceptional qualifications for the job of administering a tropical sea-port colony like Lagos and improving its communications, sanitation, and trade; McCallum's experience had included both military and civil engineering, harbour works, telegraphs, 'peaceful penetration', central and local government. Although McCallum's ill-health forced him to leave West Africa after only one tour of duty, Chamberlain managed to find, in MacGregor, a man with even more varied but even more apposite experience and talents to continue the intensive work of development.[1]

Sir William MacGregor was a man of impressive talents, a kind of

[1] Sources, for biographical details of the lesser known Governors and other officials, are a combination of material from civil lists, staff lists, Colonial Office lists, *Who's Who*, and *Who was Who*, press obituaries, mentions in memoirs of others, references in archives, etc. For MacGregor, the author is indebted to Mr. R. B. Joyce's biography in course of publication.

'Admirable Crichton' to whom little was impossible. He began life as the second of eight children of a farm worker in Towie, Aberdeenshire, in a tiny cottage. Poverty seemed likely to deprive him of the opportunity of higher education, but his brilliance and application at the village school greatly impressed the local dominie (schoolmaster), minister, and doctor. They were able to arrange that the boy remained as a kind of pupil teacher at the village school, while studying, during intervals when not working at the plough or as a herdsman, for a bursary at the Aberdeen Grammar School. MacGregor, who is said to have learned his arithmetic tables as a boy from the cover of a copy of the Shorter Catechism which he read while herding his cattle, won the bursary and reached the grammar school at the age of nineteen. In two years he was at the university, graduating M.B. in 1872 and M.D. in 1874. Later, he made himself, in the words of the *Dictionary of National Biography*, an 'excellent linguist, botanist and ethnologist'. He was expert in many unexpected subjects: he led explorations in New Guinea and Labrador, was learned in Italian law, kept a private diary[1] in French, German, and Italian (presumably to ensure its privacy), and read his Greek testament daily.

MacGregor's first official appointment abroad was as an assistant medical officer in the Seychelles, in 1873. In the following year he went to Mauritius, and then was promoted to Fiji as senior medical officer. In 1884 a ship was wrecked in stormy seas near Suva, Fiji, and MacGregor by great courage and physical strength rescued three people from drowning. For this he was decorated by the Royal Humane Society. Other unusual distinctions later came his way, like the medal of the Royal Geographical Society for exploration in New Guinea during his ten years there, beginning in 1888. For his anti-malarial work in Lagos he was awarded the Mary Kingsley medal of the Society for Tropical Medicine. After a tour of duty in Newfoundland as Governor, during which he led an arctic expedition in Labrador, MacGregor ended his career as a Governor in Queensland, where he helped to found the new university and became its first Chancellor.

The five years spent by this remarkable man in Lagos were one part, the African part, of a career of distinction in all the inhabited continents of the world, and in several very different fields of activity.

[1] Mr. R. B. Joyce, of the University of Queensland, MacGregor's biographer, has not been able to trace more than a few pages of this diary (in English), now preserved in the Australian National Library, Canberra.

Neither his simple background nor his intellectual distinction can be made to fit the popular stereotype of the British colonial Governor as a gentlemanly mediocrity. Neither he nor his predecessor McCallum can be regarded as men of less than outstanding, exceptional ability and experience. The choice of such men to govern Lagos seems to emphasize the importance, in Chamberlain's eyes, of Nigerian development.

Despite a suggestion that MacGregor first took a post abroad because he was threatened with pulmonary tuberculosis, his physique seems to have been as prodigious as his intellect. The *Dictionary of National Biography* describes him as 'a great block of rough, unhewn granite', but as distinguished by 'tact, patience and firmness with native races, and determination to prevent their exploitation by Europeans'. The entry goes on:

> Reticent by nature, and with a certain ruggedness in his character, MacGregor was essentially a strong man and an inspiring leader: yet he was entirely without boastfulness or egotism, and his qualities of strength and restraint combined to make him, in the words of Lord Bryce, 'a model of what a Colonial Governor should be'.

It is typical of the difficulties of writing Nigerian administrative history that so little is recorded about the work in the South of men like MacGregor, Moor, and Egerton. There is as much or more on record about MacGregor's previous work in New Guinea, where a missionary drew this vivid if not wholly accurate pen-picture of him:

> Sir William MacGregor is a hardy Scotsman, with a tall gaunt frame and possessed of great strength. He began life as a ploughman on a farm. He was mainly self-taught, and by industry and perseverance rose to the position of a doctor of medicine. . . . A better man for the post it would be difficult to find. His energy is untiring, and by his dogged determination he manages to overcome difficulties that would appear to others as insuperable . . . His manners are rather uncouth, but they are suited to a wild and rugged country like New Guinea.[1]

'Uncouth' or not—and there is plenty of evidence that MacGregor had both tact and dignity—and suited or not to a 'wild and rugged country', MacGregor seems to have been widely respected and liked in Lagos, in Newfoundland, and in Queensland—all of them colonies in which tactlessness would have ensured failure. There is no sign of uncouthness in his own published work on New Guinea (*British New*

[1] W. D. Pitcairn, *Two Years Among the Savages of New Guinea* (1891).

*Guinea, Country and People*, 1898) or in what is recorded of his speeches in Lagos; they are all distinguished by lively frankness, humour and modesty, and by a constant, courteous, kindly, and imaginative sympathy with the governed and the underprivileged which is a refreshing contrast to the ugly and contemptuous tone of many contemporary references to 'coloured' peoples—particularly references to literate West Africans. It was no doubt this gift of imaginative sympathy which made MacGregor ready to consult the governed on all occasions, to stress their desire for liberty and independence, and to show such ingenuity in finding new ways of making contact, to supplement the formal organs of Crown colony government.

The Lagos which MacGregor found on his arrival in 1899 had already felt the impact of the new forward policy of Chamberlain, as applied by McCallum. The most easily visible move forward was the railway, urged upon Chamberlain in 1895 by the Liverpool and Manchester Chambers of Commerce, and actually begun in the following year; in March 1900 the line between Lagos and Ibadan was opened for traffic. Other first fruits of Chamberlain's policy were already ripening in 1900. McCallum had completed the telegraph line from Lagos to Shaki, near the northern border of the Lagos 'hinterland'. The dredging of the Lagos harbour had begun, and the draining and reclamation of the swamps. The installation of electric street lighting had begun, and the Marina was being made into the first decent road in the capital. These, of course, were only beginnings, but they were at the same time tokens and reminders that it was as a city planner and developer of his own home town, Birmingham, that Chamberlain, having already by industry achieved a private fortune, first achieved fame and acquired experience of government at the local level, before entering national politics.

The legacy of past inactivity was still visible, in the Lagos of 1900, in the dirt and squalor of the town, in the unmade roads, and in the disease and mortality figures for Africans and Europeans alike. Not all the legacy of the past was bad, although it was certainly complex and untidy. At least, the idea that Britain might soon pull out altogether had given Africans opportunities of advancement to more comfortable positions in the Government service than they were to enjoy again for several decades; indeed, the static, sedentary service of the Lagos headquarters was soon to be swallowed up in a larger service liable for transfer to much less comfortable and much less advanced outposts; a 'mobilization' of the civil service for constant active service in rough conditions.

As early as 1891 the Colonial Secretary of Lagos had been able to report with pride to the Governor that the *Blue Book* for the year had been almost entirely compiled, with little reference to him, by the chief clerk in the Secretariat, Mr. Henry Carr, the African who was later to become Inspector of Schools, Director of Education, and Resident of the colony. In those days, most of the Africans who reached senior office were not, strictly speaking, Nigerians. There were men from the Gold Coast (like Mensah, clerk to the Legislative Council and confidential clerk to the Governor) or from Freetown—who had been either specially recruited for service in Lagos or posted there from Freetown or Accra in the period when Lagos was a mere settlement ruled from the Gold Coast or Sierra Leone. Often Governors and heads of departments on their passage out from home would select candidates for the civil service during the steamer's stay at Freetown and Accra, with as little difficulty or formality as they would engage personal servants. These strangers to Nigeria were of great service to the country; not the least of their services, although a very indirect one, was the impetus they gave to Nigerians in the search for education for themselves and their children. It was not until Southern Nigerians saw well-paid posts, posts of enviable comfort and authority, going to Creoles and other 'non-native Africans' that they began to appreciate, and to desire for themselves, something more than the smattering of English and arithmetic which had previously been considered enough to qualify a boy for trade and business. Emulation was more effectively aroused by seeing Africans in senior positions than by the sight of Europeans—who at that period were held by many in awe so great that they seemed beyond emulation. The same role of irritant, like the grain of sand forming the pearl in the oyster, was to be played later by Southerners themselves in Northern Nigeria, when, after 1948, the speedy advance in the civil service of Southern Nigerians was the belated spur to greater educational effort by the Northerners.

The early twentieth century in Lagos was recalled with nostalgia by Sir William Geary[1] as the period when 'the sound old system was to consider the African as an "Englishman with a black face" '. The statement stands in apparent contrast to the doctrine of indirect rule as developed in the North, under which it was regarded as a fatal

[1] W. Geary, *Nigeria under British Rule* (1927).

mistake to treat the African as if he were a European who had happened to be born black. An apparent contrast only; underlying both doctrines was the same idea of tact and respect for individual dignity, giving rise to different prescriptions for behaviour towards people with such contrasting codes as the Lagos élite and the Northern élite of the time.

The 'sound old system' which Geary approved was reflected in the structure and in the personnel of the Government. 'Indirect rule' had not yet been made a special mystique or technique for 'native administration' in Africa—it was still a matter of ordinary common sense and tact, rather than the object of veneration which it was later to become. Lagos was a Crown colony, one of many maritime colonies scattered over the oceans and the continents; its institutions of government for the town of Lagos, which then had a population of less than 40,000 (32,000 odd in the 1891 census), had many points of similarity to other colonies in North America, in the Caribbean, and in the Far East. These institutions were fairly advanced and elaborate, based on the time-honoured pattern, with no thought, apparently, of treating the people of Lagos, who were British subjects, many of them educated on British lines and conforming to English habits and customs, as in any way essentially different from the citizens of other Crown colonies. In particular, there had been since Lagos was acquired no serious thought of putting Lagos again under the rule of chiefs, or of including the traditional chiefs in the institutions of government. The reasons for this were simple and straightforward: firstly, the Treaty of Cession having conferred British citizenship on the inhabitants, they owed allegiance not to the chiefs but to the Crown; and secondly, the belief, rooted in the history of Lagos as a slave market and slave depot, that the primary object of those chiefs was to exploit and enslave their subjects, that they were in fact essentially cruel, evil, and oppressive rulers. By this reasoning, the acquisition of Lagos as a Crown colony was a liberation of the people, extending to them in place of tyranny the blessings of justice and the rule of law, and the rights of British subjects. By the same reasoning, the District Commissioners of the colony were not 'Political Officers' but officers of the Supreme Court, paid from the Judicial Department vote, magistrates with limited civil and criminal jurisdiction, with special functions under statute law, and coroners of their districts. But—and this was an important and all-embracing 'but'—these men, who normally had to be either barristers or solicitors, could be called upon to discharge any other duties. They had to be unmarried and under forty years of age on appointment and had to give security of £500. This liability for executive as well as judicial duties made them responsible to two masters, to the Chief Justice in their judicial work, to the Governor, through the Colonial Secretary, in their executive functions. Some idea of the prevailing trend of these other duties can be gained from the fact that they were all issued with geological equipment to help them to collect and identify mineral specimens, and that they were expected to keep a journal of 'everything of interest to the Government' which came to their notice—but in particular their journals had to contain descriptions of the country with suggestions for its development; remarks 'on the products, soils, minerals and timber found in the different districts and also on the manners, customs and language of the people with whom the Officers in question are brought into contact: suggestions for improvement in the present means of communication and throughout the interior, in trade and agriculture and [in] the general social conditions which are found to exist.'[1]

The District Commissioners of the colony were assisted, in their 'direct rule' of the four districts, by stipendiary Bales (heads) in the villages, and by the Lagos Constabulary. The 'direct rule' was essentially, however rudimentary in form, the rule of law. Within the law there was plenty of scope for African merchants and African lawyers as well as Europeans to ply their trades, untaxed. The four districts were the North-Western and the Western (based on Badagry), the North-Eastern (Ikorodu), and the Eastern (Epe). Epe had been wrested by negotiation from the domain of the Awujale of Ijebu-Ode, and Ikorodu from that of the Akarigbo of Ijebu-Remo in the same year, 1894, for the same purpose—the command of the main trade routes into the interior.

In the interior, or hinterland, at the time of MacGregor's arrival, British influence had been going forward, taking various forms—a Resident at Ibadan, a Commissioner at Abeokuta chiefly to smooth the political path of the railway through Egbaland, and Constabulary detachments at places like Ogbomosho, Ode Otin, Oyo, and Shagamu. Until Goldie's troops had disciplined the Emir these detachments were liable to attack by the Ilorins, who had long 'looked upon

[1] *Lagos Official Handbook* 1897–8. This is the main source used in this chapter for factual information about the civil service of the time, supplemented by annual reports, estimates, gazettes, and incidental references in archives.

Yorubaland as a happy hunting ground and were naturally opposed to any interference'.[1]

The alarms and excursions on the border of the hinterland must have seemed very far away from the peaceful and prosperous urban colony of Lagos, which was not only peaceful but also quite intensively administered on the new pattern, with more of the apparatus of the modern European state than could have been found in some of the states of Europe of the time. The list of Government departments in existence and the order of their creation show clearly the relative priority given to the various activities they undertook. In the absence of direct taxation, the Customs Department had long been of special importance, and in the districts the collection of Customs revenue was not the least of the District Commissioner's duties. One of the largest of the departments was the Medical Department, which in 1898 had eleven European and three African doctors. There was also a separate Sanitary Department, headed by a Sanitary Engineer, with an African 'Inspector of Nuisances' whose gruesome duties included ensuring that night-soil was deposited between 9 p.m. and midnight, and at no other times, into the lagoon, from prescribed piers and wharves; that none of this found its way back on to the island in the form of 'black mud' or 'mangrove mud' for gardens; and that the rules for the cleanliness of the meat-market and the slaughter-house were obeyed, and the users licensed.

A civil police force had been formed in 1896 from one division of the Lagos Constabulary (soon to be converted into a battalion of the West African Frontier Force). By the turn of the century the force numbered more than four hundred men in more than forty police stations. The prison, a department of one officer, had so far emerged from the era of mud walls and easy escapes that by 1898 the Lagos prison was proudly acclaimed as the finest in West Africa, with separate cell accommodation for nearly two hundred persons, and a prison hospital.

Another large department was the Public Works Department, created in 1896, out of the Department of the Surveyor-General. Its responsibilities included the construction and maintenance of public buildings and roads, of the electric light, telegraphs, telephones, piers, and the new sanitary tram line. The department's staff included three engineers and more than a dozen foremen, a brick-maker, and a road

[1] Short history and description of the colony of Lagos by F. B. Archer, *Lagos Official Handbook* (1898).

constructor. The Lagos Railway was already a separate department, and there were other departments concerned with public works; the Engineering Department, for instance, formed in 1897 to look after the engines and boilers of the flotilla of the Government Vessels Department—launches, boats, and steam canoes. One of this department's more picturesque achievements was the transportation to Lagos in 1897 of more than three thousand people, Obas, chiefs, and their retinues and horses, for the Royal Jubilee celebrations.

The separate Harbour Department was responsible for the surveying and marking, by buoys and beacons, of the treacherous bar and channels, for regulation of the port, lifeboats, licences of seaworthiness, maintenance of lighthouse and signal stations, and occasional duties like the laying of a telegraph cable across the harbour.

The Post Office, although in its infancy, operated mail services from Lagos as far inland as Shaki, and had an inland money order system operating between Lagos and the colony districts. Telegraphic communication with the outside world had been established since 1886 by the African Direct Telegraph Company.

One small department already headed by an African was the Education Department of Henry Carr, B.A., Inspector of Schools. Carr had reached this office through the chief clerkship in the Secretariat, where he had been Secretary of the Board of Education and Examiner for the civil service. His principal function as Inspector of Schools was to determine the eligibility of the schools (mostly mission schools) for the Government grants-in-aid administered, after 1888, by the Board of Education. The Board was an impressive one, consisting of the Governor and the entire Legislative Council, as well as three or four school managers from the missions. School fees were low, of the order of 1*s*. per month for primary and 30*s*. per quarter for secondary education. Lagos was already an examination centre for Matriculation, and for the degrees of B.A. and LL.B. of the University of London.[1]

The civil service which linked the departments, through the colonial Secretariat, with the Governor and the central organs of government was a surprisingly sophisticated one, with standards of competitive entrance and advancement higher than it would be practicable to enforce sixty years later in some parts of Nigeria. Entrance to the lowest clerical grade was by competitive examination in a very practical group of subjects. They were arithmetic,

[1] *Lagos Official Handbook* (1898), p. 18.

handwriting, English composition (writing 'a clear and grammatical account' of some recent local occurrence, and writing a simple letter), dictation, conversation, and knowledge of Yoruba. Promotion from the junior to the middle grade (£54 to £96 per annum) was dependent on passing a further examination in typing at 20 words per minute. To obtain promotion to the senior grade at £108 per annum middle-grade clerks had to undergo a further examination in the Government system of account, the drafting of letters, the docketing and scheduling of dispatches and letters, local Ordinances and Orders in Council, interpretation in Yoruba, and shorthand-writing at the rate of eighty words per minute.[1] All promotions were centrally regulated 'by merit and ability and not necessarily by seniority nor length of service'. The probation period was six months, and annual confidential reports to the Secretariat by heads of departments had to include details of each clerk's ability, intelligence, and—showing how deep the Victorian zeal for self-help had bitten—'endeavours after self-improvement since joining the service'. The senior grade consisted of chief clerks, £240–£300, 1st Class clerks £168–£204, and 2nd Class clerks £108–£150. Vacation leave for officers on £150 a year or more was three months in any two years. Such conditions, for those times, when combined with security of tenure and pension, and the improbability of senior clerks being uprooted by posting away from the amenities of Lagos, were very good; they represented solid comfort and dignity for their occupants. The salaries of senior chief clerks, for instance, were higher than those of young medical officers, and higher than several categories of European officer—not only the Foremen of Works, but the Assistant Commissioners of Police and the officer in charge of the prison could be earning less than the respected, stiff-collared, African chief clerk.

Office hours were from 8 a.m. to 11 a.m. and 1 p.m. to 4 p.m. on weekdays and 8 a.m. to 12 noon on Saturdays. These hours were so arranged to fit in with the Government's daily business with the Bank of West Africa—the only bank, financed by Sir Alfred Jones, managed by Mr. Neville, who was a member of Legislative Council and played a very considerable part for many years in developing the exports of the colony, notably rubber and cotton. The bank kept normal business hours, closing at 4.30 p.m., and the Government's

[1] Half a century later, all the governments of Nigeria, the federal Government and the regions, were recruiting shorthand-typists from overseas, alleging a lack of qualified Nigerians.

hours of opening for public business were so adjusted that the chief revenue collecting officers, like the Collector of Customs and the Postmaster, could each day pay in the day's revenue to the bank at 4 p.m., the Collector of Customs being escorted there by a corporal and four Houssas of the Lagos Constabulary. The Director of Public Works, the principal spender of the funds collected, had authority to draw on the bank, but other officers had to draw on the Treasury. All cheques of more than £200 had to be personally initialled by His Excellency the Governor in red ink, before the bank would honour them, and the manager sent to the Governor personally a monthly statement of account.

The keeping of accounts and the collection of revenue must have been made a little more complex by the mixed currency; in Lagos itself (disregarding the up-country cowries, manillas, and brass-rods) the legal tender included not only all gold and silver sterling but Spanish and South American doubloons and half-doubloons, United States double eagles, eagles, half-eagles, and quarter eagles, French twenty-franc pieces, and gold dust and nuggets.

Europeans in the service of the colony numbered less than ninety, all told, in the civil service list of McCallum's day, including the Governor himself. Africans in the list (those in senior posts) numbered about twenty; it is difficult to determine the exact number from the lists themselves, because many of the Africans have European names (e.g. Payne, Cole, Cumming, and Carr) and there was no separation by race in the lists. As for the Europeans, their origins were almost as diverse as the coinage crossing the bank's counters. There were several West Indians, and at least twenty with obvious Scottish or Irish connections; and three Thomases, a Williams, and a Vaughan among the Foremen of Works suggest that already the Welsh were present in significant numbers in the Public Works Department—another link, no doubt, with Liverpool, 'the Capital of North Wales', which many Welshmen had worked to build in the Victorian era. The Public Works Department had already adopted the formal procedure of invitations to tender for public works, all those above £100 in value being normally advertised in the newspapers and the result 'posted up in a conspicuous place'.

In contrast with the officers of the Niger Coast Protectorate, who from the beginning lived, ate, and drank in communal messes, and in even greater contrast with the officers of Lugard's new protectorate, who were under canvas or in makeshift huts of wood, mud, or metal, the Europeans of the Lagos civil service were, some of them, housed separately. This fact led to an exaggerated idea of the degree of comfort they enjoyed. In practice, although the Lagos press had caught from the British opponents of officialdom the habit of attacking the expense of housing officials, the living accommodation was austere enough by any ordinary standards. For those fortunate enough to have quarters of their own (which might also be their office in the daytime) the standard provision was two rooms (bedroom and sitting-room) and a kitchen, with nothing much in the way of furniture; in the sitting-room, a sideboard, table, three chairs, a Madeira sofa and chair; in the bedroom, a bed, a palliasse, mattress, pillow and bolster, washstand, towel-horse, small table, two chairs, and a bath-tub. This scarcely sybaritic equipment was completed by a meat-safe, a filter, a cooking-stove, a bucket, a water-drum, a latrine pan and curb, and its accompanying sand-box and scoop. This does not look like luxury for life in a capital city, but even this degree of comfort seemed enviable to their colleagues in the 'bush' and a worthy target for criticism by the press.

There were other things which set the Lagos civil servant apart from his contemporaries in the North—besides the habit of living in a house, and wearing civilian garb rather than semi-military khaki. In the Lagos of the early 1900s civil officials could be seen proceeding to their offices, not on horseback, but by rickshaw and bicycle, wearing the kind of suiting they might have worn on a summer's day in London, with the addition of a pith helmet, however cloudy the day. The only concession to the heat was to discard the waistcoat of the blue serge or light tweed suit and don a cummerbund in its stead. Significantly, there was no uniform for officials, except for the police. Outside Lagos, touring officers went by launch, by canoe, by hammock, or on foot, very rarely on horseback, still resolutely, civilly suited, perhaps adding gamekeeper's leggings or rubber Wellingtons as a concession to swamp water.

These men did not seem to seek unnecessary discomfort or arduous life, any more than their Whitehall contemporaries. The idea that there was positive virtue in hardship and discomfort to toughen the body seems to have gained strength later, under the influence of military thought. Physical toughness and constant readiness to endure physical hardship are of course militarily useful, and Napoleon's maxims of war placed the capacity to endure hardship above even courage itself among the military virtues. Lugard himself (and Lady

Lugard) believed that one of the things which ought to be placed to the credit side of imperialism was the opportunities it gave to young men to undergo hardship and so to toughen and strengthen their 'character'. In all this, militarism, puritanism, and the ideas of the survival of the fittest are curiously mingled, as they were in things like the Boy Scout movement, in the emphasis, in British education, on manly sports, and in many other fields; they reached one logical conclusion in the supreme disregard for life, comfort, and civilized values of the first World War.

But this is to anticipate developments; in the older traditions of the Lagos civil service at the turn of the century the tendency was towards formality in dress, and lack of enthusiasm for physical exercise—a tendency which suited well enough a public service with commercial, legal, clerical, and sedentary ideas of their functions, rather than military ideas of conquest and domination. It was a 'headquarter' service rather than a frontier service. The odd combination of what must have been acute sartorial discomfort with something which looks like physical lassitude was due for the most part to the obstinate survival into the twentieth century of some of the medical ideas of the mid-Victorian era, notably the idea that the health dangers in West Africa were caused by the malign influence of the 'climate' itself—the combination of certain conditions of light, temperature, air, and humidity—and that the best method of defence was to avoid exposure, excesses, and extremes, and so to escape the sudden changes in temperature and in the fluid balance of the body that violent exercise, sudden chills, and draughts might bring about. So travel by hammock instead of on foot might well be just what the doctor ordered, and not, as often popularly supposed, just arrogant indolence. It took a special effort by Governor Clifford after the first World War, by strenuous personal example on the pedal cycle while on tour, finally to wean the oldest Coasters from the 'comforts' of the hammock. The newer, opposing school which sought salvation in violent exercise numbered among its adherents such men as Lugard who believed that men who played polo often would rarely fall ill, and Willcocks,[1] his commander of the West African Frontier Force, who attributed his good health to running a mile before dinner every day—with only one good leg—and to the hardiness acquired by open-air life.

The older advice was to wear flannel next the skin, to take lukewarm baths, even to sleep between blankets rather than sheets.

[1] His autobiography has the title *The Romance of Soldiering and Sport* (1925).

Exercise, if indulged in, was to be surrounded by precautions. As late as 1898 the Lagos Official Handbook contained '*Simple Rules of Advice to Officers who have to go out in the Sun to perform their duties*', which showed clearly that the doctor who wrote them still placed greater reliance on such things as 'regularity of the bowels' and on avoiding draughts and exposure than on the new preventive medicine. The Rules merit quotation in full because of their unmistakable flavour of period and place:

1. Before going to work in the morning an officer should take a fairly substantial breakfast of Tea, Cocoa or Coffee with Eggs, potted meats or ham and eggs and fruit.

2. Regularity of the bowels is of prime importance and should be attended to as much as eating and sleeping. I strongly recommend all officers to take about 6 a.m. a glass of water and Quinine grains 5. Anyone doing this will have as good health as a climate such as this will permit him to enjoy. Personally I have done the above almost regularly since I first came to this Coast and have enjoyed excellent health.

3. Exercise to those who have been in the habit of it is an excellent thing which must never be indulged in when tired or with head improperly covered. Some men cannot take excercise in this climate as it causes fever and exhaustion.

4. When getting home for meals or after exercise all clothes soaked with perspiration should be changed, care being taken the body is not exposed to any draught.

5. As regards the bath it is most refreshing after working hours and should be tepid, the body being well soaked all over with Carbolic Soap. In the morning a wipe down with tepid water is most refreshing.

6. As few know the dangers of the sun great care should be exercised in protecting the head. A helmet which completely shades the forehead, temples, back of the head and nape of the neck should be worn and in bringing one see that it is ventilated in a lasting way. An umbrella should always be used of the tropical kind and a large silk handkerchief tied loosely about the neck is of immense protection to the neck especially in stooping.

The 'climate' of Lagos (in the sense of the health conditions) was soon to be transformed by the discoveries of Sir Ronald Ross, the great malariologist, Nobel prize-winner, and principal of the Liverpool School of Tropical Medicine, and by the work, in public health projects and in propaganda, of MacGregor and his principal medical officer, the 'rather dark' West Indian Dr. Strachan (to quote Ross's description of him). Strachan was an early convert to Ross's mosquito theory of the origin of malaria, corresponded with him, and soon converted MacGregor. The three men met and became friends. But Lagos's reputation as an unhealthy place lived on for many years, kept alive partly by the protagonists of the North and its open spaces, who wished to focus interest and effort on the development of the North, and tended to claim both health advantages in the Northern climate and health disadvantages in the South and along the coast, in the older colonies, which were not borne out by the medical statistics. And as for the climate, so for the people; the protagonists of the North, in particular Lady Lugard, were to claim that the peoples of the North were greatly superior to the peoples of the coast.

Ross's memoirs, published in 1923, give vivid sketches of the Lagos he visited in MacGregor's time, and of some of the chief figures engaged in the development of West Africa, including Chamberlain himself, MacGregor, and Sir Alfred Jones. Ross greatly admired Sir William MacGregor ('Of all the men I have met I honour him perhaps the most'), describing him as 'full of thought and knowledge', and leaving the following portrait:

> Wise, grave, but humorous, bearded, thick-set, with wrinkled forehead and a high and somewhat conical bald head, his low voice and kindly manner filled all with trust in him. He drank no wine and did not smoke, but was no fanatic in these respects, and kept a hospitable table. Every night he read his Greek Testament, and was also skilled in French and Italian, and knew something of many barbarous tongues. He was a mathematician, a practised surveyor, a lapidary, and a master of many arts, but always proud of his medical upbringing and his nationality. Simply dignified, he did not allow his dignity to obscure his personality, and he had no trace of that meanest and most mischievous vice, jealousy. He was not a politician, but a genuine administrator careful of all the interests of the people entrusted to him—still more, a scientific administrator who added knowledge to his solicitude. He went minutely into every question submitted to him, and it would have been impossible for him to deal with our deputation as Chamberlain had done—in fact he would have made a much better Secretary of State for the Colonies.[1]

The rather bitter comment on Chamberlain in this tribute to MacGregor's memory was a reference to a deputation from Liverpool to London on 15 March 1901, led, inevitably, by Sir Alfred Jones, to urge upon Chamberlain the need for a large-scale attack on African health problems. Ross, meeting Chamberlain then for the first time, was disappointed. He found him 'acute but not penetrating, sharp but

[1] Sir Ronald Ross, *Memoirs* (1923), p. 445.

not sure, deft but not deep, straight but clever', 'a man of display rather than of possession, and not very capable of any profound analysis or integration'. 'As usual with politicians, he deprecated expenditure, not recognizing that sanitary expenditure is an insurance against the much greater expenditure, caused by sickness, as that on fire-engines is against fire.'

Ross left the Colonial Office after the interview bitterly disappointed and angry:

I remember thinking to myself angrily, as I left Whitehall: 'These people are no longer fit to hold the hegemony of the world.' Probably the fault lay with the permanent officials: but in either case my dreams of general British action against malaria vanished at that interview.

MacGregor too was having his difficulties over health problems with the Colonial Office, writing to Ross, in a letter quoted in Ross's *Memoirs*:

I shall be very glad to send you a few notes on malaria in the field, what we are doing, and what lions roar at us in the path. So far the greatest obstacle is the Colonial Office. It is bad enough to have to deal with malaria alone: but malaria entrenched behind Sir . . . . . . . . . . . . . . . is impregnable.

This was after Ross's visit to Lagos on the new Liverpool School's research expedition to West Africa to study malaria—largely financed, when the Colonial Office declined the honour, by Sir Alfred Jones of Elder Dempsters. Jones had also made himself responsible for the greater part of Ross's salary, although, as Ross noted, Chamberlain and the Colonial Office managed to obtain, cheaply, much of the credit for encouragement of the School and its work.

Ross was met on his arrival at the Lagos bar by the Governor's little steamer, and on the steps of Government House by the resplendent bearded figure of the Governor himself, wearing 'a white pith helmet, his ribbons, and a kilt of the MacGregor tartan'. Afterwards, still in the same impressive attire, MacGregor took his compatriot and guest on a tour of the market, where they met 'many large and loquacious ladies', to several of whom the Governor bowed, and doffed his topee, inquiring after the health of their husbands and their children.

These two like-minded medical Scotsmen (continuing the contribution to scientific discovery in Africa that men of their race and profession like Mungo Park, Livingstone, and Baikie had begun) were later to visit the Suez canal zone together, studying malaria and solving the serious malarial problem of Ismailia; and MacGregor confided to Ross his great ambition (characteristically, an ambition of useful service to humanity rather than one of dominion and 'power' in the ordinary sense). This ambition was, to be allowed by the Colonial Office to give up his Governorship, and to be appointed as Malaria Commissioner for the British Empire, with Ross and an engineer to help him, and with the Colonial Office, the War Office, and the India Office jointly footing the bill for public health schemes to eradicate malaria. A tremendous scheme, but there was what MacGregor called 'a dead pull' against them, somewhere in London. 'Ah!' sighs Ross, in his memoirs, 'the things which might have been but for that dead pull!'[1]

Despite the frustration and disappointments caused by the Colonial Office, Rose looked back with great pleasure to his visit to MacGregor's Lagos, admiring the Governor's medical and administrative work, recalling with pleasure a champagne lunch at Government House attended by the Ladies' League, African and European, and ending his account thus: 'I was to meet him again soon on happy occasions; but the low land of wood and water, swept at that season by tropical rain, from leaden skies, has only sunny memories for me.'

It is odd how often—far more often than the Lagos weather itself would suggest, to writers accustomed to British skies—the phrase 'leaden skies' was used about Lagos and its climate, inevitably conveying an impression of gloom and depression. *The Nigerian Handbook* of 1953 preserves the tradition, predicting that the visitor to Lagos 'will probably be met with leaden skies, drenching rain and steamy heat'. Lugard's biographer refers to 'the often leaden skies reflected in the grey waters'.[2] It was this kind of refrain which maintained the bad climatic reputation of the coast long after medical science had shown the way to healthy life in tropical conditions. Lugard himself, deeply antipathetic to Lagos, played a notable part in the condemnation of Lagos in his *Amalgamation Report*: 'Its

[1] Julian Amery, in *The Life of Joseph Chamberlain*, vol. iv, has suggested (p. 232) that Ross meant yet another Scottish (Aberdonian) doctor, Sir Patrick Manson, then Colonial Office medical adviser. Certainly, friendship between Ross and Manson had turned sour. But the then Permanent Under Secretary, Sir Montagu Ommanney, is also a possible candidate for the title of 'the dead pull'.

[2] Perham, *Lugard, The Years of Authority*, p. 420.

climate is enervating, with damp winds from the sea. . . . It is surrounded by evil-smelling swamps, the complete reclamation of which is impossible. . . '.

It is but a short step from Lugard's description to the even more libellous description in P. C. Wren's famous *Beau Geste*, read by millions of British boys in the twenties and thirties, first published in 1924, and resolutely helping to stamp on the British mind the same simple Lugardian message about Nigeria, 'North good, South bad': 'From that wonderful and romantic Red City, Kano, sister of Timbuktu, the train would take him, after a three days dusty journey, to the rubbish heap called Lagos, on the Bight of Benin on the wicked West African Coast.'

So the city which held nothing but 'sunny memories' for the great sanitarian who visited it at the turn of the century, and was already being so transformed by an able medical Governor that it did not seem ridiculous to think of it in terms of a new Venice in Africa, a great and beautiful mercantile centre built around a lagoon—this city, some twenty years of British rule later, could be described without effective contradiction as a 'rubbish heap'. What went wrong in those twenty years?

At the beginning of the century, before Lagos was joined up to any larger unit, there was a form of civic commercial government which was up to date with the best public health practice, and even ahead of Britain, in some respects, in the way of active Government interest in education, health, railway construction, and forward planning of economic projects. Lagos was the civil capital, the seat of both government and commerce; there was money to spend, and Lagos was an obvious and proper place to spend it. Neglect of Lagos and of the health needs of a rapidly growing city was not then the sign of virtue and right thinking which it later became, when exiguous revenues had to spread over the whole of Nigeria, when 'direct rule' and the embryo constitution of the Crown colony had been merged in the more autocratic form of protectorate.

But this again anticipates later developments, in particular the 'centrifugal' tendency of the new 'indirect rule', in which 'provincial administration' was given higher priority and held in greater esteem than the work of development and municipal improvement in the capital city. In contrast, MacGregor's system of administration showed the opposite, centripetal tendency which befitted a Government interested more in economic and commercial development than in establishing a uniform alien system of rule and of authority over a wide area.

It was logical, therefore, for MacGregor to decide that the commercial centre, the communications centre, should remain the governmental capital, and that the public health standards must not fall short of those needed in the capital city. The largest departments were those most closely concerned with trade, communications, and public health—they were the Railway and Marine Departments, the Public Works Department, the Medical Department—exercising their functions within the capital, around it, and along the communications by rail and water. There was an adequate colonial Secretariat serving the Governor, in which MacGregor had taken care to reserve at least one of the three posts of Assistant Secretary for a Nigerian, insisting that he should be on exactly the same footing as regards salary and status as the two Europeans. In the provinces the Government was represented by the necessary functionaries of the modern state, placed according to need and availability—postal staff, police, doctors, District Commissioners in the colony districts where 'direct rule' had long been established.

The central Government would not have claimed to be a system of local or provincial government, outside the colony area, any more than the British Government in the nineteenth century would have claimed to regulate local affairs in detail; to criticize it as an inadequate system of uniform provincial government, as compared with what later became renowned as indirect rule, is to miss the point that peaceful economic development, not dominion, was the prime object of its existence, and that MacGregor's idea was to retain and strengthen provincial government *by* the chiefs, not *through* them. Help to the chiefs, in the shape of the services of the Chief Justice sitting with the Alake's judges at Abeokuta, for instance, was provided as a kind of technical assistance. Its object was to enable the Alake's government to deal successfully with the kind of case involving European merchants, or capital punishment, which might otherwise, if left entirely in the hands of the Alake's judges, have led to loud demands by influential interests (by merchants and by missionaries) for the abrogation of the guarantees of independent statehood for Egbaland. And the administrative representatives of the central Government, like the Resident at Ibadan and the Commissioner at Aro, had diplomatic and commercial functions; they were not 'rulers'.

The immediate verdict on MacGregor's five years' Governorship was given, on his departure, in the annual report for 1904:

Sir William MacGregor left the Colony early in January after holding the office of Governor for nearly five years. That five years has witnessed a most remarkable development in the resources of the territory, and in the general condition and prosperity of the people.

The town of Lagos has been improved almost out of recognition, the revenue has been nearly doubled, many public works of great utility have been carried through, others have been commenced, and others again have been brought within the range of practical politics.

This extract has been quoted because it illustrates clearly enough the practical, utilitarian standards of success which the Southern administrators were apt to apply to their work—economic, commercial standards, on the old liberal principle, later stated very clearly by Lord Hailey in his contribution to Calvin W. Stillman's *Africa and the Modern World*:[1] 'If we can adequately improve the standard of living of any backward people, we need not trouble overmuch to seek to arrange their political future, for they will see to that for themselves.'

MacGregor's five years had seen an extraordinary outburst of energy, after the stagnation of the pre-Chamberlain era, not confined to the efforts of the administration alone, but channelled in precisely those directions which the merchant pressure-groups of the time had prescribed—and so, wholeheartedly supported and approved by them. His administration of Lagos is now remembered, when it is remembered at all, as the period of the digging of the MacGregor canal, and the draining and reclaiming of the Lagos swamps—the most conspicuous parts of the public works involved in improving the sanitation of the capital.[2] Later changes in policy did not obliterate this kind of work; but what is perhaps more significant than the work itself was the approach to it—the method of persuasion and consultation with the people concerned which MacGregor adopted. Because all this was later discredited and superseded by Lugard's methods, there has been little detailed study or description of the achievements of the older and gentler ways.

Unlike their Northern colleagues, the Lagos administrators of this generation left no published account of their methods, and founded

[1] *Africa and the Modern World*, edited Calvin W. Stillman (1955).

[2] The only mention of MacGregor in Sir Alan Burns's *History of Nigeria* is a footnote explaining the name of the canal.

no new 'school' of administration. So it is fortunate that MacGregor's methods involved him in a good deal of thinking aloud and public discussion, in consultations of which records survive, and also that he was impelled—probably by the attacks on Lagos and its people by influential speakers and writers like Lady Lugard—to place on record his impressions of Yorubaland and the Yoruba.

The discussions of which the record survives[1] include those in the Legislative Council; those in the Central Native Council which MacGregor set up to associate the chiefs with the Government and with each other; in the Lagos Institute 'for the mutual improvement in general knowledge' which he began for the gentlemen of Lagos, with himself as president; in the Lagos Ladies' League, the voluntary association of European and African ladies which he inspired, in which the better-off ladies of Lagos undertook the distribution of quinine and other medicines in a campaign to reduce the appalling infant mortality in the town—a strange but effective campaign in which the weapons of the teetotal, reticent Governor were socialite champagne lunches supplementing the heavier artillery of canals, drains, drugs, lectures, examinations, and sanitary inspectors.

In all his consultative arrangements MacGregor did a good deal of listening, as well as explaining and expounding, which seems to have achieved peaceful co-operation and understanding, as well as respect and liking. Repeatedly he emphasized in his reports the desire of the people to manage their affairs without interference, their ability to do so, and their readiness to consider suggestions made to them. In his last report, that for 1903, he sought particularly to emphasize these points:

> The position and authority of the hereditary and elected chiefs has as far as possible been maintained; but development had been proceeding so rapidly that many chiefs have been placed in a somewhat difficult position between the older and more conservative elements on one side, and the younger men that wish to go faster on the other side. There is, however, on all sides an intense desire that they, the natives, should continue to manage their own domestic concerns. This desire is largely met by the regularly established and recognised Native Councils. There was not in the course of the year a single question of trouble or anxiety in connection with these Councils, which are generally conducted with great decorum, order and regularity. Councils of this kind are, indeed, very ancient institutions in the land, and now, when regulated and officially recognised

[1] Details are given in the Nigerian National Archives, *A Handlist of Nigerian Official Publications, Provisional*, vols. i and ii (Ibadan, 1961).

are of the greatest use in preventing oppression and in improving native administration generally. They invariably showed themselves to be ready and willing to consider any suggestion made to them.

There is very little suggestion here of 'imposing' any particular form of 'rule' outside the colony area, whether 'direct' or 'indirect' rule. In keeping with orthodox economic and political liberalism, and the realities of the funds available, there were strict limits to legitimate interference. It was enough to establish peace and essential public services and stable currency, to provide trade, and then let each native society and each enterprising individual get on with their jobs without unnecessary official interference. Lack of interference did not necessarily mean neglect, or lack of interest or attention; many commentators have since thought so, contrasting the lack of systematic imposed rule with Lugard's structure linking the district head, through the hierarchy of the reformed Emirate, to the Resident and the Governor. This latter was a system in which there was one master or ruler to whom all paid deference, an organization with distinct grades and ranks like an army, in which everyone knew his place. It was not that MacGregor was in favour of letting the Yoruba kingdoms and chieftaincies disintegrate; on the contrary, he did intervene, continuously but steadily, in the direction of strengthening the chief's position. It was because of this policy that there was no attempt to link the central and local authorities into one machine of government, with the threads of control, discipline, and command running into the Governor's hands.

MacGregor's method of enhancing the chiefs' dignity and influence, widening their knowledge, and getting the benefit of their advice was to establish a Central Native Council of chiefs, and to take pains to associate them with him in his plans—just as he took pains to associate the leading citizens of Lagos with him in his plans for both the town and the protectorate, through the new voluntary institutions as well as through the official bodies like the Legislative Council and the Boards of Education and Health. As chairman or president of these bodies, the Governor kept in touch with both the educated public and the traditional authorities, and could both persuade and be persuaded through discussion.

The proceedings of the opening session of the Lagos Institute on 16 October 1901 (preserved in the National Archives at Ibadan) are an example of MacGregor's use of such occasions to expound, to popularize, persuade, and take soundings. On that occasion, after a brisk outline of the events leading to the new forward policy, he gave his own assessment of problems and priorities for action—an assessment very close in all essentials to the policies advocated by the merchants and adopted by the Selborne Committee. One of his remarks—'the locomotive is preferable to the Maxim'—practically summed up the merchants' philosophy. The detachment, lack of 'jingoism', and frankness with which he described the old period of inactivity and the change brought about by the threat of military action by France are striking; mentioning that the French had at the time of speaking about sixty thousand troops in Algeria, he went on:

> From the military and political points of view perhaps the best way for us to deal with all this would have been to continue and persevere in doing nothing, as we industriously did for so very many years.
>
> But this easy-going inactivity was rendered no longer possible by the doctrine of effective occupation, new to international law, created by the cupidity, the civilizing furore which recently in epidemic form seized the great nations of Europe.

It was in the same address that he summed up the needs of Lagos: 'Soundness on Railway extension, on provincial government by the chiefs, and on Sanitation should be the great political tests applied to the political men of this country.'

This was in 1901; in an address to the Legislative Council in 1903 (26 February) he varied the emphasis slightly, choosing as the three most important questions affecting the colony 'Agricultural Development, Sanitation, and Railway Extension'. But this did not mean that he had overlooked 'provincial government by the chiefs'. Much of the speech was devoted to explaining measures to enhance the position of the Obas and chiefs, including symbolic stipends to the Alafin of Oyo and the Oni of Ife. In his speech to the Lagos Institute in 1901 he had had this to say on the subject:

> Perhaps the most interesting and the most important question connected with administration at the present moment is that of provincial government. This is one of those critical questions on which men's minds are very apt to differ. My own personal views are that the Government of the hereditary chiefs of the country should not only be retained, but should be steadily and consistently strengthened and developed. Reasons for this policy may be found in these facts. In the first place some form or degree of native rule exists now in each Province. Certain men and certain families have long exercised it. They are accustomed to it; the country is used to it. It suits the genius of all classes of these communities, and it is

therefore better adapted to their economic and social development than any other form of rule.

MacGregor's avoidance of interference was based on policy, therefore, on a respect for Yoruba institutions, a realization of their complex balance, and a belief that traditional society should be left as free as possible to adapt itself to the great economic changes which were taking place: 'the future development of this country must be by its own people, through its own people, and for its own people'.

Referring to the weakening of the Alafin's powers, in his 1903 speech, MacGregor said:

I humbly think it was carried too far. Ever since I made the acquaintance of this chief I have consistently endeavoured to strengthen his rule, because I entertain a high opinion of his wisdom, and of his loyalty to the King and to his own country and people. . . . Were it practicable to do so, it would be very desirable that the authority and influence of the Alafin should be extended beyond its present limits, over districts formerly ruled by him and his predecessors. But it is a fact that if the prestige and authority of a chief are once seriously weakened, it takes time and care to repair the damage.[1]

Like much of what MacGregor said and wrote, these seem wise words, in the light of almost half a century of subsequent unavailing efforts to put the clock back and restore some of the Alafin's authority over Ibadan. In any event, his greatest contribution to provincial government was not a backward step, nor yet an effort to hold back the clock, but the forward step of the Central Native Council, already mentioned, which his successors allowed to fall into disuse and disfavour. It was this council which first brought the Yoruba Obas and chiefs out of their various kinds of seclusion into conference with one another and with the Governor. On the memorable occasion when the Oni of Ife first attended he sat at the Governor's side, with his back to the rest of the assembly, his face concealed from them as custom demanded. But he did come, and spoke, and with his help MacGregor solved the delicate question of chiefs' entitlement to wear beaded crowns. Within a very few years, partly as a result of the initiation into the modern world which the frequent visits to Lagos for council meetings represented, the Yoruba chiefs' horizons were widened. The Alake of Abeokuta, for instance, visited England (and Scotland) with the Governor, was presented to King Edward VII, and

[1] Address to Legislative Council, 26 Feb. 1903.

by his dignified presence did something to counteract the odd reports of the inhabitants of the West Coast which were then current. By 1902 the Alake had agreed with the Governor that the Chief Justice from Lagos should sit with Egba assessors to try mixed cases and serious cases like homicide. It may not be too fanciful to see in these events the beginnings of the processes which led to an Oni of Ife (and former railway official) becoming the first Nigerian Governor of a region, and to a son of the Alake of Abeokuta becoming the first Nigerian Chief Justice—to mention only one of the many Egbas who have distinguished themselves in the law since these beginnings only sixty years ago.

But the distinctive features of the Yorubaland Protectorate of MacGregor's time were the peace which prevailed, and the ease with which, on the whole, the people were absorbing the rapid changes, amounting to an economic revolution, which were taking place as a result of the Governor's other main objects of concern—railway extension, agricultural development, and sanitation.

On the question of railway extension north from Ibadan, MacGregor himself surveyed and decided upon a suitable route[1] through the populous palm-oil zone (and later cocoa belt) from Ibadan to Oshogbo, in preference to the alternative and at first sight more natural route through Oyo to Ogbomosho. Construction was delayed, partly because of cost, partly because of Lugard's dogged preference for an interior railway, starting from the highest navigable point on the Niger, so that it should be entirely independent of Lagos and its railway. It was not until 1907, after Lugard had been replaced by the Royal Engineer Girouard, that the Lagos railway reached Oshogbo and the Secretary of State authorized both the interior railway from the Niger at Baro[2] to Kano, and also the extension of the Lagos railway to meet it—a compromise solution of the problem which had divided the Selborne Committee and inspired Antrobus's statesmanlike indecision. As it turned out, it would probably have been better to concentrate from the beginning on strengthening the links of the North with Lagos, by rail and other means, but Lugard's unwillingness to accept the railway link was a sign of the intense antipathy which any idea of dependence upon Lagos or association with Lagos aroused in him.

[1] And ever since, the most profitable section of the Nigerian railway.

[2] The name Baro is said to come from the railway milestone inscription —o (= bar o).

In agricultural development, to take another of MacGregor's subjects of first importance, there was in the first few years of the century an unprecedented burst of activity, of experiment, and of enterprise, in which all the agents of development joined with enthusiasm and energy—officials, merchants, missionaries, chiefs, and farmers. One of the forms which this enthusiasm took, one which appealed to officials, missionaries, and people alike, was a greatly extended distribution and a greatly intensified testing of economic plants from all the countries of the tropics, through the Government botanical gardens. Farmers were supplied with many thousands of seeds, seedlings, and saplings by these gardens, which in their day did useful and important work, giving instruction in cultivation and training gardeners and demonstrators as well as supplying coffee, kola, cocoa, maize, rubber and oil-palm seedlings, and citrus and other fruits from places as far apart as Malaya and the Caribbean, mostly obtained through the network of enthusiastic botanists linked together by the Royal Botanical Gardens at Kew and the Imperial Institute. These institutions were inundated with specimens for identification and with requests for advice as to their economic possibilities.

All this activity—largely amateur—helped greatly in the transformation of the staple diet of the people, as well as in the development of the important economic crops and of useful specialist trades in gums, dyes, fibres, resins, and oils. Peace, and the new matchet or cutlass of stronger steel, made it possible to clear the bush and so increase the area of farmland; the crops then grown, whether for food or for export as cash crops, were nearly all of exotic origin. Despite the traditional conservatism of farmers, there seems to have been no long hesitation in adopting new crops which thrived, commanded a good price, and did not require constant or intensive labour; labour indeed was a difficulty, for with the abolition of slavery came the unpleasant but salutary shock, for the landowner, of being forced to work himself and to pay for labour. Equally, there was little hesitation in dropping any crop which did not pass these tests—in the Lagos Protectorate at different times coffee, cotton, and maize failed to maintain the farmer's interest when prices or yields failed to justify the labour involved. This tendency was taken by some observers—not those best qualified to judge—as proof of what E. D. Morel called 'the damn' nigger theory', the theory that the Negro race of man was incorrigibly lazy. This theory was to the advantage of many powerful vested interests in Africa at the time, and those who accepted it were ready to justify by it such things as depriving the people of the Congo of their land by a system of foreign concessions, and importing Chinese labour into South Africa—all on the basic assumption of the black man's 'laziness' and 'inferiority'. It is to the credit of the Nigerian administrators that their official reports repeatedly reject and refute this theory—except for a few reports from some parts of the protectorate of Southern Nigeria where agriculture was scarcely practised at all. MacGregor himself took great pains to combat the vilification of the people of the West African coast, saying, at a meeting of the Royal African Society in June 1904:[1] 'The Yoruba farmer is a very hard-working, industrious man, who is an enthusiastic agriculturalist.'

In the same address MacGregor praised the Yoruba as 'deeply religious', patriotic, with a high sense of justice, and a passionate desire to manage their own domestic affairs, and said that it was the courtesy of chiefs and people which at first sight struck one most forcibly; the chiefs could 'serve as a model of politeness to any people in Europe'. This might be thought somewhat fulsome and exaggerated praise, until one realizes the kind of thing which MacGregor was presumably trying to counteract, exemplified in an address by Lady Lugard to the Royal Society of Arts a few months before, contrasting 'the higher types of the Northern states' with the 'cannibal pagans' of the South.[2]

There was, however, even in MacGregor's eulogy, a reflection of the current perplexity of the older generation of Africans, of Carr, Blyden, and of official Europeans—a feeling of disappointment and concern about the untoward effects of social engineering by education. In the 1900 annual report there was a typical expression of these doubts: '. . . it is deplorable that among the large number of unemployed there are such a large number of able-bodied men who, because they have been taught at school to write a few ungrammatical sentences in a fairly legible hand, consider it beneath their dignity to follow agricultural pursuits.' MacGregor's address in 1903 touched upon the same ominous dissatisfaction felt by elders with the younger generation of a society in rapid transition: 'It is at the same time a fact, that parents and persons in authority complain that children and young people are now less respectful and obedient than was formerly the case. Rightly or wrongly, this change is imputed to contact with Europeans.' The 'troublesome' scholars of Lagos, who seemed so

[1] Royal African Society *Journal* (1903–4), p. 464. [2] See pp. 158–161.

advanced to their elders, were quite soon to seem reactionary and out of date to their own juniors.

The cure for the shortcomings in the younger generation was felt by the eminent Africans and enlightened Europeans to be an even greater, even more massive dose of the education and the development which in small doses were to blame for the disease—not, as those in authority in the North advocated, a slowing down, even a reversal of the process of change, in the belief that education in English, and mission influence and contact with Europeans, 'detribalized', 'denationalized', and 'spoiled' Africans, leading by a primrose path straight to the inferno of racial deterioration, disease, and undisciplined chaos. Another, related idea which Europeans experiencing the green warmth of Southern Nigeria expressed then, and have often expressed since, was the idea that the gods had been too kind to the Yoruba by making subsistence too easy, with none of the compulsion to work which harsher climates induced—the natural corollary of the idea that British supremacy in the world was due largely to the challenge of an adverse climate and to the toughness it produced.

Nevertheless, despite the easy climate and doubts as to the industry of the modern young men, there was a rapid growth in the area under cultivation, and in the back-breaking work of clearing bush and forest to grow both food and cash crops. Enthusiastic and indiscriminate felling of the most saleable and accessible timber for export, and the rubber boom, showed that there was no lack of the acquisitive instinct when the rewards were high enough. But the over-tapping of latex-bearing plants and trees, and the destruction of trees for export (which often went to waste because of teredo-worm damage while the logs lay in brackish water awaiting shipment), were like killing the goose that laid the golden eggs, destroying the jungle wealth and not replacing it.

So official efforts in agricultural development were directed into two channels, the development of economic crops and the conservation of forest resources. During one leave MacGregor himself studied cotton-growing in Egypt; the Cotton Growing Association began operations; the Botanical Curator visited the West Indies in 1901 to bring back more economic plants; and American experts in cotton-growing and stock-raising visited the Lagos Protectorate.

Forest conservation was not so popular as new cash crops, for the obvious reasons. As early as 1897 the rubber boom depredations had led to the tabling of the first ordinance 'To provide for the Establishment and for the proper Regulation of the Forests'—prompted by officials' fears for the future if these depredations were allowed to continue unchecked. So vehement was the opposition to the Bill in local opinion that it was withdrawn, and the man already recruited to head the embryo Forest and Botanical Department, Cyril Punch, a former planter and trader, was diverted for his first tour to perform the duties of Private Secretary to the Governor. Only after this period of diplomatic training did he assume duty as Superintendent of Forests. His indoctrination in the methods of diplomatic 'peaceful penetration' must have been adequate, because in the same year he persuaded the chiefs of Ibadan to grant the Mamu forest as 'a gift to Queen Victoria', and in the following year the Alake and the chiefs of Abeokuta leased for 999 years the Olokomeji Reserve, later to become the centre of forestry in Nigeria. The episode of the withdrawn Bill illustrates the real strength of public feeling at the time against bureaucratic control and interference, and the Government's responsiveness to public opinion, after the first false step taken in haste to adopt legislation too far ahead of public opinion.

There can be little doubt that the suspicion of bureaucracy, and the vociferous opposition to its extension in Lagos, were fostered by the European merchants and independent-minded sea-captains in Lagos, and by the contacts Lagosians had with Liverpool and Manchester. E. D. Morel, who became after Mary Kingsley's death the most eloquent publicist of the West African merchants' point of view, quotes a speech by the president of the Manchester Chamber of Commerce in the nineties, Mr. Arthur Hutton, which shows how far they were prepared to go in putting the claims of trade above those of official rule: 'I sincerely hope that the day is not far distant when the African community will rise up and protest against the Crown Colony form of Government.'

But these oddly seditious imperialists heartily approved MacGregor's methods (cf. Morel, 'Lagos alone, under the able guidance of Sir William MacGregor has known the blessings of peace'). In particular, they liked his success in improving trade, communications, and public health, and his avoidance of war and punitive expeditions, of direct taxation and expensive civil and military establishments. MacGregor himself described his system as one designed to take native character, customs, and susceptibilities into account and to allow, and even require, the native authorities to take such a large share in their own government that punitive expeditions and plots against the Government were unknown. To the merchants this system must have seemed a perfect illustration of the beauty of free trade, where avoidance of military intervention brought rewards in trade and friendship, where better communications and better sanitation, designed to improve traders' conditions, became an unmixed blessing for the whole community; where God and Mammon co-operated, and only the official needed careful watching and control by constant criticism.

The most complete statement of the traders' point of view is contained in E. D. Morel's first important book on West Africa, published in 1902, *Affairs of West Africa.* It was based on knowledge acquired from work and study in England, in France, and in Belgium. The link with Liverpool and Sir Alfred Jones was strong. Until 1901 Morel worked for Jones as head of the Congo department of Elder Dempsters; he left them to avoid embarrassing their business by his increasingly outspoken and hostile criticism of King Leopold's personal empire in the Congo, a regime which he played a chief part in bringing to an end by unwearying pressure of publicity directed against it. It is typical of the way in which most of the main threads of interest and influence led back from West Africa to Liverpool that this important book should have been written by the naturalized British citizen, Morel, working in Liverpool, with a foreword in memory of Mary Kingsley, and a chapter on sanitation by Dr. Ronald Ross, the great malariologist, then recently appointed to the new Liverpool School of Tropical Medicine, and like Morel himself a close associate of Sir Alfred Jones and John Holt. Ross's chapter was written at first hand, since he had just returned from his visit to Lagos, whereas Morel's first-hand acquaintance with West Africa, at that time, was limited to a brief spell in his youth when he was a purser on the Antwerp–Congo line acquired by Elder Dempsters.[1]

Ross's contribution to Morel's book was concerned with the subject of sanitation which was so close to his and MacGregor's heart. Ross expressed himself with great vigour, blaming the failure in West Africa to advance civilization on the health conditions, condemning the bad houses, the bad food, the lack of segregation of European and African residential areas, the absence of mosquito nets, of punkahs,

[1] His employer, Alfred Jones (like Stanley, explorer and developer of the Congo) had a humbler start in life, as a poor Welsh boy shipping from Liverpool as a cabin boy.

of organized games and recreation, and contrasting the squalid life of Europeans in West Africa with the greater comfort and the more gracious amenities of European life in India; he rejected utterly the argument of economy:

Do not talk to me of lack of funds. There are plenty of funds, but they are thrown away on military expeditions; on the salaries of useless legal officials—chief justices and attorney-generals of little villages.

This country should be made to understand that it is has more to do than to watch processions of colonial troops and to brag about its Empire. It is its duty to see that the Empire which it boasts of is properly administered, and that our countrymen who are sent to carry on the affairs, both official and commercial, of that Empire are not left to die there unnecessarily.

There was a new robust professionalism in these remarks, no doubt derived from Ross's years in the Indian medical service. There had not, previously, been such an emphasis on the medical services' duty to care first for the white official and trader as the agents of civilization. This was a dangerous innovation, and there was the even more ominous idea that it was the official's duty—and a matter of life and death—to segregate himself from the administered population. These ideas, perfectly logical and justifiable on strictly medical grounds, were destined to prevail over the previous notions and to have far-reaching consequences in social relations and in increasing inter-racial misunderstanding, especially in the few large centres where there were Europeans and educated Nigerians in significant numbers. There was soon to begin a change in emphasis from a general responsibility for the cure of the sick to a prior responsibility for the official and commercial community; this led, within a few years, to the creation of a West African medical staff to which it was far more difficult for a Nigerian to get himself appointed than it had been before under 'the sound old system'. Eventually it came to be forgotten that there had been a time, in Lagos at least, when medical facilities were available to all comers. It is significant, however, that these changes were not effected in MacGregor's time. There is no hint, in his approach to public health in Lagos, of any capitulation to what was really a counsel of despair, the segregation of Europeans in the interests of their health and efficiency. On the contrary, having first satisfied himself that it was after all practicable to make Lagos a reasonably healthy town, at moderate expense, and that there was no need to go to the even greater expense and upheaval of the proposed move of the seat of government inland to Olokomeji, he set about making Lagos healthy for all, rich and poor—not simply for the resident Europeans—and made no move towards separate residential areas, cantonments, or hospitals for Europeans. All that came later, in part cause and in part effect of a hardening of the divisions between black and white in the official hierarchy, with Nigerians relegated more and more to the lower rungs of the ladder as the older men who had won distinction in earlier days retired, as the civil service became more of a pioneer, frontier service in the unrulier parts of the protectorate, and so less attractive in almost every way to educated Lagosians; and as civil service discipline came, in these hard conditions, to resemble military discipline, with an almost exclusively European officer caste often too hard pressed in their ordinary duties to pay sufficient attention to the welfare of their junior staff.

MacGregor, in his public health measures, characteristically sought, and obtained, willing public co-operation rather than the respectful obedience which, in medical matters at least, he might have been tempted to consider his due. As has been mentioned, he formed the Lagos Ladies' League, for health work amongst the children of Lagos. He formed the Lagos Board of Health, taking the chair himself; this, after some vicissitudes and periods of suspended animation, later developed into the Lagos Town Council. He introduced hygiene courses and hygiene examinations for primary school teachers and primary school pupils, with lectures given by medical officers, and a course of instruction printed and distributed to schools, with certificates of competence for the teachers and moneys provided by the Legislative Council for prizes to the children who distinguished themselves in the hygiene examinations. Government subsidies to schools depended as much on the efficient teaching of hygiene as on reading and writing. Medical officers were sent on courses at London and Liverpool in parasitology and anti-malarial work. The Director of Public Works was given as much money as he could use on contract labour for swamp reclamation; prisoners too were dosed with quinine and employed on swamp reclamation. A scheme was devised for Crown leases of plots reclaimed by the lessees from the swamp. In commending this work of reclamation to the Legislative Council MacGregor said: 'It is a work that I trust this Council will never allow to be interrupted while there is an acre of swamp left in Lagos.' But the biggest single public health or public works project (in MacGregor's time the two were not easily distinguishable) was the digging of the MacGregor canal across the island, as a great drainage project, the result of MacGregor's own investigations, in Amsterdam, into the effect of salt-water canals in anti-malarial work. A scheme for sewerage for Lagos was also considered, but eventually rejected on grounds of expense—to be resuscitated sixty years later in the first, post-independence National Development Plan, with little more hope of immediate construction.

Development of this kind, carried out peacefully and tactfully, carefully avoiding conflict and occasions for riot, punitive expeditions, and heroism, is not news; nor is it the stuff of romance and adventure stories; better drains, commercial progress, and financial statistics do not make exciting reading. No doubt this is the chief reason why the administrators of the old Lagos colony and protectorate were not inspired to record their achievements as Lugard and many of his officers did. It is not a complete explanation, however. Even if there had been a public at home sufficiently interested in peaceful colonial administration to stimulate official writing of books it is difficult to see how MacGregor himself, for instance, could have said or written much more than he did in public praise or defence of his territory, its peoples, and his own philosophy and methods of government without immediately seeming to criticize adversely the very different, military methods being applied elsewhere in Nigeria, in conditions on the whole more dangerous, more arduous, and more difficult than those in Lagos. Further, MacGregor's methods, although brilliantly and tactfully applied, were orthodox; there was no criticism on the score of militarism, oppression, or obstruction to civilizing influences to answer or forestall, and the ever-increasing prosperity and independence of the territory from imperial subventions must have seemed evidence enough of the soundness and the solid value of what his administrators were doing. But even so, there were aspects of the swelling revenues and increasing prosperity which prevented the heads of conscientious administrators from swelling in proportion—in particular, they were aware that much of the government of the country depended upon the proceeds of the duty on trade spirits, around which a fierce and unhappy controversy raged.

With direct taxation out of favour, and with great commercial clamour against indirect taxation penalizing other trade goods, particularly those of British manufacture, it was by no means surprising that a heavy burden of duty should be imposed on 'square face' gin, chiefly imported from Germany and Holland; and inevitably, this duty raised very substantial revenue. To many, including 'that sincere but tactless, misinformed and pugnacious cleric, Bishop Tugwell' (Morel's description), it seemed a terrible, disgraceful thing that the Government should be financed so largely by demoralizing liquor. So the duty went up and up, in an effort to restrict the trade, which thrived on this kind of punishment throughout the period before the first World War. As the spirit revenue increased, so did the criticism of the Government of Southern Nigeria for depending so largely upon it—as compared with Northern Nigeria, where trade gin was prohibited and the Government claimed that direct taxation had an altogether bracing and salutary effect on the people, very different from that of trade gin.[1] But in practice, there was little sign of excessive drinking of trade gin or of any demoralizing influence. MacGregor himself, although a total abstainer and in general sympathy with the missions, was not convinced, by his own observations, that the ill effects they reported were attributable to trade gin. As in all things, he took the sane and common-sense line; he had the spirit analysed, and passed legislation prescribing proof strengths. So dependence on schnapps for revenue continued. Gin was a sound investment and a valuable currency when there was an annual increase in value as duty rose; also, it was credited with great medicinal powers and used in ceremonial libations.

For the administrator, the reflection that his life's work, his salary, and his pension were financed by possibly noxious spirits may have served to cast doubt on any idea that an ideal form of government had been discovered. Another influence in the direction of official silence and reticence was the articulate and critical Lagos public and press, influenced, as we have seen, by their Lancashire trading partners in the radical tradition of dislike of officialdom and hatred of taxation; so, for the official, silence was golden. Yet another influence towards silence must have been the fact that there was so little in the way of a visible, tangible new system or model of provincial administration which could be shown as a tidy pattern on a map. The Yoruba in the protectorate were still governing themselves—not as a result of neglect, but as a matter of principle and of mutual agreement. The chief merit of MacGregor's system was that it worked constantly on the side of human freedom and dignity, without causing friction or explosions, and left room for each community to develop, in Macgregor's own words, in a way suited to the genius of all classes

[1] See p. 146.

of the community, and better adapted to their economic and social development than any other form of rule. It was in fact as near freedom from alien domination as it would have been possible for an alien officialdom to devise; and it worked. It was as kindly and bountiful as the climate itself—too soft, some would say, for the lasting good of the people and the inculcation of the sterner virtues.

# CHAPTER IV

## The Protectorate of Southern Nigeria, 1900–1905

If the system of a European Government, adapted gradually and by experience earned to native customs is of advantage to the country governed, so (paradoxical as it may appear) must the employment, where necessary, of force be. Diplomacy may win a point here and there, but in the person of the administrative officer it is often sent, unless supported by a strong escort, flying out of a town somewhat quicker than it entered it.

Annual Report for 1903.

The first battle is with superstition and the old order of things.

Henry Carr, 1901.

WHILE Lugard in a predominantly military way and MacGregor in a predominantly civilian way had been tackling the problems of the North and of Lagos, respectively, Sir Ralph Moor, a somewhat more shadowy figure than either, had been steering a systematic course through difficulties of a kind which they did not have to face, and devising to meet them a kind of government half-way between the civil and commercial of Lagos and the military and authoritarian of the North.

The chart by which Moor navigated had been drawn in outline by his predecessor and former chief in the days of the Foreign Office protectorate, Sir Claude MacDonald; but it was left to Moor, who succeeded him in 1896, to fill in the detail and to do the actual navigation.

From the beginning of the Oil Rivers Protectorate under MacDonald until the amalgamation of Nigeria under Lugard just before the first World War—a period of more than twenty years—there was remarkable continuity of policy and direction in what now forms the Mid-Western and Eastern regions of Nigeria. That there should be administrative continuity throughout the changes from Foreign Office and chartered company rule to Colonial Office rule is at first sight surprising, but continuity of policy was a natural consequence of continuity of staff and of the similarity of the problems they faced, as each new stretch of country was systematically opened up for trade; and continuity of staff, so far as the unhealthy conditions allowed, seems to have followed naturally upon the decision by Chamberlain that Moor should remain in charge when the territory was transferred to the Colonial Office. Moor, as a member of the Selborne Committee, was aware of what was intended as well as of what had been done. He was accompanied into the colonial service by several administrators and heads of departments experienced in the arts of peaceful penetration. Many of the senior men had by the early years of the century spent up to ten years in the difficult and often deadly Oil Rivers and Niger Coast Protectorates; and several, including Moor himself, asked for transfer to healthier climes—Cyprus being one of the favourite choices—but little heed seems to have been taken of their requests. The requests seem to have been prompted by weariness, ill-health and family separation, and by the depression caused by seeing so many friends invalided or dying, rather than failure of local leadership or team spirit. But there was a feeling that after five years or so it might well be the turn of another young man to bear the weight of a very heavy end of the white man's burden.[1]

It was still a very young service, however; one of the 'old hands' who had petitioned for transfer to another territory was Widenham Francis Widenham Fosbery, who at the age of thirty-four was already a C.M.G. and Acting High Commissioner. Another senior officer who, like Fosbery, would have liked a change was F. S. James, first appointed in 1896, aged twenty-six; by the time he was thirty he was in charge of the Eastern Division (about one-quarter of the whole protectorate and the least settled part); at the age of thirty-two he was appointed C.M.G. for work done as Divisional Commissioner of the new Cross River Division, comprising five districts (Afikpo, Obubra, Bende, Okuni, and Aro-Chuku), an area of about 7,250 square miles, with a population guessed (in 1905) at more than half a million; salary. £650 per annum. It was only in 1902 that this area was 'opened up' by the Aro Field Force, and, as the annual report for 1902 hopefully put it, the protectorate thus 'freed for ever from the evils of slave-raiding and slave dealing on an organised scale'.

The line of policy so steadily and continuously pursued throughout

[1] The C.O. 444 and 520 series contain much correspondence on these topics.

these years was essentially as explained by MacDonald, in 1892, to the Liverpool Chamber of Commerce:

> The nature of the natives, the climate, everything is against hasty and precipitate action. To advance slowly, leaving no bad or unfinished work behind, to gain the respect and liking of the natives, and only to use force when compelled to do so, are the means which in my humble opinion lead to success in West Africa.

Like McCallum and MacGregor in Lagos, MacDonald was a steadfast believer in consulting native opinion and in basing policy firmly on the wishes and the aspirations revealed in the process of consultation. It may not have been Scottish egalitarianism which inspired this respect for African self-determination; but these men may well have been influenced by the unhappy ancestral memories of the MacGregors and the MacDonalds—memories of the terrible mistakes made by alien governments in the treatment of the Scottish highland clans.[1]

Whatever the source of MacDonald's sympathies, there can be no doubt about their strength. Dr. J. E. Flint in his biography of Goldie describes MacDonald's approach in the following words, based on a study of MacDonald's report in 1889 to the Foreign Office on the future of the Niger territories:

> He simply assumed, without any discussion or attempt to justify his method, that his task was to find out the wishes of the Africans, and implement them. For him 'Imperial Interests' were the interests of the Africans. He therefore went from town to town, and in the most thorough fashion open to him, proceeded to conduct what was in effect a rudimentary kind of plebiscite. In each place he tried to collect together a cross-section of the local society, chiefs, influential traders, elders, literate Africans, European managers, even those who could give some idea of the wishes and aspirations of the poor and the slaves. They were then asked to indicate which form of rule they preferred; chartered company, colony, or Foreign Office protectorate. A full, and often lengthy discussion followed, MacDonald explaining the implications of each system in a factual way. The results of all these meetings were often correlated, and MacDonald put forward the general view as his own recommendations. This was indeed government by consent. Though the acquisition of territory by treaty was in a sense a form of 'consultation' this was probably the first example of African opinion being allowed to determine the *form* of colonial government.[2]

[1] cf. Maclean, of the Gold Coast, for whom also claims have been made as a tactful exponent of indirect rule, 'the White man in whose time all slept sound'. See G. E. Metcalfe, *Maclean of the Gold Coast* (1962), p. vi.

[2] Flint, *Sir George Goldie and the Making of Nigeria*, p. 130.

It was as a result of this investigation (instigated of course by the Liverpool shipowners and merchants campaigning against the Niger Company's 'monopoly') that the Oil Rivers Protectorate was set up, and MacDonald appointed to run it. The apparent enthusiasm for Her Majesty's protection shown by her new wards—rather like the Lancashire merchants' imperialist interest—was due not so much to a liking for official rule as to a cordial hatred of the Niger Company, and to the prospects of economic advantage to those whom MacDonald had visited and consulted, the people of the coast and of the oil rivers, in places like Bonny, Opobo, Calabar, Forcados, and Brass. These were people who had long had contact with white men, were used to business dealings, and were well placed to profit by trade with the interior under British protection. It was when efforts were made to consolidate by law and order the opening up to trade of the interior that administrative problems and friction really started, with many warring tribes speaking hundreds of different languages and dialects.

Except for Benin, there were no large kingdoms, and the leaders thrown up in the confused years of the nineteenth century—such as Jaja and Nana—had all at one stage or another fallen foul of the British authorities and been exiled or otherwise made powerless, leaving behind them, instead of the enlarged and vigorous states that their leadership and ability might otherwise have established, a legacy of greater disorganization and of fear and suspicion of the white man. With things as they were, there was no convenient administrative solution to hand comparable with the continuance of Fulani rule in the North or the strengthening of the traditional rulers in Yorubaland.

MacDonald, and his lieutenant and successor Moor, were therefore driven to adopt a painfully slow and testing form of peaceful penetration, the pace dictated by the temper of the people, the large number of 'arms of precision' possessed by them, and the availability of revenue to consolidate territory penetrated before moving on again.[1] Sometimes, as in the Qua Ibo country whose inhabitants were found to be 'exceedingly unruly', 'excessively turbulent, aggressive and dangerous', it was necessary to temporize for several years, simply maintaining some kind of peace sufficient for trade to do its

[1] Written before publication of J. C. Anene, *Southern Nigeria in Transition, 1885–1906* (Cambridge, 1966). See his chapter vi, which suggests that Moor lacked Macdonald's patience and love of peace, at first, but (pp. 237–8) underwent a conversion to the pacific approach about 1902.

mellowing work, until new supplies of money and of men permitted something more ambitious. The process was described twice in connection with the annual reports of the period, in the clearest terms, once in the report for 1899–1900, and later by Egerton, on taking over Southern Nigeria, in a covering dispatch on the report for the year 1904.

The report for 1899–1900 gives this summary:

> The natives of the Protectorate, without exception, are conservative to a degree, especially among the older chiefs, and it is with the greatest difficulty that improvements of any kind can be introduced among them, and the only way by which this has been achieved has been by the use of the greatest patience, energy and tact. It is needless to say that from time to time punitive action has had to be taken to put down wholesale massacres, cannibalism, and closing of trade routes, but such primitive means are never resorted to unless all efforts of a pacific nature have utterly failed. This factor, the conservatism of the people, must also be considered when the work which has been performed in this Protectorate during the nine years of its existence is looked into. The work of opening up inland from the Coast has been slow, and must always be so, for if done in a hurry and with no thought for the welfare and improvement of the people, it would take a very short time for the country to fall back into its former state.

Egerton's recorded impression on his arrival was as follows:

> The history of the Protectorate is, I believe, unique both for Africa and for other portions of the British Empire. Throughout the whole of the territory now under our control settled government has only been established by a show of military force, and yet the whole cost of introducing and maintaining law and order—involving the maintenance of a large military establishment—has been defrayed from the local revenues without incurring any debt. As each year a larger area has been pacified, a proper system of justice established, free trade between town and town and with the coast rendered possible, the increasing revenue has enabled a further area to be similarly dealt with in the succeeding year. In addition to this, large sums have been annually contributed towards the cost of the administration of Northern Nigeria.
>
> I have so recently assumed the administration that I cannot claim any credit of these excellent results which are due to the efficient administration of my two predecessors and the loyal assistance rendered them by the civil and military officers of the Protectorate Service: but it is nevertheless a pleasant duty to draw attention to the gratifying results obtained.[1]

Egerton had long and varied administrative and judicial experience in Malaya before his appointment to Southern Nigeria—he was the

[1] Egerton's covering dispatch to the 1904 annual report for Southern Nigeria.

first Nigerian Governor to have what later came to be regarded as a 'normal' colonial administrative service background, a public school education (Tonbridge) and a degree (in law). His great gifts were a flair for finance, and for economic and commercial development (his remarks about 'gratifying results' and his tribute to staff in the report quoted above have much the same flavour as the company chairman's report to the shareholders on a successful year's business), and secondly an even more marked flair for avoiding personal publicity. Despite his long career as Governor in Nigeria and later in British Guiana he managed to avoid fame and notoriety; he almost avoided mention—no published works, no mention in the *Dictionary of National Biography*, no great involvement in controversy. He died in March 1947, at the age of eighty-nine, having quietly outlasted all his coast contemporaries.

Moor also is an enigmatic, even tragic figure. He was the son of a doctor; his career in West Africa began after his resignation from his chosen career in the Royal Irish Constabulary, the result of his being involved in a divorce case. A few years after his retirement from Nigeria, in 1904, on grounds of ill-health, he was found dead in bed in circumstances pointing to suicide. The years of his retirement he had spent advising Sir Alfred Jones, and the Cotton Growing Association, on the development of West African trade. Among those who paid tribute to his ability as an administrator were Mary Kingsley, E. D. Morel, and Geary. Geary quoted in his *Nigeria under British Rule* the systematized procedure which Moor laid down in 1896 for the ten stages in the process of 'opening up' Southern Nigeria:

1. Small, peaceable expeditions
2. Reports of officers on economic products
3. Native Councils of chiefs in friendly towns
4. Route surveys
5. Treaties
6. Consideration of complaints
7. Patrol of waterways
8. Opening of landways and suppression of tolls
9. Native travellers
10. Establishment of permanent posts

This process, obviously aimed at the peaceful development of commerce, did not always go peacefully and smoothly; at any stage of the proceedings there could be sudden danger and death, with ' "Diplomacy" . . . in the person of the Administrative Officer . . . often sent, unless supported by a strong escort, flying out of a town somewhat quicker than it entered it'.

When this happened, the alternatives were a show of force or a decision to leave the area until it became rather more 'ripe for development'. There was nothing in the terrain or in the organization of the people which permitted the speedy deployment of mounted infantry on punitive expeditions, there was no room for the rapid exemplary humbling of power which the open spaces of the North permitted Lugard to administer to the Emirs. The desperate, dangerous work of the early pioneers in the South, on the other hand, produced a service in which cheerful resourcefulness and a sense of humour were more valuable than impressive personal dignity. When, usually after a convincing demonstration of naked power, peace was established, the District Commissioner found himself sitting in the midst of the people, in the often noisy and highly informal native council. This setting and background were different from those of the 'Political Officer' in the Northern Emirate receiving with careful ceremonial robed Moslem dignitaries, a ceremonial based on rank and precedent, and prescribed in great detail in Lugard's *Political Memoranda*. (The Resident was to follow a drill—to rise to receive a chief of the first grade, to shake hands and offer a chair; for a chief of the second grade, no chair, but a raised seat 'such as a box covered by a carpet'; third, fourth, and fifth-grade chiefs to be seated on a mat on the floor, etc.)[1]

The very greatest importance was attached by Moor, and his officers, to the native courts and native councils. They were intended to be the chief instruments of progress employed directly by the Government, supplementing the civilizing influences of commerce and education. At the end of the period of Foreign Office jurisdiction there were twenty-three native councils and minor courts (in addition to consular courts) under the ultimate direction of the judicial officer and under the immediate supervision of administrative officers. From the beginning these courts and councils were held to be of great value, not only in the administration of justice but in 'providing the means of instructing the people in the proper methods of government'—as the 1898–9 report put it:

Not only are they engaged in direct judicial work, but the Native Councils as distinct from the native run of Courts, are allowed and encouraged to make necessary native laws affecting the tribes which they represent and

[1] See p. 145.

over which they have control. All these Councils and Courts have practically the control of their own funds under the supervision, of course, of European officers; and the expenditure of these funds for the general advantage of the country and people provides an object lesson in civilized administration. By this means Court houses are erected for the administering of justice and good roads made from village to village, and other works of general utility carried out. It is anticipated that the value of the work done by these Courts will greatly increase in future years, and if proper attention be paid to their organization and control they will relieve the European officials of a large amount of labour, and indeed carry out work of administration and control which otherwise in all probability could not be coped with.

It is unnecessary to go into the question whether this is a description of direct rule or of indirect rule; what matters is that it was a deliberate effort to teach, to 'elevate', and to influence by direct contact. The essential point, of contact and supervision, was repeatedly emphasized in subsequent reports. In the 1902 report, for instance, written by Probyn, later Governor of Sierra Leone, the point was made thus:

The expansion of a wholesome trade will itself spread cultivation among the natives: the natives will also gradually become more cultivated through the influence of the increasing number of those educated in the Protectorate Schools; the most widespread, powerful and rapidly acting influence tending to elevate the natives will, however, be found in the Native Councils, *provided the latter are constantly supervised by European officers.*

The same point was made again in the annual report for 1903 (the last year of Moor's service):

Patient work and time will do much with the native but, only when he is in constant contact with the European. Given sufficient European supervision, the work done, and to be done, will the more easily be consolidated and made firm and lasting.

It was not only the Europeans themselves who had this firm belief in the benefit their presence could bring and was bringing. The first inspection of education in the protectorate of Southern Nigeria was carried out by Henry Carr, lent by MacGregor to do a schools inspection at Calabar and Bonny, and to make recommendations on education generally. After observing that missionaries tended to look on schools as the instruments for making converts, while other men looked on them as instruments for making good and useful citizens, he observed that the children the missionaries were training to live in heaven had first to get through the world. He conceded, however, that the first battle was 'with superstition and the old order of things', and that the missions were indeed winning this battle, however disappointing the academic standards might be:

> I am convinced that small as is the actual result in school learning produced by the missions, the result which they have produced on the temper, intelligence and social conditions of the people has not been unimportant, and this is the work which it has as yet been possible to achieve.[1]

But as in the native councils, so in the schools, supervision, direct, constant supervision, was essential; otherwise 'the tendency is to under-staff them, to under-pay the teachers, and to ambition a multiplicity of subjects without a thorough grounding in the elementary matters of instruction'.

The backwardness of the peoples of the Southern Protectorate seems to have called forth a special effort from the Government in both education and administration, a tendency to reach for the new broom and sweep as clean as possible. They saw less to admire in the existing situation and the existing institutions than their contemporaries in the North and in Yorubaland, and so there was less temptation to use those institutions—how, for instance, could a proper system of rule be based on the terrible Long Juju of the Aros? As Carr had said, the first battle was with this kind of superstition and the old order, the oppression, which ignorance and superstition permitted. In the absence of large states, in the absence of communications other than waterways, it was possible, and indeed necessary, to base the area of each new district as it was established on the principle that the boundaries should not usually be more than about two days' march, or thirty miles, from the district stations.

The districts were grouped in divisions, staffed by a Divisional Commissioner and a Travelling Commissioner. So far as possible, each district had two officers, a District Commissioner and an Assistant District Commissioner, so that one could be on tour while the other was in the station. Direct governing powers were limited to the collection of Customs duties, the trial of serious crimes by 'natives' and of cases involving 'non-natives'. The 'indirect' powers lay in the control which the administrative officer exercised through *ex-officio* presidency of the native courts and councils. These were held responsible for the good government and order of the area under their jurisdiction, and had powers of local legislation. The declared

[1] See annual report (1899–1900).

principles under which Moor exercised his power as High Commissioner to grant or withhold assent to rules made by native councils were these three: first, no unnecessary interference with customs and habits; second, no creation of class privileges; third, persuasion to include provisions which experience in other countries had proved to be beneficial.

The second of these principles—avoiding the creation of class privileges—is of particular importance and interest, as showing a conscious effort by British administrators not to do what Lugard was endeavouring to do in the North; for at that time Lugard was endeavouring to preserve and strengthen the class structure in the North, and deprecating the tendency of some missionaries to preach the equality of men, 'which, however true from a doctrinal point of view, is apt to be misapplied by people in a low stage of development, and interpreted as an abolition of class distinction'.[1]

Moor's administration had as its declared object 'the education and improvement of the native' and his 'elevation'—a position somewhat different from the school of MacGregor and of Egerton, more concerned to improve conditions and services and let the human plant flourish and develop as it would; different also from the Northern school, more concerned to protect the plant from outside influences or too rapid change of any sort. As a result, Moor's administration soon became more closely and directly involved in education than the other governments, through the combined influence of official zeal, missionary endeavour, financial assistance from the merchants, and growing popular demand. Out of Henry Carr's visit grew, first a post of Inspector of Schools, in 1901, to advise the High Commissioner on the systematic allotment of grants to schools; and next, in 1903, an Education Department under a director, J. A. Douglas, an Oxford graduate in modern history, with experience in Indian universities and schools.

As Carr had said, mission education had at first been evangelical in purpose, mainly bible classes in the vernacular; but under the influence of Government grants and of practical necessity the missions were already branching out into other teaching, in the places where they were established. At Calabar, for instance, the Hope Waddell Institute of the United Free Church of Scotland was already a large and well equipped residential school for a hundred boys, the first institution to give an education in English combined with practical

[1] Annual report, Northern Nigeria, 1905–6.

instruction in carpentry, printing, and tailoring. Printing and tailoring were extensions of evangelism; carpentry was in demand by the chiefs or heads of houses and the people, for the purposes of trade, and so was coopering, in an economy so dependent on palm-oil trade in puncheons. The Catholics and the Church Missionary Society also had started education in English, and instruction in trades like brick-making, brick-laying, carpentry, and building. Beginnings had even been made in girls' education with a Convent School at Calabar opened in 1904, and a Girls' Institute at Creek Town giving elementary education and household training—run by the United Free Church.

Not all places in the settled part of the protectorate were reached by mission efforts, and in many districts chiefs and councils wanted schools, free from mission influence, which would give a secular education. 'Pidgin English' was already a *lingua franca*, but the demand was in all cases for 'English book proper' and for carpentry and coopering instruction—so that the children could grow up into successful traders, with a sufficient knowledge of spoken English, the ability to read and write an English letter, and a knowledge of arithmetic and elementary book-keeping. The Government too had its own ideas about the syllabus, wishing to educate boys up to the standard required for employment as clerks and as telegraphists, and to give instruction in the simpler processes of agriculture and market gardening. Douglas was by no means as keen as the missions on the teaching of tailoring and printing, observing caustically that the undesirable use to which a knowledge of 'the art of Caxton' was habitually put in other parts of the coast furnished 'an instructive object lesson', and that tailoring encouraged too widespread a tendency to wear European clothes 'instead of the more becoming and serviceable native costume'. Douglas, whose Indian experience was in the Punjab, would have felt more at home, in spirit, in the North of Nigeria!

By 1910 there were about fifty schools run directly by the Government, in the places where the missions had not established schools, from the beginnings in 1903 when the first director was appointed, with a staff of four Europeans—two inspectors and two schoolmasters, the latter 'enjoying' a salary of £180 per annum. The director (£500 per annum) was Secretary to the Board of Education, of which the High Commissioner was chairman. In 1905 the only official who was a member of the Board was the puisne judge, the others being representatives of the three principal missions and one representative of the merchants—all Europeans.

There is no doubt that the progress in education in the early years of the century, with all its consequences in later years, owed much to Moor's own personal efforts. He raised £5,000 in England during one leave to help build new premises for the Bonny Government school, helped by merchants' donations; Miller Brothers and the African Association were shamed into helping by the example of Sir Alfred Jones, who wrote to Moor, when sending his contribution, 'If what we have given is not enough, you can have as much more as you want'—but commented on the absence of firms like Miller Brothers from the list of subscribers.[1]

The whole process of the spread of education in the newly pacified districts of the Southern Nigeria Protectorate, despite the difficulties of finance and the lack of teachers, is a remarkable illustration of the degree to which Moor was able to combine the resources of the officials, of the chiefs, of the traders, and of the different churches in the mission field, content to develop education on the foundations built by the missions, where they existed, but educating directly wherever the missions were not established, if there was a local demand. It was in these early years that the Easterners seized with both hands the possibilities of acquiring the education and the skills which placed them in the van of the advance towards independence.

In medicine, there was by the time of Egerton's arrival a considerable Medical Department, sufficient, in theory at least, to provide a medical officer for each district. Unlike the Lagos Medical Department, the medical service of the protectorate had from the beginning conceived its first clinical duty to be the care of the official community, military and civil. The numerous military expeditions and patrols which had to be accompanied by a doctor, and the health conditions (ranging from bad in the best stations to appalling in the pioneering outposts), made the medical care of the Europeans and of African officials, police, and troops a full-time occupation for most of them. There was still little demand for European medicine among the public at large, but each medical officer was also responsible for sanitation in his area, and for the training of subordinates. Although there was no campaign for public health instruction comparable with MacGregor's efforts in Lagos, Moor himself wrote what was called

[1] C.O. 520/3. Miller Brothers, the Glasgow merchants, were not loved by their Liverpool competitors.

a 'treatise' on sanitation, for use in the schools as a textbook.[1] Perhaps the most striking achievement in the field of public health was the progress made in vaccination against smallpox. The vaccine was manufactured at Sapele, from 1902, and smallpox was in consequence no longer quite the same terrible scourge which it had previously been throughout the territory. Sapele, incidentally, was regarded as the unhealthiest place of all, for Europeans; in the first annual report to the Colonial Office the grim statistics for Sapele give some indication of the amount of a medical officer's time which must have been taken up in attendance on his colleagues. In the year, at Sapele, there were, with an average European population of fourteen, one hundred and nineteen cases of sickness among them; there were eight cases of invaliding and five deaths, 'which totalled would appear effectually to dispose of all but one of the average European population within a year'. In the same year, the medical officers of the protectorate treated in all just over a thousand African cases. Many of these were commercial, mission, and Government employees, but there was already the beginning of the demand for medical attention and European medicine, which later swelled to a flood, greater than the medical staff could cope with. The success of smallpox vaccine played a part in this.

In 1905 there were thirty-two district medical officers and four senior medical officers, under the principal medical officer and his deputy. As in the administrative service, there had been remarkable continuity, despite the arduous active service involved. Dr. Allman had been appointed as principal medical officer in 1891 by the Secretary of State for Foreign Affairs, and was the only substantive holder of the post for a period of sixteen years, until the merger with Lagos. During that period he had accompanied the expeditions to Benin city, and the Cross River, Eket, Okrika, Ekuri, Ishan, and Aro expeditions, with several mentions in dispatches and the award of the C.M.G. He served on the Colonial Office committee in 1901 for the reorganization of the West African medical services which started the trend towards 'unification' of the medical service, and away from 'Africanization' or 'localization'. The reasons for this trend were that the first duty was to provide for the European officers of the Government, especially in the bush, the best possible medical attention; that African doctors were not equal in professional competence to Europeans, except in rare instances, and did not possess the confidence of

[1] C.O. 520/3.

European patients; that social conditions were against African doctors, particularly where Europeans lived together on the 'mess' system, and where many of them were officers of the regular army. It was later stated that African doctors had been 'tried without success' in Southern Nigeria, but in 1905 there were no African doctors on the strength. Indeed, the conditions of life and service can have had little appeal for African doctors, who at that date were all men from the older colonies and settlements, who could be assured of more congenial conditions on the coast, in Lagos, or elsewhere, among their own people. It would have taken a man of quite exceptional gifts and strength of character to overcome the prejudices and distrust an African doctor would have encountered, serving, for instance, on a Cross River military expedition. The senior nursing staff were five European nurses in the hospital at Calabar, originally Presbyterian mission appointments, later taken over by the Government and paid at the rate of £100 per annum each. In terms of senior staff, the Medical Department was one of the two largest, rivalled only by the Marine Department.

The Marine Department under Lieutenant H. A. Child, R.N. (who later helped to site and develop Port Harcourt),[1] was responsible for the maintenance and improvement of harbours and waterways and the maintenance and operation of the Government fleet of steamers and launches; this work occupied a European staff of more than thirty marine officers and engineers. By contrast, the Public Works Department was small, with a mere half-dozen engineers and assistants. There was a separate Roads Department, with one officer, in 1905. The complement of official departments was made up by a few small units directly concerned with economic development and regulation, on much the same lines as those in Lagos, a Forestry and Botanical Department, and a Commercial Intelligence Officer, appointed in 1905.

The Forestry Department was started by Moor in 1899, as soon as he knew that he was to be appointed High Commissioner of the new protectorate. He sought authority from the Colonial Office for two officers; he was allowed one. By 1905 the establishment had increased to eight Conservators and Assistant Conservators under H.N. ('Timber') Thompson, the originator of scientific forestry in Nigeria, a product of the Cooper's Hill Indian Engineering College, with twelve years' experience in the Indian forest service and, in Burma, 'a

[1] See pp. 186–190.

widely read, cultured and able man' who 'earned the deep respect and trust of all the Governors with whom he served in his long career of twenty-six years'.[1]

From the beginning, with the appointment of the first officer (P. Hitchens, a 'Eurasian'), the main preoccupation was with the rubber-producing area of Benin, and with attempts to control and regulate the rubber boom by declaring close seasons for rubber-tapping, and by the licensing of rubber-tappers. The rubber 'rush' of the nineties had brought many strangers, some of whom were not content with permanently damaging the trees and tapping the roots, but also slaughtered elephants indiscriminately for their ivory, demanded provisions and lodging from the local people with menaces and actual force, and in some cases seized captives, demanding ransom for their release. The new Forest Department took over from the Administration the work of protecting the rubber and the similar work of controlling the boom in mahogany, by prohibiting the felling of trees less than nine feet in girth at ten feet above the ground, by collecting royalties, and by levying export duty on lumber shipments from the docks.

The Forest Department was destined to remain responsible for agriculture as well, and for the botanical gardens, until 1910, when Thompson realized his long-cherished ambition to separate forestry and agriculture, and to concentrate the efforts of the Forest Department on the creation of the permanent Forest Estate. Until then, about half of the senior staff had to be employed on tasks like the care of the botanical gardens, and service on secondment to the B.C.G.A., growing cotton.

As in the colony of Lagos, the early years of the century were a time of energetic experiment in agriculture and in the introduction of exotic crops and plants; some succeeded, some failed, but the net result was to enrich the economy and the diet of the people. Amongst the failures must be counted the untiring planting by Hitchens, in the Benin forests, of thousands of the latex-bearing tree *Funtumia elastica*. The idea was to provide communally owned rubber plantations. In the first year of his work it was claimed that two hundred and fifty miles of Benin roads or paths had been planted with rubber seeds, four deep, on each side. When, years later, the trees began to bear, the superiority of the *para* rubber from the East Indies was just becoming apparent. The market for 'Lagos rubber' collapsed, and the

[1] D. R. Rosevear, chapter xvi, *Nigeria Handbook* (1953 edition).

plantations were left untended. Plantations of mahogany and of iroko were tried and proved unsuccessful, the trees being subject to unexpectedly severe attack by pests when grown in plantations. The coffee plantations taken over from the Niger Company at Nkissi proved unremunerative, and were abandoned. The same fate attended the B.C.G.A.'s experimental cotton plantations on the Sobo plains. A cattle ranch was started with cattle from Barbados shipped, in 1902, by way of the Canaries (because of the British quarantine rules which precluded shipment via the United Kingdom); all the cattle were dead within a year. Some of these vain efforts must have been heartbreaking for the enthusiasts who put their hopes and trust in them—not for material reward, but for the satisfaction of assisting in the development of the country and the 'elevation' of the people.

But some ventures succeeded, such as the mangoes from Trinidad, the tobacco from Virginia, and the firewood plantations of teak and *cassia siamea* from the Far East. And cocoa, piassava, kapok, cinnamon, rafia, and kola succeeded; there was also experimentation with jute, castor oil, bananas, maize, and ground-nuts.

All this had been put in hand before Egerton's arrival, by Moor and his officers, but it was the economic development of the country which dominated Egerton's thinking and determined the nature of his proposals for day-to-day administration and for the merger of Lagos and Southern Nigeria. Very soon after his arrival, in 1904, he was suggesting to the Secretary of State that at least some of the administrative officers for Southern Nigeria should be selected by means of the competitive examinations held for the Home and Indian civil services and for cadetships in Malaya, Hong Kong, and Ceylon. He also proposed that those selected should be given training in surveying, map-making, geology, and botany, a clear indication of the overriding importance, in his eyes, of economic development—there was no question of learning law, or the more arid, routine functions; he wanted officers with brains of good quality, trained exclusively in subjects useful for development of the country's resources. The reasons recorded in the Colonial Office[1] for not accepting his recommendations were not very inspiring: the chief reason was that a committee was already examining the question of administrative selection and training; others were the defeatist counsel that selection on the basis of a written examination would simply mean taking those who just failed to get into the Home and Indian services, which were more

[1] C.O. 520/25.

attractive, with no guarantee that these men would have the requisite qualities of character; and that the written examination would tell particularly against those candidates of slightly more mature years whom they wished to find for Nigeria because conditions there demanded some maturity and experience.

At about the same time, soon after his arrival, Egerton reported in a dispatch to the Secretary of State dated 17 September 1904:

> Had this Protectorate received the financial aid which has been given to Northern Nigeria, or had it even not had to contribute to the support of that Protectorate, and had the money been well spent, there is very little doubt that the revenue might now have been a million sterling and the trade that commensurate with such a revenue.[1]

In fact, the Southern Nigeria revenue for that year was £470,606; so that what Egerton meant was that the revenue could have been doubled, by the expenditure in the years 1900–5 of a very few hundred thousand pounds more on communications and on the investigation and development of natural resources. The Colonial Office decided not to reply; it was probably the best course, since it is difficult to see what they could have said which would not have displeased the Treasury, or Lugard, or Egerton himself, and exposed the Office to further criticism.

Egerton had no criticism of his predecessors, however; he thought the systematic opening up of the country without external aid, while also providing a contribution to Northern Nigeria, a unique achievement. It was, in fact, most systematic; each year the military submitted estimates for the dry-season campaign to extend the efforts of pacification, and each year the protectorate was extended as planned, within the financial means available.

The gist of the orthodox teaching about this period of Nigerian history, derived chiefly from Lugard's own admiring accounts of his work, is that British rule in the North was planned, skilful, and systematic, while in the South it was unplanned and untidy, and somehow discreditable. In Dame Margery Perham's view (expressed in *Native Administration in Nigeria* and other works) there was in the North 'confident and rapid action which in three years put the whole country into British hands', while in the South there was 'reluctant, uncertain and rather haphazard penetration from the coast'.[2]

[1] C.O. 520/25.

[2] Perham, *Native Administration in Nigeria*, p. 3. See also her introduction to Joan Wheare, *The Nigerian Legislative Council* (London, 1950).

In point of fact, such a comparison can be sustained only if the new North of 1900–5 is compared, not with the South of the same period, but with the confused coast settlements and administrations of the pre-Chamberlain era. If a comparison is made between the protectorates of Northern and Southern Nigeria in the period of their implementation of Chamberlain's policy and of the Selborne Committee's plan of commercial, economic, and social development without unnecessary interference, and without direct taxation, the inescapable conclusion is that both in Lagos and in Southern Nigeria the action taken was neither reluctant nor uncertain, nor haphazard, but remarkably rapid, exact, and systematic, and justified by immediate success, both in financial terms and in terms of solid, measurable improvement in the conditions and prosperity of the people, and in their increasing freedom from the tyranny of ignorance and superstition.

# CHAPTER V

# The Amalgamation of Lagos and Southern Nigeria, 1905–1912

Give me roads—good, broad straight roads right through the jungle from one tribal area to the next—then we'll be able to let in the light.

Sir Walter Egerton.

EGERTON'S scheme for the joining together of Lagos and Southern Nigeria, submitted to the Secretary of State in a confidential dispatch of 29 January 1905,[1] was not a scheme for complete fusion. It seemed to him that the different methods of administration which had been adopted in the two territories forbade complete fusion. The basic difference, of course, was that the institutions of Lagos, and of its protectorate, were in the tradition of the colony, while those of Southern Nigeria (without Legislative Council or Executive Council) were the institutions of a protectorate.

As a newcomer to Africa from the other side of the world, appointed as both Governor of Lagos and High Commissioner for Southern Nigeria, Egerton seems to have observed both systems in action with an impartial eye, passing adverse judgement on neither method of administration, and recommending minimal changes for the time being. His idea was that a partial fusion would permit the retention of the different methods of administration, until the time came to amalgamate the whole of Nigeria, or, in his words, to 'add Northern Nigeria to this administration'.[2] This latter step he believed, at the time he wrote his dispatch, to have been already decided upon. He believed also that joining the two protectorates would be easier, and offer greater economy, than the operation of joining Lagos and Southern Nigeria.

Egerton did not give a detailed recital of the administrative differences prompting his proposal for partial fusion only—concentrating, characteristically, on a scheme based firmly on the economic life and communications of the country. But it is when these factors are con-

[1] C.O. 520/29. [2] Ibid.

sidered that the difficulties of fusion from east to west seem most obvious, as compared with the idea of spreading northwards from the various sea ports into the interior of the continent. It is also when the communications and economic life of the two coastal territories are considered that the differences in administration as between them emerge most clearly.

The Lagos colony and protectorate had one main centre and obvious capital, Lagos, which was the centre of trade and of communications by rail, sea, and creek, and administrative capital, with the full apparatus of Crown colony government, already being talked of as the 'Bombay of West Africa' and as the 'Liverpool of West Africa'.

There was no comparable centralization in one capital in the Southern Nigeria Protectorate. Calabar, the seat of the Government, was but one of eight small ports, no one of which contained representatives of all the competing firms. It had a small Secretariat, no Legislative Council, no commercial press, little so far in the way of an educated class of Nigerians, no railway. But when the provincial organization of the Government was examined, there was much more to show in the settled parts of Southern Nigeria than in the Lagos hinterland—areas neatly and systematically divided into districts of roughly comparable size, with district medical officers and district engineers, as well as the administrative staff, and with native councils and native courts, supervised closely by administrators—quite different from the quasi-independent states of Yorubaland, irregular in size as in advancement, some with Residents (like Abeokuta and Ibadan), some without, depending on the scope for commercial diplomacy offered by trade and railway construction. These men, like Elgee in Ibadan (who had been MacGregor's Private Secretary), regarded themselves as Residents in the original sense, that of an agent of the British Government in an almost independent state, and were following MacGregor's policy of maintaining, preserving, and strengthening the rule of the traditional and elected chiefs, avoiding unnecessary interference, and following the spirit and the letter of the treaty agreements with the chiefs.

Egerton hesitated before recommending Lagos as the capital. He believed it was not, and he feared it could never become, so healthy a place of residence for Europeans as Calabar. But the economic arguments, particularly the fact that there was free mercantile competition between the firms ('sadly lacking' at Calabar), made him choose Lagos, and resolve to continue its development into a great port and worthy capital.

He proposed that the revenues should remain separate, a natural consequence of his proposal that the legislatures should remain separate. He felt that the Lagos Legislative Council's powers could hardly be extended to cover Southern Nigeria, about which the unofficial members knew and cared very little. There should, however, be one Governor and High Commissioner (by analogy with the Straits Settlements) who would have a Colonial Secretary in Lagos and a Secretary to the High Commissioner in Calabar.

The new territory formed by amalgamation should, Egerton thought, be called Southern Nigeria, 'as good a name for the entire territory as can be found'. He wished to limit the number of provinces to three, giving both geographical (or economic) reasons as well as administrative reasons. The three should be, first Lagos and its hinterland, with Lagos as the provincial capital, second Forcados and its hinterland, with Warri as the capital, third Calabar and hinterland, Calabar being the provincial capital. He wished the existing divisions to remain undisturbed.

The chief reasons for having three large provinces were purely administrative; a very small number of large provinces would permit the appointment, as Provincial Commissioners, of officers with a reasonable salary and seniority, to whom the Governor would be able to delegate a good deal of responsibility, and from whom a senior man to act for the Governor himself would come. Either the most senior man would normally be at Calabar, where considerations of distance from the capital at Lagos demanded a greater delegation of authority, or he could be permanently at Lagos where he could conveniently relieve the Governor. Significantly, Egerton thought the men to fill these posts should preferably come from services whose administrators had been selected by competitive examination; he also suggested that there should be consultation with Sir Frank Swettenham of the Straits Settlements on the question of the posting of the man who would act for the Governor. Since Southern Nigeria, although still undeveloped, was much larger and potentially more important than Lagos, he thought more than half the cost of the joint machinery should be provided from Southern Nigeria revenue. There should be an amalgamation under a Financial Commissioner of the Treasuries and Customs Department—but other departments would remain much as they were, borne on the separate estimates of the territories.

Egerton's proposals lay for a year in the Colonial Office before the answering dispatch, dated 12 January 1906. The delay was rather odd, because the proposals had been specially called for in 1904. Egerton himself might have submitted them earlier if the same kind of mischance had not overtaken the dispatch asking him for proposals as befell the Selborne Committee's proposals. In that important case the Colonial Office had mislaid the file; now again, when a very important step was being taken, the dispatch asking for Egerton's plan was landed by mistake at Forcados and sent up river to Lugard's headquarters at Zungeru.

The more creditable reason for the delay in answering the proposals was the decision to await Egerton's arrival on leave, for discussions. In these discussions Antrobus was the sole survivor in office of the planners of 1898, in the Selborne Committee, and seems to have played the principal part in finally shaping the approved plan of amalgamation. He considered 'the weak point' of Egerton's scheme to be the proposal to leave legislature and finances separate—not least because loans secured on the revenues of a protectorate did not have trustee status, whereas loans to a colony, or to a combined colony and protectorate, would have this advantage. No doubt this argument weighed with the financially and economically minded Egerton, although it seems more an argument for altering the domestic law than for determining the constitutional form of a dependent country.

Unfortunately, there is little on record of the Colonial Office deliberations prior to the submission of the draft dispatch in reply for the approval of the Secretary of State—merely Antrobus's laconic submission: 'Mr. Strachey and I have discussed these questions with Sir W. Egerton; and the conclusions arrived at are embodied in the accompanying draft of a despatch to the Acting Governor which is now submitted for approval.'[1] The Secretary of State, with a sense of the constitutional niceties, thought it proper to obtain His Majesty's approval of the dispatch before it was signed and sent, because it did after all involve a fairly considerable alteration to the King's dominions.

The scheme prepared with so little fuss and recorded discussion differed from Egerton's proposals (apart from the fundamental difference of the decision to join the legislatures, estimates, and departments fully) only in matters of comparatively minor detail. His scheme for the provinces was not tampered with; this meant that

[1] C.O. 520/29.

three provinces, based on Lagos, Warri, and Calabar respectively, came into being, styled the Western, the Central, and the Eastern Province.

Each province had a Provincial Commissioner, with an Assistant Provincial Commissioner as Provincial Secretary who was also deputy for the Provincial Commissioner. The three provinces shared a staff of seven Senior District Commissioners, thirty-three District Commissioners, and fifty-five Assistants. The Provincial Commissioner and the Provincial Secretary of the Western Province were given offices in the Lagos Secretariat. The head of this Secretariat was designated Lieutenant-Governor and Colonial Secretary. In addition to these senior administrative posts in the Secretariat there were the new posts of Financial Commissioner and of Commercial Intelligence Officer, and five 'pure' Secretariat posts of Chief Assistant Secretary, Assistant Secretary, and Junior Assistant Secretary. Departmental representatives in each province were responsible to the Provincial Commissioner, except in purely professional and purely departmental matters. So, by 1906, there were three 'regions' in Southern Nigeria, with the principal seat of government at Lagos; the provinces of West, Centre, and East of the period 1906–12 corresponded more or less to the short-lived post-independence regions, West, Mid-West, and East. The capitals in each case moved inland, to Ibadan, Benin, and Enugu from the former port sites of Lagos, Warri, and Calabar. Ethnically and economically the Egerton pattern was probably as sound as any that could have been devised; it is a pity it was destroyed.[1] It is unfortunate too that the legislatures and estimates were joined together, and the Lagos Legislative Council's powers extended to cover the whole territory. Hindsight suggests that it might have been practicable to aim from the first at three provincial legislatures; the three provinces were big enough and viable enough to justify such an arrangement.

Incomplete though it was, the joining together of Lagos and Southern Nigeria meant that Egerton was in charge of a large 'going concern', partly at least of his own devising, and adapted for the work of economic and social development as he envisaged them. Each year the new Government's organization spread its activities further into the interior, with revenues and expenditure rising to record heights. The annual report for 1906 recorded the achievement, for the first time, of one million pounds in revenue.

[1] See pp. 205–6 and map.

This compares with the Northern Protectorate's own revenue (excluding subsidies) of a mere £150,000, against expenditure of about half a million pounds. The Northern deficit was made up by an imperial grant-in-aid of £315,000 and a contribution of £25,000 from Southern Nigeria. Furthermore, unlike the North, the South was not dependent upon direct taxation. Eighty per cent of the million pounds came from Customs duties, £600,000 odd from spirits, £82,479 from tobacco.

To quote a phrase from the contemporary Colonial Office files, the Southern Nigeria estimates 'swelled like mushrooms'—as well they might, since there was a great deal to be done; and otherwise, in a strange reversal of ordinary fairness, the contribution to the North of the duty paid by Southerners on allegedly injurious trade spirits would almost certainly have been increased, to relieve the Colonial Office of the perpetual strain of begging money for the North from the Treasury. Egerton most certainly would not have liked this; as early as March 1905 he asked the Colonial Office how the South's contribution to the North was calculated, and the Colonial Office thought it best not to answer ('we need say no more unless he raises the question again').[1]

The point was that in the South the flag was not preceding trade; 'the flag' and what it connoted in the way of better facilities for trade was itself being financed by light duties on trade; while in the North the flag not only went in front of trade, but was wagged and displayed in such a way that traders were actively discouraged from following it.[2] Egerton would have relished the opportunity of bringing the North into the stream of world trade; soon after his arrival, and even before the amalgamation of Lagos and Southern Nigeria, he was showing his 'tycoon' quality by making the first of a series of 'takeover bids' for those parts of the North which seemed within reach of the communications, the trade, and the dynamic enterprise of the South.

In September 1906, on the announcement of Lugard's resignation, Egerton followed this up by suggesting to the Colonial Office that even if an amalgamation of North and South was not to be carried out then, at least the provinces of Ilorin and Kabba should be absorbed into Southern Nigeria. Already, with the Lagos railway pressing north, these two provinces were finding it easier to get mails and supplies from Lagos; and there were 'geographical

[1] C.O. 520/30. [2] See pp. 134–5.

and ethnological reasons' for their being administered from the South.

It was the prospect of extending the railway northwards which formed the chief reason advanced for 'capturing' Ilorin and Kabba. The Colonial Office's West African Department noted with pleasure the ex-Malayan Egerton's 'tremendous admission' that railway construction in Nigeria had gone, and was still going, better than railway construction in Malaya, thanks largely to MacGregor's legacy of better medical provision for the construction teams and to his deliberate policy of paying well for the land on which the line was built—a policy outlined by MacGregor himself at a meeting of the Royal African Society in 1904:

> It costs very much more to build the railway without giving concessions of land, but the just and more expensive method will pay best in the end, as it robs no-one of any part of his property. The Yoruba has as clear ideas as to the rights of property as Englishmen have.[1]

A separate Colonial Office file was opened for the consideration of Egerton's amalgamation proposals, and the arguments for and against were weighed.[2]

To the officials in Downing Street the chief obstacle to progress seemed to be Lugard himself and his work. The difficulty of one administration pushing the construction of its railway into the territory of another was seen and analysed by Olivier (later Lord Olivier and Governor of Jamaica), who concluded that it was not insuperable: 'This difficulty, however, can be got over if the Northern Nigeria Government will co-operate properly, and not treat Southern Nigeria (as they are rather prone to do) as a hostile or rival community.' He doubted, however, whether Ilorin could safely be taken into the South, because of Lugard's policy of maintaining Fulani rule there, over the predominantly Yoruba population, and because of his system of direct taxation:

> To detach Ilorin from that connection, especially if we did away with the tribute tax, which is not raised in Southern Nigeria, would almost certainly create suspicion and unrest. Its abolition in one Emirate would certainly raise awkward questions in others.

Olivier went on to recall that the Selborne Committee had 'advisedly' left Ilorin in the North; they had, but without showing the working which had led them to that answer. Olivier also commented that the

[1] *Journal of the African Society*, vol. iii (1903–4), p. 464. [2] C.O. 520/37.

Fulani were 'superior to the Yorubas in military and administrative capacity', showing, incidentally, how far this particular racial myth had progressed.

It was not a new myth, for Europeans had long been fascinated by the mystery of the origin of the Fulani; the lightness of their skin was doubtless enough to suggest some kind of inherent superiority, to those conditioned to react in such a way.

From Olivier's automatic acceptance of the idea of Fulani superiority in 'military and administrative capacity' (as if there were a necessary relation between the two) it can be seen that the myth was prevailing over the efforts of people like Mary Kingsley, MacGregor, Moor, and Morel to refute this particular version of the 'damned nigger' theory. Men like MacGregor and Moor had great respect for the people they governed, particularly perhaps for the Yoruba, as soldier and farmer, and for the Yoruba chief as a wise administrator. MacGregor in particular had taken pains to refute the idea of Negro inferiority; he did not take issue publicly with the public utterances of Lord and Lady Lugard contrasting the noble, healthy, 'bracing' North and its people with an unhealthy, 'low-lying' South,[1] but he spoke out in public a few weeks later in terms like the following, sticking to matters of which he had knowledge:

> It is difficult for one that knows the Yoruba race to believe that in point of intellectual capacity they are inferior to Europeans. . . . The Yoruba can fight also. He was able to defend himself from Dahomey. Sir Ralph Moor, for example, entertains a high opinion of the Yoruba as a soldier.[2]

But this was not a matter in which rational observation and argument could dispel the fumes. By about 1908 or so military opinion of the peoples of Nigeria had followed a pattern strangely similar to that adopted in India. Opinion changed, if not the character of the Yoruba himself. There was already a tendency to divide Nigerians into 'martial' and 'non-martial', almost on the lines of the similar divisions in India. As in India, the North was apt to be regarded as 'martial' and the South as 'non-martial'. This division corresponds broadly with the types of government established by the British in India and in Nigeria. Where, as in Bengal and Madras, the Government was the lineal descendant of John Company, the people were adjudged by the military authorities as 'non-martial', and their early military record was forgotten. But where, as in the Punjab, the Government was

[1] See pp. 158–70.

[2] Address 'Lagos and the Alake', *Journal of the African Society*, vol. iii, p. 464.

more widely typified by the military officer turned 'political officer', the people themselves were apt to be regarded as 'martial'—particularly the Moslems. Mary Kingsley observed that the Moslem religion required a sandy soil; she might well have said that military empire thrived best in open country where the horse could be used to advantage, rather than in the forest, creek, and estuary, where every tree and every bend could conceal a dozen 'unsporting' enemies, ready to launch a concealed and 'cowardly' attack. At any rate, the military conquerors in Northern Nigeria, as in Northern India, were in no doubt as to their own preference for the open country and its inhabitants, and in no great hurry to 'spoil' their sturdy military virtues and simple loyalty to their officers by too much education.

Olivier for one seems to have taken the assessment by Lugard of Fulani superiority as axiomatic, revealed truth, but neither he nor his seniors were disposed to accept Northern superiority when it came to European administration. Olivier's recommendation was that the Secretary of State should authorize the Southern Nigeria Government to proceed with the railway, into the North, as far as Jebba, and that the North should be told 'to co-operate in aid of its construction fully and loyally'. Ommanney, the Permanent Under Secretary and former Royal Engineer, with long experience in organizing railway construction, grimly noted in the margin of Olivier's minute: 'co-operation has been the last thing thought of in the past', while Antrobus wrote that he had always hoped that amalgamation would be possible, on Lugard's departure.

The problem of posts and of persons to fill them was then tackled. Egerton, Olivier suggested, already had so big a task in hand that he could not be expected to take over the North in addition; and it would be a pity to set a Governor-General over him. The idea of a single public service was a good one, but the country was too big for the appointment of only one Governor for the whole to be true economy; and 'the right sort' was difficult to find (Antrobus agreed, 'very difficult').

So, it was advisable to fill Lugard's place without delay—Wallace, the Deputy High Commissioner, relic of Goldie's Company, did not impress Olivier as a candidate: '[Wallace] does not seem to me very brisk or energetic, and I think he would be too much of a King Log.' Egerton would do, of course, but it would be a pity to take him from Lagos, and he could hardly be expected, immediately on top of his Southern Nigeria service, to do a full Governor's term in Northern

Nigeria. There was an application from Clifford, Colonial Secretary, Trinidad, 'a candidate worth considering'. This was the second time that this future Governor of Nigeria was considered for a Nigerian appointment: the first time was in 1900, when, had he not been required in Pahang, he would have been offered the post of Secretary, Southern Nigeria, at Calabar. Eventually, instead of succeeding Lugard as Governor of the North in 1906 he succeeded him as Governor of Nigeria in 1919.

The papers finally reached the Secretary of State, Lord Elgin, with the suggestion by Ommanney that there should be discussion by the Secretary of State with the Parliamentary Under Secretary (Winston Churchill), himself (Ommanney), and Antrobus. There the Colonial Office file on amalgamation closed.

From the apparently unrecorded discussion arose what can only be regarded as a very neat and logical decision to appoint as Governor Percy Girouard, Royal Engineer, expert in railway construction and operation in Africa—he had been in charge of the Sudan Railway, the Egyptian Railways, and the railways of the Transvaal and Orange River colony, now granted responsible government.[1] He must have been known to Ommanney, himself a Royal Engineer who had become one of the Crown Agents in 1877, as a Captain, R.E., on completing a tour of duty as Private Secretary to the Secretary of State for the Colonies. In 1900 he became Permanent Under Secretary of State at the Colonial Office. There was probably little in the way of finance and materials for railway construction which Ommanney did not know about, because these were the most important side of the Crown Agents' business in the years from 1870. The Crown Agents had helped to build and run railways in many countries, among them Queensland, Natal, Cape Colony, Ceylon, Mauritius, and Lagos. And, as Permanent Secretary from 1900, Ommanney was at the receiving end of the strong pressures from men like Chamberlain himself and Sir Alfred Jones, from Governors and merchants in Nigeria, from Chambers of Commerce in Lancashire—Liverpool, Manchester, and Oldham, the constituency of the Parliamentary Under Secretary. All were pressing for railway construction. Little

[1] Girouard was a French-Canadian, a graduate of the Royal Military College at Kingston, who had been trained on the Canadian Pacific Railway. He is pictured, in youth, as one of Kitchener's favourites on his staff—'privileged and indispensable' and as the possessor of 'rare good looks, bubbling high spirits, and that happy transatlantic ability to express himself crisply and tartly without causing offence' (Philip Magnus, *Kitchener*, 1958, p. 108).

wonder, then, that Lugard's lack of co-operation with the South on railway construction was resented, and that the opportunity of his resignation was eagerly taken to replace him by another expert in transportation—but this time one whose expertise lay in African railways, not in the mule-trains and bullock carts of mid-Victorian India.

Girouard lost no time in starting the advance of the railway into the North. Meanwhile, Egerton's reports from thriving Southern Nigeria continued to make cheerful reading, with 'peaceful penetration' on classic principles from the three coastal provincial capitals of Lagos, Warri, and Calabar. Each improvement made in communications—roads, harbour works, railways—helped to weaken and destroy the cherished Northern hope of making the Niger the chief outlet to the sea through the 'rival' territory of Southern Nigeria, although it was not until 1926 that the fleet of Northern sternwheelers plying between the coast and Lokoja or Baro finally dwindled to a few old vessels, and the service came to an end.

A few extracts from Egerton's annual reports are enough to show the main themes and purposes of his administration, close to those of his predecessors and of the Selborne Committee, but with a new boldness and largeness of scope in finance and economics. Egerton's was essentially the approach of an experienced professional administrator of his time—humane but businesslike, concentrating on material advantage to the people. It had not yet become fashionable to speak of material, economic development as something less worthy and less noble than 'good government' practised as an end in itself—although the tendency was there, and growing. The old idea was expressed in Victor Hugo's phrase 'Améliorer la vie matérielle c'est améliorer la vie morale, faites les hommes heureux et vous les ferez meilleurs',[1] and in Goldie's motto 'physical development first'. It was not material development as an end in itself which the older liberal philosophy sought, but material development as a means to other good things, as a means of spreading civilization, of 'letting in the light' on dark places. What Egerton expected from the material development he worked for with such energy is clearly shown in the report for 1905, mentioning the creation of the new post of Commercial Intelligence Officer:

[1] 'To improve material life is to improve moral life; make men happy and you will make them better.' Egerton's reference to 'moral and material gain' seems a direct echo of Hugo's aphorism.

It would be difficult to over-rate the importance of this office, or the magnitude of the results that may be achieved if, as is anticipated, it is possible for him to collate such facts and figures as may induce British merchants whose operations are now confined to the fringe of the Protectorate to push further ahead and emulate the growing enterprise of the German trader. If the interior is by this means opened up to civilising influences the moral and material gains will be enormous.

The material gain was great—the moral gain, with no agreed basis of measurement, more open to doubt and question. Birtwistle, the man appointed, through the Board of Trade, was a man of great energy and knowledge, indefatigable in his efforts to match markets and products. When after some seven years he left Nigeria Lugard did not succeed in replacing him, and the department lapsed. Lugard's conception of government and its duties seems to have been one of activities not directly concerned with material development: that was the business of businessmen. This attitude is shown in a talk he gave to the Liverpool branch of the Royal Colonial Institute in October 1921, when, using a favourite railway metaphor, he envisaged progress in Africa as lying along two parallel lines together forming 'that dual responsibility which they as a nation had accepted'. The 'engine of progress which ran along the track of material development' was 'guided and controlled chiefly by the great commercial, banking and mining corporations which had supplied the energy, the capital and the brains'—but the engine which ran along the parallel line of 'moral, political and educational development' was chiefly 'under the control of the home Government and the local Government in West Africa'.

This is a far cry from the ideas of the Selborne Committee, of Egerton, of MacGregor, and Moor who saw themselves clearly as creating the conditions in which commerce, and through commerce civilization, could flourish, bringing to the Nigerian enslaved by his environment freedom, knowledge, and greater power over his environment. For them the imagery would not have been a railway with two parallel tracks and two engines steaming along separately, in the same direction, but something more like the words which are the theme of this chapter, words used by Egerton in conversation with the new commander of his army of one battalion, Hugh Trenchard, words never forgotten by Trenchard, who quoted them nearly half a century later to his biographer:[1] 'Give me roads—good broad

[1] Andrew Boyle, *Trenchard, Man of Vision* (London, 1962).

straight roads right through the jungle from one tribal area to the next—then we'll be able to let in the light.'

There were other significant words used by Egerton to Trenchard at their first meeting, in 1904, when the soldier, newly arrived in Nigeria, sought Egerton's approval of his decision to prohibit the whipping by his men of captives taken on punitive expeditions. Egerton said 'You did right. In degrading others we degrade ourselves.' This too greatly impressed Trenchard: 'It was the first of many audiences with a colonial Governor whom Trenchard learned to revere as one of the wisest, noblest and most under-rated of British pro-consuls.' Once again, there was a decided contrast here between Egerton's attitude to corporal punishment and that of the more famed proconsul Lugard in the North; he, at about the same time, was doubtful whether the flogging administered by the authority of the native courts was hard enough, and suggested in the 1906 edition of his *Political Memoranda*, issued for the guidance of administrative officers, that whipping 'should, I think, be made deterrent and more severe . . . since mutilation, etc., is prohibited'.[1] It is no surprise to find Lugard taking pride in introducing the 'cat' as a new punishment in Hong Kong.[2]

Trenchard, a Royal Scots Fusilier, was a soldier of a quite different kind, unusual, brilliant, later to be one of the founders of the Royal Air Force, Commissioner of the Metropolitan Police, and head of the the United Africa Company. In a regular army officer of the time Trenchard's combination of humanity and commercial acumen was remarkable; he was well suited to the task of 'opening up' the territory to trade. One of the most unorthodox steps which he took—and perhaps one of the most useful—was to have himself appointed as the Nigerian agent of Harrods of London. Although Trenchard lacked some of the orthodox inhibitions of his rank and profession (he had been educated at an army crammer's, not at a public school) he certainly did not lack military ability or the military virtues of courage and endurance. He finally left Nigeria with one of the most common but most deadly malarial complications of the time, an abscess on the liver. Not long after his return to England he was at the ripe age of

[1] Lugard, *Political Memoranda* (1906), Memo. no. 8—'Native Courts'.

[2] Perham, *Lugard, The Years of Authority*, p. 361. The C.O. 446 series also contains Lugard's proposals, rejected by the Colonial Office, for legislation which would have permitted Europeans, unofficial as well as official, to have their carriers whipped, after inquiry but without trial, for looting or pilfering, in the villages through which they passed.

thirty-nine one of the first volunteers to begin flying training. More extraordinary still, he had been shot in the lung, during the Boer War, and half paralysed from the waist down by the same bullet. He was told there was no hope of his recovery; but within a few short months he had contrived to cure his paralysis, to conceal the fact that he had only one lung in working order, and to get himself sent back to the fighting in South Africa.

His method of curing his paralysis was typical of the toughness of his generation: while convalescing on sticks in Switzerland he decided to take up tobogganing as the only form of adventurous sport which seemed remotely possible for a paralysed man—although, whenever he had a spill, he had to be picked up and put on his feet again. One day a violent crash from his toboggan at high speed cured his paralysis, and he promptly engineered his own return to active service. For a man of this quality the opening up to peaceful trade of Southern Nigeria was a memorable and enjoyable adventure; one column of his, after the murder of Dr. Stewart, collected and impounded nearly 18,000 arms of precision—an indication of the enormous trade in arms which had been helping to keep the whole of the protectorate in a state of seething warfare of town against town. On two other columns Trenchard was accompanied, as his 'political officer', by the great little missionary, Mary Slessor—they must have made, between them, a truly formidable combination of civil and military power.[1]

'Letting in the light' remained Egerton's slogan. It was a principle consistently and energetically followed. In his report for 1905 Egerton wrote:

> The people are typical of the country, in that they are mentally undeveloped and afford an enormous field for the efforts of the pioneers of civilization. They are free from direct taxation: they live in comfort and have few or no cares. On the whole their lot is a happy one.

In the report for 1906 he recorded the progress towards development, away from '*dolce far niente*', and, maybe, away from happiness:

> The year under report has been one of rapid progress in every direction. The opening up of the country has been continued and the remote districts have been brought into closer touch with the civilizing European influence. . . . The traders have pushed their way further up country, and the Cross River for the first time is being properly developed. The means

[1] Details taken from Boyle, op. cit., Anene, op. cit., and annual reports.

of communication have been improved, making the work of the administration more effective and giving greater security to life and property.

The report for 1907 was a further instalment of the same cheerful story:

Progress in the social condition of the people and expansion in the trade of the country have been remarkable during the year under review. There has been no relaxation in the efforts of the Government to make remote districts easily accessible, improve the means of communication and transport, promote friendly intercourse between the natives of various tribes, and to suppress the slavery, cannibalism and barbarous practices of the natives of the interior districts. The improvements in the means of communication, besides resulting in an increased trade, have tended to establish peace and good order in the remote districts of the country, and to lessen the difficulties of administration.

The report for 1909 returned to the same theme:

. . . with the steady advance into the interior, and rapid construction of good roads, the extension of the railway, and the systematic clearing of waterways, trade should continue to develop, and with the advent of the trader and the closer contact with civilization the work of administration should be rendered easier and more effective.

To the average officer in the 'bush', progress may not have seemed either so rapid or so easy in the battle against 'juju' and the evils of superstition and ignorance,[1] but these extracts do make clear what the guiding principles and hopes of the administration were in 'opening up' the country.

First, there was a belief in civilization—a belief perhaps not so naïve as the reaction from two later World Wars waged by 'civilised' nations has since made it appear. Before the barbarities of these wars there was still good reason to believe that there was a universal, attainable state of civilization just around the corner, in which rational, humane, peaceful, and prosperous societies would flourish, outgrowing warlike, violent impulses and hatred of foreigners. Egerton believed that 'evil communications corrupt good manners'; he saw himself as 'improving manners', extending peace and civilization, by improving communications. This was the process of 'letting in the light'.

Intrinsically, this process had little to do with the conscious, de-

[1] For a frank and very readable account of the process see *Juju and Justice in Nigeria* (1930), written by G. Lumley from the reminiscences of Frank Hives, an (Australian) administrator in the old Southern Nigeria.

liberate extension of the British *raj*, or with nationalistic imperialism, or with advancing the claims of any particular system of rule. It was more like the exuberant slogan 'Life more abundant' which the Action Group chose for itself fifty years later—all the good things, the freedoms, the powers, the resources which a modern state in a modern world could provide.

Also, there was the hope that after a few years of supervision the native councils could take over more of the functions of local government—so permitting the administration to devote more and more energy to the tasks of administrators in a modern state.

Compared with the North, there has been very little written about provincial administration in the Southern Nigeria of Egerton's period. As in the Lagos of MacGregor's day, this was not a sign of inattention or neglect. In fact, the machinery of provincial government with three Provincial Commissioners, each in a thriving commercial capital, with a departmental staff responsible to him, and an adequate staff of administrators guiding the native councils, presents a very sensible, workmanlike, and tidy pattern. Egerton had other plans and schemes for tidying up the system which could hardly be pursued, with the prospect of an all-Nigeria amalgamation, until that amalgamation became a reality. One of these was the adoption of the Indian penal code, and another was the assimilation of the differing local government growths in the various parts of the South. At one extreme was the quasi-independent state of Egbaland, at the other extreme the most rudimentary forms of House Rule. It was implicit in the administrator's approach that all these societies should be allowed to grow, in the hope that they would coalesce, without the necessity to impose on them any hierarchical system of rule; but there was a clear need for a law comprehensive enough to govern the relations of central with local government. It was this kind of development which was inhibited by the indefinite prospect of amalgamation with the North.

There was one Southern Nigerian Government officer, however, who was moved to take up the cudgels on behalf of his administrative colleagues, and defend them against the current criticisms, mostly inspired by the missions, of the system known as House Rule, and of administrative support of House Rule. This was R. E. Dennett, a forest officer who had spent some twenty years in other parts of West Africa before beginning his Nigerian service in 1902, and whose duties had made him acquainted with administrators and their charges throughout Southern Nigeria. Dennett was a prolific writer of books and articles on African religion and folk-lore, as well as travel books and articles on forestry and agriculture.

According to Dennett, the Southern Nigerian administrator was a 'disestablished' administrator: he was deliberately not pushing the wares of any particular national or religious creed. Dennett attempted, in an interesting article,[1] to summarize what the 'disestablished' administrator had been trying to do in the last decade, as it seemed to him, an onlooker.

Dennett saw the administrator as a man earnestly endeavouring to weld together the primitive forms of 'Father Rule' or 'House Rule' into 'one great native kingdom or confederation of kingdoms'. In his view, to have followed up the abolition of slavery by the abolition of House Rule—as some missionaries thought Moor or his successor should have done—would have meant taking over the direct rule of the country, and making of Southern Nigeria not a protectorate but a colony. Instead, Moor had decided to maintain the authority of the heads of houses, while protecting their members against acts of oppression and cruelty by their heads. In other words, Moor, like MacGregor, had followed the policy of the Selborne Committee in maintaining native institutions—indirect rule, in fact.

It is clear from Dennett's account that Egerton, having created three very senior posts of Provincial Commissioner, was prepared to leave the problems of provincial administration to be settled by them and their staff, but Dennett saw everywhere the same practice, the administrator 'endeavouring to help the natives of the country to rule themselves in accordance with all that is good in their own native laws and customs'; and determined, 'however great the popular pressure may be, to guard the interests of the people he governs against the inroads of fanaticism and sentimentality from whatever direction these attacks may come'.

Dennett traced the growth of institutions of rule and social organization from what he called 'Simple Father Rule' (e.g. the family of an isolated fisherman) to House Rule (as found in fishing, hunting, farming, and trading settlements), which included, with the father's kin, others, strangers seeking refuge, 'rolling stones come to rest', and 'pawns' or persons pledged by themselves or others as security for loans. It was Moor's greatest hope that under the guidance of the administrator the native councils and native courts could

[1] *United Empire*, vol. ii (1911), pp. 612–22.

bring these houses together, under chiefs elected as 'Fathers of the Country'.

This system of indirect rule—for such it was—was dynamic, not static, aimed at change and development, like the economy itself. It was completely undermined in the end by Lugard's decisions as Governor-General in 1914 to end House Rule, to remove the administrative officer from the councils and the courts, and to set provincial courts above them in which neither British nor native lawyers would have any say; this was done despite the emphasis placed throughout the previous years on the supreme value of administrative supervision, guidance, and contact, despite Lugard's own professed belief in continuity of policy.

When Lugard's successor Clifford spoke with regret of 'the abolition of House Rule, since nothing was contrived to take its place', Lugard had ready his double-edged weapon of defence. He claimed first that he had not abolished House Rule, but that the Secretary of State, with his entire concurrence, had repealed the ordinance which gave 'its worst features' the support of the law and the policy. And the return stroke of the double-edged blade was that the Secretary of State had not approved a scheme which he, Lugard, had proposed 'with the hearty support of those who know the country best' to strengthen the 'legitimate functions' of the houses.[1]

Professor Dike has since shown how these 'Houses' were an adaptation to the needs and opportunities of trade between the white man and the people in the interior; they were a new kind of social organization fashioned for commerce and for the cash economy.[2]

In the field of communications and their development the contrast between Egerton's approach and Lugard's was even more marked. While Lugard was experimenting with bullock carts, drivers, and farriers imported from India, and blaming their failure on the bad workmanship of the carts, Egerton was already bowling along the first motor road in Nigeria (the Ibadan–Oyo road on which Nigeria's first university was built) in a motor car at the rate of '35 miles in a little over two hours'. Not long afterwards, there was the first motor-bus service between Ibadan and Oyo, with European drivers and Albion lorries. The Ibadan–Oyo route was important as a feeder road to the railway at Ibadan, and as a consolation to Oyo for not having the railway. It was begun in 1905; in March and April 1905 Egerton

[1] Lugard, *The Dual Mandate*, pp. 372–3. See pp. 219–20.

[2] See Kenneth Dike, *Trade and Politics in the Niger Delta, 1830–1885* (1956).

travelled overland from Lagos to Calabar by Ibadan, Benin, Onitsha, and Aba, a journey which 'had previously neither been accomplished nor attempted'. In the same year work was begun by the specially formed Roads Department (absorbed in 1909 by the P.W.D.) on the road linking Benin city with the port and capital at Sapele and Warri as part of an extensive programme of trunk roads until 1913. The transformation of Benin city from the terrible state of 1898 to the orderly, rebuilt town of 1910, with a pure water supply, good schools, churches, and wide roads was indeed one of the oftenest quoted justifications for British rule. Dennett and Morel both pointed to it with pride.

From Lagos itself the trunk road towards Abeokuta reached out as far as the new Lagos waterworks at Iju by 1911, but it was 1920 before it reached Abeokuta, and not until 1922 that the road reached Ibadan—the same year in which the Oshogbo–Benin road link was completed.

Meanwhile, the Lagos railway reached Oshogbo in 1907, and Ilorin, in the Northern Protectorate, in August 1908. A year later it had reached the Niger at Jebba where a ferry operated until the bridge was built in 1915.

On the amalgamation of Lagos and Southern Nigeria work began in real earnest on the improvement of the Lagos harbour. The work followed the original recommendations of the consultants (Coode and Partners) who had carried out examinations between 1892 and 1898, proposing training banks and moles 7,000 feet long, together with extensive dredging estimated to cost nearly one million pounds.

At that time the revenue of the whole colony of Lagos for all purposes was only about one-fifth of the dredging costs, and there was no chance of starting work, but Egerton did start as soon as the revenue of the combined territories reached £1 million. The conveying of stone for the mole from Abeokuta, the dredging of the harbour, and the reclamation of adjacent swamp accounted for much of the mushroom swelling of the estimates—but Egerton remained unrepentant, recalling later with particular pride that he had taken over a territory free of debt and left it with five millions of debt incurred on public works.

The first decade of the twentieth century was indeed a decade for optimism. Economic resources showed great promise, and the search for wealth was vigorous. Coffee and cotton might prove failures, and the younger generation arouse misgivings, but the Imperial Institute's mineral survey of Southern Nigeria, and the independent discoveries of administrators and others, were revealing some potential wealth—the brown coal and lignite of Asaba, the gold fields of Ilesha, coal at Udi (1908–9), lead and zinc at Abakaliki, and widespread deposits of limestone suitable for cement. Perhaps the most exciting of all in promise (although in outcome a disappointment), oil and natural gas 'in quantities' were discovered, by drilling near Epe in the colony, carried out by a company partly financed (in an early and little-known state venture into oil exploration) by Egerton's Government. His intention, in financial participation, was to ensure that the search would be thorough and painstaking.[1] There had long been signs of oil and bitumen, but the real striking of oil was reported in triumph to Egerton by the managing director in November 1908—the very same year as the first major discovery of oil in Persia. As it turned out, the oil was very thick and not marketable at that time; and so, like some of the other mineral discoveries, such as the Asaba lignite, mineral oil was not an easy way to wealth. The mystery of the ending of the oil search and of the Government's financial share in it no doubt has its solution somewhere in the archives, but the only relevant subsequent reference to the oil discovery which the present writer has been able to discover is one sentence in Lugard's *The Dual Mandate*—a cryptic reference which suggests that he may on the amalgamation of North and South have withdrawn official financial support from the oil search in the South, on grounds of financial prudence and orthodoxy: 'If, as in a case of oil-boring within my experience, a company asks for financial assistance, the Government is not justified in accepting a speculative risk which financiers will not incur.'[2] To have continued the search might have changed the course of world history.

One significant point about these early discoveries, however, is that they were all made quickly, in the first few years of official, Colonial Office rule, not by private enterprise, but by official agencies or agencies officially sponsored, without any massive expenditure or large numbers of technical staff. There was simply an informal co-operation between officials, private industry, and academics like Professor Dunstan of the Imperial Institute—an easy and remarkably

[1] C.O. 520/37.

[2] Lugard, *The Dual Mandate*, p. 484. 1957 is the date usually given for oil discoveries in Nigeria, not 1908; an illustration of the official amnesia which accompanied World War I and 'amalgamation'. See pp. 218–20.

untroubled co-operation of which the art seems since to have been lost amidst the complexities of large-scale organization.

If in the provinces the method of developing local government did not give the appearance of order and tidiness which a more static, more authoritative system of rule from above would have given, at the centre itself the organization of the Government was becoming a model of order. The clearest outward sign of this new order and elegance was the building begun in 1906 to house the new public offices. These, fully adequate for Southern Nigeria, were to serve as the increasingly overcrowded headquarters of the Government of Nigeria until 1948. Previously, the public buildings had been typical of the old pre-Chamberlain regime—poor, inadequate in size, badly lit, with roofs designed on the model of the roofs built between the masts of the hulks which served as the merchants' warehouses. The new building (which could accommodate the whole headquarters, including those officers who previously had been forced to use the downstairs room of their house as an office, and so to live above the shop) was equally expressive of the new era in government.

For one thing, it was elegant and gracious, one of the first buildings not to be erected at the lowest possible price. It is still, with its twin towers and clock and its classical pediment, and its flanking wings, looking over the quadrangle and gatehouses across the harbour, one of the finest buildings in Lagos. It was Egerton himself who conceived the idea of the building as being a planned development over ten years or so. (The architect, E. O. Cummins, would have preferred, as any architect would, to have done the whole in one operation.) For that reason the building now known as the Old Secretariat is really a monument to the first Southern Nigeria development plan; it was designed in seven blocks to be completed as and when staff requirements made it necessary—first the centre, containing the 'dignified parts' of the constitution—the main entrance and staircase, the Legislative Council chamber, with offices, press gallery, and visitors' gallery; next the flanking wings on either side, in line with the centre; next the wings out towards the harbour, forming three sides of the central quadrangle. Gatehouses were built closing the quadrangle on the seaward side, which could be (but never were) replaced by a further permanent block completing and enclosing the quadrangle.[1] When, in 1948, the concept of planned development had at last regained favour, the extension to the public offices was a remark-

[1] C.O. 520/37.

ably plain cube of concrete dwarfing and overshadowing the older, more graceful building of mellowed brick—by that time defaced also by an old captured German gun from the Cameroons and a huddle of black 'temporary huts'. Most of these huts have since, mercifully, been removed; the main front, once more visible from the Marina, has been admiringly likened to a Wren church, and more unkindly to a Virginian country gentleman's stables; either way, it reflects a long and gracious tradition of architecture and is an apt reminder of the prosperity which Egerton brought to Southern Nigeria.

In the civil service itself there were signs of the drawbacks which accompany increasing efficiency in formal functions. Now that Lagos governed the whole of Southern Nigeria the senior Yoruba and other African civil servants were no longer so favourably placed—they had the difficulties of transfer, of educating children when transferred, of finding accommodation among peoples who still had not set foot on the road to 'civilized' standards of living and sanitation, peoples in many ways more prepared to accept the white officer than they were to accept the African. It was in this period that the idea of being a civil servant became less attractive and less attainable for the young Nigerian; the civil service was beginning to be accepted as 'white man's work', without explicit change in official policy. But, also important, there was, as in any other form of organization, a growing tendency to work as a machine, once the early pioneering was done; to work by rule and by precedent rather than at full stretch, creatively and imaginatively.

The best illustration of this tendency—still in its infancy, not reaching maturity until long after the first World War—is given by D. R. Rosevear in his brief history of the Forest Department in the *Nigeria Handbook* of 1953. In many ways the Forest Department can be seen in its various stages reflecting the changing ideas of the Administration as a whole. When in 1905 the time came for the merger of the Lagos and Southern Nigeria governments it was the Forest and Botanical departments which were the first to be joined, under 'Timber' Thompson, who therefore became responsible for more agricultural ventures, in the shape of the Lagos Government's botanical gardens at Ebute Metta and Olokemeji and model farms at Mamu. It was partly due to this combination of forestry, agriculture, and botany that the forest reservation programme, the main task of creating and maintaining the proposed permanent forest estate of twenty-five per cent of the country's land surface, was somewhat delayed; other contributing reasons were the deep-rooted public suspicion and resentment which had bedevilled the department's efforts since the first attempt at legislation in 1897, the protracted debate over land rights, and the unpopularity of the regulatory functions of the department, the permits, licences, fines, and imprisonment which dated from the Benin rubber boom. This unpopularity was increased after 1908, when, under the authority of the Forest Ordinance of that year, the department embarked on a policy of restricting the felling of the best timber trees throughout the country, inside and outside the areas proposed for reservation, by licences, fees, and prohibitions. The idea was protection of the best timbers pending the establishment of the reserves, in the hope and expectation that the reservation programme would soon be completed. In practice, this hope was not fulfilled; the needs of war, the vexed question of land acquisition, popular suspicion of official motives, and the sheer momentum of bureaucratic routine proved apparently too strong for the really creative work of the department to make good progress. Rosevear[1] analyses this unhappy process in the following words:

In the face of rebuff and inactivity the real goal was lost sight of and the general protection laws developed into a monster which took charge of forestry.

The moment the laws were passed and permit books for felling protected trees printed the forest officer became more and more tied to an office. The making out and signing of permits, the checking of money and bringing it to account, the Treasury work and auditing, the continual look-out for fraud, innumerable court cases and a dozen other related things absorbed his energies and filled up a good part of his time that should have been devoted to more enduring forestry. He quickly became converted from a highly-trained technical officer into something but little removed from a tax-gatherer. Further, because of the continual demand for payment for what they regarded as their activities on their own farm-lands, and the distress caused by fines or imprisonment, all hope of ever gaining the sympathy of the people for the true work of the Forest Department was lost. Gradually even the Administration, upon whom reservation ultimately depended, quite excusably came to regard the settlement of the forest estate as a thing of no particular urgency; and, worst of all, a considerable number of forest officers came to believe that in the tropics permit-issuing outweighed all else in importance.

The end of this cautionary tale comes after, and not before, amal-

[1] D. R. Rosevear, chapter xvi, *Nigeria Handbook* (1953), pp. 181–2.

gamation and the first World War; but the experience of the Forest Department mirrored a gradual process which was taking place in Nigeria wherever the idea of British Government as a bountiful provider of benefits and economic betterment gave way, under the force of financial stringency and the deadening weight of routine, to 'keeping the peace and collecting the tax'. Perhaps the first step of the Forest Department away from development and towards a kind of police function came with the separation of the Forest Department from the main stream of agriculture and botany; if so, it was the opposite of what was intended and hoped at the time the separation was made; then, the idea was that experts in each function should be more free for creative work in their own special fields, not the opposite.

But this fault, this 'institutionalization' of the civil service, cannot be blamed on the early Governors of the South. Justice has not yet been done to them for their wisdom and energy in endeavours to make of their territory a modern state fit to take its place in a modern world, and to give scope and opportunity for its peoples to develop their full potentialities, in freedom, but with help and gentle guidance. It was this freedom, interpreted as 'licence' and 'insolence', which was the chief offence in Southern Nigeria to those who preferred the 'coherent system', to use Dame Margery Perham's words, of Lord Lugard.

# CHAPTER VI

# The Protectorate of Northern Nigeria, 1900–1912: Reality and Myth

Governments are not philanthropic institutions

Lugard

LUGARD'S biographer writes of his work in Northern Nigeria from 1900 to 1906:

By the time Lugard left Northern Nigeria, he had constructed both upon paper and in the practice of the men, British and African, who worked under him, what can claim to be the most comprehensive, coherent and renowned system of administration in our colonial history. This was his greatest and most famous work, the achievement of his prime.[1]

At first sight, this seems an extravagant claim to make on behalf of what was, after all, a very rudimentary form of one-man rule which could not pass the normal tests of colonial administration: financially, it was far from viable, depending for the bulk of its revenue on subventions from the governments of the United Kingdom and of Southern Nigeria;[2] 'pacification' included, during the last hectic months of Lugard's rule, the massacre of thousands of practically unarmed peasants. There was none of the ordinary physical plant of civil government—hardly anything in the shape of civil departments, or a normal Secretariat, or roads, or railway, no beginning made in the social and economic service which alone might have been some excuse for the use of armed force—or 'pacification', to use Lugard's own preferred euphemism.

The claim is, however, more meaningful than the almost entirely threadbare apparatus of government left to Lugard's administrative heirs would suggest. Lugard had succeeded in two fateful ways. First, in defiance of the policy of his distant and often preoccupied civil masters he had carried out an occupation of the whole country by

[1] Perham, *Lugard, The Years of Authority*, p. 138.

[2] In Lugard's last year local revenue was £142,000; total expenditure was nearly £500,000.

force of arms and introduced the rule of the sword—a system of rule as 'comprehensive' and 'coherent', given the resources in men and money at his disposal, as military ideas of discipline could make it. Secondly, he had succeeded in a propaganda campaign directed to the creation and manipulation of his own fame as an administrator, and of the myth of the superiority of his territory, and his methods, over all others. These achievements of sword, pen, and tongue wrecked the plan for ordered, peaceful development of the new 'undeveloped estate'.

The Lugard myth is one which current studies of the archives of the period, by Nigerians and others, must surely dissipate; but it has lasted a long time. At the beginning of the century the Lugards' use of current ideas of race, evolution, prestige, patriotism, civilization, and duty managed to cover the whole scene with a swirling mist which concealed what they wished to conceal, and threw at the same time a kind of romantic glamour of heroic chivalry over Lugard himself. Even now it is difficult to peer through this mist of propaganda and identify the dominant features of the 'renowned system', but the attempt has to be made, because Lugard's actual and legendary achievement set Nigeria's history, for good or ill, on a permanently altered course, at a crucial time.

The bare statistical facts of the administration which Lugard set up are plain enough in outline; it was the tale of the events in the process of pacification—the feats of arms recalling the oldest militaristic myths of medieval chivalry, of the Crusade, and of King Arthur and his Knights of the Round Table—which assured a sympathetic hearing for the chroniclers. They made a strong appeal to the nostalgia for feudal times still so strong in English life, particularly in the kind of English public whose attention and support the Lugards sought to capture. This public was not primarily the industrial and mercantile interests—although there was something in the propaganda for them too[1]—but the other England of the ruling and officer classes, the gentry, and those who sought identification with the gentry. This was a world still agrarian, conservative often to the point of strong reaction against the complexities and the ugliness of the modern industrial world,[2] and disdainful of all but the richest of the new

[1] Prospects of railways, cotton, and mineral resources, and a general emphasis on the wealth of the territory in the past, and its prospects for the future.

[2] G. M. Trevelyan's *England under the Stuarts*, published in 1904, catches exactly this feeling: 'One condition of modern times is, that what pays best is generally ugly, and that whatever man now touches for a purely economic reason,

industrialists, merchants, and millionaires. This was the 'public' to which the Lugards belonged and to which they directed their propaganda. One immediate result was the projection into Nigeria of the great schism in British or, specifically, English life, with Northern Nigeria attracting the attention of the consciously 'superior' classes, the officers and gentlemen—and that helped to repel and antagonize the rest, the traders and missionaries busy and influential in the South, who might have had much to contribute to economic and social development in the North also, had their presence been encouraged.

Dame Margery Perham's own admirable marshalling of evidence of Lugard's work, and in particular her quotations from the Lugard papers, are invaluable as sources, but the conclusions drawn in this chapter are diametrically opposed to the conclusions drawn in her biography of Lugard. Her conclusions tend to confirm the legend of Lugard as 'a great public servant' and 'a great administrator'. That, as the biography itself makes clear, was not the view of the officials to whom he was responsible in the Colonial Office, the only men of their time who were in a position to study comparative colonial administration, even from a distance.

The biography concedes that 'Lugard's standards were wholly different from those of the department he served' and that 'this now famous piece of work was carried on under an almost constant fire of disapproval from the Colonial Office which was bitterly repelled by Lugard.'[1] There is no great mystery about the standards and ideas of the Colonial Office of the time. Certainly, there was the usual tendency to concealment and to secrecy which is the inevitable accompaniment of the British civil servant's preoccupation with the defence of his Minister. With Lugard departing from the accepted standards and ideas they had more than the usual amount to cover up from public gaze, but the department's standards were being observed, and their ideas being put into effect more or less exactly and more or less openly, by the more experienced and more loyal administrators in Southern Nigeria. The essence of their ideas was peaceful and largely self-financing progress. Nothing else made

he mars.' This was the school of thought of Carlyle (one of the Lugards' favourite authors) and of Ruskin (with whom Flora Shaw had had 'a deep friendship'—Perham, op. cit., p. 57) rather than the utilitarian school which was so dominant an influence on contemporary commerce and administration.

[1] Perham, *Lugard, The Years of Authority*, p. 187.

sense, politically or financially, and 'the man on the spot' was expected to realize this and behave accordingly.

What, then, were Lugard's very different standards and ideas? Here his biographer stops short of a rational analysis, preferring to suggest that he possessed some gift denied to lesser mortals: 'The word instinct must not be misused, but at least he had such an aptitude for administration that he hardly seemed to need the process of reasoning or discussion, either with himself or with others, or even of experiment.'[1] Since reasoning and discussion are of the essence of administration, this looks ominously like an aptitude for minor military rather than major civil business, for 'command'. This shows in the 'instinctive', irrational quality of Lugard's decisions, and in his unvarying choice of the militaristic solution to each problem capable of a peaceful solution. First there would be the 'instinctive' militaristic reaction, and then, at length, sometimes preceding action, more often following it, a welter of verbiage which often defies rational analysis but never fails to find some kind of 'moral' basis.

In such a case it is no use looking for administrative achievements in concrete terms. As Dame Margery Perham says, the achievement was upon paper and in the practice of men. It was a question of power over men: in Nigeria, both naked power and power to 'mould' men, to determine trends and courses to be followed for the future; outside Nigeria, it was a question of moulding and influencing opinion.

In detail as well as in the overall concept, the method was the militarism of the age, nourished in the anti-intellectual, anti-commercial tradition of the officer class. Lugard's work represents the high-water mark in British life of the militarism which in other European countries at the same period of history (notably in France and Germany) went further and usurped many of the institutions of metropolitan government. Britain's domestic institutions escaped the direst effects, because the officer class was not quite so professional, not quite so powerful, not quite so wholly military as the same class in France, in Germany, and in Russia. And in the new colonial Empire, although the imprint of militarism was strong elsewhere, it was in Northern Nigeria alone, far removed from the civil influences of traders, lawyers, missionaries, and an established civil service tradition, that the military class gained the upper hand, and superimposed itself on the existing form of rule by the Fulani Emirs, themselves a military ruling class.

[1] Perham, p. 140.

If one ignores, for the moment, the myth of Lugard, and concentrates on the actual decisions which he took, and the steps by which he built up his power in Nigeria, this emerges clearly enough.

From the first day of his appointment his 'instinct'—a trained aptitude for command—showed him the path to pursue:

Arriving at the end of December 1899, I took over the administration from the Royal Niger Company, and the Union Flag was hoisted in place of the Company's, at 7.20 a.m. at Lokoja, on January 1st 1900, in presence of a parade of all arms, at which all civilians were present in uniform.[1]

Military ceremonial, the flag, civilians in uniform; the pattern seems clear enough already. The same evening, after a formal dinner in the W.A.F.F. officers' mess, he showed his concern for the creation of a style and precedent of rule, rather than any tendency to identify and discuss actual problems of administration and development: 'It is in the hands of each one of us: it is we who are selected to mould the young beginnings, to set the precedents and set the tone, and, in short, to make or mar this work.'[2]

Lugard's written attempts to 'mould the young beginnings' in the next few years were massive; the most important were: the annual reports, the long-range artillery of the propaganda war, nominally addressed to the Secretary of State but deliberately directed over his head to 'the public'; the 'confidential' *Political Memoranda* (revised and printed in 1906) for the 'guidance' of his successors' administrative officers; and his and Lady Lugard's published writings and addresses of the period. These earlier documents show, with a clarity which his later contributions did much to conceal, just what kind of priority and what kind of precedents Lugard had in mind. Even the style of his writing reveals the man; an old Gladstonian Liberal and Congregational Minister had described it ten years before in words which have not been bettered: 'Captain Lugard writes as though he were the Special Commissioner of Heaven invested with authority.'[3] Sir William Geary's word 'dithyrambic' also conveys the essence of

[1] Annual report, Northern Nigeria, 1900. This, Lugard's first report, is the only one in the series of the year which displays the author's name—'by Major-General Sir F. Lugard, K.C.M.G., C.B., D.S.O.'. Such self-advertisement was a break with civil service tradition, although customary in military dispatches.

[2] Perham, *Lugard, The Years of Authority*, p. 25.

[3] J. Guinness Rogers in a strikingly prescient article in *The Nineteenth Century* (vol. xxxiii, Feb. 1893) condemning Lugard's activities in Uganda and remarking on the 'strange glamour' with which they were surrounded.

the annual reports. It provoked hostility in Geary, even though Lugard was aiming at 'pacification' on paper. And if he could provoke hostility on paper, he could do so on the ground even more readily: 'I lost no time in sending out survey parties . . . instructed to avoid hostilities.'

There was not much danger of armed reconnaissance parties, led by military officers, young professionals eager for 'a show' and for medals, succeeding in the avowed object of avoiding hostilities. In view of his own experience, it is not easy to believe that Lugard seriously expected them to do so. As soon as these officers came too near for each community's peace of mind, in the state of war between town and town which then existed, there was bound to be trouble. Each officer in turn reported an 'attack without provocation' and each commander 'found himself compelled to fight' and 'inflict serious losses' on 'the enemy'. For Lugard, anything was 'defiance' or 'insult' enough. 'These people used poisoned arrows'—an obvious offence against the code of chivalry—'and are a constant source of trouble, firing at canoes proceeding up the river, and defying authority in the dense forest and undergrowth which cover their country.'

This was to be the recurrent pattern, as it had been the pattern of Lugard's previous career.[1] But Lugard's experience on charges of provoking hostility and of inhumanity had unfortunately taught him one useful lesson—the utility of withholding reports of such incidents, whenever possible, until he could give his own carefully worded version of an accomplished fact.

The big question-mark which hung over Lugard's career and fame, even when it was at its height, was of course the degree of 'provocation' and 'hostility' which inspired his onslaught by force on the Northern Emirates, particularly on Kano and Sokoto. David Muffett's researches[2] have done much to remove the question-mark, suggesting that both Sokoto and Kano had shown an unrequited desire to avoid hostilities with the British, and that Lugard made no real effort to establish peaceable and friendly contact with them. This suggests that Lugard's reports should be treated as partly fiction, and this would indeed resolve the puzzle of the contrast between the aggressive, high-handed style of writing and the protestations of peace and patience which they contain. The reports were in the

[1] 'Peace has not exactly dogged his footsteps.' Stephen Gwynn, in the *Fortnightly Review*, Mar. 1903.

[2] D. Muffett, *Concerning Brave Captains* (1964).

militaristic tradition of generals' dispatches, the product of a mind dominated by considerations of weapons and tactics, using the annual report as an extension of war, as an additional weapon.

One of the best illustrations of this dominance by military considerations is the story of Lugard's capitals. Had Lugard thought in terms of peaceful penetration his choice of a capital must surely have fallen upon the great commercial centre of Kano, and he would have based his plans on making it the centre of government.[1] Everything would then have fallen into place; the Lagos–Kano axis of communications and trade could have been established early, without bloodshed, despite local 'sewage' difficulties at both ends. But Lugard's choice of a headquarters made sense only in military terms divorced from administrative and commercial reality. First, he proposed to move his headquarters from Lokoja, for the ostensible reason of 'avoiding rocks and sewage'. This, he said, was prevented by 'the collapse of the Public Works Department' and the 'delay' in the arrival of a new head of department—both, of course, things for which he accepted no blame. So, because he was 'compelled' to put up a bungalow for new arrivals, and the ridge was 'healthy', and 'a fine polo ground' had been made, he decided to stay for the time being, and, instead of moving his headquarters, to move the town itself downstream—'and so to do away with the pollution of the water, and with other evils such as the proximity of a haven for thieves and prostitutes, the infection of mosquitoes with malarial germs, and the insanitary conditions inevitable round a large native town'.[2]

It is in arguments of this kind that Lugard reveals the limitations of his mind; so far as he was concerned the problems of urbanization could be solved by moving the town away. And then, after a spell at Jebba, on the Niger (where he had established his military headquarters in 1898, when raising the W.A.F.F.), he planned a new 'permanent' headquarters. Given his as yet unrevealed intention to conquer the country, given a strong desire to have nothing to do with Lagos and its railway, and not to be near a centre of population, his choice of a command headquarters was confined to the vicinity of the

[1] The C.M.S. mission under Bishop Tugwell which reconnoitred the North in 1900 made a bee-line for Kano as the obvious centre of the country, hoping to spread their influence outwards from there. And the Selborne Committee clearly thought of Kano as the 'natural' starting point of the railway which was to be the instrument of development and communication.

[2] Annual report for 1900–1—sent in 1902.

highest navigable point on the river system (about which there was in practice no agreement).[1] But Lugard did not wish to be in a river valley, ostensibly because of the presumed greater health hazards. Thus it was that he came to move his capital to the economically, commercially, and administratively irrelevant site of Zungeru, abandoned after a few years, and to squander money and labour on the construction, from there to an equally irrelevant point on the Kaduna River, some ten miles away, of a light railway—which then had to be extended for about ten more miles to 'a more convenient terminus' on the river. It was an expensive operation.

It was by further steps of this kind (e.g. ideas of mule-breeding and ostrich-farming, ideas of importing bullocks, carts, farriers, blacksmiths, and clerks from India, and similar 'price-indeterminate' schemes)[2] that the militaristic bias of Lugard's mind turned Northern Nigeria inexorably further and further away from the path of administrative progress and financial solvency. His railway was an 'administrative' railway—part of the command system; his telegraphs were command communications, nothing to do with commerce. Not to have a normal Secretariat made sense only if the policy being followed could not be subjected to the ordinary processes of discussion and formulation. Since Lugard's plan was fully formed, and too secret, too personal for a Secretariat, he was driven to nepotism to secure the appointment of his own brother, an army officer like himself, as 'Chief Clerk' in his office, and the appointment of a personal friend to command his army while he fought against the War Office's attempts to exercise their constitutional, civil control. It was Lugard who won most of the engagements in this battle also.

But before conquest could begin, a 'moral' justification must be thought out. The annual reports for the first years show the first workings out of this justification. For this, the Fulani rulers had to be both good and bad. Strange ideas of race and of intelligence had to make them 'decadent', 'degenerate', and 'cruel' enough to be

[1] Lokoja, at the Niger–Benue confluence, was perhaps the highest practicable point for all-season navigation. Lugard's expectations of navigability further up the Niger and Kaduna rivers proved over-sanguine, and efforts to improve navigability proved expensive failures.

[2] These 'experiments' are detailed in the annual reports: the scheme for bullock-carts to replace carriers 'with their thieving and looting propensities' is obviously the product of a military transport-officer's Indian experience. Its failure was everyone's fault but his—the carts' 'bad workmanship and faulty construction', the aninals 'badly selected'. One hundred carts were bought in England, and 1,538 oxen bought in Sokoto and Bornu.

attacked and conquered, whether they resisted or not, and yet in the next breath they could be 'born rulers' and 'incomparably above the negroid tribes in ability'—and so fitted, if they submitted promptly, to be used in the new command structure.

For the upper part of the command structure the experienced civil administrators offered on transfer from other territories by the Colonial Office clearly would not do; Lugard fought with the Colonial Office to resist their posting to Nigeria, and won. He preferred to use his own selected army officers for 'political' duties. His reasons for this are worth quoting at length as an example of his concept of administration and of his method of self-justification:

> Objection has been taken in some quarters to the appointment of military officers as civil residents. Failing the supply of men with African administrative experience I have found that selected Army officers are an admirable class of men for this work. They are gentlemen; their training teaches them prompt decision; their education in military law gives them a knowledge of the rules of evidence and judicial procedure sufficient when supplemented by a little special study to meet the requirements of a not too technical system of court work, and their training in topography enables them to carry out the surveys of all their journeys.

He went on to clinch his arguments, in a superb example of militaristic thinking, by the assertion that military officers were 'less militaristic' than civilians, and more opposed to punitive expeditions.

The 'not too technical system of court work' meant that 'justice' was incorporated into the structure of discipline and command, with the Chief Justice and the Attorney-General reduced in importance to fit into something that bears a close resemblance to military discipline. Although the Chief Justice and the Attorney-General might make recommendations (and the first Chief Justice resigned in protest)[1] it was the Commander who took the decisions, and Lugard took pride in not accepting the Attorney-General's advice in the cases that came before him. In a private letter to Lady Lugard the High Commissioner gave his own complacent account of this judicial system in which he was not 'hampered by legal technicalities', but brought to bear 'a long African experience and a knowledge of native custom' and a 'strong "common sense" point of view', 'frequently'

[1] The first Chief Justice, Gollan, was appointed first as Private Secretary to the High Commissioner, and promoted later; his independence of mind by 1904 distressed Lugard, who 'was relieved at his departure later the same year and the substitution of a chief justice who, it seems, gave no further trouble upon the points at issue' (Perham, op. cit., p. 163).

setting aside the Attorney-General's recommendations: 'I think that for substantial justice it would be hard to beat this system.'[1] The accused, deprived of means of defence, must indeed have found it hard to beat; one thinks of the many hundreds of death sentences which Lugard must have personally confirmed under his 'not too technical system of court work' on wretches tried by unqualified judges whose military training had taught them 'prompt decision'.

If civil law and civil rights were one important part of the influences which Lugard's 'instinct' prompted him to exclude from his territory, civil trade and civil enterprise fared no better. Civil law and trade are so closely interdependent that the one can hardly flourish without the other. Lugard's attitude to traders and trade was entirely of a piece with his attitude to other civil influences which would work against his dream of a regimented Empire. He was to express that dream at length later, when 'Mandates' became fashionable and when he was a candidate for appointment to the League of Nations Permanent Mandates Commission, in his book *The Dual Mandate*. But by that time the simple outline of administration which had served his purpose in Northern Nigeria had become pretty confused, and he never again returned to the stark simplicity of this statement, which dates from 1905:[2]

> The aims of West African administration are comparatively simple. Unconcerned with that large range of subjects which provide material for the domestic legislation of most civilized countries, its problems are confined to two main branches:
> (1) The treatment of native races, who are centuries behind ourselves in mental evolution, and the steps by which they may be gradually brought to a higher plane of civilisation and progress: and
> (2) economic development by which these tropical countries may develop a trade which shall benefit our own industrial classes by the production, on the one hand, of the raw materials—rubber, oils, cotton, hides, etc.—which form the staples of our own manufactures, and by the absorption in return of our manufactured cottons, hardware and other goods.

One need look no further for reasons for the lack of schools, hospitals, and social services; he was 'unconcerned with that large range of subjects'. But the most significant thing about the idea of 'trade' expressed here is that it is conceived in terms of caste and status: in Africa, the docile peasantry producing raw materials; in Europe, the docile 'industrial classes' producing manufactures; and

[1] Perham, op. cit., p. 162 (Lugard to Lady Lugard, 23 Jan. 1906).
[2] Lugard's chapter in C. S. Goldman, ed., *The Empire and the Century* (1905).

over all, godlike, the English gentleman, 'ruling' both. It reflects an attitude of mind 'centuries behind' capitalism in 'mental evolution'. And despite this dream of an Empire 'swapping' raw materials for manufactures, in which traders would presumably have had some kind of role to play, Lugard showed no sign of grasping the idea of an administration devoting itself to creating favourable conditions for trade.

In the field of trade, there were three possible agents of modernization whose activities, if wisely fostered, would have speeded up the introduction of the cash economy, of currency, and of cash crops, and the end of the old economy of barter, slave-raiding, and slavery. These were: the trader from the coastal areas, the European trader, and the Hausa trader.[1] All three main categories Lugard seems to have regarded with disfavour, particularly the man from the hated coast: 'The immigrant black trader is by no means a desirable person.' One of his alleged vices was 'a fondness for litigation'.

This left the European and the Hausa. For the European trader he showed in extreme form the distrust typical of the officer class:

> They are a class I much distrust . . . I could never have the patience to sit at the same Council table with them. They would loathe me and I them, and I should forget and become sarcastic, which irritates a commercial magnate more than cayenne pepper does a dog.[2]

His biographer's comment on this is that he seemed mainly concerned 'to control, or even in some spheres to prohibit, the business enterprise of his nation. Such governors could not be reckoned very effective agents of the forces they are supposed to represent' (i.e. the forces of economic imperialism as depicted in Marxist literature, built upon Hobson and Lenin). However this may be, an administration which does not make economic sense, imperial or non-imperial, can hardly make progress. Lugard's antipathy to traders from the outside, whether white or black, might conceivably have been redeemed by active encouragement of the Hausa trader. But here again the old Adam of his 'instinct' seems to have got the better of him, and his chief concern was to see that they and their caravans did not go untaxed. In the areas where there was sufficient security of life and property to permit the trader to take the risk of travelling alone, and

[1] This excludes the Arab trader plying between Tripoli and Kano, the Levantine trader on the west coast, and the flourishing trade between the northern part of the Gold Coast and Northern Nigeria; these trading systems were less susceptible to administrative control.

[2] Perham, op. cit., p. 170 (letter from Lugard to Lady Lugard).

not in convoy, he could avoid the caravan toll-stations by striking off the road.

This made the Hausa trader a criminal, and legitimate quarry. According to Lugard's way of thinking, every Hausa trader was one toiler less in the fields; he deplored the Hausas' 'keen trading instinct' which brought about 'an undue tendency to desert the paths of productive industry and to go to and fro through the country carrying goods on their heads for the pleasure of making a profit by barter. The problem is, how can this class be taxed except by tolls'[1]

So far in this chapter the quotations from Lugard's writings have been taken either from his published writings or from the biography. There is however in the first 'confidential' edition of Lugard's *Political Memoranda* (1906)[2] a unique source of evidence of his dominant ideas of administration. To read these three hundred odd pages of close print carefully is to enter into a dream world, a looking-glass world where, amidst a forest of impossible instructions for its custodians, the ordinary principles of civilized government and of justice become grotesquely distorted and reversed. Lugard went to some lengths to conceal from the Colonial Office the existence of these memoranda, prohibiting their removal from the territory, and later having them printed in England without the Office's knowledge. When the Colonial Office got wind of them, and insisted upon seeing a copy, Lugard was markedly hesitant about sending one, and finally sent the revised, printed version, not the originals. Nothing obviously wrong was seen in them by the Colonial Office, although Antrobus remarked: 'Sir F. Lugard's jealousy of our seeing these instructions is absurd. They can have no "confidential character" in regard to the S of S.'[3]

Perhaps they did not yet know their man. The *Memoranda* can be taken at first (if one accepts the myth of Lugard as a laborious and humane administrator) for the rather dull work of a perfectionist, with only occasional qualms about the repressive possibilities they reveal. In them, like Bernard Shaw's 'Englishman', for whom Lugard

[1] Annual report 1906—a specially long one written to 'guide' his officers.

[2] Although these were never made public, and copies are hard to find, much of their content (slightly diluted) is reproduced in his published writings, particularly in the chapter on 'West African Administration' in *The Empire and the Century*, in *The Dual Mandate*, and in the annual reports. The printed and bound edition of 1906 bears two dates—'February 12, 1905, Revised September 1906'—the latter date being two months after Lugard's resignation—under Lugard's own name.

[3] C.O. 446/44.

might well have been the original model, he was 'never at a loss for a moral attitude'. If they are read with a more critical eye, however, they begin to seem rather different. Here is one example, from the memorandum on 'Political Offences and Punitive Expeditions':[1]

> Every effort will be made to avoid bloodshed; time and opportunity will be given for surrender, and no shot will be fired until the troops have actually been fired upon, or are beyond all possible doubt about to be attacked. This, in Pagan districts, is usually indicated by the raising of the war-cry.

A cursory reading reveals only the unexceptionable moral attitude of the first sentence, and the really humane officer could and did risk his life before giving the order to fire. But Lugard is having it both ways: the less humane or less courageous commander might ignore the spirit of the first sentence and follow the letter of the second, with its clear hint that a few shouts were a sufficient excuse.[2]

The main purpose of the memorandum from which the quotation above is taken was to stop up the gaps in the system of discipline after 'normal' processes had been followed. Some account of this 'normal' process of administration and justice as conceived in the *Memoranda* ought therefore to be given before further details of what he called 'abnormal or "administrative" procedure'.

The first of the *Political Memoranda*, and the most important for its lasting influence on the shape of the Nigerian public service, was entitled 'Duties of Residents'. The portion quoted below[3] was the source, whether deliberate or not it is difficult to say, of most of the confusion which was later to develop about direct and indirect rule:

> A Resident, as the name implies, is an Officer charged rather with Political than with strictly Administrative functions, and the degree to which he may be called upon to act in the latter capacity will depend upon the influence and ability of the Native Chiefs in his Province, or in different parts of his Province. Generally speaking, it will be his endeavour to rule through the Native Chiefs, and to educate them in the duties of Rulers according to a civilized standard; to convince them that oppression of the people is not sound policy, or to the eventual benefit of the rulers; to

[1] Lugard, *Political Memoranda* (1906), Memo. no. 7, p. 162. Page numbers given here refer to the 'confidential' print by Waterlow (1906).

[2] Perham, op. cit., p. 524, quotes as 'a very encouraging compliment' to Lugard the words of one officer in 1918 about the *Political Memoranda*: 'Reading them was like reading the Bible, the more you read it, the more you found there was in it!'

[3] Lugard, *Political Memoranda* (1906), Memo. no. 1, p. 7.

bring home to their intelligence, as far as may be, the evils attendant on a system which holds the lower classes in a state of slavery or serfdom and so destroys individual responsibility, ambition and development among them; and to inculcate the unspeakable benefit of justice, free from bribery, and open to all.

In those Provinces, or rather in those parts of Provinces, which are under the rule of a Chief of the first or of the second grade, this will be a Resident's primary duty and object, though the institution of direct taxation, and the consequent duty of assessing all the towns and villages himself, will throw upon him a considerable amount of purely Administrative work, even in such districts. In this work he should invite the co-operation of the Chief, and endeavour to enlist his cordial assistance by making it clear to him that his own interests are deeply involved. In Provinces where there is no Chief of the first or second grade, a Resident's functions become more largely Administrative, and among uncivilized Pagan tribes he must assume the full onus of Administration to the extent to which time and opportunity permit. The position of Native Chiefs is dealt with in Memo. 9.

It is the duty of Residents to loyally carry out the policy of the High Commissioner, and not to inaugurate policies of their own. The High Commissioner is at all times ready and anxious to hear, and to give full and careful consideration to, the views of Residents, but, when once a decision has been arrived at, he expects Residents to give effect to it in a thorough and loyal spirit, and to inculcate the same spirit in their juniors.

Shorn of the moralizations, and ignoring the semantic difficulties presented by the unusual use of words like 'Resident' and 'Administration', one can see that Lugard's idea of rule was simple autocratic rule from himself downwards. Whether Residents or administrators or Political Officers, his officers were to obey him, and to see that his orders were transmitted down through such intermediaries as were available without any nice regard to social organization. It is typical of Lugard's approach that the 'Memo. 9' to which he refers deals mainly, not with 'Native Chiefs', but with what he called 'aliens who won their position by conquest'[1]—the Fulani rulers. Substantive Residents were 'not to inaugurate policies of their own',[2] but Acting Residents should 'endeavour to carry out the policy of the Resident in charge and inaugurate nothing without the concurrence of the High Commissioner'.[3] Thus trusted with little or no initiative, Residents were to trust their subordinates not at all: 'Constant supervision and careful enquiries are necessary to check any malpractices on the part of the Native Staff and to prove which of them are really honest and reliable.'[4]

[1] Lugard, *Political Memoranda* (1906), p. 190. [2] Ibid., p. 7. [3] Ibid., p. 8.
[4] Ibid., pp. 8–9.

The Resident was ordered to set up a native court, 'in every city or village where it appears feasible to do so' and to supervise its work, 'seeing that the judges do not accept bribes, or impose sentences of a kind which we regard as inhumane or cruel (e.g. mutilation, etc.) and that they administer substantial justice'. 'The powers he exercises in respect of these Courts . . . enable him to entirely control their actions, and, in fact, to use them as auxiliary courts.' But they 'should avoid becoming engrossed in Court work to the neglect of their other duties. Such work induces a tendency to stop in one place, generally the Provincial Headquarters, and hear cases, while all the rest of the Province is left to take care of itself, or, at best, to the control of Junior Officers'. So, with a quotation from a soldier-administrator of another age and continent, Sir Henry Lawrence, adduced in support of the superiority of work in the district 'surrounded by the people' over 'the work done in office surrounded by untrustworthy officials', Lugard ordered his officers to 'pass from place to place' and endeavour 'to lessen oppression and bribery' and 'to deal with alien scoundrels from whom the natives cannot defend themselves'.[1]

The 'alien scoundrels' Lugard had in mind were not the British, nor yet the Fulani, but the petty extortioner, often a soldier or a Government employee, who would use an official envelope or wear some article of uniform to convince villagers that he represented 'the White Man', and then demand money, women, cattle, or supplies, with threats that if they were not forthcoming he would arrange a punitive expedition. It is a sad commentary on Lugard's administration that these crimes of 'personation, extortion, and robbery' were so easy and so prevalent that they were made the subject of a special memorandum. Lugard's way of dealing with this epidemic, the result of the terror in which his new administration was held, was a general sanction for flogging of the culprits:

Flogging should usually be awarded for these offences (unless the convicted person is an influential Chief . . . ) and above all it should be administered at the scene of the crime, in order that the ignorant villagers may have ocular proof that Government itself is not a participator in the exactions which have been made upon them.[2]

But if a false representative of the white man could bring a real punitive expedition to destroy a village, and a real representative of the white man could be publicly flogged for trying the same trick, this

[1] Ibid., pp. 10–11.

[2] Ibid., p. 244. Floggings were in addition to long sentences of imprisonment.

lesson may have been a difficult one to grasp: 'fear the White Man' was the simpler message which the real Government and the false personators all passed on.

The memorandum concludes: 'It is, perhaps, the most serious difficulty of Administration in tropical Africa that it is so hard to find honest Native subordinates.'[1] It is legitimate to suggest that a High Commissioner who was himself an honest subordinate treating his own subordinates fairly might not have found it quite so difficult.

For 'influential Chiefs' who oppressed and extorted, the punishment could vary, at Lugard's discretion, from 'lenient' treatment for 'offences arising out of old custom and habit' to deposition and removal from the province; each of the old Emirs was in fact removed. But: 'The important Chiefs, and the persons holding high rank in a Native State, will never be arrested, or kept under detention in the common prison or otherwise, unless such extreme measures are necessitated by a very serious political crisis.'[2] This was a neatly executed exercise in the politics of power; it put the important chiefs above the law but directly under the personal power of the High Commissioner, strengthening his position while weakening both that of the Resident and that of the chief.

The touring Resident, passing from place to place, inspecting, assessing for tax, surveying, reporting, sending returns, fixing boundaries, and 'becoming personally acquainted with the various peoples' in the provinces must not think, however, that he could thus dodge his court work. He must 'hold his court' wherever he might be 'in a formal manner in various centres and towns in his Province'. And he should submit 'his own reports and returns to the High Commissioner at whatever place he may be, without necessarily returning to Headquarters', and was solemnly warned, on top of all this: 'Travelling, it must be remembered, costs money for transport, and is not undertaken for pleasure. Each journey, therefore, should achieve some definite and useful result'.[3] Yet not travelling was worse—'There should never be more than two Political Officers at Headquarters simultaneously.'

The miscellaneous duties imposed on the Resident were so fantastically detailed that no one could possibly have thought it possible to carry them all out, not even Lugard, who had had no experience as district officer or magistrate to guide him. Why then pile on to these men the duties of postal officer, the supervision of the issue of

[1] Ibid., p. 245. [2] Ibid., p. 195. [3] Ibid., p. 11.

stamps and receipts by the telegraph clerk, and all the rest? Lugard never explained his reasons for this, but it allowed him to blame the Treasury and the Colonial Office for meanness; and since the tasks were impossible any officer he wished could be disciplined or dismissed on some pretext or other. And, of course, the enormous range of activities listed for performance gave the desired appearance of a coherent system, at least on paper.

Residents were saddled with all the civil duties, including judicial, police, Customs, and Transport Department responsibilities. This last was no sinecure, involving the arranging and paying of carriers and labour, the arrangements for fodder and transport animals for the army and the Public Works Department, and the fixing of wage rates and the control of prices of foodstuffs. The instructions about prices and wages had at least the merit of clarity, although it is difficult to see how anything could have been a more effective discouragement of trade. Both wages and prices were to be kept as low as possible. Foodstuff prices were to be fixed by the Resident 'in consultation with the local Chief, who will be warned that he will be held responsible if higher rates are demanded from Government servants passing through, and an "executive" fine may be inflicted if the warning is disregarded'.[1] 'Residents, when engaging men for transport or labour, should endeavour to keep down the rates (remembering that it only costs a man about 1d per diem for his food).'[2]

On the other hand, having done his best to keep prices and wages down, the Resident with quite exceptional stamina might endeavour to follow the instruction 'to encourage trade by every means in his power'—'an important part of the duty of each District Officer'. There was little guidance contained in the one paragraph on trade, which outlined this duty as 'informing the people of the nearest European trade-centres and the products they should bring to market, especially encouraging the growth of cotton, and reporting fully as to the output and the possibilities of increase of all products sylvan or agricultural'.

There was however a complete memorandum on 'Currency and Payments in Kind'. Much of it was devoted to instructions: 'to bring pressure to bear, by insisting on payment in legal currency, whenever it can be done without manifest injustice'.[3] But this was for payments

[1] *Political Memoranda* (1906), p. 13. [2] Ibid., p. 12.

[3] 'Manifest' in this context is a particularly Lugardian choice of words; the implication is that injustice not 'manifest' would pass the test.

of fines and taxes to the Government. Lugard was anxious to ensure that traders did not 'step in' and acquire the currency and remit it out of the country, because this would 'add to the difficulties of Government', by leaving taxes to be paid in cowries or produce instead of money. So, to make the trader pay cash for produce intended for export, and to force him to accept payment in kind for goods imported, he deliberately did not introduce a money-order system into centres like Kano, refused escorts or protection for currency being transported to the coast, and refused facilities for the conversion of copper or silver into more easily transportable gold. These measures made trading prospects less inviting; together with the delaying of the railway extension into the North from Lagos, the taxes, and the caravan tolls, they were formidable obstacles to development. In this memorandum Lugard gave what he called 'a simple illustration' of the way in which he saw his system working:

Currency itself, of course, remains a mere token of values, and is of benefit in facilitating the conversion of values, according to the requirements of the individual. Thus the Government requires the services of certain soldiers, and pays them cash for those services. The soldier requires various kinds of food, and other articles of necessity or luxury, and pays away his cash to obtain them. The supplier has a tax to pay, and thus converts the value of the food brought from his fields into the tax value, and this again when received by Government is disbursed in soldiers' pay: so that in this simple illustration it is clear how the Native of the country by his own industry and produce pays for the soldiers which maintain him in peace and security. If he further requires cloth or salt from a trader, the want is a stimulant to extra exertion that he may have additional produce wherewith to purchase these requirements.[1]

Fortunately for the peasant, these strange words from a twentieth-century administrator were not quite true; the main financial burden fell upon the United Kingdom Treasury, and to a lesser extent on the revenues of Southern Nigeria, where slightly more sophisticated economic policies prevailed, and trade gin duties paid most of the expenses, civil and military.

The memorandum on the courts of justice shows the same subordination to the imperatives of military rule. Of the Supreme Court system there was the barest vestige.[2] Junior police officers had more

[1] Ibid., p. 23.

[2] In *Nigeria under British Rule* (p. 241) Sir William Geary maintains that the Northern Region Supreme Court tried no criminal cases in the whole of its existence 1900–14, and only one civil case, in which he himself appeared.

judicial scope, being declared 'Justices of the Peace throughout the Protectorate', rather than for a particular district; 'it is therefore within the competence of one of these Officers to finally adjudicate upon a petty case which he has fully investigated'—and also, presumably, to judge whether he had 'fully investigated' the case. No nonsense was allowed about any right of convicted persons to appeal to a higher court: 'The monthly list of Criminal cases sent to the High Commissioner operates as an appeal on behalf of the convicted persons. In Civil actions . . . Natives have no right of appeal.'

The provincial court, in which the Resident was the judge, was an 'innovation' meriting a longer quotation to show how remote it was from the fundamental ideas of civil justice:

> The Provincial Courts are under the more immediate control of the High Commissioner rather than of the Chief Justice, since the cases are often concerned with political questions, and the Courts are, as a rule, held by officers without legal training. The fundamental principle is that the Provincial Court shall not be hampered with more legal technicality than is absolutely necessary; and that working with the Native Courts, and using their powers of arbitration and conciliation, Residents may combine judicial and administrative work.[1]

The memorandum[2] goes on grimly to underline the 'fundamental principle' of combining what should be separate and of ensuring the dependence of the judiciary on the will of the executive: 'An Officer who betrays carelessness when acting as a Judge . . . shows himself to be incapable of becoming a good Administrator.'

Subordinate 'Native Courts' were 'established by Warrant, under the hand of the High Commissioner and the Seal of the Protectorate,

Significantly, this was a case in which the Government had sought to eject the London and Kano Trading Co. from premises leased to them. Geary appeared for the company; 'the Government sought to prevent his appearing, by a special law, but the Colonial Office disapproved it'.

[1] The 'fundamental principle' of mixing judicial and executive functions stems mainly from what Lugard admitted elsewhere (his chapter in *The Empire and the Century*) to be the 'dilemma' of the abolition of the legal status of slavery, and the need, as he saw it, to keep 'domestic slavery' for 'the Moslem gentry' going for a time. No British judge would have returned a runaway slave to his master, but a 'Political Officer' could be instructed—and was instructed—to use 'tact and common sense'. The problem was one of ensuring 'the creation of a labouring class to till the lands of the ruling classes'. On the assertion by slaves of their freedom, he wrote: 'It is not the policy of Government to hasten, but rather to retard, this inevitable outcome'. *Political Memoranda* (1906), pp. 137–8.

[2] Ibid., Memo. no. 4, 'Notes on Judicial Procedure', pp. 62–5.

on the recommendation of a Resident'. But Lugard hastened, characteristically, to disclaim responsibility for the decisions taken by these courts of his own creation. Persons sentenced by these native courts—the overwhelming majority—were never to be sent to 'a British Gaol': 'It is my view that, as the Government is not directly responsible for the justice of the sentence inflicted, it should not undertake to carry the punishment inflicted into execution.'[1]

This convenient way out, typical of Lugard's methods, is as old as Pontius Pilate's dilemma. Always, in Lugard's system, although power was concentrated in his hands, there was someone to blame, some convenient scapegoat. This was one of the chief advantages to him of the decision to retain Fulani rule; he could have things both ways all the time. Using them, he could and did claim that he was perfecting a system of indirect rule through native chiefs; since they were not native chiefs at all in one sense but 'aliens' they could be deposed and others appointed, bound to him by ties of discipline, fear, and self-interest, whereas native chiefs in the ordinary sense would have been bound rather to the people by ties of kinship, religion, and social organization. If his new Emirs did well, and obeyed him, he would get the credit—as he did in 1906 when the Fulani Emirs remained true to their vows, when Lugard's whole ramshackle empire was suddenly threatened by a rebellion of Hausa peasants at Satiru armed with hoes and axes. If they all did ill, he could claim that the use of them in his system was (a) unavoidable, given his resources, which were too few, the fault of the Colonial Office and the Treasury, (b) an 'experiment' of which not much should be expected from the first generation, although the next should prove better rulers. If individuals among them did badly, it was the fault of the Emir, or of the Resident. These were a few of the possibilities of self-justification. In the course of time, there were elaborations of the theme, in which his administrative successors could be blamed either for following his instructions too slavishly, or for departing from their real purpose through lack of understanding. But by then the myth of Lugard's wisdom had so prospered that even the most scathing critics of the system almost automatically absolved its founder from blame, and looked elsewhere for the culprits.[2]

[1] Ibid., p. 80.

[2] The most startling example of this tendency is contained in the books of Dr. Walter Miller, perhaps the most searching criticisms of Lugard's system ever published, as seen from the point of view of a missionary resident in the North,

In practice, the decision to retain Fulani rule flowed, like so much else in Nigeria's history, from his 'instinctive' militarism and his highly irrational decision to subdue the whole territory by force of arms with no prospect of revenues adequate to administer it. Given that insubordinate decision, he had little choice in the matter of retaining Fulani rule, if the country was to be ruled in the military way which was the only way he knew. And it was military thinking that suggested to him that they, or the next generation, could be moulded like clay to the pattern, not of 'black Englishmen', but of 'English gentlemen', and that they should also mysteriously retain what was 'good' in their own heritage, losing only the 'bad'.

After the shock of crushing defeat, the 'prestige' and influence of his chosen rulers were to be restored and upheld by

letting the peasantry see that Government itself treats them as an integral part of the machinery of the Administration. That there are not two sets of Rulers—the British and the Native—working either separately or in co-operation, but a single Government in which the Native Chiefs have clearly defined duties, and an acknowledged status, equally with British officials. These duties should never conflict, and should overlap as little as possible. They should be complementary to each other, and the Chief himself must understand that he has no right to his place and power, unless he renders his proper services to the State.[1]

In other and simpler words, the Fulani Emirs, or captains, were to be incorporated into Lugard's hierarchy of military command. In this

from the beginnings in 1900, for nearly half a century. Miller singled out for special criticism 'the error in administration' of retaining Fulani rule and deliberately extending it, the bias towards the *status quo* and the ruling classes, the dispersion from the capitals of the guilds and of the chiefs who had formed part of a system of restraints on the Emirs' tyranny, and the discouragement of education, and of the missions. He described the system as something as near to fascism as it was possible for it to be under the British Colonial Office. Of all these things Lugard was 'the only begetter', and he and Miller met frequently. Yet, amazingly, Miller absolved Lugard from all blame, actually dedicating his first book to 'Lord Lugard, Africa's friend'. The blame for failure was that of his officers, able men trying to carry out the policy of 'our great chief, Lugard, but not realising that they were perpetuating the rule of lawlessness and cruelty'. Lugard played with Miller 'as a cat with a mouse', as a fellow-missionary said—(Perham, op. cit., p. 506). One must assume that Miller never saw the *Political Memoranda*. See W. R. S. Miller, *Reflections of a Pioneer* (1936), *Yesterday and Tomorrow in Nigeria* (1938), *Have we failed in Nigeria?* (1947), and *Success in Nigeria?* (1948).

[1] *Political Memoranda* (1906), p. 191.

system they were to be the 'Viceroy's Commissioned Officers', sworn in publicly with full military ceremonial to serve and obey the King. They were gazetted, in five grades according to their importance, paid substantial salaries, and presented with their staves of office 'by the High Commissioner personally, when possible, at a Review Parade of Troops, in the presence of the Resident and of their assembled people'.[1] Protocol was detailed: no chief should sit on a chair in the presence of the High Commissioner; those of the first grade would be provided with a raised dais, such as 'a native bed covered with rugs and carpets'. 'All other grades will sit on mats and carpets on the ground.' Only chiefs of the first and second grades would be allowed 'royal trumpets'; no one except a chief could wear a sword, or assume special dress and titles.[2] The symbolic presents given by the High Commissioner to the new Emir of Kano when he was installed were a sword, a dagger, and an umbrella.

There is no room for doubt here about the precedents, the tone and style of rule which Lugard was introducing. Whoever received the staff of office, whether the silver-headed staff of the first grade, or the brass-headed staff of the second, or the 'short batons of an entirely different pattern' of the third, fourth, and fifth grades, was going to be a cog in the machine of military autocracy. Residents were instructed to support their authority in every way, to 'enforce' their 'just tribute' from surrounding villages. He even made provision for previously independent tribes to be included in the new model Emirs' jurisdiction—with, of course, 'the concurrence of the High Commissioner'.[3]

With ranks and status settled, the question of pay and rations for the officers had to be considered. The 'previous Administration' (i.e. Goldie) had, Lugard noted, accurately enough, encouraged some of the Fulanis' subjects to revolt, and this was a trend he wished to reverse. According to him, the British conquest meant that the Emirs had lost to him all rights of taxation, of title to land and land revenue, and his new appointees as Emirs 'expected a declaration of policy' on taxation—'and it was even reported that there was a widespread feeling of unrest pending its announcement'.

The 'instinctive' militarist reaction was to restore social discipline and ensure adequate pay for the new cadre of 'officers' by direct taxation; this Lugard did, making it the responsibility of his Residents to

[1] Ibid., p. 192.
[2] Ibid., pp. 193–4.
[3] Ibid., p. 264.

assess and supervise collection, because he did not trust the Emirs themselves.[1] With little indirect revenue, and no prospect of the Treasury providing the kind of emoluments he considered necessary[2] to ensure that self-interest and the fear of dismissal from lucrative office reinforced the Emirs' loyalty to him, direct taxation was obvious enough. It is Lugard's justification of it that reveals the man and his talent for clothing naked oppression in the garments of liberty and progress. Having conquered a country of peoples allegedly oppressed and enslaved by aliens, and having reinstated the 'aliens' as 'native chiefs', giving their silver and brass staves the backing of imperial steel and gold, he then taxed the people directly to pay for as much of the new disciplinary system as possible, claiming that direct taxation was the 'moral charter of independence' of the people.[3]

The reasoning which led to this satisfactory conclusion was curious. Firstly, he claimed that 'all civilized nations' recognized the principle of direct taxation of the individual 'in proportion to his wealth, and the protection and benefits he receives from the state'. So, if direct taxation was to be introduced 'at some not remote time', it was 'the more far-seeing policy' to introduce it simultaneously with 'the inclusion of the country under British control, when it is looked upon as a natural corollary of the assumption of rule'. This took no account of the difficulties it would make in the intended amalgamation with the untaxed South, or of the benefits which 'civilized nations' conferred on their citizens, or of the feelings of those who had been encouraged by the British to revolt against Fulani rule, who could scarcely look upon the reimposition of taxes as 'the natural corollary' of British rule. Next, Lugard asserted that direct taxation was unsuited to a people held in a state of slavery or serfdom, who could not be expected to recognize an obligation to maintain the efficiency of the state. But, slavery ended (it had not been ended; it was allowed to continue), direct taxation ought to be introduced: 'Direct taxation,

[1] ' "Jekadas (tax collectors) are corrupt", says Sir F. L. "Sweep 'em away; natives can't be trusted. Residents must personally assess", etc. etc. and so we are being broken down with overwork and the natives are sullen and discontented.' C. P. Orr, Resident, Zaria Province (1905), quoted in Perham, op. cit., p. 185.

[2] Geary, *Nigeria under British Rule*, p. 235, gives the following figures for the 'net income of chiefs' at this period: Emir of Kano, £8,500, Sokoto, £5,515, Bornu, £5,009, Zaria, £2,500, Katsina, £2,000.

[3] *Political Memoranda* (1906), pp. 85–6.

therefore, as being the State recognition of the rights and responsibilities of the individual, is the moral charter of independence of a people.'

This is 'aptitude' indeed: but there was more refinement of the 'principle': 'Experience (I wrote in a former Memo) seems to point to the conclusion, that in a country so fertile as this, taxation is a moral benefit to the people, by stimulating industry and production.'[1]

So, with himself at the apex of this closed system of military discipline in which his largely army-trained cadre of officials and his alien rulers turned into native chiefs were all directly subservient to him, with the system of justice similarly tamed and subservient, with few lawyers, few traders, few missionaries to argue and protest, with no one except his own brother privy to the secrets of policy,[2] it would seem that the work was complete; but one thing was missing. Individuals who disobeyed could be quickly dealt with, but what should be done in the event of collective defiance by whole communities resisting authority, actively or passively? This gap must be filled; there must be no mutinous behaviour.

Lugard therefore devised what he called 'Abnormal or administrative procedure'—a procedure whereby 'offending communities' could be brought to heel without delay or judicial inquiry, on a specious basis of morality and humanity, set out in a memorandum on 'Political Offences and Punitive Expeditions'.

The offences Lugard had in mind were those 'in which a community as a whole voluntarily accepts responsibility for a crime, by shielding the criminals, thwarting investigation, or refusing to give evidence which they undoubtedly possess. The offence may or may not have been aggravated by opposition to the forces of

[1] There is an interesting comparison between the 1906 and the 1918 editions of this memorandum which illustrates the 'slipperiness' of Lugard's mind; the 1906 version read: 'Communities, however, who have only recently emerged from such a state of servitude, are not, at first, wholly fit to appreciate those rights and to assume those duties, and they take some time to acquire the sense of responsibility and its obligations. Mohammedan rule in Africa is vicious, in that it usually holds a large section of the people in this state of irresponsible tutelage, thereby arresting all progress' (p. 86). By 1918 the second sentence did not look so good, so it was changed: 'Mohammedan rule in Africa, purged of its greatest drawback—viz. that it creates and maintains a large class in a state of bestial servitude—can thus be made an instrument of enlightened progress. Direct taxation may be said to be the corollary of the abolition, however gradual, of forced labour and domestic slavery' (p. 166).

[2] Appointed as 'Chief Clerk, Office of the High Commissioner' with the status of a second-class Resident in 1903.

the Protectorate.' The 'moral' basis must in fairness be set out in Lugard's own words:

The ultimate sanction for such a course of action is derived from the same source as the right to inflict a judicial penalty. In either case it is consequential on the assumption of the right to govern. That, in turn, may, or may not, be directly based on the right of conquest; but in any case, it is assumed by the more powerful over the less powerful, and carries with it the obligation to protect all sections of the community from outrage and violence. A Government, therefore, unable or unwilling to discharge this duty to the least of the governed race, ceases to be worthy of the name of a Government. Judicial powers, however emanate directly from Government itself, being, as it were 'a divine right' inherent in Government, not necessarily vested in, or even exercisable by, the Head of the Government. Administrative powers, on the other hand, are vested solely in the Head of the Government, and the extent to which they may be exercised by any official is limited by the extent to which they are delegated to him by the Head of Government. This is necessarily so, for, whereas judicial powers are limited by the penalties attached to each crime by law, and hedged around with many safeguards in their application, Administrative powers are arbitrary, and partake of the nature of the punishments or indemnities inflicted by a victorious force.[1]

So, might is right. The High Commissioner is above the law, and can punish the whole community, ostensibly for the protection of 'the community', with more force than the law could ever permit. But an even better method of enforcing discipline than wholesale punishment was in prospect, none other than the ancient device of tyranny, spies, and secret agents:

Though coercive and Punitive expeditions are still unfortunately a necessity in this country, in order to protect the weak from outrage, and to put a stop to lawlessness and brutal outrages, they are only applicable to a very early stage of organization. An effective Administration, by means of secret agents, etc. should soon be able to discover who are the ringleaders and chief culprits, and so to effect the arrest of guilty individuals, instead of inflicting punishment on the whole community.[2]

Meanwhile, pending the realization of this 'ideal', life must be taken, in the name of 'humanity':

When, however, the use of force is necessary, I prefer the destruction of life to the destruction of food; for the former falls upon those who are directly responsible for the original cause, and has an immediate effect, whereas the latter causes suffering later on to the non-combatant portion

[1] *Political Memoranda* (1906), p. 161.

[2] Ibid., p. 163.

who are the less responsible—for women and children, the aged and the weak, are the first sufferers from famine. Experience has shown that, where the resistance is determined, the only way of avoiding recurrent expeditions is to inflict severe punishment, for uncivilized man, regrettably, only recognises force, and measures its potency by his own losses. The punishment must, therefore, be such as will thoroughly deter the people from a repetition of crime.[1]

Further comment on Lugard's system of military despotism seems unnecessary; there remains only the need to show that he regarded the whole system of 'justice' and 'administration' as an enjoyable fulfilment of his own wish to command:

I love this turgid life of command, when I can feel that the sole responsibility rests on me for everything, whether it be a small crisis like this, with the necessary action to be taken to preserve life, and to re-establish prestige or whether it be, as my day's task has been, to confirm the hanging of criminals or the penal servitude, or the petty punishment of others, watching jealously that the executive officer does not inflict punishments which are unfair, or that the legal adviser does not hamper true justice by technical objections.[2]

In Lugard's last few months as High Commissioner and 'pacifier' there was more bloodshed, massacre, destruction, and loss of life than there had ever been in the course of British intervention in Nigeria. The full story has been told, and does not need to be repeated here.[3] It was the other campaign fought in London, the propaganda campaign, which affected the future of Nigeria and of the Nigerian public

[1] Precisely what this representative of twentieth-century British civilization meant by urging his military officers on to 'severe punishment' is not entirely clear. He maintained in the confidential print that 'the burning of a village is not a very serious punishment' (p. 162). In the published version, in *The Dual Mandate* (p. 584), this became 'the burning of a hut'. He elsewhere makes it clear that he had no objection to things like the stocks and flogging—so long as they were made severe enough: 'Native courts now appear to err on the side of leniency, and Residents report that flogging is a mere farce, and prisons do not exist.'

[2] Letter to Lady Lugard, 2 Feb. 1906, quoted Perham, op. cit., p. 248. The year which began thus so enjoyably for Lugard with 'the small crisis' of the Tiv people in revolt and burning the Niger Company's store saw the flames of revolt rising at Satiru in the same month, repressed with great slaughter and destruction of the town after a massacre by machine guns of peasants armed with hoes and axes, in March; in this larger crisis Lugard's system was saved only by the Fulani Emirs' bonds of loyalty remaining firm; soon afterwards came another massacre at Hadeija; Lugard was recalled by the new Liberal Government 'for consultations' and left Nigeria in May 1906, resigning shortly afterwards.

[3] Perham, op. cit., and Muffett, *Concerning Brave Captains*.

service more deeply and more permanently than the actual facts of Lugard's 'pacification' of Northern Nigeria.

Before examining the simple but effective mechanics of the campaign which made this 'form of sultry Russia'[1] appear to be a triumph of colonial administration, one must make the point that the very success of this campaign in presenting a romantic picture of Northern Nigeria captivated and attracted to careers in Northern Nigeria many English gentlemen more typical than Lugard of those vintage years when the English gentleman seemed, not only to himself but to many others, the pinnacle of human evolution. But the traditions of their country and class and their public school training, their youth, their inexperience of government and their innocent acceptance of imperialist propaganda made it impossible for them to think in terms of revolutionary, radical questioning of the whole concept of government. What they could do, and did, under Lugard's less dictatorial and less pugnacious successors, was to make the despotism something more moderate, more humane—gentler, in fact. There developed the paradox of a system devised by an extreme, professional militarist being modified (in the erroneous belief that the founder's intentions were revealed in his moralizings about progress) by more normal, more kindly amateurs. In this, they were being true to the long English tradition of compromise between coercion and freedom, between progress and reaction, between injustice and justice, which found expression in the ideas of gentlemanly behaviour and of 'fair play'.

Even the penury and the poverty which were the most obvious outward signs of Lugard's 'price-indeterminate' administration helped to save it from the worst condemnations of later visitors and critics from the outside world. In contrast to places like Leopold's Congo neither the inhabitants nor the resources of the country were being 'exploited', and the rulers lived on poor pay in poor conditions; thus even Morel, the chief critic in his day of the Congo and of militarism, and no lover of powerful officialdom, was moved to record the most striking tribute of all to the new élite service which had been

[1] Winston Churchill's description of Lugard's Nigeria, written in the Colonial Office the day after Lugard wrote glorying in the feeling that the sole responsibility for everything rested on him (Perham, op. cit., pp. 247–50). Churchill's view was that there had been too much nominal occupation of territory which was 'disturbed' rather than governed, and that there should be a withdrawal and concentration on economic development of the more settled regions, i.e. a return to the policy of the Selborne Committee. Lugard's subsequent resignation, and later appointment to distant Hong Kong, suggest the classic treatment for dangerous 'political' generals (cf. Marchand, Macarthur, etc.).

built up, by 1911, out of Lugard's rudimentary beginnings.[1] This was not Lugard's achievement, but the achievement of his milder successors. He had left to them a system of one-man rule and command; they had made a few almost unconscious changes which moved in the direction of that other model of social organization and of training with which the officer class was familiar—the public school; in a sense they became headmasters, and ceased to be 'commanding Officers'. Girouard started the process by forming a Secretariat and by letting the Chief Justice deal with the judicial work Lugard had retained in his own hands, decisions unnecessarily attributed by Dame Margery Perham to a failure to measure up to Lugard's standards of industry. Residents were given greater freedom and initiative, becoming house-

[1] 'When one sees this man managing, almost single-handed, a country as large as Scotland: when one sees that man, living in a leaky mud hut, holding, by the sway of his personality, the balance even between fiercely antagonistic races, in a land which would cover half-a-dozen of the large English counties; when one sees the marvels accomplished by tact, passionate interest and self-control, with utterly inadequate means, in continuous personal discomfort, short-handed, on poor pay, out here in Northern Nigeria—then one feels that permanent evil cannot ultimately evolve from so much admirable work accomplished, and that the end must make for good.'

Asking himself 'how is it done?' he went on: 'And the answer forced upon one, by one's own observations, is that the incredible has been wrought, not by this or that feat of arms, not by Britain's might or Britain's wealth, but by a handful of quiet men, enthusiastic in their appreciation of the opportunity, strong in their sense of duty, keen in their sense of right, firm in their sense of justice, who, working in an independence and with a personal responsibility in respect to which, probably, no country now under the British flag can offer a parallel, whose deeds are unsung, and whose very names are unknown to their countrymen, have shown, and are every day showing, that, with all her faults, Britain does still breed sons worthy of the highest traditions of the race.

'Northern Nigeria still poor, a pensioner upon the Treasury, in part upon Southern Nigeria: unable to stir a step in the direction of a methodical exploration of its vegetable riches; its officials housed in a manner which is generally indifferent and sometimes disgraceful, many of them in receipt of ridiculously inadequate salaries, and now deprived even of their travelling allowance of five shillings a day.

'The salaries paid in Northern Nigeria fill one with astonishment. The salary of a first-class Resident appears to vary from £700 to £800; that of a second-class Resident from £550 to £650; that of a third-class Resident from £450 to £550. Kano Province when I visited it was in charge of a third-class Resident, admittedly one of the ablest officials in the country, by the way; that is to say, an official drawing £470 a year was responsible for a region as large as Scotland and Wales, with a population of 2,571,170. The Bauchi Province was in charge of a second-class Resident, drawing £570 a year: it is the size of Greece, has a population of about three quarters of a million, and additional administrative anxieties through the advent of a white mining industry' (E. D. Morel, *Nigeria, Its Peoples and its Problems*, London, 1912).

masters rather than commanders of military outposts. The 'Viceroy's Commissioned Officers' of Lugard's regimental system now began to play something like the role of the head boy and the prefects in the public school model of 'indirect rule'. Below stairs, imported Nigerian and Creole clerks under 'second division' British officials performed minor but essential functions which did not entitle them to join on equal terms in the society of their betters; it would have been as unthinkable to promote one of these men, British or African, to 'the Administration' as it would have been to promote a domestic servant in a public school to the teaching staff. When Lugard returned as Governor-General he naturally disapproved of these changes which had come about in relaxation of his system of discipline; but paradoxically it was just these changes which helped to save the reputation for wisdom and humanity which he and Lady Lugard had contrived to establish by the propaganda campaign, begun in the early years of the century, and continued by them until the end of their lives.

It pays to advertise, and the Lugard myth was the greatest achievement of two old hands at the game, allied by marriage in 1902. Lugard's own experience of arraignment ten years earlier on charges of inhumanity and war-mongering in Uganda had taught him the use of propaganda methods in self-defence and self-advertisement. Then, by diligent writing, speech-making, and private intrigue, helped by briefing of *The Times* through that august journal's colonial department head, Flora Shaw, Lugard had won all along the line, emerging with fame instead of lasting ignominy, having made the useful friendships which led to his appointment, by one of those friends, to a position of autocratic power. Once appointed, Lugard did not propose to fulfil the expectations of Goldie and Chamberlain that he would proceed peaceably and steadily, or to heed their warnings against war. Instead he planned his two kinds of war, in which the pen would consolidate and defend the work of the sword.

Marriage in 1902 to Flora Shaw gave him a formidable ally, a whole diplomatic, intelligence, and publicity service in one person. This general's daughter, now a general's wife, was like her husband an ardent imperialist; like him, she had experienced arraignment for her part in an imperial scandal (the Jameson raid) and had escaped with considerable skill; like him, she had suffered a somewhat mysterious mental and physical collapse. They were well matched, and fit for the work they had to do.

Circumstances were in their favour, particularly the current combination of enthusiasm for empire with ignorance of West Africa. Official reticence being already a firmly established tradition in the civil (although not the military) service of the Crown, the Lugards did not need to fear open contradiction by Lugard's brother officials, or by the employees of the Royal Niger Company. These latter had been sworn to secrecy by their master, Goldie, who took his own knowledge to the grave with him, swearing to return to haunt his son and daughter if they sought to publicize him.

Outside Liverpool, there was in Britain only a very faint image of West Africa as an unhealthy coast where British efforts had not been a great success—and this in an age of great success in most other continents. Of Northern Nigeria's peoples, and of the country itself, practically nothing was known, so there was a clear field for a skilled publicity campaign to make a lasting first impression on the public consciousness. The friend and publicist of the 'unofficial' West Africa —Mary Kingsley—was dead, and her mantle as spokesman for the interests of trade and peace was about to fall on E. D. Morel, just embarked on his career as a full-time journalist and author. Morel at that time had no first-hand knowledge of the country, and was easily misled by the opening moves in the propaganda campaign. His first book on West Africa shows how this unusually alert keeper of the 'conscience of Empire' was duped by the timing and content of Lugard's first annual report into dismissing his earlier forebodings. He greeted with eager relief the indications in Lugard's first report that 'getting in touch with people' was better than military expeditions.[1] This seemed to belie the previous scanty news of 'numerous expeditions against native rulers' and 'the "smashing" of this chief and the other'. Round one—the concealment of his real intentions from the Colonial Office itself and from the self-appointed public watchdogs—went to Lugard. The report for 1901 did not appear

[1] The first report was published in February 1902, when Morel at Hawarden and in Liverpool was preparing for the press the first of his two important books on West Africa, and was concerned 'whether the present fashionable policy of force and hurry is found by practical tests to be even more sterile in useful results than the apathy which preceded it'; he compared the 'blessings of peace which Lagos and Yorubaland enjoyed under MacGregor' with the rumours of warlike preparations in the North, where 'the military element appeared to reign supreme'. 'Whether General Lugard, with his military instincts and training is the right man in the right place is a matter on which opinions may differ . . . Nobody doubted his capacity, but it was suggested that the delicate problems of internal politics existing in Northern Nigeria required civilian rather than military habits of mind to cope with.' Morel's doubts were stilled by Lugard's first report (*Affairs of West Africa*, London, 1902).

until 1903, and that for 1902 and the first eventful months of 1903 was published in 1904. These were not so much plain factual reports as deliberate attempts to sway public opinion, attempts to prove as authoritative truth that conquest was forced upon him.[1]

The next objective in the propaganda campaign was the 'vindication' of the 'pacification' of the Northern Emirates planned in 1902 and carried out in early 1903. The Colonial Office's first intimation of such a campaign being planned was a Reuter report on 5 December 1902, and there were embarrassing questions in the House of Commons before the Christmas recess, to which, of all personages, it was the Postmaster-General, Austen Chamberlain, in his father's absence in South Africa, who replied as best he could without information, denying any plan to attack Kano, and surmising that Lugard's moves must be measures to protect the Anglo-French Boundary Commission. It was not until Parliament reassembled in the following February, when the success of the Kano expedition was mentioned in the King's speech, that Parliament paid any further attention.

By then the Kano campaign was over, and a practically deserted Sokoto was about to be occupied. The field campaign was over, Lugard was rebuked for secrecy before the act, but given the credit for a speedy victory, and the first sighting shot in the propaganda campaign had been fired by Lady Lugard in an anonymous article in *The Times* of 20 January.[2] Lugard was soon making his way home on leave to prepare his publicity, designed—against an opposition as unprepared and disorganized as he had encountered in Nigeria—to prove that the conquest had been a necessary and glorious feat of arms worthy of the finest British traditions, that Northern Nigeria was worth more than the price paid in blood and treasure, and that an era of peaceful progress had now begun under his own heroic but humane guidance. The Lugards were to devote much of the rest of

[1] 'My full account and vindication of my acts will be reserved till it is all done' (Lugard to Lady Lugard, 28 Feb. 1903, quoted in Perham, op. cit., p. 120).

[2] The article concluded that the expedition had become necessary 'to maintain the unbroken record of dignity and authority upon which the position of Great Britain in North Nigeria has depended', and sought to show that 'the prestige of the white man' was the instrument by which British supremacy had been achieved—that, 'the military superiority of the white man', and the efficiency of the W.A.F.F. 'There have been conflicts, some of them scarcely less picturesque in their accompaniments than the tournaments of medieval times'—but 'the unregenerate British public does not, as a rule, mind a fight, but it likes to know what the quarrel is about.'

their lives to preserving the myths which they succeeded in building up in the next two years. It is an indication of the strength of the imperialist, jingoist spirit of the time, and of the confidence that was reposed in the honour and the word of a 'gentleman', that they should have succeeded so easily both in their immediate task and in the long-term consolidation of their achievement.

Their version was accepted. Those who knew better were unable, for one reason or another, to speak out. Of these, MacGregor was one who diagnosed the disease with professional accuracy, and saw it flourishing, not only in Northern Nigeria, but in other parts of West Africa, and in London.[1] He did what he could, with partial success, to counter Lugard's disparagement of the West Africans for whose protection he was responsible, but Lugard had the big guns, and used them ruthlessly. In a private letter to a friend written just after his final departure from Lagos MacGregor revealed his sense of powerlessness against the forces of militarism:

I am not able to return to West Africa. I have given a new trend to government there, and I met with great, almost virulent opposition to my peace policy. Lagos is the only British colony we possess there that has had no war since I went out. I alone can travel without a great military escort to the most remote corner of the territory. West Africa is the arena for ribbons and crosses, and medals. A man of peace is not wanted nor liked there. Those who at first opposed me bitterly, now ask the Colonial Office that my methods may be maintained. I have not shed a drop of blood in Africa. That is considered phenomenal but is it not a sad and woeful commentary on British rule? The policy of smash in West Africa is I fear an outcome of military imperialism.[2]

Both the Colonial Office and the Treasury knew well enough that whatever Lugard was, he was no great administrator in any ordinary sense, although party politics might make it necessary to cover up his most aggressive departures from normal standards, when it was expedient to do so. The archives, both in England and in Nigeria, bear

[1] The Permanent Under Secretary at the Colonial Office at the time, Ommanney, was a former regular army officer, who had served as a Crown Agent for many years, responsible throughout for railway construction. Although MacGregor was normally reticent and always a man of peace, Morel's quotation of critical remarks by him on the Crown Agents' expensive and dilatory railway construction in *Affairs of West Africa* incurred the displeasure of the Colonial Office, and may have affected his subsequent career.

[2] MacGregor to Sir Samuel Griffith, 14 July 1904, quoted in R. B. Joyce, 'Sir William MacGregor, a Colonial Governor', *Historical Studies, Australia and New Zealand*, vol. xi, no. 41, p. 18.

mute but unmistakable testimony to the justice of the frequent strictures on that part of the military autocrat's work which was open to inspection in London—the correspondence, the arguments, the words and the figures presented to them in the form of dispatches and proposals. Compared with the standard of work coming from Lagos and Calabar, and from other territories, Lugard's efforts seem indeed, as they were called by those who had to make sense of them, 'slovenly' and evidence of a 'vicious habit of mixing subjects', of a facility for ignoring correspondence, and of untidy, muddled presentation of estimates and proposals.[1] In 1905 the Treasury, having complained before that the form in which Lugard's estimates were submitted 'expended much time and patience', wearily returned them to the Colonial Office with an appeal to have them typed legibly, and to 'do something' about 'the Zungeru typewriter'.[2] Antrobus had been moved on different occasions to express regret that either MacGregor or Moor had not been given the job of opening up Northern Nigeria instead of Lugard. In the circumstances his comment about one of Lugard's schemes seems charitable enough, if not exactly admiring:

> Sir F. Lugard has many good qualities. He has plenty of 'go', he is full of ideas, and he is not afraid of taking responsibility. But he is not a prudent or far-seeing administrator, his schemes are not well thought out, and he has more than once involved us in heavier expenditure than contemplated. We have not hesitated to let him try experiments when it seemed worthwhile to do so.[3]

Sir George Goldie was another who knew enough of the truth to quarrel with the Lugard version of events; but Goldie took issue with Lugard privately, not in public. In Goldie's case it was not so much official reticence which sealed his lips as a whole-hearted revulsion from self-advertisement and self-glorification, and enough is now known about both Lugard and Goldie to suggest that it was Lugard's attempts to minimize Goldie's work and glorify and advertise his own which must have occasioned Goldie's lasting disgust and lasting silence.[4]

[1] Perham, op. cit., p. 188 cites these examples of 'harsh minutes penned in Whitehall'.

[2] C.O. 446/44 (May 1905).

[3] Minute in C.O. 446/40, dated 16 Sept. 1904, quoted in Perham, op. cit., p. 190.

[4] There is a mysterious clue on the fly-leaf of *Sir George Goldie, Founder of Nigeria* by Lady Dorothy Wellesley and Stephen Gwynn; this bears the words (from Sir Thomas Browne): 'Herostratus lives that burnt the temple of Diana: he is almost lost that built it.' This work, an attempt after Goldie's death by one of

Apart, therefore, from a few lone voices in Parliament, and critics like Stephen Gwynn in the *Fortnightly Review* of March 1903, the silence of those who knew something of the facts—no one knew them all except Lugard himself—left Lugard with a clear field for propaganda.[1] The full spate of propaganda which launched the myth of Lugard as a great and humane administrator began immediately after the Kano-Sokoto campaign, when he arrived in England on leave in May 1903.[2] It was a joint effort by both the Lugards, their greatest, most durable victory.

It would be impossible to retrace all Lady Lugard's steps through the maze of secret diplomacy, and her movements from the offices and houses of Ministers to Parliament and to Printing House Square 'spinning her web of charm and persuasion', as Dame Margery Perham puts it; but her book, and her public performances, show the basic propaganda technique in stark clarity. The biography of Lugard gives details enough of her work behind the scenes, in the dining-rooms and drawing-rooms of the great, to show how assiduously she used her talents and the information improperly supplied to her by copies of confidential dispatches and correspondence from Lugard himself, and by the indiscretions of the public men in London with whom she sought contact. If, as must be assumed, her secret contributions to the cause were as effective as her public contributions,

his friends and one of Lugard's chief critics to ensure that his work was not allowed to fall into oblivion, came near to the discovery of the hollowness of the Lugard myth. Who was 'Herostratus', if not F. D. Lugard? And whom did Goldie have in mind, in the later cryptic remarks which escaped him, to the effect that no man could be trusted with power, and that self-advertisers 'from Caesar to Napoleon' were 'the worst enemies of human progress'—if not F. D. Lugard? For the breach between the two men caused by Lugard's attempts to discredit Goldie in his paper read to the Royal Geographical Society in November 1903, see Perham, op. cit., pp. 206–10.

[1] Critics of imperialism like Hobson were more concerned with the major upheavals in South Africa, and the interplay of economic and financial power, than with individual manifestations of 'sword-rattling' adventurers of Lugard's type, although his name was frequently given as an instance.

[2] One of the peculiarities of the alleged 'open hostility' shown to Lugard's administration was that it never interfered with the leave arrangements which permitted him to enjoy a summer leave from May to November in 1901, a mid-summer honeymoon in Madeira in June to July 1902, a summer leave from May to November in 1903, and a summer leave from May to November in 1905. His final recall from Nigeria by the Secretary of State again brought him home in May 1906, but this was unplanned. This arrangement permitted Lugard to conduct his efforts at 'pacification' in the dry season and return home to write them up for the public amidst the spring flowers at Abinger.

this side of the campaign was in most efficient hands throughout.

Between May 1903 and the end of 1905, at the crucial time when the most populous country in Africa was just emerging, the Lugards published their version in two annual reports, one book, and a handful of addresses to learned societies. These were so skilfully attuned to the taste of the public to which they were addressed—then the most influential public in the world—that they established the 'renown' of Lugard and his territory. In the words of modern Nigerian critics of British nation-building in Nigeria, 'they made the North too big'. How was it done?

The method may be seen most clearly if Lady Lugard's addresses to distinguished London audiences are taken as examples; the first of these was her address on 18 March 1904 to the Royal Society of Arts, for which, appropriately enough, she was awarded the Gold Medal of the society. In the chair, with a most distinguished audience present, was the Duke of Marlborough, Parliamentary Under Secretary of State at the Colonial Office. The Government had censured Lugard for not telling them of his proposed campaign against Kano, but had accepted the necessity, on grounds of 'self-defence', of the campaign; the King had sent his congratulations on its success, and of course, now that all was over, it was in the Government's own interest that it should appear in a favourable light. The title of the talk was simply 'Nigeria'.[1] After the talk, the chairman remarked that he had had the pleasure of listening a few weeks before to 'a very similar paper given by Sir Frederick Lugard' to the Royal Geographical Society. In fact, the title of Lugard's paper was 'Northern Nigeria'; but it made no difference; both were designed to suggest that only the North mattered, that Lugard's territory *was* Nigeria, and Lugard himself the best asset of Nigeria. But there was a difference, too: there was what the Duke praised as Lady Lugard's 'light and delightful touch'. He was right; this was the touch of a fairy wand.

At the touch of Lady Lugard's magic wand Lagos and Southern Nigeria became something at once loathsome and yet insignificant, and Northern Nigeria became suddenly 'a wonderfully fertile and well-watered country—rich, too, in mineral indications'. The Gold Medal was earned; the paper was a work of art.

She began by assuming, rightly, that 'with notable exceptions' her audience knew nothing about Nigeria. Interest in the Empire had

[1] *Journal of the Royal Society of Arts*, vol. lii (18 Mar. 1904).

previously been directed solely to the white colonies, but now there was a quickening interest in the tropics and their 'vast fields of potential wealth'. This she approved; 'we, who are the ruling factor'[1] in the new Empire, although not responsible 'for conscious statesmanship', should learn the 'facts' because 'we are responsible for that unconscious part of statesmanship, which proceeds from the general standards of opinion'. She then proceeded briskly to the first of the 'facts' which she wished to mark indelibly on the almost empty slate of public opinion: 'You have to think of the whole territory as running north, and south, not east and west, from the sea.'

This 'fact' established, she said there were two governments (Lagos and Yorubaland thus being left out of account). There was the South, of which she gave an odd description: 'a coast Protectorate which, under the name of Southern Nigeria, stretches for upwards of 100 miles in a strip along the coast'. And there was the North—here Lady Lugard warmed to her work—'an inland Protectorate which, under the name of Northern Nigeria, extends from the borders of Southern Nigeria and Lagos into the relatively healthy uplands bordering on the Sahara, and comprises within its limits an area of one third of the size of British India'.

The analogy was stressed: 'I have spoken of the size of the country as being one third of India, and I have purposely compared it with that great dependency.' The purpose was soon made clear: it was to emphasize the superiority and the importance of the territory 'pacified' by Lugard, and it was achieved with the aid of all the authoritative pseudo-scientific racial theories of the day:

> In India, before the coming of the Europeans, native races of a lower order than the present ruling castes allowed themselves to be driven by successive invasions down to the sea shores of the extreme south, or up into the wild fastnesses of the hills. It is equally true of Nigeria . . . In India the great 'native' invasions[2] were ever from the North . . . So it has been with Nigeria . . . As in India, so in Nigeria. We meant to trade but conquest

[1] 'We' here meant 'the British public'; the 'British public', for the Lugards, connoted roughly the readership of *The Times*; it did not include 'the democracy', or 'the mob' or the 'masses', terms which they used on other occasions as more or less synonymous.

[2] 'Native' invasions is particularly good, making Alexander the Great and the Moghuls presumably 'natives'—but 'native' here seems to mean 'non-British'. For a lady with a French mother and an Irish father, Lady Lugard had a surprisingly high opinion of the British race: 'It is a great idea . . . this conception of an Empire which is to secure the ruling of the world by its finest race . . . ' (Lady Lugard to Chamberlain, 29 Sept. 1902, Perham, op. cit., p. 81).

was forced upon us. Having conquered we are now obliged to administer, and the hope that lies before us is to develop from the small beginnings which have been made in Nigeria such another great prosperous dominion as our ancestors have created for us in India.

And now, after this orchestral overture, the theme of the hero is introduced; the hero with his gallant band struggling against vast odds and surmounting terrible obstacles:

When my husband, Sir Frederick Lugard, took up the High Commissionership on the 1st of January, 1900, he and his little handful of civil and military officials looked around them at just such a position as Englishmen have seen themselves called upon to deal with again and again in the three hundred years during which our Empire has been made. They were, I forget how many, but an infinitesimally small number . . . They numbered among themselves some of t e very best types of Englishmen of all ranks, men loving adventure, devoted to their work, accustomed to the hard exercise of sport and war, and carrying with them into all they did the inexpressible advantage of having been bred in the fair and kind habits of our public schools and homes. This fairness and kindness in dealing with native questions and with the individual natives themselves has perhaps, had more to do with the rapidity and completeness with which our administration has been established in Nigeria than any other single quality. Without brains, initiative and decision it would, however, have been insufficient. These qualities were not wanting.[1]

Turning from the conquering heroes, each in 'a position of authority', 'from the High Commissioner down to the lowest subordinate' in this 'school for the development of character' in which 'the larger atmosphere of patriotism' was 'all around personal life', Lady Lugard turned to the conquered—the Emirates, the 'states with tottering thrones' acknowledging 'a certain vague allegiance' to 'the great Foulah of Sokoto' whose former state she likened to that of the Great Moghul of India of Clive's day. Neatly working in a mention of her husband's 'first entering' the country and raising the West African Frontier Force, she went on to describe the pagan tribes 'defending themselves from attack by being generally ready to take

[1] There is a good deal more in the same strain of false and cloying sweetness; the brutal realities described by one of these officers, later General Crozier, are a sharp corrective (*Five Years Hard*) to Lady Lugard's version; her personal experience of Nigeria was five months spent in what she called 'solitary confinement' at Zungeru and Lokoja and on the voyage up and down the Niger from Burutu. Crozier, on the other hand, describes how at Kano (with six Wellingtonians present amongst twenty officers) he and his brother officers shot 'beasts, birds, and people . . . fugitive traders' indiscriminately: 'Real red murder reigns.'

the offensive'.[1] A reference to 'the strangest rumours current' about other tribes, including one 'reported to have tails' and 'another which would appear to justify the Greek legend of the Amazons' led naturally, as a bridge passage, into a summary of the racial composition of Nigeria which mentioned the South only to press home the denigration of its peoples:

Thus we may roughly divide the population of Nigeria into three parts: There are Fulani, who are the military and ruling class, fast falling into a degradation by the vices which are apt to undermine the despotism of uncurbed power but still representing authority as it has existed in the eyes of three or four generations. There are the Hausas, once themselves the ruling race and now representing the industry, the agriculture and the commerce of the country. And below these are the tribes too numerous to catalogue . . . These tribes vary very much among themselves, and the higher types of the Northern States would legitimately protest against a classification which should seem to lower them to the level of the cannibal pagans of the Southern Coast.[2]

There was, however, 'one blight which fell on all prosperity'—slave-raiding; this she described in terms which served not only as justification of the process of conquest but also as a further ingenious illustration of the North's 'superiority':

It is no matter for surprise that the lower types of the inhabitants of Nigeria should be found on the further outskirts of the country to the south and east for the centre of wealth and power and civilization, the centre also of slave-raiding was in the north west. . . . Here in these far inland States, remote from touch with European civilization, is all the light and leading of the country.

The message that the Emirates were thus both good enough and bad enough to be conquered was skilfully transmitted; even the soldiery was presented as seekers after truth and enlightenment:

The process has of course necessitated many military expeditions. The little army of the West African Frontier Force has borne its gallant part in winning this country not only for the Empire but for civilization. And these expeditions have not meant only fighting even in their actual conduct. They have served to obtain knowledge of the country and the people which

[1] It was this trait (shared incidentally by Lugard himself) which played into the hands of the system of punitive expeditions already described.

[2] Lady Lugard's book *A Tropical Dependency* published in 1905 marked the height of her vituperative powers in regard to the people of the coast (p. 334): 'The nearer to the coast the worse was the native type. . . . Sorcerers, idolaters, robbers and drunkards, they were indeed no better than their country.'

owing to the awful disorder and desolation to which we succeeded were fast dying back into primitive barbarity.

So, the 'blight' was removed, and—in a figure of speech which had been for many the grim, literal truth—'The people have been restored to the soil.' Lugard's policy of retaining domestic slaves for 'the gentry' was touched upon very lightly indeed: 'In Nigeria it is judged that the time has not yet come for dealing directly with the question of domestic slaves.'

The heavier touches were reserved for the achievements of the heroes—'what toil, what pluck, what initiative, what sturdy endurance it has needed'; 'A vast country has been brought under one flag. It has been organized for administration on an English basis of justice and clemency.'

Then, after a happy reference to Sir Walter Raleigh's landing in Guiana, the Eldorado of the Elizabethan age, the peroration rose to new descriptive heights:

> We have here a wonderfully fertile and well-watered country, rich, too in mineral indications. In its more southern limits, and especially in the river valleys, it suffers from the curse common to all low-lying tropical countries, of an enervating climate, which, in the case of the white man, predisposes him to malarial fever. . . . But, as the country stretches inwards and upward from the coast, it rises to fine and healthy plateaux, across which the dry air of the Sahara blows with invigorating force.

This brilliant essay in suggestion of the false and suppression of the truth ended with brief but encouraging hints of future wealth and progress; the newly established peace had enabled the natives 'to fling themselves on the soil to cultivate it'. There were prospects for trade, prospects of a light railway to Kano, prospects for cotton growing and for white settlement: 'There seems no reason why, in these districts, white men should not before long go out to settle.'

This was heady stuff, but precisely compounded to produce a state of euphoria in the distinguished audience who heard her, and in others who would read the full press accounts of this and similar talks, Lugard's reports, her own book; she was shaping British public opinion. Behind the words appealing to racial pride and complacency, to cupidity and to romantic notions of empire, chivalry, and history, there was a serious and simple message which was to be repeated, reinforced, and rammed home. Lugard was a great hero, a great administrator, his Empire was valuable and good, his peoples worth reclaiming from the barbarity into which oppression was plunging them, from a previous eminence in cultivation and prosperity. To make Lugard and his achievements stand out sharply, the rest of West Africa, its country, its climate, its people, and its administration, were painted in the darkest tones.

The audience on this occasion, as on the others, had no difficulty in identifying the hero of the epic, the chairman setting the example in the discussion which followed and pointing the lesson. He thought he was right in saying that there were not more than two hundred white men in the whole of Nigeria (understandably he too had lost sight of the Southern portions); and when one considered that fact, it was marvellous to think of the work that Sir Frederick Lugard had been able to accomplish in the six years[1] he had been there. Except that he had not lost the confidence of his fellow countrymen, Lugard was like Sir Warren Hastings; he enjoyed 'the goodwill and admiration of the Colonial Office'; the Duke was sure his administration would continue to commend itself 'to all British men and women, as being a sound, a careful, a prudent, and above all, a humane administration'.

Other friends in the audience added their tributes of praise—some tinged with a word or two of caution. Lord Scarbrough, the new chairman of the Niger Company (after an expression of hope that Goldie 'the founder of Nigeria' might one day be induced 'to fill in the picture and to describe the birth of a great idea, solely and entirely his own, which culminated in 1900') wished to refer to 'material advantages'. For 'imperial reasons' it had been necessary to 'act promptly', but the pace had been too hot from the commercial point of view, and it would be some years before 'the revenue of Nigeria' (he too seems to have taken Nigeria and Northern Nigeria as synonyms) overtook the expenditure. There was a first duty 'to give the natives confidence', but there should be a concentration on the district close to the river, and a Council for Africa at home to stop 'hot and cold fits of government'. Sir John Kirk's contribution was in the same strain, politely suggesting development near the river first. Sidney Buxton, the Liberal M.P. wrongly 'tipped for Colonial Secretary' in these last months of Conservative government, one of the

[1] Including, presumably, the period before 1900 when Lugard was engaged in the transfer of staff, arms, stores, and stock from the Royal Niger Company to the Government.

many public men Lady Lugard had been carefully cultivating,[1] did his duty by her, saying that everyone felt that in Sir Frederick Lugard they had 'a great public servant', and that he for one hoped it might not be long before he was called to a higher place and higher service in the country for which he had done already such admirable work.[2] Mr. Alfred Emmott, M.P. for Oldham, one of those who had expressed alarm the previous December when the Reuter report of a plan to attack Kano was published, had now by some means been reassured and won over; he was particularly loud in his praises; he thought that England had in Sir Frederick Lugard one of the highest types of British administrators that the country had ever produced—there was not much to fear for the old country so long as she could produce men like Sir Frederick Lugard—but the cotton industry couldn't wait for a heavy railway, so could they please have a light one! The same speaker, addressing the same society three weeks later on world cotton supplies, repeated with even greater enthusiasm the lesson he had learnt at the feet of Lady Lugard:

[1] See Perham, op. cit., p. 231. Buxton's support for the Lugards was apparently won by her promise to make inquiries for him in the City for financial people interested in journalism who might help to cure the Liberals' lack of a supporting press.

[2] This looks like a 'push' for Lugard towards the Governorship of an amalgamated Nigeria. In Lugard's own paper read to the Royal Geographical Society in November 1903 he had made what looks like a public bid for the appointment, showing himself prepared even to sacrifice 'the moral charter of independence of a people' (direct taxation) in his haste to peg out his claim: 'It is a policy of doubtful wisdom to enforce direct taxation in the very early stages of British rule, and I feel myself that economy can only be effected by the realization of Mr Chamberlain's scheme of amalgamating Northern and Southern Nigeria and Lagos into one single administration. It is only in this way that Northern Nigeria which is the Hinterland of the other two, can be properly developed, and economies introduced into the triple machinery which at present exists. The country which is all one and indivisible can thus be developed on identical lines, with a common trend of policy in all essential matters.'

The rest of Lugard's paper (the occasion of his quarrel with Goldie, who was shown a copy by the Secretary, Keltie, before it was delivered) is notable for its adherence to the propaganda pattern of 'facts', except that Lugard was not so free as his wife to condemn the achievements of his colleagues in other territories, and at this time left much of this dirty work to her. The pattern was (a) 'chaos' when transfer took place in 1900, in the Southern part of the Protectorate (i.e. Goldie's part); the ancient regime had been broken and nothing substituted for it, (b) Fulani were 'an alien race detested for their misrule' for purposes of conquest, and 'native chiefs' when it was a question of 'ruling through native chiefs'—'their misrule compelled interference: their over-weening confidence has rendered conciliatory measures abortive'; (c) 'the extraordinary advances' (not specified) since Lugard himself had been in charge.

I allude to Northern Nigeria, of which Lady Lugard gave us such a graphic account three weeks ago. It is not too much to say that our greatest asset there is the Governor, Sir Frederick Lugard, who has shown such a splendid combination of energy and pluck, of patience and endurance, of firmness and fairmindedness in that country, qualities which have quickly achieved a remarkable success.

A remarkable success indeed, and greater success was to follow, but it was not to be in the direction of peaceful development for which Lancashire interests had campaigned for so long. Emmott's own cry was taken up by others and the bubble of Lugard's reputation swelled. The chairman at Lady Lugard's next recorded public performance,[1] Earl Grey, himself quoted Emmott's verdict that Lugard was Nigeria's chief asset, adding for good measure that his value was not lessened by Lady Lugard's 'lofty idealism, untiring industry and sound common sense' placed at her husband's disposal. On this occasion Lady Lugard was no doubt greatly encouraged by the success of the conjuring trick at the Royal Society of Arts meeting by which she had made Southern Nigeria and Lagos practically vanish, leaving only a little odorous smoke behind. She now tried even bolder magic, taking as her subject the whole of what she called 'West African Negroland', beginning very briskly with the perfected vanishing trick in which Southern Nigeria disappeared and Lugard appeared twice as large as life, in a matter of a few seconds; she did this in her first sentence: 'I was asked to read a paper tonight upon Nigeria—that portion of West African Negroland which my husband is engaged on administering for the Crown, and the only portion with which I have any personal acquaintance.'[2]

But she had been asked so often where Nigeria was, and questions of that kind, that she thought it would interest her audience if she gave 'a short general sketch of the little known section of the world to which it belongs'. The name of the country, Nigeria, was 'not properly a name': 'It is only an English expression which has been made to comprehend a number of native states covering about

[1] Meeting of the Royal Colonial Institute (later Royal Empire Society, now Royal Commonwealth Society) in May 1904 (*Journal of the Royal Colonial Institute*, vol. xxv, June 1904).

[2] This leaves the impression that she arrived in the North by broomstick; in fact, she went out and came back by the usual route, calling at the West African ports *en route*, and sailing up and down the Niger; in comparison, she had seen less of the North than of the South.

500,000 square miles in that part of the world which we call the Western Soudan.'[1]

There followed a vivid kaleidoscopic jumble of myth and history, bringing in the Phoenicians, the ancient Egyptians, the Berbers, the Arabs, the Copts, Tyre and Sidon, Rome and Carthage—and particularly the Moorish Arabs 'who carried civilization into Spain'.[2] The object of this was to assert that in what she called 'the fertile belt' just south of the Sahara there had been 'white' Berber and Arab influences 'potent in modifying the character of the leading black races of Negroland'—and that there had also been through the ages a remarkable 'continuity of life' through trading and cultural contacts with Europe and Asia.[3] So, 'the superior races' were in posses-

[1] A case of fairly acute 'Kilometritis': by 1904 it was known that Nigeria was much less than 500,000 square miles. The actual figure now given for Nigeria is 356,669 sq. m. (281,782 sq. m. for the north, including the Sardauna Province).

[2] If this seems to stray a long way from the development of modern public services in Nigeria, it does no more than the whole of the Lugards' teaching was designed to do. The skill with which Lady Lugard summoned in aid of her spell the most potent spirits of darkness, prejudice, and ignorance shows cool deliberation, rather than self-deception. For the dark colours depicting the south and the coast colonies she used Moslem Arab prejudice and fear of the forest belt into which they had been unable to penetrate, and medieval Moslem prejudice against the heathen, as well as the deep-seated European belief in the deadly 'miasma' of swamp country, and strong 'taboos' against cannibalism, human sacrifice, and so on. The brightness of the colours used in painting the north depended on contrasts, and on European racial and colour prejudice—in favour of the non-negroid, 'white' influences she revealed in the north—and on the prejudice of her upper-class British public in favour of 'gentlemanly' rule. It is significant that in choosing their audiences the Lugards did not choose the African Society (not yet 'Royal'), recently founded in memory of Mary Kingsley, in which the traders and southern administrators were prominent—and in which there were African members like Dr. Blyden.

[3] This idea of 'continuity of life' permitted a deft and felicitous comparison of her husband Lugard with another great historical figure with some reputation for wives and wisdom—King Solomon: 'My husband wrote to me only one or two weeks ago of deputations sent down to him with presents from the Sultans of Sokoto and Kano and Kantagora . . . In reading one might imagine it a description of embassies sent to King Solomon a thousand years before Christ, instead of to a British governor nearly two thousand years after Christ: and when we compare the progress made by the British people in the intervening period with the fate of Negroland there is some ground for understanding the relative positions which we occupy to one another.'

After the talk, the only administrator from Nigeria who seems to have put in a word on these occasions, Dr. Cargill, Resident, Kano Province, after confessing that much of what Lady Lugard had said was news to him, and describing the Emir's ceremonial visit to the High Commissioner (2,000 people coming 240 miles through 'a waterless country with few inhabitants'), introduced a sober note by reading, from a letter from the Emir, these words: 'All the people in this country, our women, our children, and our goods, are in your hands; it is not your doing,

sion of 'the Uplands bordering more nearly upon the desert and civilization', while 'the inferior black races were driven back towards the then impenetrable regions of barbarism and equatorial Africa', creating 'a belt of cannibalism' attested by 'the Arab records' of 'every one of the superior Negro kingdoms' to the north of the alleged belt of cannibalism.[1]

After another broad panoramic sweep over thousands of years and thousands of miles—from the ancient Persians to the glories of Arab civilization in Spain, and the Arabs' introduction into Europe of the gift of civilization[2]—the long and inconvenient route back to Nigeria wound through the fourteenth-century kingdom of Ghana.[3] From Ghana, the road lay down river through the lands of Melle and Songhai[4] to the Nupe kingdom of the same era:[5] 'Thus we have come gradually eastwards to our own territory of Nigeria, where the Hausa states, probably of mixed Berber and Coptic origin, were founded at a period of which the narrative takes us back to mythical history.'

This route served her purpose better than the more usual sea route

it is God's will; if you do ill, the discredit is yours; if you do well, the praise is yours. Ponder over these words.' Cargill ended: 'I think those words are worth pondering over, and I commend them to you.'

[1] The maps at the front and the back of Lady Lugard's book *A Tropical Dependency* (published the following year, with a specially bound copy presented to the King and others to the Prime Minister, the Colonial Secretary, and many other leading men) are masterly pieces of tendentious propaganda. At the front, a map of 'the Western Soudan' showed peoples in red ink; right across the map the so-called 'cannibal belt' is shown with the names derived from legendary sources of the mythical inhabitants, reading, from west to east, Lem-lem, Rem-Rem, Dem-dem, Gnem-Gnem. A M. de Lauture, who had written fifty years earlier, was quoted as fixing this 'cannibal belt' as running south of the line of 10° north latitude, with 'the finer races of Mussulman Negroes' between 10° and 17° north. This was in the talk—in the book the following year she pushed the cannibal belt further south, making Northern Nigeria an even better proposition. At the back of the book there was a map of Northern Nigeria; as in the text, there was no room for Southern Nigeria to be shown.

[2] The compass, clocks, cotton, gunpowder, paper, sugar, the peach and the pomegranate are mentioned; also 'They taught us how to wash our clothes, and they introduced the habit of changing them, which was even more important.'

[3] Where the king, although a pagan, 'was nevertheless sufficiently enlightened to allow himself to be largely governed by Mussulmans', where (*sic*) 'there were white women who were beautiful and charming, and among the negresses there were excellent cooks, who made delicious dishes of macaroni and honey and other sweet things.'

[4] Where 'distinguished professors, black and white' had taught in the university and the schools.

[5] Then 'the greatest district of the Soudan'—its people 'clever in weaving, dyeing, metal-work and other arts'.

by one of Sir Alfred Jones's Liverpool steamers to the 'West Coast' that she was determined to overlook as much as possible in boosting Northern Nigeria. But at the same time the state of the North before Lugard must be depicted as one of chaos and decadence from previous heights, and the impression must be left that the coastal areas were a sink of iniquity and a wretched failure of British administration. The peoples and the states of Northern Nigeria were described. The Hausas[1] had seven legitimate states, to which had been added 'illegitimate' states[2]—'many of the principal states of Nigeria' which 'stretched almost to the southern coast'. There was Bornu. In the time of Queen Elizabeth of England, when England's arsenals contained 'chiefly bows and arrows', Bornu possessed an institution obviously regarded by Lady Lugard, general's daughter and general's wife, with special approval—'a standing army equipped with muskets'. On the Fulani people she added 'a few words', speculating for a moment on their unknown origin (Jewish, Phoenician, Indian, Roman, or Egyptian ?) and noting their attainment of 'ascendancy and power' in these cunningly chosen words:

In dealing with them and with the Hausas we seem to be in the presence of one of the great fundamental facts of history, that there are races which are born to conquer and others to persist under conquest . . . Yet both are persistent races, and it will be curious and interesting to see what development each will take under a rule at once stronger and more peaceful than any they have known.

The implication was that 'decadence' would be reversed by Lugard, that his rule would soon prove even more prosperous than the golden age when all the inland states 'carried on an important trade with Europe and Asia. They had their large standing armies, and they enjoyed at home a very high degree of intellectual, scientific, industrial and political development.' Undeterred by the impossibility of explaining 'decadence'[3] she gave a version which supported the concept of a superior North and a coastal fringe so inferior as hardly

[1] 'An interesting people, of whom we are far from having as yet sufficient information' but 'the best fighters' of Nigeria. Her husband had however made do with 'a small bodyguard' of about seventy Yoruba during his mysterious movement behind his army in the campaigning from Kano to Sokoto, a fact she did not mention.

[2] Listed as 'Zangara, Kebbi, Nupe, Gwari, Yaura, Yoruba and Kororofa'.

[3] 'The mystery of the decadence of peoples is among the great operations of Nature for which we have no explanation.'

to merit attention. Negroland's 'ups' had coincided with the prosperity of civilizing 'white' or non-Negro influences from the North, and Negroland's 'downs' with evil times across the Sahara. Negroland's ancient civilization, inspired by Egypt, disappeared as Egypt declined; 'it rose again with the rise of the Western Arabs, it fell with their fall.' Then, at the end of the fifteenth century, there began 'a new chapter of foreign influence' from the coast, which was not of much account: 'The European coast colonies came into existence, but they were founded for the most part in the midst of the very lowest class of pagan natives. It is impossible for me to speak of them tonight.'

But she did find it possible to speak of them; what she found impossible was to speak anything but evil, because they were the dark background against which Lugard's North was to shine out in full radiance:[1]

> Through unfortunate circumstances and by lack of knowledge, European influence on the West Coast has been exerted to little purpose. What has been done there bears no comparison which can flatter our pride with what was done by Egypt of old or the Saracens of the Middle Ages across the whole broad breadth of the upper Negro belt. The continent of Africa was no dark continent to them. Nor need it be a dark continent to us. Our hope is now that, in following the example of our illustrious forerunners in penetrating beyond the coast and carrying British administration for the first time into the fine uplands of higher Negroland, it may be our happy fortune to initiate a new era of prosperity, and to introduce into those countries blessings of peace and justice under which the qualities these peoples showed themselves to be possessed of in the past may ripen to a finer fruit.

The phrase 'flatter our pride' gives Lady Lugard away; in this 'la belle époque', the zenith of pride, pomp, wealth, and privilege for the English upper classes, an able woman in her unique position could flatter the pride and influence the policies of the nation without stepping outside the narrow world of London society, except for visits to Printing House Square to influence further the breakfast reading of the public whose post-prandial complacency she flattered at her Royal Society meetings, giving them a hero to applaud and feats of arms artistically told to admire.

[1] In her book *A Tropical Dependency* she pictured the traveller coming up-river from the coast: 'leaving the nude savage of the coast to prowl in dusky nakedness through the mangrove swamps of Southern Nigeria at its mouths, the traveller . . . sees the natives on the banks ever increasing in dignity and decency as the latitude recedes from the equator.'

The picture of West Africa she and her husband painted was vivid, plausible, and effective, needing only constant repetition and reinforcement through the columns of *The Times*, and of *Encyclopaedia Britannica*, her own long book published the following year, Lugard's annual reports, both the Lugards' chapters in the imperialist publication *The Empire and The Century*[1] of 1905, and her contributions to mammoth publications like *The Historians' History of the World*. Very soon they had not only succeeded in painting the 'halo of imperialism' around Lugard's whiskered head, but had made a joint reputation as 'authorities' on African history, government, economics, slavery questions, labour questions, trade—everything African. It was to one or other of the Lugards (during Lugard's official service usually to Lady Lugard) that academics, journalists, politicians, and administrators turned for articles, contributions, talks, information, forewords; in return they received 'authoritative' confirmation of the Lugard myth; the ripples of confusion spread from the original small circle first through the whole British consciousness and then outwards until it permeated what passed for world opinion. Their dominance of opinion was as extraordinary, as 'comprehensive', and 'renowned' as Lugard's system of tyranny—and based on no firmer foundations. Just a little more intellectual curiosity at the crucial time, on the part of professional students of the subjects on which the Lugards so easily became 'authorities', a little less reverence for authority and prestige, and the myth could not have survived. But it did survive, and grow, and spread, and lives still.[2]

[1] This imperialist symposium (with a poem 'The Heritage' by Kipling) contained a chapter by Lugard which purported to describe 'West African Administration' but in fact was devoted in roughly equal portions to dispraise of 'West Africa General' and shameless praise of his own work in Northern Nigeria: 'Our Colonies on the West African Coast were located among the lower negroid types, who had been ousted from the interior uplands by the superior and civilized races from the North, and I have already shown that the result for three centuries has been a thankless task.' 'In 1900 the British Government came for the first time in contact with a type of humanity greatly superior in intellectual ability to the coast population.'

[2] It was the process thus begun which resulted in the appointment of the man who had done most to discourage trade and finance as director of a Unilever Company, of Barclays Bank, of the Empire Cotton Growing Association; the man who had kept wages to a minimum became an I.L.O. expert on native labour; the man whose policy was to keep slaves for the gentry became 'the chief living authority' (Perham) on anti-slavery questions, and a League of Nations expert on slavery; the man who despised and opposed the development of intellect became an 'education expert', a member of a Colonial Office Advisory Committee on education, a university council member, a Governor of the London School of

Volumes could be written about the disastrous results of the success of the Lugard's propaganda; while it would be absurd to claim that they were wholly responsible for such failure as there has been in British administration in Nigeria, or for subsequent political and economic imbalance in the federation, or for the spectacular growth of colour problems and racial prejudice in the twentieth century, their extraordinary version of people and events, doggedly maintained throughout the rest of their lives, has played a terrible part. Many of the ramifications lie outside the immediate period of this chapter, and outside the scope of this book, but one example must be given to show something of the technique by which the Lugards sought to preserve their victory and authority. The example chosen is that of one of the chief propaganda vehicles which they selected, the successive editions throughout the century of the *Encyclopaedia Britannica*, to broadcast their simple message—Lugard good, rest bad; North good, rest bad; North a success, South a failure.

The tragi-comic battle of the *Britannica* began for the Lugards in earnest in the 1911 edition, when their reputation as 'authorities' on Africa had been established. So far as Lady Lugard was concerned, it ended in 1929, the year of her death, also the year of publication of the last edition to contain a signed contribution from her on the subject of Nigeria. But even the 1964 edition contains a few scattered relics of the long polemical battle the Lugards fought, a few shattered fragments of the triumphal arch they had built; and the 1902 edition contains Lugard's own first contributions to his own fame. So it is necessary to go back in time and then forward to study the myth of Lugard and the North in its rise and fall.

The *Encyclopaedia Britannica* had already a long and honourable history by 1898, when the modern business methods and journalistic methods of *The Times* took over, bringing it from Edinburgh to London, modernizing it, and making it a financial success.[1] In 1902 it was

Oriental and African Studies; the exponent of autocratic government had a legislature named after him in Nigeria, and became a member of the Upper House of the Mother of Parliaments; and the national imperialist was appointed to the League's Mandates Commission as an official critic of imperial policies more enlightened than his own had ever been; most ironic of all, perhaps, the destroyer of civil law received honorary doctorates of civil law from two English universities. Poacher into gamekeeper?

[1] Born in Edinburgh in 1768, in the Age of Enlightenment, the *Encyclopaedia Britannica* had always been distinguished by a Caledonian sternness of purpose, by high scholarly standards, and by a deliberate reticence about recent events.

estimated that there were 50,000 copies in use in the United Kingdom alone, and 500,000 in the United States. In the new world of the twentieth century no publication could have suited better the purpose of 'indirect rule' over world opinion than this. The departmental editor for geography and ethnography was the Scotsman, J. Scott Keltie, Secretary of the Royal Geographical Society, editor of the *Statesman's Yearbook*, and known to the Lugards. The Lugard contribution to the 1902 edition, at least in the shape of signed contributions, was limited to an account by Lugard himself of 'the Uganda Protectorate',[1] written in collaboration with Sir Harry Johnston.

In the 1902 edition the main article 'Africa' was contributed by Keltie himself jointly with Heawood, the librarian of the Royal Geographical Society, who also contributed the article 'Nigeria' covering Northern and Southern Nigeria. Both articles tended to reflect 'travellers' tales' to some extent, and some of the unfortunate effects of the 'widespread application' of the theory of evolution to ethno-

These were not taken into account until they could be seen in the historical perspective of half a century. By the end of the nineteenth century this meant that the encyclopedia's contents were related to a different world, a world transformed by steam, steel, railways, exploration, Empire, science, machine guns, imperialism, and all the rest—not least the revolution in thought caused by Darwin's work on evolution. The encyclopedia's old exacting standards had left them far behind. *The Times* took over, halving the price the Edinburgh publishers had been charging, introducing payment by monthly instalments, boldly bringing the edition up to date, and greatly increasing sales, in the new world of widespread education, rapidly growing English-speaking populations throughout the world. A. and C. Black had sold 9,000 copies in the 14 years before 1898: *The Times* sold 18,000 in their first year, for £365,000, and 18,000 more in the United Kingdom alone before 1902, when a new, handsomely bound set of volumes was brought out. There was to be no more waiting for perspective, no more reticence about recent events. Departmental editors were appointed, who invited contributions not only from scholars but from 'sailors and soldiers, men busied in commerce and finance'—and from explorers and empire builders.

[1] This was a mixture of self-justification, self-praise, and criticism of the unfortunate officer, Macdonald, who had been invited by the Government to report on Lugard's Catholic–Protestant war in Uganda, and later had to deal with some of the endless complications which were to arise from it. A few extracts strike the authentic Lugardian note: 'Both sides rushed to arms, and in spite of strenuous efforts on the part of the British administrator to avert war (which at one time appeared to have succeeded) the French party, confident of victory, determined to fight, and committed fresh outrages, and finally attacked the British who had assembled round Kampala.' Captain Macdonald's report 'was set aside by the Government who, however, agreed to pay a sum to the French priests without admitting liability, and the Foreign Office published a categorical reply by Lugard to the accusations made'.

Needless to say, the contemporary French encyclopedia *Larousse* gave a rather different account of these events.

graphy.[1] But facts were given, briefly, of physical features, population, and administration of this 'British protectorate occupying the whole lower basin of the Niger, with adjoining territories up to Lake Chad'. Lagos was separately described, and came off best of all, because the contributor was none other than the Yorubas' friend and Lagos Governor, Sir William MacGregor. It is a pleasure to read his article, particularly after the Lugards' prose; it was brief, factual, and libelled no one, although some of his enthusiasm for health and education comes through, and perhaps a little disapproval of luxury[2] in the description of the Government House as 'sumptuous' and in the mention of 'an elaborate club, provided from public funds'. The article breathes a sane and sensible utilitarianism. There was an article on the 'Hausa' by the 'muscular Christian' Canon Robinson, one of the first British students of the people and the language, and an article on Benin by Gallwey, who had taken part in the Benin campaign and remained to administer the district.

It was not until 1911 that Lady Lugard achieved her breakthrough into the columns of the *Britannica* with signed articles on 'Nigeria' and on a range of subjects—Sokoto, Kano, Katagum, Fula, Hausa. By this time, in the 1911 edition, a new authority had been given to the publication, in addition to its long tradition, and the respectable authority of *The Times*: the 1911 edition had the authority of the University of Cambridge as well.[3] So any respectable person would turn with some confidence to the article 'Nigeria' in such a

[1] 'The chief postulates of all branches of enquiry have been revolutionized by the widespread application of the theory of evolution and of new methods of research' (preface to 1902 edition, *Encyclopaedia Britannica*).

[2] 'The principal buildings in the town of Lagos are a large and sumptuous government house; the Glover Memorial Hall, used for public meetings and entertainments; an elaborate club, provided from public funds; police quarters, and many substantial villas that serve as quarters for the officers of the civil service. There are many solidly built, handsome private buildings.' 'The great majority of the civil servants are natives of the country, some of whom have been educated in the Colony, others in England and elsewhere. The European officers number generally about 112; the native officers about 259.' Much of the rest was statistical with emphasis on education, health, and trade—the last showing a doubling of exports in the five years before the end of 1899. (37 schools, and 7 Moslem teachers for instruction in Islam, 15,000 vaccinations in 1899, 5,000 iron roofs in the town, mention of the hospital, the lunatic asylum, the chemical laboratory, the leper asylum; Lagos population 33,000, protectorate estimated at 'upward of two million'.)

[3] The University's association with the publication was in fact a simple commercial agreement with the University Press, whereby the latter acted as agents for its sale.

publication, written by 'a lady of title', none other than Lady Lugard (herself mentioned in the encyclopedia as a distinguished lady journalist), wife of the great administrator soon to return as amalgamating Governor-General to the scene of his administrative triumphs. And what would they find?

First of all, they would find a 'factual' description contrived by ingenious expansion of the 1902 version by Heawood to suggest that only the North mattered: 'Nigeria, a British Protectorate in West Africa occupying the lower basin of the Niger and the country between that river and Lake Chad, including the Fula Empire (i.e. the Hausa states) and the greater part of Bornu.'

And after that, the now familiar distortions. As in the 1902 edition, and with no recognition of improvements achieved through public health measures in Lagos and elsewhere, the coast-lands were 'extremely unhealthy'. In 1902, Heawood had gone on to give an unattractive picture, on the whole, of the peoples of Nigeria, North and South, under British 'protection':

> The inhabitants of Nigeria are distributed in accordance with the physical features, the forest-clad coast-lands being peopled by pure Negroes, some of the tribes being given, at least in the past, to cannibalism and other revolting practices, while others are harmless and peaceable. The interior possesses a mixed population, a negro substratum having been modified by contact with the northern races of the continent, and by them converted to Islam, which forms, however, but a thin veneer.

Lady Lugard was able to touch up this picture; the 'touching-up' reveals both her purpose and her method. Where Heawood had put 'pure Negroes' and 'broad placid channels' it was sufficient for her to replace a few epithets by delicately pejorative ones: 'pure Negroes' became 'typical Negroes', 'broad placid channels' became 'broad sluggish channels', and so on. And new matter was inserted, like the assertion that some of the peoples of the Niger Delta 'occupied a low position even among the degenerate coast negroes', and, in her contribution 'Hausa', the opposite assertion: 'Morally and intellectually, however, they are far superior to the typical Negro.' The information about 'harmless and peaceable' peoples on the coast disappeared, and the old evils to which Heawood had referred were made to appear widespread and current, with a broad hint that the British administration in the South had not really done very much about them:

> In the delta district and the forest zone the inhabitants are typical Negroes . . . In colour the majority are dark chocolate, others are coal-black

(a tint much admired by the natives themselves) or dark yellow-brown. Cannibalism, human sacrifices and other revolting practices common to the tribes, are being gradually stamped out under British control. Trial by ordeal, and domestic slavery are still among the recognized institutions.

Heawood's idea of a 'modification' of the Negro substratum in 'the interior' did not suit her purpose; she introduced this version: 'In the northern parts of Nigeria the inhabitants are of more mixed blood, the negro substratum having been to a great extent driven out by the northern races of the continent.'

But all these touches were a mere darkening of the background and setting for the jewel-like brilliance of Lugard's administration of the North. After one paragraph on Southern Nigeria's history from 1885 to 1906 she sailed into a description eight times as long of the North under Lugard—including a list and summary of his 'enactments', making all appear splendid, advanced, and progressive. Then, after a paragraph on the amalgamation of Lagos and Southern Nigeria, there was one on the 'Northern Nigeria railway'—omitting mention of its financing by Southern Nigeria: 'The route chosen for the line was that advocated by Sir Frederick Lugard.' There followed a paragraph on Girouard's administration, the purport of which was to suggest that, while he 'devoted much attention to land tenure', this was unnecessary: 'He adopted the land policy of Sir F. D. Lugard.' Poor Sir Hesketh Bell, Girouard's successor, was mentioned only in a footnote. The whole article, in fact, was meant to show Lugard as the sun, the sole source of light; the rest was darkness. Look up 'Lugard' in the (unsigned) biographical article, and he is there; look up Sokoto, Nassarawa, Kano, Katagum, etc., and Lugard is there; one discovers that his 'pacification' was preceded by 'the refusal of the Sultan of Sokoto and many other Fula princes to fulfil their treaty obligations', that 'defiance' and 'open hostility' led to a briskly successful campaign, followed by peace and progress—but no health, education, or trade statistics. In all these accounts, as in the case of Uganda, it is the Lugard version which prevails.[1] In the handsome

[1] Oddly enough, however, the unsigned 'Lagos' articles reveal a different hand, not Lady Lugard's, and not MacGregor's, although they reproduce the substance of MacGregor's defence of the Yoruba, at the African Society in 1904, the emphasis on their peaceful disposition, industry, friendliness, courtesy, and hospitality—despite their patriotism and 'proved capacity as fighting men'. 'Beauty is indeed in the eye of the beholder'—a simple verity illustrated also in the brief, ludicrous, and anonymous contribution under 'Ibo': 'The Ibo are a strong, well-built Negro race. Their women are distinguished by their *embonpoint*.'

leather-bound volumes of the 1911 edition, the only one to bear the coat of arms of the University of Cambridge, Lady Lugard had done a remarkable 'public relations' job for her husband and for military imperialism.

But if one looks next at the 1922 edition it seems as if the old witch's spell has been suddenly broken; a new champion has arisen and scattered the powers of darkness and obscurantism. The new contributor of signed articles, both on 'the Gold Coast' and on 'Nigeria,' is the former Governor of the first and the current Governor of the second, Lugard's successor Sir Hugh Clifford, an author and publicist of no mean ability himself. The article 'Nigeria' leaves no doubt that he has understood Lady Lugard's game, and has enjoyed having a tilt at the Lugard myth. Nigeria is described fully, factually, and fairly, but in terms which seem calculated to cause the Lugards the greatest annoyance. A clean sweep is made of the racial nonsense and the Northern bias, other names besides Lugard's are given honourable mention, a balance is struck between the various parts, and there is even a suggestion that the great Lugard made rather a mess of some of the amalgamation arrangements.[1]

It was a short-lived victory; when one turns to the 1926 and 1929 editions one realizes the full force of the Lugards' combined pugnacity and persistence. Once again it is 'F.L.L.'[2] who returns to the charge, in the article on Nigeria. Then, at the time of writing for the 1926 edition, she must have been in her seventy-fourth or seventy-fifth year, but she was still capable of striking back. No overt polemics in the *Britannica's* dignified columns, since this was work for the dagger and the umbrella, not the sword; but there was a riposte in her article to every point in Clifford's article which could have been taken as damaging to the Lugard myth.[3] The war served

[1] Particularly in the lack of a normal Secretariat for Nigeria, in the troubles in Egbaland, and in the practical abolition of the Legislative Council.

[2] Flora, Lady Lugard.

[3] Clifford's 'serious rising' in Egbaland became 'an easily suppressed rising' which 'gave momentary uneasiness'. In fairness to Lugard, it should be noted that it gave him uneasiness for the rest of his life. Dame Margery Perham (*Lugard, The Years of Authority*, p. 456) quotes his largely unfulfilled prophecy to her: 'You will blame me for Abeokuta.' Clifford's introduction of a Nigerian Secretariat on orthodox lines was disparaged in the 1926 article as 'a step which in practice tended to curtail the responsibility and initiative of the lieutenant-governors and residents of provinces'. Where Clifford had said that the outbreak of the 1914 war had for a period paralysed the activities of the Government of Nigeria, Lady Lugard wrote that 'the outbreak of war postponed the consolidation of the system'. The material prosperity of Clifford's administration after the work was

as an excuse for administrative shortcomings in Lugard's work, which was given reverential treatment, and as an excuse both for a panegyric and for a reassertion of Northern superiority, in 'loyalty' this time:

> Every department was depleted by volunteers for active service, and it was with difficulty that the administrative machine was held together with the remnant of overworked staff retained. For four years, the first thought of every Englishman in Nigeria was given to the War. And not of the Englishmen only. The War served at least to test and exemplify the solid results of British rule. Throughout the War period the great native Chiefs of the North were constant and unflagging in their loyalty . . . they rendered the great service, when the country was practically denuded of troops, of maintaining absolute tranquillity in their dominions.

These later stages of the battle of the *Britannica* belong properly to a later period; they are inserted here to show the persistence and the pervasiveness of the Lugard myth, shaping the course of events and the development of opinion throughout the world, doing incalculable harm. Lady Lugard died undefeated; her husband's fame was firmly established, and he ended his career with greater honour than Raleigh and Warren Hastings and some of the others with whom she had led him to be compared. If one looks up the entry in the 'Lugard' article in the *Encyclopaedia Britannica* of 1964 one finds the lapidary inscription which is the fruit of their efforts; the summary of his achievements survived unchanged from words which can be found also in the 1911 edition:[1] 'Throughout his African administrations Lugard sought to ameliorate the condition of the native races,

delicately attributed to good luck rather than good management, and grave doubts were expressed as to the wisdom of reintroducing a Legislative Council and of introducing 'the elective principle'.

[1] One of the oddities of this memorial is that when it was first written Lugard had administered only one territory, Northern Nigeria, in which the 'problem' of the liquor trade did not arise, and he had sought to defer the ending of domestic slavery. Slave-raiding he did suppress, but many other administrators had suppressed slave-raiding without suppressing truth, or justice, or peaceful enterprise, or the spirit of liberty and independence. Lugard is also given credit for Uganda, where he secured British predominance and put an end to the civil disturbances, though not without severe fighting, chiefly notable for an unprovoked attack by the 'French' on the 'British' faction. In Northern Nigeria 'Lugard's task in organising this territory was impeded by the refusal of the Sultan of Sokoto and many other Fula princes to fulfil their treaty obligations . . . In 1903 a successful campaign . . . and when in September 1906 he resigned his commissionership, the whole country was being peacefully administered under the supervision of British residents.' He was, we learn, 'author of many valuable reports' and his wife 'a distinguished writer on colonial subjects for *The Times*'. The 1966 edition contains a revised article, by Sir Alan Burns, based on the biography.

especially by the exclusion of alcoholic liquors, and by the suppression of slave-raiding and slavery.'

Of other and greater administrators, there is no memorial, no trace.

This digression from the realities of Northern Nigerian administration before the amalgamation of Nigeria has been necessary to show how the Lugard myth succeeded in obscuring these realities, and how unfavourable to radical reform the Lugards' propaganda efforts had made the general background of information, assumptions, and opinion. It was impossible for his successors to free themselves or the country from this *damnosa hereditas*, just as it was impracticable, within the finance available, to turn what had become a heavily encumbered military training ground and gentleman's sporting estate back into the viable economic venture which its founders had intended it to be—as well as much else.

Within the strict limits of what was practicable, much was done; administrative miracles were accomplished by hard work in appalling conditions, and by unobtrusive reforms within the overall framework.[1] After Girouard's two eventful years from 1907 to 1909 there was another period of administration by Olivier's 'King Log', Sir William Wallace, until the arrival of Sir Hesketh Bell in December 1909. Olivier's description of Wallace as a King Log may have been a little unkind; at any rate he had been responsible, off and on, for administering the territory, by the end of his first decade of British rule, for a longer period than anyone else, Lugard excepted.[2] Wallace's

[1] Lugard's successor Girouard in his two years (April 1907 to April 1909), broken by a period of leave in 1908, personally surveyed the Baro–Kano railway and personally superintended the first construction efforts, had soundings taken in the Niger to determine its real potentialities for navigation, organized a normal Secretariat, handed over judicial work to the Chief Justice, sorted out relations between the civil service, the police, and the military, putting them 'on a sound and definite basis' (Orr, *The Making of Northern Nigeria*, p. 191), started an Education Department, appointing a director and writing a memorandum, obtained the appointment of an important Land Committee to determine policy for land tenure, and found time also to tour the Northern Emirates to reassure the Emirs that there was to be continuity of policy, and no breach of the undertakings his predecessor had given them. In practice, within the limits of finance, and of those undertakings, Girouard, who 'came like a breath of fresh air', had briskly done what he could in the way of reform. And the chief change was probably the devolution of initiative and responsibility to Residents; there was no longer a central 'dictator'.

[2] Wallace was in charge for about four years in all, Lugard a few months more. Wallace had been one of the Royal Niger Company's agents-general on the Niger and Benue before 1900. It is a pity he was not moved by the flurry of interest in Northern Nigeria caused by the successful exploitation of the tin-fields

contribution to reform was the abolition of caravan tolls and taxes, before Girouard's arrival, and it is to him that Morel attributes the 'initiative of perpetuating, under British rule and with the modifications required, the system of land taxation indigenous to the community'.[1] An important change was the establishment of native treasuries, another significant step towards devolution of government and increased local initiative.

But despite the railway, despite improving communications, despite the increasing experience and the very great efforts of the thinly scattered administration, despite the successful exploitation of the tin-fields, Lugard's framework of a non-commercial, martial system of command remained intact, static, and bankrupt, and a heavy burden for the white men on whose shoulders he had placed it. It is appropriate that the chapter should close with a few words by a Northern Nigerian describing these men, rather than with the warmer but not dissimilar tributes paid to them by their British colleagues and contemporaries; the writer, the Premier of Northern Nigeria, was himself born in 1910, great-grandson of the Sultan Bello who founded Sokoto in 1809:

> Whatever the rights and wrongs of the attack on Kano and Sokoto may be, the British were the instrument of destiny and were fulfilling the will of God. In their way they did it well. Even at the actual time there was no ill-will after the occupation. We were used to conquerors and these were different: they were polite and obviously out to help us rather than themselves. We soon realized the difference between Lugard's government and the ambitions of the Royal Niger Company. Though they chased the Sultan across the country and killed him, they supported the new Sultan Muhammadu Attahiru, my father's first cousin, who was ruler when I was born, and his Councillors.
>
> They made no drastic changes, and what was done came into effect only after consultation. Everything went on more or less as it had done, for what could one Resident, an assistant and a few soldiers in Sokoto do to change so vast an area as Sokoto Emirate?[2]

in 1909–10 to add to the number of books then published by Northern administrators, looking back in justifiable pride and wonder at the achievements of their service in its first decade. Of these the best is probably Orr's *The Making of Northern Nigeria* (London, 1911), although it suffers from belief in Lugard's annual reports, on which it is largely based, and from belief that 'service under him was a liberal education' (*The Making of Northern Nigeria*, p. 179).

[1] E. D. Morel, *Nigeria, its Peoples and its Problems* (London, 1911), p. 150 (this, Morel's second book, was dedicated 'to the memory of Mary Kingsley').

[2] *My Life*, by Alhaji Sir Ahmadu Bello, K.B.E., Sardauna of Sokoto, Premier of the Northern Region of Nigeria (Cambridge 1962).

# CHAPTER VII

# Lugard's Amalgamation of Nigeria, 1912–1918

The whole system and policy on which this country has been run, not only in the old days but right up to now, seems to me wrong. Lugard[1]

I regard continuity of Administration as a matter of paramount and indeed vital importance in African Administration.

Lugard, *Political Memoranda*.

EASILY the most remarkable thing about Lugard's 'amalgamation' of Nigeria is that it never really took place. In the past, the chief and practically the only source from which published accounts of this period have been drawn is Lugard's own official report, published in 1919.[2] Fifty years later, when the Colonial Office records are available for study, his departures from veracity can be measured. The discrepancies do not make pleasant reading, but they cannot be glossed over; at this turning point it would have been possible, under wiser guidance, for public administration in Nigeria to have made progress; instead, there was some reaction, and a good deal of confusion.

The general claim made by Lugard was to the effect that (despite difficulties and disappointments caused by the war of 1914–18) he extended to the South an orderly and 'better' system of administration, founded upon the principles of indirect rule which he had himself developed in the North. On one point there has never been any doubt: there was indeed an upheaval and reversal of the policy and practice followed by MacGregor, Moor, and Egerton in the South. Lugard's attempts in the same period to destroy the work of his own successors in the North are less well known, and were less successful, since he was less free to destroy and then to remould into his own personal system of command an administration whose 'success' was the chief ingredient in his own fame. In both areas the chief result of

[1] Letter of 18 Oct. 1912 from Lugard to Lady Lugard (quoted in Perham, *Lugard, The Years of Authority*, p. 423). By 'this country' it is Southern Nigeria which is meant.

[2] *Report by Sir F. D. Lugard on the Amalgamation of Northern and Southern Nigeria and Administration, 1912–1919* (Cmd. 468).

his work was a lasting confusion—two confusions, rather than one amalgamated confusion—worse confounded by attribution to forces outside his control operating against him. These forces included 'opposition' and 'hostility' in the Colonial Office, the baneful effects of Western education on Southern Nigerians, the work of Lagos 'agitators' and a 'mischievous' press, the unfortunate effects of the war, the general cussedness of the peoples on whom he sought to impose his benefits of taxation and discipline, and the mistakes and inadequacies of 'lesser men' in the public service, before him, under him, and after him. The simpler and more consistent explanation of all three confusions—the confusion in the North, the worse confusion in the South, and the confusion in the reporting of both performances—is to ascribe them all to their begetter, Lugard himself, and to his 'heroic' defects in mind and character.

The problem of amalgamation of North and South was of course not an easy one, but it could have been solved. The main difficulties have been traced, in the previous chapters, back to Lugard's own achievements in the North. There, instead of administering 'things' and developing 'services', Lugard had been preoccupied with the widespread extension of rule over 'people'—an undertaking so unprofitable that it made amalgamation of the viable South and the bankrupt North both far more urgent, from the point of view of the home Government, and far more difficult, than the joining of two viable administrations would have been. The immediate task was to free the home Government from the expensive millstone which Lugard had fastened round its neck, and to transfer the whole burden to a new amalgamated Nigeria. Whether there was any idea of poetic justice in choosing Lugard to achieve this is not clear. What is clear is that the Secretary of State at the time, Harcourt, was under Lady Lugard's magic spell, and had as yet an unshaken belief in Lugard's administrative prowess.[1] Perhaps, too—although this is pure conjecture—Harcourt may have hoped, since Lady Lugard's work had helped to build Chamberlain's fame as a great Colonial Secretary, that the Lugards would perform the same service for him. It is doubtful whether his department shared any such hope. For more than a

[1] In announcing to Parliament Lugard's appointment Harcourt said: 'Northern Nigeria is in the truest sense the product of his foresight and genius. He reclaimed it from the unknown; he gave it a legal code, differing only in its civilization from the essential lines of native custom; he established a land system which, combining altruism with revenue, may well be a model and inspiration to other Protectorates.' All this is myth, not fact (Parl. Debates, 27 June 1912).

decade they had been describing Lugard's proposals, from Northern Nigeria and from Hong Kong, in such terms as 'fatuous', 'monstrous', and 'preposterous'. But whatever doubts the officials in London and in Nigeria may have felt, they could have had no doubt about Lugard's fame, or about his industry and drive. These were established facts. Harcourt was so anxious to secure Lugard's services that he was prepared to agree—despite the Office's misgivings—to special terms. These included the extraordinary arrangement whereby Lugard would serve short tours in Nigeria, and work, while in England, at the Colonial Office, retaining his gubernatorial powers at all times. This was one of the most fruitful sources of conflict and of confusion in the years from 1914 until 1917, when the 'Scheme of Continuous Administration' (Lugard's description) was cancelled by the Secretary of State. The difficulties over papers, the delays, and the paralysis of local initiative in Nigeria in Lugard's absences finally became intolerable.[1] But the damage had already been done. The 'Scheme' had been Lugard's main reason for not altering the old division of the country into North and South and for not having a central Secretariat for the whole country. Retaining the existing unequal divisions and making no provision for a normal central Government permitted him to argue that he could direct affairs equally well from London as from Lagos. And much of the thought and consideration which the Colonial Office might have been able to give, under more normal arrangements, to closer study of more thoroughly prepared proposals had to be devoted to efforts to mitigate the Scheme's worst effects, and to end it.

Against all the authority of the received version of events—symbolized by Lugard's immodest adoption of 'Solomon's seal' as the badge of the new country and the emblem of his achievement[2]—it is by no means easy to analyse and describe convincingly the growing chaos in Nigerian public administration under Lugard. But one derives some encouragement, in making the attempt to redress the balance and discover the truth, from the many tantalizing clues scattered about in the writings of some of those in the public service who suffered most (and in some cases did not survive) the autocratic mismanagement of the affairs of the country to which they devoted

[1] There is a full description of 'the Scheme' and its vicissitudes in Perham, op. cit.

[2] 'A new Colonial badge was introduced consisting of the interlaced triangles known as "Solomon's Seal".' Lugard, *Amalgamation Report*.

their lives. Indeed, in one of these necessarily cryptic writings of the time there seems even to be a diagnosis of the confusion, and a method prescribed for revealing its cause. This is Charles Temple's *Native Races and their Rulers* (1918).

One of Lugard's original Residents, and the chief architect of indirect rule in the North, in the years of its development from the rudimentary system of military authority which Lugard had bequeathed to his successors, Temple was Acting Governor of the North and then Lieutenant-Governor of the Northern provinces from 1911 until his retirement through ill-health in 1917, after years of conflict with Lugard. Dame Margery Perham treats the continuing dispute with Lugard fairly fully, mentioning Temple's dismay on hearing of Lugard's appointment, his uneasy personal relations with Lugard, their opposed ideas of indirect rule, Lady Lugard's discussions of Temple's service future with the Secretary of State, and Lugard's poor opinion of Temple's intelligence; she attributes his retirement in part to the wearing effect upon him of his 'continuing difference with his Governor not only over his concept of Indirect Rule but over the closely related issue of the denial to the Residents, as he saw it, of a proper measure of freedom'.[1] The issue was certainly freedom, but not for Residents only—it was the issue of freedom for the governed as well.[2] Dame Margery Perham detects, in Temple's whole book, 'only one very casual reference to Lugard'. This is surprising, because Temple went as far as he well could within the law and service tradition to characterize the chief 'ruler' of 'native races' and his methods, without actually naming him. There are two passages in particular which seem to hit the unnamed target with great precision and effect.

The first passage occurs in a chapter 'The Anatomy of Lying', the main purpose of which was to convey to the reader a sense of the

[1] Perham, op. cit., p. 485.

[2] Briefly, Temple's thesis was that there were three possible methods of rule open to a handful of white men responsible for vast populations and areas: the first, direct rule, though honest, was impracticable, and not the best; the second, indirect rule, required delegation, devolution, a free hand for the Resident, and 'scope for native leaders'; the third, which was dishonest, and worst (and Lugard's way, although Temple did not say so outright) was to use indirect rule as an expedient while building upon it a machine of tight, detailed control and coercion. 'Scope for native leaders' was the essence of Temple's plea, rather than 'bossing about' by white men. He served happily under Girouard and Bell, and could have done so under MacGregor, Moor, and Egerton; although there is no trace of 'utilitarianism' in his philosophy, there is no trace of 'militarism' either.

abnormal situation in the North, where a handful of administrators sought to administer vast areas and assess each village for taxation. The inevitable result was to create an atmosphere favourable to the art of lying and deceit amongst the governed—lying, either from evil motives, to conceal extortion and corruption, or lying, from better motives, to protect themselves and the peasantry from European 'official' interference. According to Temple, the administrator had to develop a great analytical skill in order not merely to detect the lie, but also to discern the motive behind it, good or bad, praiseworthy or blameworthy. After this account of the art of oral lying by the natives of the country, he went on to give an analysis of written falsehood which clearly applies to the writings of Lugard, and of Lugard alone among the Nigerian Governors:

The purveyor of the written untruth, on the other hand, is deprived of the assistance which a charming manner and an appearance of bluff honesty confer. He must depend, in order first of all to create an atmosphere of truth and absolute accuracy favourable for the operation of the lie, chiefly on a liberal use of true but more or less irrelevant statements of fact. Next, in order to produce confusion of the mind, on great prolixity and redundancy of expression, so that the recipient, after reading away for some time may say: 'This is all very fine and certainly all very true, but hanged if I can make out what he is driving at. All this seems beside the point, but I suppose we shall get there presently. I confess to feeling rather confused all the same.' Thus drifting along, he soon becomes an easy prey. But what a disaster should he detect even one inaccuracy in all this mass of irrelevancy. In place of being lulled into a confused but dreamy credulous, receptive state of mind, he becomes at once alert, sceptical, and repellent.

But there was a method of getting at the truth. Temple goes on:

There are in the world dull, studious persons who seem to take a pleasure in hunting out the lies of others. Such marplots, kill-joys, call them what you will, do not scruple to examine written documents in a sceptical frame of mind. They will segregate any number of irrelevant facts, supply the missing portions of the plausible half-truths, detect the apparently trifling but really very important omissions. Thus proceeding they will plod through all the baffling intricacies of the maze, capture the lie in the centre, drag it out into the light of day, and exhibit it right before the eyes of its horrified parent.

The second cryptic passage in Temple's book becomes clear, once the key is found. It is in the concluding portion of the book, entitled 'Parthian Arrows'—where he quotes at some length, from Motley's

*Rise of the Dutch Republic*, the masterly description of the despot King Philip of Spain:

'A petty passion for contemptible details characterised him from his youth, and, as long as he lived, he could neither learn to generalize, nor understand that one man, however diligent, could not be minutely acquainted with all the public and private affairs of fifty millions of other men. He was a glutton for work. He was born to write despatches, and to scrawl comments on those which he received. He often remained at the council board four or five hours at a time, and he lived in his cabinet. . . . He spoke no tongue but Spanish, and was sufficiently sparing of that, but he was indefatigable with his pen. He hated to converse, but he could write a letter eighteen pages long, when his correspondent was in the next room, and when his subject was, perhaps, one which a man of talent could have settled with six words of his tongue. The world, in his opinion, was to move upon protocols and apostilles. Events had no right to be born throughout his dominions without a preparatory course of his obstetrical pedantry. He could never learn that the earth would not rest on its axis while he wrote a programme of how it was to turn. He was slow in deciding, slower in communicating his decisions. He was prolix with his pen, not from affluence, but from paucity of ideas. He took refuge in a cloud of words, sometimes to conceal his meaning, oftener to conceal his absence of any meaning, thus mystifying not only others but himself.'[1]

Temple goes on to reflect, on the quotation from Motley:

To liken a brother official to that monarch would certainly be actionable; and indeed probably an exaggeration, as such a combination of detestable traits is, we may safely assume, very rare. At the same time splinters of that beam we may sometimes find even in our eyes. The rage, it may rightly be termed a 'furia' for writing is not rare, else had this book, for instance, not been written.

Although thus careful to remain on the lee side of the law of libel, Temple leaves little doubt that it was Lugard he had in mind:

The habit of writing . . . is liable to restrict the usefulness of an official who has climbed to a position where his energies were better employed in doing things rather than discussing actions at great length on paper, both before and after performance.

On the whole an official need not fear the pricks of conscience as long as he is addressing his superiors, for they can generally protect themselves; though it is true that he may have to support pin-pricks, or stabs, should

[1] Apart from his book, Temple's chief contribution to this labour was perhaps his exposure of Lugard's attempts to juggle with the native administration finances in the Northern Region—thus encouraging, in the officials of the Colonial Office, the 'alert, sceptical and repellent' frame of mind towards Lugard's proposals which characterized the Office more and more through the years.

he go too far. It is rather when addressing screeds to juniors, who are at his mercy, that an official should remember how sharp the stings of remorse can be. For juniors must not only read what he writes but try to fathom what he means also; and more, they are very generally compelled to furnish a coherent and quite understandable reply. Moreover, it is hard to bring a senior official to book for any damage he may thus work to the brains and intelligences of his juniors. Who is to know whether he is abusing pen, ink and paper and wearing down his own health and that of his staff to the detriment of all executive capacity? The juniors are far too loyal to complain, and generally, by making extraordinary efforts, succeed in pulling their chief out of the quagmire, or the ink-stand, in the nick of time.[1]

Fifty years after the event it is possible for 'dull studious persons who seem to take a pleasure in hunting out the lies of others' to apply to Lugard's writings Temple's technique of segregating the 'irrelevant facts', supplying 'the missing portions' of 'the plausible half-truths', detecting 'the apparently trifling but really very important omissions', and plodding through the maze to 'capture the lie in the centre'. Lugard wrote so much that the technique is a laborious one; but, applied to the *Amalgamation Report* and to *The Dual Mandate* and the *Political Memoranda*, it yields some startling results.

Take, for instance, one of the more specific, concrete, and therefore more verifiable of the supposed achievements on which Lugard's reputation rests—his happy initiative in discovering the site of Port Harcourt, as a port terminus for the proposed Eastern railway. There is a carefully worded account in the *Amalgamation Report* (§§ 123–4) which contrives to suggest that, whereas Lugard's predecessors like Moor had blundered and been deterred by difficulties, he, Lugard, after a glance at the map, went at once, found the right place, and developed it—brisk, energetic, masterly leadership. The story which

[1] The passage from Motley and commentary are at pp. 239–40 in C. L. Temple, *Native Races and their Rulers*, against a marginal note 'Writing, writing, writing!' Temple used the same technique of quotation to give speed, point, and direction to another of his Parthian arrows, aimed at 'The Pushful Secretary'—who appears to be Donald Cameron, Lugard's 'Central Secretary' and later Governor of Nigeria. Recounting Washington Irving's story of Abdullah ibn Saud (employed by the Prophet to write down the revelations of the Koran, who fell into disgrace through making absurd alterations and making them 'matter of scoff and jest among his companions, observing that if the Koran proved Mahomet to be a prophet, he himself must be half a prophet') Temple concludes (prophetically): 'All Secretariat officers will be glad (I used to be one myself so I know) to hear that Abdullah nevertheless was subsequently readmitted into the fold of the faithful, and was even made Governor of Egypt during the Kalifate of Omar. Verb. sap.' (Temple, p. 243).

can be pieced together from the Colonial Office archives is a very different one: but first, 'the lie in the centre'—Lugard's version:

It naturally strikes the eye when looking at the map, that the great Bonny estuary, situated in the very centre of the coastline of this area, would form an ideal port. When, however, questions of general railway policy were discussed some 15 years ago, Sir R. Moor stated that it was altogether impossible to make a port on this arm of the sea, or to obtain railway access to it, by reason of the mangrove swamps by which it was bordered. . . .

With the object of investigating this problem, I visited the Bonny Creek in December, 1912, shortly after my arrival in Nigeria, accompanied by Captain Child, R.N., Director of Marine, and Sir J. Eaglesome, Director of Railways and Works. The Bonny Bar at the entrance to the creek, 325 miles east of Lagos, shows 21 feet of water at high tide; which contrasts favourably with Forcados or Lagos. The forbidding expanse of mangrove swamps which border this great estuary for miles had apparently discouraged investigation heretofore. Deep water was found up to Okrika, 30 miles, and Sir J. Eaglesome reported that no insuperable difficulties existed to the construction of a railway terminal; he was in fact, at first sight much impressed with its possibilities.

Beyond this point the estuary was uncharted and had been little explored. It was reported that navigation was difficult. A careful survey of the whole estuary, up to and surrounding this point, was at once put in hand. In the course of this survey it was found that the deep water extended for a considerable distance beyond Okrika, and some eight miles north-west of it the mangrove swamp suddenly gave place for a distance of 1,400 yards to red cliffs 45 feet high, which appeared to offer a much better site for a railway terminus. There was at this point a fairly large basin for a harbour with deep water 200 yards across at the narrowest point. The site was cleared of dense forest, and it was found to be well adapted for the purpose, though limited in area. Further investigation established the fact that access could be obtained to the mainland, without crossing any swamp or tidal waterway—a piece of good fortune which could not have been anticipated in a district so intersected by back waters—mangrove swamps and creeks. Approval to the project was at once given by the Secretary of State, Mr (now Viscount) Harcourt, who took a keen personal interest in the scheme, and the port was named after him.

It needs only a suspension of disbelief in Lugard, and literary skill, to make of this raw material a romantic epic of adventure and discovery, such as the account given in the biography:

Lugard now sailed eastward, past the Niger mouths and along the coast. One of the main purposes of the tour was to explore the south-east coast for a site at which he could build a port. This would be the outlet for the projected eastern railway. In a canoe, drenched with sweat, Lugard and his staff probed the steamy hot creeks and mud flats, over which the canoe had at times to be hauled. A fringe of uncanny looking mangrove trees stood in the water, while behind rose the densely forested banks. Lugard and Eaglesome found the head of an inlet near Okrika which seemed suitable and which Lugard afterwards named Port Harcourt in honour of a Colonial Secretary towards whom, at that date, he still felt extremely friendly. That then virgin site is now Nigeria's second port with a population of 72,000.[1]

It is certainly the stuff of heroic mythology, but this does not seem to have been the way the site was selected at all. Lugard certainly never saw the site until after the Secretary of State had approved the project and work had started. He cuts a very sorry figure when his account is compared with the original accounts in the archives, the figure of a man unscrupulously endeavouring to gain credit due to others, and to discredit those others. Piecing the evidence together, one finds that the maligned Moor, who died in 1909, had devoted a considerable proportion of the growing revenues to building up the Marine Department under Child (who was accidentally drowned when the *Ivy*'s whaler capsized, on active service in the Cameroons campaign in 1914). One of the department's main tasks, an uncomfortable one, had been the charting of the whole coast, a labour carried on, year after year, systematically and carefully.

Lugard arrived in Nigeria, with orders to amalgamate, on 3 October 1912. His voyage from Lagos to the Southern Nigerian ports in December 1912 was a part of the formal inspection of his new dominion undertaken in a hectic and hurried five months' residence in the country before returning to spend five months in London. He left Lagos by the Government yacht *Ivy* on 2 December, with a formal, pre-arranged itinerary of inspection of the port towns, Forcados, Bonny, Opobo, and Calabar. There was no suggestion at the time of a voyage of exploration up the River Bonny; indeed, Lugard was in a tremendous hurry, throughout his five months, endeavouring to demonstrate to the Secretary of State that he could cram into this period all the travelling and inspection and office work which took other men a year to accomplish. The original report on the discovery of the site of Port Harcourt seems to have been a report by Sir John

[1] Perham, op. cit., pp. 394–5. The December weather at Port Harcourt is not so trying as this description might suggest; it is dry (average rainfall in the month is less than 2 inches), with a mean maximum temperature (*Nigeria Handbook*, 1953 edition, p. 9) of 87° and a mean minimum temperature of 73·3°.

Eaglesome[1] which makes it clear that what Lugard had in mind, on this formal tour of inspection, was the choice of one of the existing ports as the railway terminal—not the discovery of a new port site. On arrival at Forcados (the headquarters of Child's Marine Department) Lugard told Child, Moorhouse (the Provincial Commissioner, Central Province), and Eaglesome to look for deep water near high ground for a railway terminus. Child, who knew the coast, said there had been a survey of the Bonny River as far as Okrika, where there was the required combination of deep water and high ground. Child suggested that the gubernatorial party should go in the yacht straight away, and have a look at the possibility.

This was done, and the only difficulty found was the mangrove swamp, between deep water and high ground. Lugard then left, in *Ivy*, to resume his planned tour to Opobo and Calabar. After Lugard's return to Lagos, when the *Ivy* was again free, Child sent the vessel back, under Lieutenant Hughes, to survey the creeks just beyond Okrika. Hughes discovered and charted deep water for seven miles reaching right up to the forty to fifty-feet cliffs where Port Harcourt now stands. On 7 March 1913 (when Lugard was on his way to London) Eaglesome, Child, Hughes, and Cotton, the District Commissioner, made a landing, climbed up the cliffs by rope, cut a path through the bush at the top, and came out through fallow farmland on to the main road from Diabo to Omokoroshi. Eaglesome gave the Southern Nigeria Marine Department the whole credit for the discovery:

> . . . this discovery has been due to the years of careful investigation and hydrographic surveys made either by, or under the direction of Lieutenant Child, R.N., the Director of Marine . . . it is a tribute to the accuracy and care with which the maze of creeks has been surveyed by Lieut. Child assisted by officers like Lieut. Hughes that when such an unexpected call upon it—viz., the site for a railway terminus was made, the survey should not be found wanting.[2]

Lugard did not question Eaglesome's account, and later, in August 1913, he wrote again to the Secretary of State[3] suggesting (in a form

[1] Sent to Lugard in London about March 1913, and forwarded to the Secretary of State under a formal dispatch from Lugard himself, without comment, on 5 June 1913 (C.O. 583). There are some odd alterations in the date of Eaglesome's report, but it seems to have been dated by him 9 Mar. 1913.

[2] C.O. 583/3. Enclosure 2 to dispatch Nigeria no 110, Lugard to Harcourt, dated London 5 June 1913.

[3] Dispatch 183 of 18 Aug. 1913.

of words which reads strangely, when viewed against the background of his later claim of the discovery as his own) that 'great credit' was due to Lieutenant Hughes—not for the fruitful discoveries he had made, but for something not precisely stated: 'I am sure you will concur with me in considering that very great credit is due to Lieut. R. H. W. Hughes, R.N.R. who has worked indefatigably to produce this chart.'

It was in this dispatch that Lugard proposed that the new port should be named Port Harcourt, after the Secretary of State. Agreeing, Harcourt minuted: 'I hope some method may be found of making it known publicly that the name was not suggested by me, but is adopted at the express request of Sir F. Lugard.'[1]

This story of the 'discovery' by Lugard of Port Harcourt serves to illustrate his use of the technique Temple described, a use skilful enough to deceive his biographer, among many others, and to discredit the dead men (Moor, Child, and Hughes) to whose long and arduous years of careful work the real credit was due.

It is much the same story with others of Lugard's vaunted achievements. Once Temple's 'alert, sceptical and repellant' state of mind is fully aroused, the exposure of the complex web is simply a question of assiduous detective work, as the Secretary of State and his officials were to discover—but not, unfortunately, before he had been permitted to introduce, mainly as a result of his first, hectic five months' tour of the country, the measures, administrative, judicial, and legislative, which brought about, not amalgamation, but severe and lasting disorder. Examples can be given of these measures; but in what order can disorder in public administration be comprehensibly described? Even the chronological order is confused by Lugard's own reporting, long after the event; when war and peace, progress and reaction, administration and judiciary, slavery and freedom are all jumbled, even the alphabetical order offers no solution,[2] since 'A' would be for an amalgamation which did not take place, and for an amalgamator in whose eyes upheaval was 'continuity of policy' and

[1] In the *Amalgamation Report* account Lugard contrived to suggest what Harcourt, whom he now hated, wished to avoid. By a coincidence, which did not escape the C.O., the Asst. Provincial Commissioner at the time was also a Harcourt (A. B. Harcourt, I.S.O.).

[2] Mr Justice Maule (cited in *The Magistrate*, by Sir Alison Russell, p. 15)—'It may be my fault that I cannot follow you. I know that my brain is getting old and dilapidated. But I should like to stipulate for some sort of order. There are plenty of them. There is the chronological, the botanical, the geographical—even the alphabetical order would be better than no order at all.'

destruction was 'reform'. One hypothesis which seems to make sense of Lugard's acts and language and of the confusion they caused is that, continually seeking power and fame as ends in themselves, yet knowing them to be impossible to declare openly and frankly, Lugard was constantly driven to deception, to concealment, and to mystification both of others and perhaps also of himself; and, as confusion grew, the need for further concealment grew, bringing further confusion in its train.

Things began in 1912 auspiciously enough. The South prospered, the North was poor, but peaceful. Amalgamation was accepted as an overdue necessity. Lugard's fame ensured good will and general welcome to his appointment. In May 1912 occurred the last of the great Edwardian[1] dinners at which the lions of Nigerian administration were fed and praised.[2] Lugard was guest of honour, and advice was proffered to him by Goldie, by Girouard, by Hesketh Bell, by Egerton, and by John Burns (an 'old Coaster', now Cabinet Minister)—sound and characteristic advice from each, which Lugard had no intention of taking. His objective was straightforward—once again, it was 'one-man rule'—but the means to the end were labyrinthine.

His insistence upon 'the Scheme of Continuous Administration' was in keeping. Not only did it prevent his work being touched in his absence on leave by the hand of an Acting Governor, but it offered the opportunity of gaining ascendancy in London as well as in

[1] 'Edwardian' in style still, although a new reign had begun; the unmistakable style changed with the first World War's beginning.

[2] *Journal of the African Society*, vol. xi (1911–12). Dinner at the Trocadero restaurant, 16 May 1912, when the society entertained Sir Frederick Lugard. The record shows signs of a carefully prepared occasion. Sir Clement Hill, in the chair, introduced Goldie as first speaker, in the firm clear words: 'Sir George Goldie was the Founder of Nigeria.' Goldie in his speech paid tribute to others present, John Burns, Egerton, Girouard, Bell, before a brief and ironic introduction of Lugard: 'I shall not presume to dilate on Sir Frederick's great record, which is as well known to you and to the world at large as it is to me. But I know him to be as modest as he is great, and that any prolongation of these remarks must be painful to him, so I will at once propose the toast of "Nigeria" coupled with the name of Sir Frederick Lugard.' Lugard responded. Burns urged compassion, justice, and fair play instead of force, Egerton said 'push on with roads as well as railways', urged the importance of agriculture and of the mineral survey and development of the port of Lagos. Girouard described the loyal, enthusiastic staff Lugard would find in the North, and paid tribute to Strachey of the Colonial Office as 'a firm friend of all our work in Nigeria'. Hesketh Bell urged development of economic exports from the North, particularly agricultural development. Lugard closed the meeting with a few words about 'continuity of policy' being 'the very first essential'.

Nigeria. It was 'the Scheme' which made him decide (despite plenty of advice to subdivide the territory)[1] to retain the two unequal divisions of the enormous estate as they were before. Ostensibly designed to cause 'the minimum of administrative disturbance', and accepted by the Colonial Office for that reason as a temporary expedient, it was this decision which in practice let him keep all the power in his own hands. Under this arrangement, the two Lieutenant-Governors, to whom he would delegate powers in the limited field allowed to them, would carry on the routine of government, while he, as Governor-General, would retain as much control as he saw fit, at all times, wherever he might be. The salaries he proposed for them, compared with the Governor-General's salary (£6,857 p.a.), show how he saw their relation to him (£2,000 p.a., plus duty pay, £600 in the South, £400 in the North, and £1,500 plus £300 duty pay for the Administrator of Lagos). The departments placed under the Lieutenant-Governors were, for both, Medical, Public Works, Forestry, Agriculture, Education, Police, and Prisons—and the South also became responsible later for the Marine and Customs departments.

The central (or combined) departments included the Railway (railway amalgamation being of course one of the most obvious necessities), Audit, Treasury, Posts and Telegraphs, Judicial, Legal, and Survey departments.[2] Inexplicably, except as a strengthening of his own hand, he also retained at the centre Directors of Medical and Sanitary Services and of Forests and of Railways and Works to 'superintend' departments North and South, 'without interfering with their departmental organization'. These central departments were to look to the central Secretariat, but this office had 'nothing to do with political matters and native affairs', the central Secretary's functions being thus reduced to routine matters, while Lugard and his 'Political Secretary' held the strings of power which ran out to the Lieutenant-Governors direct (and to the heads of departments, and to the Chief Justice).

[1] Proposals to make anything from three to seven 'states' are mentioned in the *Amalgamation Report*. Temple proposed seven divisions, three in the North, four in the South. Of Boyle, the senior administrative officer in the South, Lugard said in his summary: 'Mr Boyle's views are so nearly identical with my own that it is unnecessary to give them separately.'

[2] The salaries adopted in 1914 for these senior posts were not princely; they included Chief Justice £1,600 + £320 duty pay, Attorney General £1,400 + £280, Treasurer £1,000–£1,200 + £200, Customs £900–£1,100 + £180, Marine £1,000–£1,200 + 200.

This was Lugard's executive dispensation, which included the supreme judicial authority as well, and, by restricting the Southern Nigeria Legislative Council to the area of the colony, he also became the legislature for almost the whole country. More must be said separately about the judicial and legislative new order, although they were never separate from the exercise of personal power, in Lugard's thinking. The logic behind these executive arrangements, if such it can be called, is that they were answers to the questions which Lugard seems always to have put to himself—perhaps not consciously—when considering any aspect of organization: 'How can I use this to preserve or increase personal power and authority, and at the same time explain my actions in the language of progress and reform?'

Thus, these executive arrangements, with their conspicuous lack of strength in the places where British colonial government was usually fairly strong,[1] seem to have flowed directly from the submission to Lugard in 1912 (as Governor of the North and Governor of the South) of the separately prepared draft estimates of the two separate administrations. Instead of appointing a man or men with appropriate knowledge and experience to devise a workable scheme, in consultation with those who had prepared the estimates, Lugard secluded himself at Offa with both sets of estimates for some three weeks of his crowded five months' tour—out of touch with all three of the Governments concerned (himself being the fourth, the new Government of Nigeria). There he re-cast the drafts to produce something nearer to his heart's desire, leaving also on record, in a private letter to Lady Lugard, his own description of his work.[2] Dame Margery Perham describes him as showing, in this work, 'an ingenuity bordering on trickery—that legitimate trickery to which most devoted colonial officials, from the District Commissioner upwards, have resorted in the interest of their people'. Questions of ethics in administration are difficult, but this was a remarkable example of introducing confusion for the sake of personal power:

I think you would laugh if I explained the lines on which I have done this thing. I amalgamate the Railways—an absolute and immediate necessity—also the Marine, equally necessary for different reasons. The bulk of the

[1] i.e. in the offices of Chief Justice and of Colonial Secretary, and in the Legislative Council.

[2] Perham, *Lugard, The Years of Authority*, p. 420. In these estimates Northern native administration Treasury surpluses were included by Lugard as part of the general revenue, which was regarded by everyone else as a most unpleasant piece of 'trickery'—see p. 211.

Public Debt I transfer to Railways on which it has been incurred, and I therefore take over the Public Debt (Interest and Sinking Fund) into my Combined Nigeria Estimates. This involves a net expenditure of about ½ a million. So I take over the Customs also (of course in each case both the Revenue and Expenditure) and as this has a Rev. of about 1½ millions, I have nearly a million at my disposal to meet the deficit of both Budgets. The S.N. revenue is reduced to £108,000 from £2,000,000 by this process! and in order to make the process palatable to S.N. I tell them that it is necessary to transfer the Customs to the Central (Combined) Estimates in order to save them paying the usual £70,000 to N.N.! They will never arrive at the fact that in reality they leave me with a large sum which I can devote to either N. or S. Nigeria as I like. . . .

If good use had been made of the revenues thus reserved, the 'trickery' might conceivably have been classified as 'legitimate', although it is hard to see its necessity, since the object, clear to all, was to unite a prosperous administration with one in deficit. But the same will to power, the same secretiveness and inability to seek expert advice ensured that Lugard's schemes for using the money were ill-judged.

A few examples must suffice, from a fairly wide range. Most striking of all, perhaps—even wilder than the proposals for moving the capital to Kaduna and some of the Lagos departments to Ebute Metta, near Lagos, and running the civil servants back and forth by special train—was the 'new ostrich industry' which Lugard determined to start in the Northern Region. For the sake of this venture Lugard cancelled the work of geological survey of the South which had been proceeding steadily since 1903, started by Moor, and carried on under the direction of Professor Wyndham Dunstan of the Imperial Institute. Dunstan himself, expressing his regret at the cessation of the survey, described the work done as 'the most fruitful economic investigation of mineral resources which has ever been conducted in a British Colony'.[1] The 'new ostrich industry'—in remote Bornu—was hardly a fair exchange; it was accurately described by the Colonial Office as 'a miserable fiasco'.[2] It seems to have been Lugard's own feather-brained idea, and he was assured before the start that it would fail. He sought to buy the birds from one Count Poniatowski, whom he had met in Paris, the head of a French syndicate which had de-

[1] C.O. 583/22.

[2] A pencilled note by A. J. Harding, dated 24 Oct. 1917, on Lugard's dispatch of 7 Jan. 1914 proposing deferment of geological survey because, *inter alia*, 'a new ostrich industry is about to be started' (C.O. 583/8).

cided to end an experiment they had been conducting in ostrich-breeding in Africa. To his credit Count Poniatowski honourably declined 'to do a trade' with Lugard, because he was sure the project would fail, as theirs had, with heavy casualties and any feathers produced unsaleable. In understandable perplexity, he replied to Lugard's offer to buy: 'What object is there to choose a country offering every possible difficulty?' Lugard wrote: 'I intend to give the matter a trial nevertheless in Nigeria.'[1] His motives remain an inscrutable mystery: it may have been a case of finding any enterprise in the North to deprive the hated South of economic benefit, it may have been a search for a valuable export which could be sent from Bornu by parcel post, there being neither railway nor road transport; it may have been some obscure symbolism of power associated with the plumes worn by proconsuls and, in Edwardian days, by their ladies. But whatever the reasons were, the failure was rapid and complete, as may be judged by the words of the administrative officer to whose lot it fell to exercise direct rule over the ostriches in their last days, in 1914, just before the war:

> The Political Officer has grown accustomed to being made a jack-of-all-trades, and I therefore showed no surprise when I had the supervision of an ostrich-farm added to my countless duties. The farm was about as successful as most State-run enterprises. French experts having failed under favourable circumstances in the north, it was not likely that an amateur was going to achieve success. . . . But the net dividend amassed from this venture was one egg, excavated from the body of a dead ostrich, which I converted to my own use, and to the entertainment of my friends, in the shape of buttered eggs for four days.[2]

So one ostrich egg can be added to the Lugard list of tragi-comic failures, which already included new capitals in the North, and light railways, and mule-breeding, and bullock-drawn and man-drawn carts—which the men concerned found easier to carry, despite their weight, than to pull or push. But if one looks at *The Dual Mandate*, published years later as a guide to African administrators, one looks in vain for any sign that Lugard might have learned from his experience; instead, one sees, at p. 532: 'Ostrich-farming, bee-keeping (a lucrative industry in India), the domestication of the elephant,

[1] The correspondence can be followed in the C.O. 583 series.

[2] *Up Against it in Nigeria*, by Langa Langa (H. Herman Hodge), p. 142. There is a photograph of the ostriches in their pens on the farm in this entertaining book of reminiscences.

eland and zebra, and the breeding of zebroid mules—all these and a hundred other problems offer inducement to the scientific investigator.' And, best of all, a footnote on the same page, in reference to the ostrich-farming: 'In West Africa, the French have experimented largely in ostrich-farming and claim success. The cost is estimated at £4 per bird per annum (Revue Coloniale, 1901).'

There is no mention of Lugard's own ostrich industry or of the outcome of the French 'experiments' subsequent to 1901—although *The Dual Mandate* was published nearly twenty years later!

But this glimpse into the 'ostrich industry' (although useful as an example of the irrational proposals which were to destroy confidence in Lugard's judgement and even raise doubts, in the Colonial Office, as to his mental health) is one of the departures from order only too easy to make in an attempt to portray disorder. Perhaps the chronological order, after all, is the best guide through the maze. At least, there is one period, Lugard's first five months' tour of inspection in 1912–13, in which he can be seen fairly clearly, before the fog of war finally made the already confused scene hopelessly obscure. Thanks to the care with which the biography documents this period of Lugard's life, there is a record of his moves and thoughts as he set about the destruction of the old order. This 'running commentary on his official activities',[1] together with the official material since released for study, shows how the tragic blunders in administration, like the more farcical ones, sprang fully formed from the autocrat's own prejudices and temperament.

Lugard arrived in Lagos on 3 October 1912, and took the oath as Governor of Southern Nigeria, administered by the Chief Justice of Southern Nigeria, Willoughby Osborne. The next day he departed for Zungeru by special train to take the oath as Governor of Northern Nigeria. At Zungeru he 'found it necessary' to explain to Temple, whom he thought 'muddle-headed', that 'he was now Secretary and I was the Governor'. Within a few days, back in Lagos, he was writing to his wife to say that he was 'not in sympathy' with 'the educated native'. 'His loud and arrogant conceit are distasteful to me, the lack of natural dignity and courtesy antagonize me.' Within three weeks he was in Ibadan, finding the local officials and traders (including the locally famous Resident, Oyo, Captain Ross) 'a bit casual', and detecting signs that the Lagos people and press were stirring up the people of Yorubaland 'to resist loss of their lands and taxation' and

[1] Perham, op. cit., p. 383.

to resist being reduced 'to the futile condition of North Nigeria'. 'They regard it with suspicion if I blow my nose, and think it means some deep-seated plot. I am beginning to think they are hopeless and that any attempt to make any reform with their co-operation is impossible.'[1]

At Ibadan he noted that the Government had paid rent for the land needed for the railway, and observed with distaste: 'Government pays to be allowed to confer benefits.' It had been MacGregor's policy to pay rent for land required for Government purposes—a deliberate and sensible policy, as well as an honest one—and the Resident at Ibadan, Captain Elgee (still remembered there with respect), had been MacGregor's Private Secretary. He had been given by Egerton a free hand to carry on MacGregor's policy of indirect rule, but 'as soon as Lugard learned that he was still working towards the goal, attributed to Sir William MacGregor, of building up little independent states'[2] Elgee was posted away from Ibadan. When he protested, he received brusque treatment from the new master: 'My policy, I said, was the very opposite of MacGregor's . . . It was time that he was made to understand the position for his head is swollen exceedingly.'[3]

So heads, swollen or muddled, were already beginning to roll. For Lugard, even before he had begun his inspection, the administration was like the Augean stables, with himself cast in the role of Hercules (as well as that of Solomon):

[1] Since Lugard's idea of 'reform' was in fact to reduce the South to 'the futile condition' of the North, and to introduce taxation, he was right to expect a lack of co-operation; and his Lagos critics were right to regard his nose-blowing with suspicion.

[2] Perham, op. cit., p. 406 (the quotations from Lugard's letters to Lady Lugard on this tour are also taken from the biography, chapter xix).

[3] In his pamphlet *The Evolution of Ibadan* (Lagos, Government Printer, 1914) Elgee left a modest and interesting record of the work which he and his predecessors had been patiently trying to achieve over the years in Ibadan. Sir William Geary made a point of mentioning in *Nigeria under British Rule* that he had deposited his personal copy of this work in the British Museum—where it still is, one of the few extant copies, if not the only one. It is an important little work, not only for the facts it contains but also because those facts cannot be reconciled with Lugard's condemnation of the Administration in general or of Elgee in particular. Their offence, in Lugard's eyes, was that these societies had not been broken in, in preparation for autocratic rule Instead, these administrators had taken seriously the 'protection' of the rights and the vitality of native institutions, and in some cases were prepared to resist the kind of domination Lugard wished to impose. So they, like the Emirs of an earlier decade, must submit or be scattered. Elgee was given a punitive posting to Ijebu Ode, where there was not even a habitable house, and rescued by the Colonial Office, who found him a West Indian appointment. He died in 1917.

In Administration there seems to be perfect chaos, and a great deal of crime and also of official incapacity, etc. Yesterday I had a case of 744 murders by ordeal, also accusations in a different district against a Gov. officer of horrible things, including aggravated rape and possible murder.... It is clear that this Administration wants regularly cleaning out like the Augean stables ...[1]

Lugard's next move from Lagos was the Odyssey to the south-eastern ports in early December. Although he did not discover the site of Port Harcourt as he claimed, he did make one startling 'discovery'—the 'discovery' that 'native policy' there was 'non-existent':

... his first impression of south-eastern administration was poor. He quickly decided that nothing less was required than 'the creation of an administration, for but little exists . . . native policy is non-existent. The two Provincial Commissioners were in practice Lieutenant-Governors who did what they pleased.... My policy is revolutionary, and these fellows do not know where they are. But I find them a nice lot and I find I have a reputation here which makes it easy for me to do what would be practically impossible for any other man.'[2]

As to the assertion that there was very little administration, this was a grotesque travesty of the facts, and a libel on his predecessors' work—belied by the very existence of ports like Calabar, with prosperous traders who impressed Lugard with their command of English, and by the Provincial Commissioners 'who were in practice Lieutenant-Governors', with their staffs of secretaries, departmental officers, and District Commissioners. Even the flourishing mission institutions, 'so many that he had to spend an extra day in order to make a really thorough inspection', were evidence of the success of his predecessors and the direct result of their policy and practice. Perhaps, since Lugard was already determined to smash the system, he could ease his conscience by pretending there was little to smash.

[1] Perham, op. cit., p. 392 (letter, Lugard to Lady Lugard, 13 Nov. 1912). The bringing to trial of cases of murder by ordeal seems to be evidence of introducing order and justice, rather than one of perfect chaos—as also, the investigation of accusations against Government officers.

[2] Perham, op. cit., p. 396, quoting what appears to be a rather 'swollen-headed' *and* 'muddle-headed' letter from Lugard to Lady Lugard, 12 Dec. 1912. In this and other quotations a key is required for the understanding of Lugard's language. Expressions like 'native policy' can usually be replaced, with benefit to the sense, by publicly and perhaps even privately unavowable expressions like 'chain of command' or 'dictatorship'. When applied to his own ideas, 'revolutionary' means 'reactionary'. 'Continuity of policy', of which he made great play later, usually meant 'doing as I say'.

Back in Lagos on 12 December 1912 after this voyage, he left again towards the end of the month, stopping at Abeokuta, where even he could not claim that administration did not exist. There a United Egba Government had been built up over the years on the model of the Lagos Government, with a Secretariat, directly recruited British officials, a printing press, official gazettes, water-works, roads, and much of the essential forms of modern government.

These arrangements, so much more businesslike than any Nigerian local government was to see again for many years, were a grave offence in Lugard's eyes. He chastised J. V. Young, the Commissioner at Abeokuta, 'with unmerciful logic' for his achievements, pointing out that his success in persuading the Alake and his council to make laws made 'our position more difficult'—(i.e. the policy of reaction and the 'smashing' of the Egba treaty). Young was apparently too taken aback, or too 'loyal', to argue with the new Governor: 'He would not gainsay me, and only urged (as all others do) that he thought he was doing what Mr W. Egerton wanted but had never been able to get any instructions and guidance.'

Lugard's conclusion, faced with this, the product of the older, more honourable tradition of indirect rule, in which the old institutions were adapting themselves to modern needs, was a revealing one: 'all I can do at present is to put a stop to progress on wrong lines and try to find a way through the wood to the right path.'[1]

But when he arrived in the Northern Emirates Lugard saw something more to his taste and liking. A 'Durbar' was arranged in his honour at Kano on New Year's Day, 1913. Here was militarism triumphant, with no unwelcome trace of merely utilitarian progress—instead, provisioned at heaven knows what cost to the country through which they had marched for weeks, there were 'some fifteen thousand horsemen, and an uncounted number of footmen, each grouped around their chief'.[2] There were 800 West African Frontier Force, and about 300 mounted infantry, with turbans and lances, and there was the galloping 'Salute of the Desert', with Emirs dismounting to kneel and make obeisance to him. Here, apparently, in contrast to the South, there was nothing to criticize; the walls of Kano were crumbling, but otherwise, when Lugard 'inspected' the city, the 'new clean prison', a new Treasury, and 'the first rather tentative

[1] Perham, op. cit., pp. 449–50 (letter, Lugard to Lady Lugard, 23 Feb. 1913).

[2] Perham, op. cit., p. 400. Lugard's own figure, in the *Amalgamation Report*, was 'some 30,000 horsemen'.

schools' were the only things of note—no need to spend an extra day here inspecting new institutions!

Lugard went on to the plateau, where he discovered 'the whole of the mining law in a muddle', with 'none of his officers' seeming to have 'any understanding of this complex subject'.[1] He felt obliged to spend 'the best part of a week hammering out the substance of a new Minerals Ordinance and new Mining Survey Rules, drafting them himself and, in the interests of the natives, forcing some unpalatable restrictions upon the mine managers'.

Then began the journey back to Lagos, via Zungeru, Onitsha, Benin, and Sapele. Lugard spent four weeks there, before sailing home to submit his amalgamation proposals. 'Lugard had not been there a week before it was reported that all the officials were at breaking point and longing for him to go and relieve the intolerable pressure.' But Lugard was satisfied on one point; he had done in five months what others would have taken a year to do:

> The amount I have learned about the Administration of S.N. and all its chief questions and also of the Adm. up to date of N.N. is much. It seems impossible that it is less than 5 months since I landed here. I think I can claim to have done a year's work in the time.

In point of fact, Lugard had started his work of destruction of Southern Nigerian government even before he landed, setting the two Chief Justices to work commenting on his proposals for changing the judicial system in a minute dated 24 September 1912, when he had seen nothing of the system he condemned without trial:

> Nor do I agree with the principle which I understand is at the base of this complicated system of Courts and Appeal Courts, viz. that the natives, who are stated to be ignorant savages, often cannibals, should be induced to believe that they are making their own laws and governing themselves. Nor do I believe that Courts upon which they are represented as dummies will induce that belief. In my view a more hopeful means of educating them to a higher standard will be to set before them a model, of which they will gradually learn to appreciate the absolute impartiality, and at the same time allow them to have courts of their own with limited powers and under the close supervision and instruction of District Officers.

The minute to the two Chief Justices was accompanied by draft legislation introducing native courts and provincial courts into the South, on the Northern model, and limiting Supreme Court jurisdiction to the colony and a few urban centres. Speed, the Chief Justice

[1] Perham, op. cit., pp. 402–3.

of the North, who must have discussed matters already with Lugard,[1] and had no court work to engage his attention, replied promptly: 'I agree with every word of His Excellency's criticisms.' Willoughby Osborne, the Chief Justice of the South, took a little longer to reply—his comments were dated 9 December 1912, and were a careful, fully considered commentary ending with alternative proposals which would have retained the existing native courts and aimed at a planned development of the Supreme Court system. This was not what Lugard wanted at all, and it was a serious setback which had a farcical as well as a serious outcome.

Lugard was now faced with the problem of finding senior men for the new Nigerian Government he was bringing into life, among them the two Lieutenant-Governors and a new Chief Justice for Nigeria, because he proposed to amalgamate the judiciary, vesting the judicial powers under the provincial court system in the Governor-General, although the two administrations were to remain separate. Of the two obvious Lieutenant-Governors, Boyle in the South was compliant,[2] while Temple in the North was not. But they were recommended for promotion to the two posts. The way was then clear for upheaval in the South, so far as the Administration was concerned. But if there was to be one Chief Justice, who should fill the post? As in the Administration, one was Lugard's man, and ready to do what he was told, while the other was not, and was already obstructing Lugard's plans.

The details of how Lugard achieved his purposes are not clear; but there is enough on record to show that Lugard in his *Amalgamation Report* gave a misleading version of the position of the Chief Justice of Southern Nigeria, the senior of the two, and the one who would in the normal course have been appointed as the first Chief Justice of Nigeria. For the purposes of his *Amalgamation Report* Lugard used only a carefully edited version of Osborne's recorded views, omitting

[1] The evidence of prior discussion is Speed's reference to these proposals as 'our proposals'. Lugard had also written with disapproval of nine cases of alleged murder in which the Supreme Court had acquitted the accused, although 'a senior and reliable officer' had 'satisfied himself that murder had been committed'. Lugard thought this brought 'the whole system into discredit'. Speed supposed, in his reply, that 'H.E. is referring to an incident I brought to his notice' and went on to make the point that the proceedings failed 'because of some technical defect'—he could not remember with certainty.

[2] 'When I read Boyle's Minutes almost invariably I say to myself "Well, that is just exactly what I think" '—Lugard to Lady Lugard, 4 Feb 1913, quoted in Perham, op. cit., p. 407.

his well-founded criticism of the Governor-General's own proposals. Briefly, the position Osborne adopted was this: first, he agreed that the Supreme Court was not the most suitable form of tribunal 'in the opening stages of civilization' chiefly because of the quality of the influx of alien legal practitioners who employed touts to foment litigation (particularly in cases of disputed ownership of lands). Lugard used this. Secondly, Osborne suggested that the solution to this problem was to limit the Supreme Court, at first, to criminal cases, at the same time taking steps to settle and validate tribal and communal boundaries. Next, after that, the Supreme Court's jurisdiction could be extended to cover civil as well as criminal cases. Meanwhile, in the areas where the Supreme Court's jurisdiction did not already extend in the South, he considered that 'Courts of the nature of Provincial Courts seem to me to afford an excellent machinery for administering justice'. Legal practitioners should not appear in provincial courts because they would not be sufficiently under the observation of the (professional) judges (of the Supreme Court). The procedure of these provincial courts should, he considered, be 'the same as that in the Supreme Court, provided that (a) all cases shall be heard summarily, (b) in no cause or matter, civil or criminal, shall the employment of a barrister or solicitor be allowed'.

Turning to the proposed native court system modelled on those in the North, Osborne gave a specific warning against removing the administrative officer: 'I am inclined to think that the present system of native courts goes far enough, and that in the important cases native tribunals require the guiding influence and impartial judgment of a European Officer.' He thought it would be better 'to leave untouched these courts', and said 'I would most strongly urge leaving cases of homicide entirely to British Courts.' He pointed out that 'the worst evil attendant on the native court system'—'the dishonesty of Court Clerks'—was not touched by the Bill, and would 'flourish under it just as badly as it does now'. These points were all omitted from Lugard's *Amalgamation Report*, and the false impression was given that both Chief Justices condemned the old system and were in favour of the new. Dame Margery Perham, accepting the Lugard version, says of the Chief Justices that 'the case against the Supreme Court must have been strong indeed to bring them in agreement with Lugard on this issue'.[1] But only one of them agreed, and it was he, the junior, who was appointed as Chief Justice of Nigeria, while the

[1] Perham, op. cit., p. 426.

senior was retired when the office of Chief Justice of Southern Nigeria was abolished.

Lugard's recommendations for filling the post of Chief Justice survive, in the archives, in a dispatch of July 1914.[1] In it he described Osborne, fairly enough, as the senior, and 'an excellent man to work with, and deservedly popular', but went on to recommend Speed for the office, in these words:

> . . . a man of much ability, and has always shown himself ready to assist the Executive in every possible way by advising on legal matters, by drafting Special Ordinances, by reviewing the Cause Lists of Provincial Courts, and by revising the Laws. I have accepted his assistance in the reorganisation of the Courts of Southern Nigeria, and in the proposals I have laid before you for the reorganisation of the Judicial Department. I feel therefore that his claims are superior to those of Mr Willoughby Osborne, and outweigh certain drawbacks.[2] Perhaps you may consider it possible to find another post for Mr Willoughby Osborne or to mark in some way your approval of his excellent work.

This put the Colonial Office in a quandary, but finally Lugard was given the Chief Justice whom he wanted. It was suggested by Harding and Strachey that Osborne be made Chief Justice and Speed Attorney-General, but neither Fiddes nor the Secretary of State thought this a good idea. What was to be done with Willoughby Osborne? A knighthood 'to help to soften the blow' was mentioned, but the decision was that he should retire on abolition of his old office, Fiddes noting 'I understand he is reconciled to the prospect.' He seems to have departed with quiet dignity. Although there were questions in the House about the judicial system, and Osborne's retirement, and petitions in Lagos, and deputations of the Anti-Slavery Society to see the Secretary of State, all of which must have helped

[1] The C.O. 583 series contains the full correspondence both on the filling of the post of Chief Justice and on the new judicial system.

[2] Lugard's report on Speed, dated 18 Mar. 1913, contained this hint of 'certain drawbacks': 'He is of a very social disposition and perhaps a little too fond of popularity', while his report on Willoughby Osborne remarked: 'So far as I can judge, he is an excellent Chief Justice.' The salary of the Southern Chief Justice was £1,500 + £300 duty pay; that of the Northern £1,000 to £1,200 + £200 duty pay. Speed, slightly the younger (Rugby and Trinity, Cambridge) was called to the Bar earlier (1893) and his first colonial appointment was as a District Commissioner, Gold Coast, in 1899 to 1900. Willoughby Osborne (Winchester and Hertford College, Oxford) was admitted solicitor in 1897, and called to the Bar in 1904. By Geary's account, the Chief Justiceship of the North was a sinecure, while the Chief Justice of the South judged day in and day out; so Speed's judicial experience and reputation were in no way comparable with Osborne's.

to delay and delay the introduction of the new system, the outbreak of war finally drowned the protests in a larger uproar.

Meanwhile, Lugard's disruption of the executive arrangements seems to have made quicker progress than his judicial system. Indeed, at the date of amalgamation, 1 January 1914, the legislation to establish the Nigerian Supreme Court had still not been passed. In April 1914 Mr. Justice Stoker, who had served under Osborne on the Southern Nigerian bench, wrote to the Secretary of State, expressing concern about the position of the judges: since there was no legally constituted Supreme Court their judgements seemed to have no sound basis; he therefore suggested reference to the home law officers. He was told in reply that all would be made well when the law came into force. He waited until the new Ordinance was passed, and then, still dissatisfied with its provisions, he decided to follow his Chief Justice into retirement, pointing out to the Colonial Office on the way that, in his judgement, the new Supreme Court had not been constituted in time to make the appointment of the Governor-General, his swearing-in by a Chief Justice who had no legal existence, and many other judicial acts, anything other than a legal nullity. But his contention was never put to the test, and Lugard's 'reforms' came into effect. Once again, as before in the North, judicial and executive functions were intermingled, with the 'executive' in control. As often, Sir William Geary had a vivid phrase to describe it: 'The Supreme Court, as constituted, might be typified by a figure of Justice whose hands are tied and whose sword is wielded by another.'[1]

The sword was wielded by the Governor-General, through the provincial court and native court system, in which legal practitioners were not allowed, and from which there was no appeal to the Supreme Court. Sentences of over six months' imprisonment required confirmation by the Governor-General, to be delegated by him as he saw fit. He chose to delegate, for the North, to the Lieutenant-Governor, and for the South, to the complaisant former Chief Justice of the North, now Chief Justice of Nigeria. The Supreme Court itself remained a system of 'professional' justice, but its hands were tied by restriction to the colony and a few urban centres, while the bulk of the population became subject to the native courts, 'supervised' in the North by the thin sprinkling of overworked Political Officers whose numbers were to dwindle during the war and whose duties were to

[1] This is taken from a note of protest from Geary to the Colonial Office in May 1914 (C.O. 583).

increase year by year—often they were many days' march away from the remoter courts, and there was not the slightest prospect of really effective supervision or of training competent and honest judges and court officials. In the South, the administrators could clearly have done more in the way of supervision, training, and example had they been left to preside, as the Southern Chief Justice had recommended. Once they were removed, the danger of the court clerks gaining too much influence was obviously increased; and so it proved.

In any event, the Southern administration, under a compliant Lieutenant-Governor, Boyle, had already been turned inside out and upside down. The three Provincial Commissioners, who had resembled 'Lieutenant-Governors' with Secretariats and departmental staff under their direct control, in their port capitals, in what seems a straightforward and rational pattern, were abolished, and their staff scattered in nine provinces, based apparently on Lugard's wish to make provinces of comparable populations, but of differing sizes, throughout the whole country. Since population was the least static and stable basis to choose, of the various possibilities open, this had little merit. It involved immediately the building of makeshift offices and houses in the new provincial headquarters, and a wholesale disruption of departmental as well as administrative activities, besides discomfort, and confusion of the old lines of authority and co-ordination.

One of the clearest illustrations of departmental upheaval is the Agricultural Department, separated from the Forest Department in 1910, with a new headquarters at Moor Plantation near Ibadan. By 1914 the department had built up four centres for research and experiment, selected as representative of the main types of soil and climate. Apart from the main centre at Ibadan, there were experimental plantations at Calabar, Onitsha, and Agege (near Lagos)—each under the control of professional officers. Lugard lost no time in making of this reasonable arrangement something of a Tom Tiddler's ground. Here is his own record of what he did to the department, taken from a dispatch to Harcourt dated 3 July 1914.[1] In this dispatch he

[1] C.O. 583. In an address on 28 May 1919 R. E. Dennett described to the African Society the difficulties of the Nigerian Agricultural Department: although under 'the able direction' of Mr. Johnson their difficulties were lack of staff and equipment; '. . . when I think of the smallness of the staff and its poor equipment, I cannot help feeling that the powers that be have little sense of their great responsibilities in this direction . . . but when it comes to the test, what more than it has done can so badly equipped a Department do?' (*Journal*, vol. xviii, p. 266).

described the unfortunate director as 'apathetic, devoid of any enthusiasm or driving power, and content to remain month after month at Moor plantation'. But his further criticism belied this beginning: 'He appears to be always demanding an increase of staff, or capital expenditure on houses, sheds, roads and bridges in the plantation instead of making the best of what he has.' Lugard was 'not impressed' by Moor Plantation: 'I see no need of a European staff consisting of the Director, Assistant Director and one Superintendent, in addition to the Mycologist and Entomologist at that place.'

So Lugard gave the director directions: he told him that the experimental plantations at Calabar and Onitsha should be 'converted into nurseries to be looked after by a Native Overseer' and the greater part of the qualified staff should be set free 'for constant travelling and supervision of the provincial gardens which I propose to create at the headquarters of every Province'. 'These views have been pressed upon Mr. Johnson, and in the report for the quarter ending March 31st I observe a great improvement, which I hope may continue.' But look at what this extraordinary proconsul had to say a few years later, in *The Dual Mandate*, on the subject of research—particularly the work of agricultural reasearch which he had treated with such little sympathy; in *The Dual Mandate* 'research' becomes one of the two 'main lines of development' (the other, equally belatedly, being 'railways'):

> The agricultural, forestry and veterinary departments need to be greatly strengthened and brought into closer and more fruitful co-operation . . . and keep abreast of progress in the home institutions such as the Imperial Institute, and the bureaux of entomology and of mycology, and the home universities.

Drawing doubtless upon the protests of the unfortunate director whose work he had smashed and whose staff he had scattered, Lugard prescribed eloquently for the future the kind of research which in the past he had stopped: 'the investigation of the chemical and bacteriological properties of different soils—the assay of mineral ores; and, above all, with ascertaining the cause and checking the spread of disease both of animals and plants, "by which literally millions of pounds are lost each year" '.[1]

As Temple said of Lugard's 'writing, writing, writing', its main purpose was to mystify and mislead, and a long sustained attempt to fathom its meaning involves risk of brain damage. The normal reader

[1] Lugard, *The Dual Mandate*, p. 502.

ought therefore to be spared a similarly detailed account of the disparities between what was done to and what was later said about the other functions to which Lugard gave special attention. Enough has been said to show the nature and extent of the damage done to the old system before amalgamation on 1 January 1914. Within a few months, with the autocrat again running his dominion from London, Nigeria was 'wallowing in the trough'[1] when struck by the storm of the first World War. In less than two years Lugard had achieved a disorder in the whole structure of government which permanently deprived him of the trust and co-operation of the Colonial Office in London and of the educated Nigerian public, and press, and raised around him a growing fence of prickly antagonism. To use Temple's metaphor, he had made for himself a quagmire from which his subordinates many times succeeded in extricating him, while Colonial Office officials exercised as much restraint over him as they could, and so reduced his opportunities for creating further disorder. The subsequent reticence of all concerned permitted the Lugards to refurbish and regild the Lugard myth, so different from the chaotic reality of war-time Nigeria.

The general loss of confidence in Lugard, so far as the public service in Nigeria and in the Colonial Office was concerned, was sufficiently slow to develop into dogged opposition, but gathered momentum when his proposals were adopted and their implications fully appreciated. It was, of course, the governed who first showed the necessary 'alert, sceptical and repellant' attitude—particularly the educated classes who knew how comfortable the old regime had been, and where the new shoe pinched. They were not misled by his written descriptions of the old administration of the South where they lived, nor by the myth of his past achievements in the North—for various good reasons those Southerners who had tried to live there had found it uncongenial and often physically painful. As early as the end of Lugard's first five months' tour the Lagos press had decided that their new master had 'anti-black proclivities', 'a distant attitude to all men in general', and suffered from 'negrophobia' in particular.[2] The judgement was just, although often expressed in exaggerated language. It is proved by the exaggerated language in which Lugard himself gave vent to his hatred of the educated Nigerian and the people of Lagos

[1] Clifford's description of the state of affairs at the outbreak of war.

[2] *Lagos Weekly Record* 8 Mar. 1913—see Perham, op. cit., p. 585 for full quotation.

in particular: 'These people here are seditious and rotten to the core . . . the people of Lagos are the lowest, the most seditious and disloyal, the most prompted by purely self-seeking money motives of any people I have met.'[1]

For the Lagos public every major proposal and every major act of the new Governor added confirmation of his autocratic tendencies, his negrophobia, and his desire to reduce the people to submissive slavery—the amalgamation proposals first, with their destruction of the judicial system, the inauguration of provincial courts, the reduction of the embryo Parliament to the status of a municipal board,[2] the attempt to impose water-rate in Lagos, and then direct taxation, the abolition of Egba independence, the quarrel over the position of the Oba of Lagos, the proposal to enforce Government inspection of private schools, a proposed censorship of the press, a mounting total of disturbances, repressed with increasing severity. These were the chief incidents in the remaining years of Lugard's administration, and each was a proof to the educated élite of Lugard's despotic tendencies. Some of the proposals 'leaked' to the press from the Lagos and Zungeru offices, which added to public bitterness and Lugard's own increasing exasperation.

Tragically, and largely because of Lugard's reputation, both the Colonial Office and the Nigerian service were slower to realize the simple fact that Lugard's actions spoke louder than his written words; they were evidently deceived too by 'his charming manner and an appearance of bluff honesty',[3] and slow to suspect in an English gentleman the horrible traits which the governed were quick to detect. But realization dawned, and grew to conviction, and then to appalled opposition—but it was after the amalgamation proposals had been accepted that the revulsion against Lugard seemed to reach up through the Colonial Office from the juniors right up to the Secretary of State himself.

It was not so much Lugard's autocratic tendencies which offended the Colonial Office of the day as a growing disbelief in his veracity

[1] Perham, op. cit., p. 594—letter, Lugard to Lady Lugard, 9 Dec. 1916.

[2] Lugard himself became the legislature for the whole protectorate, leaving the Legislative Council, which he disdained personally to attend, practically no scope; as a final insult, its membership was made the same as that of the Lagos Town Council. For Nigeria as a whole, a Nigerian Council was set up, to meet once a year, with no function other than the respectful hearing of an address by the Governor-General.

[3] Temple—see p. 184.

and competence. Autocratic 'men on the spot' were nothing new in the Office's long experience of rule, which was almost by definition autocratic, at least in the earlier stages of each of the colonial territories. Indeed, compared with the most troublesome colonial legislatures, the autocrat, provided he retained his sanity and was amenable to Colonial Office direction, was at times useful in getting things done. In this case the thing to be done was a rapid and workmanlike job of amalgamation which would free the Office from the embarrassing and shaming necessity of annual begging from the Treasury and reporting of failure to make ends meet. The Office did not want the whole future of the country to be determined in the process, or 'Solomon's Seal' to be affixed to it; all they wanted was that it should be put into working order and made viable. This a practical autocrat might have done. When they had such a man, it was the Office's practice, or tendency—in the last resort, in protection of their Minister—to attempt, by close scrutiny of his proposals, to supply from within the Office the checks and balances to autocratic excess that were otherwise wanting. But even in the early days, as early as October 1912, the Office was detecting signs in some of Lugard's routine correspondence of a disposition 'to prejudge questions of the future divisions of his kingdom'—before his amalgamation proposals were received and considered. They were therefore increasingly on their guard during 1913.[1] By the end of that year they had decided that Lugard could not be trusted; but it was too late.

Lugard's main amalgamation, submitted on 9 May 1913, soon after his return to London from his five months of inspection of Nigeria, had been generally approved in a reply from the Secretary of State dated 2 September; an approval the Colonial Office was bitterly to regret. The proposals were greeted with very modified rapture:

Sir F. Lugard's proposals contemplate a state which it is impossible to classify. It is not a unitary state with local government areas but with one Central Executive and one Legislature. It is not a personal union of separate colonies under the same Governor like the Windwards, it is not a Confederation of States. If adopted his proposals can hardly be a

[1] It was in the most detailed field of administration—public service affairs—that Lugard's failings seem first to have come to light; the Colonial Office in 1913 received from him recommendations for promotion of officers, with confidential reports, which prompted Anderson to say: 'either these are lying and malicious statements or these men are unfit for promotion'. Other recommendations were 'absurd': 'The whole affair lowers one's impression of Sir F. Lugard's common sense', etc. C.O. 583/4.

permanent solution and I gather that Sir F. Lugard only regards them as temporary—at any rate in part. With one man in practical control of the Executive and Legislative organs of all the parts, the machine may work passably for sufficient time to enable the transition period to be left behind, by which time the answer to the problem—Unitary State v. Federal State—will probably have become clear.

This was Strachey's comment—interesting, in its contemplation, for a brief moment, of the long-term problems of nation-building, before a relapse into the customary short-term pragmatism of British colonial policy. On the 'Scheme for continuous administration' he had nothing good to say:

The plain fact is that the Governor cannot really govern from England, where he has no machinery of government and no advisers . . . If a crisis occurs, either now or under the proposed scheme, the whole fabric of pretence will collapse like a house of cards.[1]

Fiddes, sending the proposals on to Sir John Anderson, also took the opportunity to criticize 'the Scheme', observing that its worst feature was that the Colonial Office wouldn't know what was wrong until things collapsed. Anderson, having kept the file from 27 June to 15 August, submitted the proposals to the Secretary of State saying that he had discussed them with Lugard, and saw no reason why they should not be tried:

All the arrangements are of course tentative and this should be emphasised, but I can see no reason why until we can have a complete consolidation for which they will pave the way they should not work. They are anomalous of course, but so are the circumstances . . . we should give it a trial in a liberal spirit. As to Gov. Gen. I see no reason why if he is keen on it he should not have it. But he won't get any more guns or bars of the national anthem.

Harcourt agreed on this basis, and the dispatch went downstairs to the Governor-General-to-be:

The great advantage of your proposals is that they involve little change and . . . can be modified or developed at any time. . . . I have been much impressed with the ability and industry with which you have conducted your investigations and drawn up your report.

Lugard was to receive few more words of praise from this source. Evidence accumulated that he was discouraging his subordinates by

[1] C.O. 583. Minute by C. Strachey 21 June 1913. Against the reference to 'the Scheme' there is an initialled note in pencil by Strachey dated 15 June 1915: 'This actually occurred at the outbreak of war when Sir F. L. was in England, August 1914.'

not allowing them to settle even trivial points by themselves, by making them refer everything to him when he was in England, even by forbidding them to visit the Colonial Office when on leave. When the Office discovered the existence of this last instruction, he was ordered to cancel it—the Office regarded it as a method of concealing from them the views of the 'men on the spot', and Lugard's attempted explanation as 'very lame'. The tone of Lugard's dispatches became more fretful as his attempts to consolidate his power were thwarted; the 'fretful tone' was at first charitably put down to the state of his health, but not for long. On a dispatch of 26 October 1913, in which Lugard sought power to legislate without prior approval from the Secretary of State, Anderson wrote:

I do not think that one man however wise and able should have the uncontrolled power of legislating for millions of people, and that is what Sir F. Lugard claims, as his Ex. Co. may consist of only two of his officials who are not likely to offer any strenuous opposition to a masterful Governor like Sir F. Lugard.[1]

But the last straw seems to have been the discovery of Lugard's 'trickery' with the estimates, whereby he calmly took the surplus of the Northern native administration treasuries into the general revenue of government. Strachey had been sent out to Nigeria at the end of 1913—perhaps the first duty visit to Nigeria of a serving member of the Office[2]—to attend the amalgamation ceremonies and tour the country. It was a fruitful visit; he wrote from Zungeru to the Office:

I want to warn you to be particularly careful about scrutinizing all Sir F's proposals about the Native Treasury monies—I learn from Temple, Palmer and others that he wants or intends to spend some of this money on general service . . . Keep a sharp eye, I beg, on this affair.

A sharp eye was kept, from that moment on, as soon as Lugard's 'trickery' was suspected; when it was discovered and reported to him Harcourt wrote, in February 1914: 'This is all very puzzling and unpleasant.' Lugard's explanation was sought, and not accepted—'this sort of thing savours too much of trickery' (Anderson), 'it is an unpleasant business' (Fiddes), and 'in view of this correspondence I do not see how Sir F. Lugard can be safely trusted in future without

[1] This seems to be the dispatch mentioned in the biography (p. 610) from which Lugard was persuaded by his brother to delete a sentence offering his resignation.

[2] A visit 'opposed' by Lugard—Perham, op. cit., p. 412—'he found the sight of this enquiring visitor disturbing.'

some check on his proceedings' (Strachey). Forced into a corner, Lugard attempted when he reached London in the spring of 1914 to explain why he had felt entitled to help himself to the native administration money-boxes, in a memorandum to Harcourt which can be taken either as a piece of special pleading or as a confession that Lugard's real conception of indirect rule fell squarely into Temple's third and worst category—not direct, nor genuinely indirect, but a dishonest use of indirect rule as an expedient leading to the establishment of a complete alien control:

> My object was the creation of dependent States, guided and controlled by British Officers. I had not aimed at 'financial independence' viz. that the principal chief of each petty State should have power to spend a sum of money amounting in aggregate to half the Revenue, and that no expenditure from this moiety should be incurred without their concurrence. . . . The measure of responsibility which I had considered to be immediately advisable extended to practically the entire control, under the Resident, of the whole of the machinery of the subordinate Native Administration (the fixing of salaries of all Native officials, their appointment, dismissal etc.) the conduct of all Native Courts and of the Prisons and Native Police, the settlement of practically all land questions except such as affect aliens, and a limited power to originate minor capital works.

After this incident, there was a new bitterness in the Office's attitude to Lugard.[1] They questioned his financial figures, the reported numbers of casualties in punitive patrols, and, repeatedly, they detected efforts by Lugard in the field of service promotions to prejudice officers' careers, or to force the hand of the Secretary of State. Meanwhile Harcourt, urged on by Lady Lugard, made some attempt to protect her husband from the department's wrath—until in July 1914 Lugard was misguided enough, while on a visit to Belfast, to address words of encouragement to a regiment of Belfast Volunteers threatening rebellion against the Liberal Government's policy of Home Rule for Ireland. This was not unnaturally regarded by Harcourt as 'a very grave breach of the best traditions of the Colonial Service'. Lugard's apology was accepted, however, and Harcourt contented himself with a letter of rebuke which ended: '. . . this incident must in the future gravely affect my estimate of the value of your judgment and discretion.'[2]

[1] 'The attitude of the officials had hardened further: their comments became more caustic; they were quick to seize upon the not infrequent confusions caused by the mislaying of papers.' Perham, op. cit., pp. 621–2.

[2] There is a full account in Perham, op. cit., pp. 622–6.

This letter of rebuke was dated 16 July 1914. Within three weeks Britain was at war with Germany, and so was Nigeria, with a neighbouring German territory on her eastern boundary, hundreds of miles of undefended territory, her Governor-General in London in disgrace, and no one in the country empowered to plan and decide emergency measures in his absence. Incredibly, Lugard chose this moment to ask the Secretary of State for two favours: the first was *carte blanche* to introduce direct taxation in the South, the second was that the Colonial Office draft for him a law to control the Lagos press—using the war as excuse for both measures. Harcourt dismissed the first as 'a ludicrous suggestion in such a crisis as this. Sir F. Lugard had better get back to Nigeria and deal with actualities.'[1] The second was described as 'a positively grotesque idea' and firmly refused.

The war years brought their own massive contribution to the tragic confusion begun by Lugard's success in destroying and failure to remould the old system of government. The war brought a thickening of the fog, increased hardship and strain to an administration already thoroughly convulsed, public service casualties, discontents, inflation, shortages of shipping, of staff, of materials and foodstuffs, paralysis of trade and development, financial difficulties—and in the long run, the destruction of the whole system of international trade. These were piled on top of the confusion brought about by Lugard's partially successful, partially thwarted efforts to establish autocratic one-man rule; his reporting of his performance was to add to the confusion, and the whole forms a tangled mass which defies analysis.

Nigerian administration had to bear the brunt not only of the war

[1] Among these 'actualities' was the unfortunate 'Ijemo massacre' when troops fired on demonstrators in Abeokuta Province—an incident which led to the abrogation of the Egba treaty of independence in 1914. In refusing Lugard's request for 'the same discretion and initiative' as he had been allowed in the North to introduce direct taxation in the South the Secretary of State stressed the importance of doing nothing unnecessary during the war which might tend to cause unrest—'so the general question of direct taxation in the Southern Provinces . . . should stand over for the present'. Later, the Colonial Office gave way to Lugard's dogged insistence, and allowed him to introduce direct tax in Yorubaland, and serious outbreaks of disorder followed. Another 'actuality' was the war itself, but Harcourt could hardly have foreseen that as soon as Lugard arrived he would secure the removal of the officer commanding the Nigerian forces and write to his wife: 'I am more or less doing Commandant as well as Governor.' This did not prevent his believing that he never 'in any remote degree' interfered with military commanders!

with Germany but also the brunt of Lugard's private wars, as he sought to impose his will. There was the war with the Colonial Office (well described in the biography, from a point of view sympathetic to Lugard, but not blindly so); there was the war with Temple, a constant struggle to break down the freedom and local initiative and financial independence of the native administrations; there was constant war in Southern Nigeria and Lagos against the old ideas and beliefs which survived the destruction of the old legislative, judicial, administrative, and departmental pattern of government. There was the related struggle by Lugard—thwarted chiefly by the larger war, but also by bitter opposition—to convert 'education' into a means of autocratic discipline, to replace 'unreliable' and 'half-educated' Southerners in the railways and in the civil service by West Indians in large numbers, and to muzzle the Lagos press.

In the North of the time, there was a writer of genius serving in the Administration, Joyce Cary, who was able later to recreate, in his fiction, the atmosphere of the places in which he served, giving a vivid impression of the lives of the administrators, clerks, traders, chiefs, and people—drawn from real life, although a life so strange as now to seem unreal. His political writings give an equally vivid impression of the effect, upon a sensitive and perceptive mind, of experience as a district officer expected to administer, govern, supervise, and develop large areas—without experience, without money, without staff, often without any regular contact with the outside world. One can judge how different the practice of such men was from the role which Lugard had planned for them. Unfortunately, there was no writer of comparable stature to record the scene in the South. But there was one occasion, just after Lugard's departure, when the whole service was allowed by Lugard's more liberal successor to let off the accumulated steam of these years of frustration and discontent. This occasion, described in the next chapter, was the appointment of the first of several important commissions whose recommendations on salaries and conditions of service have at intervals re-shaped the public services of Nigeria. The first of these shaped public administration for the next quarter of a century, and the evidence given before it is the most vivid accessible record of an exceptionally silent service's tribulations in nearly seven lean years of Lugard.

Lugard himself, baffled in his endeavours to impose his will in its entirety on Nigeria, and succeeding only in the creation of worse disorder as the years went by, left Nigeria for the last time at the end of the war, believing that the Colonial Office 'would be delighted to see the last of him',[1] and resolved to re-create 'on paper and in the minds of men' the public image of a great administrator, whose achievement was impaired only by the opposition and enmity of misguided inferiors at home and abroad.

[1] See Perham, op. cit., p. 635.

# CHAPTER VIII

## Administocracy, 1918–1948

You cannot have an A1 administration on a C3 budget.
Sir George Fiddes.

IN 1920 Nigerian revenues topped £5 million for the first time, when the population was about 20 million. In 1938–9 Nigerian revenues (although for various reasons the figures are not strictly comparable) stood at less than £6 million, while population had risen to something like 25 million. Public service emoluments never rose much, if at all, above £1 million per annum. This was administration on a shoe-string. There was no more than 5*s*. per head of population, for all the current needs of central government, for many of the purposes of local government, and for heavy interest charges on loan capital,[1] mostly used to improve the transportation services on which the whole prospect of prosperity and increasing revenues depended. But behind these simple figures of a poverty-stricken administration (whose short and simple annals can too readily be mistaken as proof of negligence, or poverty of ideas, or plain stupidity), there is a complex ecological background. The administocracy which was to rule Nigeria for more than a quarter of a century, although it looks from the standpoint of the sixties rather rudimentary, skeletal, and static, was in fact no fixed 'scaffolding' or 'steel grid' of alien law and order, as often suggested, but something much more elastic, organic, human, frail perhaps, but resilient, the product of hundreds of major and minor decisions and adaptations to the prevailing poverty. Its shaping required a good deal of ingenuity and unremitting labour. In a more favourable economic climate than the twenties, the thirties, and the forties provided, these efforts would have reaped a richer harvest, and

[1] In 1938 it was estimated that, by 1934, £23 million of external capital had been invested in the Nigerian railway, out of a total external investment of £75 million. Much of the borrowing by the Government for the railway took place in the early twenties, on a long-term basis, when interest rates were high, and even with the guarantee of the British Government Nigeria had to pay up to 6 per cent—a heavy recurrent charge on slender revenues, setting a sharp limit to the financing of development through loans (*African Survey*, 1938 edition, p. 1324).

the administrative structure would have lost its starveling appearance. As things turned out, revenues between the wars were never ample. In the worst years of the economic depression there was even the gruesome spectacle of the skeleton administration tightening its belt.

The chief architects of Nigerian administocracy were Sir Hugh Clifford,[1] Lugard's successor, and Donald Cameron, the first Chief

[1] Sir Hugh Charles Clifford, born 1866, died 1941. Clifford was unique among Nigerian Governors, in that his background was neither 'simple' nor 'middle class' nor 'gentle', but 'noble'. A peer's grandson, son of a general (a Crimean war V.C.), Clifford was educated at Woburn Park, a private school of Catholics run by a priest who was himself a peer, Lord Petre. Intended originally for the army, he passed the Sandhurst examination, but changed his mind and joined the civil service of the Malay States, at the age of 18. Five years later, in 1887, he induced the Sultan of Pahang to accept a British agent in his state, and was appointed in the following year as the first British Resident, Pahang. He remained in Malaya until 1899, becoming expert in Malay, co-author (with Sir Frank Swettenham) of the first Malay dictionary, and author of several novels and books with a Malayan background. The novels are a key to the character and ideals of the man. Vivid, romantic, and dramatic almost to the point of melodrama, they show Clifford's love of the Malay scene and people. His heroes are white men and brown, usually adventurous, passionate men of feeling and compassion as well as men of honour; his villains are usually cruel, vicious brown and white oppressors and exploiters of the peasantry, not unlike some of the evil characters portrayed by Joseph Conrad, whose friend Clifford was. One novel in particular—*A Freelance of our Time*—bears some resemblance to Conrad's *Lord Jim*, and like it would make a stirring adventure film. Of his West African writings, the most important are his addresses to the Nigerian Council—the most lively and eloquent official papers in Nigerian administrative history—and his short book *The German Colonies: a plea for the native races*. This is exactly what the title suggests. Clifford's first wife died young, and his only son was killed in the first World War. His second wife, Mrs. Henry de la Pasture, was a successful novelist and dramatist. His step-daughter was the novelist E. M. Delafield. Descriptions of Clifford in the memoirs of Sir Donald Cameron, Sir Alan Burns, Leonard Woolf, and Sir Ralph Furse supplement Sir Richard Winstedt's description of him in the *Dictionary of National Biography* as a man of 'charming, forceful but never dictatorial personality'. Clifford was appointed Governor of North Borneo in 1899, but resigned in disagreement with the North Borneo Company's policy. He returned to Malaya as a Resident, but was promoted Colonial Secretary, Trinidad, in 1903, and Colonial Secretary, Ceylon, in 1907. Governor, Gold Coast, 1912–18, Nigeria 1919–25, and Ceylon 1925–7, in 1927 he returned to his first love, Malaya, as Governor of the Straits Settlements and High Commissioner for Malaya. But a final tragedy was about to overtake him; he became subject to fits of cyclical insanity, and a collapse in 1930 led to his resignation and permanent withdrawal from public life. He died in December 1941 'fortified by the rites of Holy Church' at the very moment when his beloved Malaya was being overrun by Japanese invaders. His widow and his step-daughter also died during the war. It is a great pity that his remarkable life has not been written, and that he was unable to write it himself in peaceful retirement; it was lived intensely, on the heroic scale.

Secretary. Clifford was perhaps the strongest card the Colonial Office could have played, at the time, from their much-shuffled pack of experienced proconsuls. When he arrived in Nigeria in 1919 he was faced with a desperate case of a sick administration, whose ailments he diagnosed and described with frankness, eloquence, and accuracy. The acute disorders due to neglect, overwork, and practical starvation he was able to cure by prompt and energetic action, but within the time and the pitifully meagre financial resources at his disposal it was beyond human ingenuity to do more than cure the most dangerous diseases and point the way towards a more complete recovery. Meanwhile, the Gold Coast administration, which Clifford had just handed over in a far healthier condition to an able successor, Sir Gordon Guggisberg,[1] was able to go ahead immediately with the first colonial ten-year plan of development. Nigeria was in no fit state to embark on any such programme. The first necessity was to get a prostrate and enfeebled administration on its feet again. The medical metaphors are not inapt, and some were used by Clifford himself. The patient was suffering from a variety of ailments which included a serious loss of memory, 'paralysis', and 'atrophy' of important organs.

Recovery was gradual and difficult. It was Clifford and his chief helper, Cameron, not Lugard, who had the herculean task of cleaning out an Augean stables of administrative chaos, after eight years of one-man rule without any proper central machinery of government. The public service—British and African—had been brought to the brink of despair by a long process of worsening conditions, and had little confidence that their situation would be improved. These were the chief internal difficulties matched by external difficulties which no Governor, however gifted, could do much to solve.

First, the internal difficulties: to describe the *damnosa hereditas* left by Lugard as a state of administrative chaos is no exaggeration. There is plenty of authoritative evidence and testimony, although it is not to be found in the writings of Lugard and his school. Clifford himself described the organizational state as he found it, in his address to the

[1] The pre-war Director of Surveys, Southern Nigeria, one of the more fortunate members of the Nigerian civil service who managed to escape from civil duty to win promotion and distinction in the armed services which qualified them for civil advancement after the war. In Guggisberg's case both were well deserved, but this was one of the discouragements which increased the discontent of the less fortunate men who had had to stay in their civil posts in Nigeria, badly paid, rarely promoted, overworked, and apt to be suspected by the ignorant as men dodging their patriotic duty to fight the war.

Nigerian Council on 29 December 1920,[1] in words which confirm Sir Donald Cameron's later comment that, in the Lugard era, there was no 'organisation' at headquarters:

> Under it [i.e. the old 'system'] the officer for the time being discharging the duties of Governor of Nigeria is daily borne down by masses of routine work, often of the most detailed and trivial character, while the absence of any central record office and of any machinery for the co-ordination of the work done by the three independent and mutually unconnected Secretariats frequently imposed on him duties of a semi-mechanical and more or less preparatory character, such as would in any other Tropical Dependency automatically be performed for him in the office of a Colonial Secretary.

In the same address, in which Clifford announced that the Secretary of State had approved the creation of the Nigerian Secretariat and Cameron's appointment as Chief Secretary to the Government, he paid tribute to Cameron and the officers of the old central Secretariat for the assistance they had given him: 'in circumstances of much difficulty and disadvantage they have discharged duties that properly belong to the office of a Colonial Secretariat—work which their Department was never designed to perform.' He went on to describe how 'over-centralisation' had had 'a paralysing effect' on the public service, had caused 'a rigid severance' between the political and non-political branches, with some Residents being reduced to 'mere ciphers', restricting their activities to the supervision of local affairs and duties on the bench of the provincial court. The 'non-political' officers were often unable to act because of the fears expressed to them by Political Officers that uncontrolled non-political activities would give rise to political complications. He condemned the decision to remould the South on the lines of the Northern native administra-

[1] This was the longest of Clifford's addresses to the Nigerian Council, written and laid on the table of the council (not read to the council, for this would have run to many hours) at the end of his first tour of service. The address—more than 300 pages of print—covered each of the major problems: the 'inutility' of the council itself, and the need to replace it by a more effective Legislative Council which would be able to exert a real influence on the Government; the remodelling of the administrative machine; the problems in personnel and *matériel* of the public service, and the revision of public service conditions and salaries; the field of 'indirect rule' in each of the main areas of the country; questions of departmental policies, including the state of the railway, agricultural development and research, plans for transport improvement, educational problems, health problems, and the need to overcome the superstitions about the West African climate. The whole was a brilliant and eloquent review, and is essential reading for an understanding of the Nigeria of the period.

tion as an attempt 'to build on quick-sand', instead of using the actual institutions of the people which still existed. He praised the old practice of his 'old friend, Sir Walter Egerton' and regretted the abolition of House Rule, with nothing put in its place. House Rule had been in many places 'an essential foundation stone . . . beneath the edifice of native policy and society', and its abolition had produced 'deplorably disintegrating and demoralising results'.

Cameron's description of the Lugard system stressed the contrast between it and the later organizational reforms, and Clifford's part in them rather than his own:

Up to August 1919 I should have left Nigeria with no regrets at all, but in 1924 I was very sorry to leave the well ordered setting of a successful administration and a respected chief. For some seven years up to 1921 Nigeria had been working without a Secretariat, without any co-ordinating machinery, without a central office in which the decisions of the Government, with their pertinent papers, might be recorded.[1]

He made his opinion of 'one-man rule' quite clear: 'There was thus no co-ordinating link save the memory of one man, the Governor, and that memory would naturally disappear with him when his term of office was concluded . . . There was in fact no "organisation" at headquarters.'[2]

The testimony of Clifford and Cameron is confirmed by the comments of another observer who had been for a time Lugard's Private Secretary, later acted as A.D.C. to Clifford, and served under Cameron in the Nigerian Secretariat; in his spare time he sought to fill the gap in the Administration's memory by writing the first *History of Nigeria* and the first *Nigeria Handbook*. Later still, he was Nigeria's Chief Secretary and, while Governor of the Gold Coast, acted also, in 1942, as Governor of Nigeria. This was Sir Alan Burns, who, writing after Lugard's death, described him in terms both more respectful and less reserved than those used by Clifford and Cameron:

He was a great man and a great governor, but he was unable to leave details to his subordinates and wasted much of his time on trifling work that others could have done for him. As a result his desk was always over-

[1] D. C. Cameron, *My Tanganyika Service and Some Nigeria* (London, 1939), p. 16.

[2] Cameron, op. cit., p. 142. An example of loss of memory quoted by Clifford was the 'recognition' of the Oba of Lagos: he discovered—after deciding the issue—that his political advisers had throughout been unaware of an important dispatch by Sir William MacGregor, which explained the issue fully, and had proposed and defined 'recognition' of the Oba.

crowded with papers, through which he worked steadily but slowly. Many a time, at the suggestion of impatient Secretariat officers, I have moved an urgent file to the top of the pile of papers on his desk, only to find it replaced later in the exact position from which I had moved it.[1]

All this represented organizational confusion, which could be, and was, fairly speedily reduced to order by organizational changes, including clearer lines of delegation and division of functions, and the creation of efficient Secretariat machinery. The human problems of a weary and disenchanted public service were not so quickly solved. They could have been solved by financial assistance from outside, on a fairly modest scale—a few hundred thousand pounds a year for Nigeria would undoubtedly have transformed the whole situation, permitting reasonable salaries, better living conditions and health conditions, and giving the service some reassurance and confidence in the future. But no such help was forthcoming; 'dependent' territories had to be independent, if at all possible.[2]

Within a few days of his arrival, Clifford had the surprising experience of meeting several members of his new Executive Council (which as a body he had not yet met) in the guise of a deputation from the Council of the newly formed Association of European Civil Servants—known to the service, from its birth near the time of the Russian revolution, as 'The Bolshie Society'. One of the deputation was the central Secretary, Chief Secretary, and Governor-to-be, Donald Cameron. They were intent on describing to the new Governor (as he put it in his 1920 address) 'without compromise or paraphrase . . . the state of feeling in the Public Service as they at that time believed it to be'. A few days later, a similar deputation from the (African) Civil Service Union, headed by Mr. Bright-Davies of the Customs Department, waited upon the Governor to describe their position to him, as he said 'very moderately and temperately, but with considerable force'. The case of the Civil Service Union was that proposals recently

[1] Sir Alan Burns, *Colonial Civil Servant*, p. 54. In the preface to his *History of Nigeria* Burns remarked that it was 'almost impossible' for him to find information about Southern Nigeria; the effect of Lugard on the South was severe concussion, followed by amnesia from which there was no complete recovery.

[2] The Colonial Office controlled no funds for helping needy territories, and if some administration could prove that imminent collapse would occur without help—a difficult thing for a collapsing administration to set out in orderly particulars—an approach would be made to the Treasury, which with reluctance and stern displeasure might—or might not—dole out a minimum sum, demanding full account and explanation of every penny; the process was made difficult enough to be a deterrent.

made for the improvement of African salaries (by Donald Cameron and Henry Carr) did not meet their needs.

With no proper Secretariat, the Governor was thus faced with a service at what one contemporary writer called 'flash-point', when he had no means of knowing what the Government could afford in the way of relief. He called on Cameron[1] to find out, as best he could from the widely scattered details in the various secretariats and departments, what the Government's financial commitments and prospects were. This done, the next step was to appoint Cameron ('the only member of the Public Service who possessed at once sufficient personal knowledge of general affairs, and of the financial position, to render possible the efficient discharge of this particular duty') to head a five-man committee, whose task was to complete within three months a revision of European salaries and conditions, first taking evidence throughout the country. The committee included some of Cameron's 'Bolshie' colleagues. Meanwhile, with strikes taking place and others threatened, the Director of Medical Services was appointed to head a new committee (containing Civil Service Union representatives) to revise African salaries. The case of the African civil service was met within a few weeks, by the doubling of an existing 30 per cent War Bonus, after emergency Executive Council meetings and telegrams to the Secretary of State, followed by a more complete overhaul of salary structure. The needs of the higher public service of the time were not so simple. Long afterwards, Cameron said that the

[1] Sir Donald Cameron, born 1873, in British Guiana, son of sugar planter; his Irish mother dying when he was young, he was brought up by grandparents in Dublin and educated at Rathmines School, Dublin; he joined the British Guiana Inland Revenue Department as a clerk in 1890, later transferring to the Secretariat and gaining promotion through the clerical ranks. In 1904 he transferred to Mauritius, and acted at times as Colonial Secretary. Acid comment by Cameron on the inefficiency of Mauritians in the civil service (while speaking in the legislature) caused a political row, and Cameron was glad to accept transfer to Southern Nigeria in 1908. He acted as a Provincial Commissioner, and as Colonial Secretary. Lugard made him central Secretary in 1914—an appointment he did not find satisfactory; Sir Alan Burns said in his *D.N.B.* article that Cameron 'never really forgave Lugard' for putting him into this post. After service as Chief Secretary and Clifford's right-hand man from 1919–24, Cameron became Governor of Tanganyika, returning to Nigeria as 'depression' Governor in 1931. Like Burns, Cameron was one of the many 'West Indian' administrators who did not come into the service through Sir Ralph Furse's process of selection, but were conspicuously more able in Secretariat duties than the average of the Colonial Office's Oxbridge graduate recruits. Like Clifford, Cameron lost a son killed in action (in the Second World War), and his last years were saddened by his wife's death and increasing blindness. He died in 1948.

conditions which his committee revealed were 'frankly disgraceful', while Clifford described the ills as 'too deep seated for their elimination to be anything save a gradual process'.

It is clear from the Governor's own description, from the evidence presented to the committee, from the committee's own report, and from contemporary published writing, that the public service was at loggerheads with itself, with the public, with traders, with miners, with everybody and everything. The African juniors were expressing their discontent in strikes, the European seniors were openly disaffected. Clifford's own public diagnosis is contained in his address to the Nigerian Council in December 1920. He traced the 'sourness of temper' and the 'disgruntled spirit' which he had found permeating the service back to the 'atrophy' of the pre-war process of 'steady and carefully calculated annual expansion, alike in *personnel* and *matériel*' to meet expanding public demands on the service. This atrophy he ascribed to the effect of the outbreak of war on a Nigeria then in the middle of the process of amalgamation, and thus caught by the storm while 'wallowing in the trough'. He went on, sparing Lugard's reputation by stressing the 'inevitability' of the subsequent failure of the Government machine to keep pace with the demands made on it, to describe the state at the end of the war:

The conclusion of hostilities found the Departments of the Government of Nigeria manned by a large proportion of worn and weary men. Those who had had an active share in the fighting were not always in the worst case. It was bitterly hard for many Englishmen, torn insistently by public anxieties and too often by heart-breaking private griefs, to plod on patiently through those years of trial, buried alive in some out-lying cranny of the Empire, devoting their energies to a round of comparatively trivial duties—as many deemed them—prolonging their tours month after month, and thereby abandoning all visible hope of early relief or respite; and conscious always that, while one man sought to do the work of many, the result of his labours could never be really efficient or satisfactory to himself or to the public. When to these things were presently added sordid money troubles and anxieties, resulting from the steady rise in the cost of living, and the uncontrollable expansion of each man's personal liabilities; and when was added a fancied reluctance of those in authority to come to their relief,—a suspicion which the delays, inseparable from the promulgation of decisions that are based upon correspondence conducted by the Secretary of State with no less than four separate Colonial Governments, helped to confirm—a certain sourness of temper manifested itself in many Public Services; and from this taint it would be idle to pretend that the Public Service of Nigeria was exempt. My first tour through the country—

undertaken within a few weeks of my arrival at Lagos—embraced a large and fairly representative area in both the Northern and the Southern Provinces: and it sufficed to impress me with the disgruntled spirit with which large sections of my new colleagues were imbued.

According to Clifford, the cure was not just better salaries, better housing, better material conditions generally, but a longer process of bringing cadres up to strength, security against frequent transfers, the laying of the bogy of the 'particular villainy' of the West African climate, an end to the 'hand-to-mouth, picnic, makeshift fashion of living' and the 'constant up-rooting' of frequent postings, which 'chilled enthusiasm' and was bound to demoralize its victims and destroy their interest in their work. He had found, on his first tour of the Southern provinces, that five of the Residents, out of the six officers of that substantive rank whose provinces he inspected, had none of them previously spent one day of their working lives in the provinces to which they had all just been appointed.

But, as the evidence presented to the Salaries Committee showed, the main, insistent grouse of the disgruntled service—placed ahead of the shocking housing conditions, the frequent postings, the under-staffing and overwork, the stagnant promotion, the prolonged tours, and all the rest—was the fact that few married officers could live on their pay, even with the most stringent economy. It was this stark fact—due to an uncompensated doubling of the cost of living since 1914—which, despite the interest of the work, was making the service 'ineligible except for bachelors and men with private incomes'. Quoting examples brought to their notice, of officers with service ranging from five to seventeen years, some in senior positions, who were quite unable adequately to support themselves and their families, the committee reported: 'We believe that these are typical cases. We know that there are others, but public officers are naturally reluctant to come forward to plead in this manner.' The examples included such cases as an officer with eight years' service clearly unable to support a wife and young child on his earnings, an officer with five years' service, living moderately, with less than £100 a year to keep a wife and child in England, an officer with fourteen years' service 'in an expensive position' with about £60 a year to keep a wife and two children, and an officer, appointed in 1919, who after four months' expenses had nothing for his wife's maintenance. One administrative officer with fourteen years' service, still an assistant district officer, on £400 a year, testified that he 'would not be able to live in West Africa but for the generosity of some of his relatives', and a Resident, on £700 a year, with four children, doubted whether he could possibly bring his 1920 expenditure to within £300 above his salary, 'a total quite beyond his private means to make up': in 1919, he testified, his family had 'definitely passed the border-line between frugality and penury', and he feared that 1920 would see them 'on the high road to beggary'.[1]

This method of supplementing the inadequate finances of a make-shift Empire from the private pockets of its employees was being achieved at such cost and hardship to the men and their families that it was impossible for it to continue. It had taken the heart out of many. The increasing strains seem to be shown in the annually rising European invalidings—77 per 1,000 in 1917, 128 in 1918, 173 in 1919. They recovered to 132 in 1920 and 68 in 1921. But improvements in conditions required money; where was it to come from?

It was here that Clifford came hard up against the external difficulty: the British public, never very interested in the responsibilities of Empire, was now utterly indisposed to take any helpful interest, and there was no prospect of financial help from its elected Government. Clifford was well aware of this. In 1919, before leaving for Nigeria, he talked to the African Society about the strong reaction against anything savouring of 'imperialism' and 'commercialism' which the 'Caesarism' of Germany had occasioned, through the war which had 'made such matchwood of the world as we knew it'. The long-standing public ignorance had been made a basis on which critics had rested 'a sweeping disapproval and condemnation'[2] of the principles and methods by which British colonial administrators had been guided. Clifford was not concerned to defend the scramble for Africa, which he (like MacGregor and others) regarded as one of the least creditable episodes in history. But he saw the work of administering the territories, whether acquired by 'sword-rattling imperialism' or otherwise, as 'one of the finest pieces of work done for humanity that any individual nation has ever been privileged to attempt'. In this

[1] *Reports and Evidence of the Salaries Revision Committee*, 1919 (C.E. 18 in Ibadan Archives). See also Cameron, *My Tanganyika Service and Some Nigeria*, and A. Lethbridge, *West Africa the Elusive* (1920).

[2] *Journal of the African Society*, vol. xviii (July 1919), p. 241. In this talk Clifford clearly had in mind the writings of a former junior colleague in the Ceylon administration (who before his resignation had been singled out by Clifford for promotion). This was Leonard Woolf, whose *Economic Imperialism* and *Empire and Commerce in Africa* were influential in shaping the Labour party's hostile attitude to Empire, at this period.

work trade and the flag went together, and should go together, if the central problem was to be successfully solved. In the modern world, the tropical territories could not 'lie fallow'—the problem was to develop their wealth without 'the speedy degeneration' which rapid changes in their peoples' environment and conditions of life were only too likely to bring. Ignorance at home, apathy, and hostility did not help at all towards a solution of this central and 'immensely difficult' problem. His own solution in principle was 'indirect rule' in the widest orthodox sense—a policy as well as a philosophy. It was to keep out the European in every field in which the native could manage things himself, and to let him in only in those fields (like deep mining, as opposed to 'fossicking about for surface deposits') where foreign capital and foreign expertise were indispensable.[1] But he insisted that official government, public expenditure, and policy proposals must be subjected to really effective local criticism by all classes, particularly 'the most able and articulate'.[2] In a later talk to the African Society, entitled 'United Nigeria', Clifford expressed the wish that the British public could be 'shaken out of apathy' and out of preoccupation with cricket, football, golf, and tennis. But this could not be done. As Clifford said, colonial officials found when they came home that 'nobody in this country knows or cares anything about the lands in which they have lived, or the people whom they have served, or a fig for them or the work they are doing.'[3]

This was plain fact; the indifference was so deep that the only really informed and effective published criticisms of British colonial administration came from within—in books and articles written by men like Woolf, of the Ceylon service, Joyce Cary, of the Nigerian service, George Orwell, of the Burma Police, Leonard Barnes, who had served in the Colonial Office, Crocker, of the Nigerian service (or even

[1] There was a dramatic confrontation between the aristocratic Governor and the millionaire Bolton grocer Lord Leverhulme on this issue. Leverhulme wanted land concessions for plantations. Clifford opposed this absolutely, claiming that peasant cultivation was more natural, better, more efficient, cheaper, and less likely to lead to oppression. Leverhulme was routed. Under careful control, 'concessions' might have been beneficial; presumably Clifford did not think such control feasible.

[2] It was this insistence on building up 'a robust public opinion' and the institutions through which it could be expressed which sets the ideas of Clifford so far apart from those of Lugard, whose constant aim was to make criticism and opposition ineffective and to silence any protest so far as he was able. Silent and unquestioning obedience—'co-operation'—was what Lugard wanted, and what Clifford abominated.

[3] *Journal of the African Society*, vol. xxi (June 1921), p. 1.

Lugard, now a 'renegade', like the rest, from the official ranks, but still seeking to exert authority). Even academic writers, like Margery Perham, came to the subject in a quasi-official capacity, as part of the work of colonial service training. 'Pure' academic interest scarcely existed; the intellectual world now so fascinated by the problems of 'under-development' seemed, throughout the inter-war years, quite unconcerned with them. Interest did begin to quicken in the thirties, but the indifference of the intellectual world, for a whole generation, was a fair reflection of the general revulsion from 'imperialism' which took place during and after the first World War.

In speaking of the revulsion against 'imperialism' and 'commercialism' Clifford had attributed both the war and the subsequent revulsion to German 'Caesarism'. But the national brand did not matter. 'Imperialism' had become a universal hate-word.[1] In Britain in 1920, when H. G. Wells published the first edition of his famous *Outline of History*, his chapter on the twentieth century was called 'The Catastrophe of Modern Imperialism'[2]—and this despite the fact that two at least of his four main helpers were themselves doughty apologists of the British Empire—Sir Harry Johnston (one of the most agile scramblers for Africa) and Sir Ernest Barker.[3] The Wells version was close to the British socialist thesis developed by Leonard Woolf from J. A. Hobson: imperialism had meant autocratic dominion of Europeans over other races, and such benefits as it had brought were outweighed by 'horrible cruelty, exploitation and injustice'. In the Marxist–Leninist thesis, founded equally on Hobson, imperialism, the last stage of capitalism, had already resulted in one World War, and would inevitably destroy itself in others. In the mythology of the defeated Germans—again based to some extent on

[1] Chapter xi of *Imperialism: the Story and Significance of a Political Word, 1840–1960* by Richard Koebner and Helmut Dan Schmidt (Cambridge University Press, London, 1964) deals with the period between the two World Wars, and is called: 'Hate-word of world struggle against Anglo-Saxon dominion'.

[2] Wells used 'imperialism' in the sense of aggressive nationalism, leading to conflict between the European powers, and found its manifestations in Africa scarcely worth mention. Since his description of the British Empire was contained in less than two pages, the work is in itself a curious example of the ethnocentric approach, the 'negligence' and the 'ignorance' he himself criticized, in the words he used to complete his summary treatment of the subject of the British Empire in 1914: 'It was a mixture of growths and accumulations. . . . It guaranteed a wide peace and security: that is why it was endured and sustained by many men of the "subject" races, in spite of official tyrannies and insufficiencies, and of much negligence on the part of the "home" public' (*An Outline of History*, p. 1025).

[3] See *The Ideas and Ideals of the British Empire* (1941).

Hobson, like the other conceptions—it was the ruthlessness, the piratical greed and cunning of Anglo-Saxon imperialism, aided by Jewish international finance, which had deliberately brought about the first World War, for the purpose of depriving Germany of her rightful 'place in the sun' and her share of the world's wealth. In the common American interpretation, the World War had been the outcome of competing European caesarism, militarism, and imperialism. The United States had joined in the war for the liberation of oppressed small nations, for their self-determination, for democracy, and for liberty—principles as inimical to the idea of French and British empires as they were to German expansion. So when educated Indians, Chinese, and Africans turned to Western liberal, communist, fascist, or socialist literature for some understanding of the threat or the accomplished fact of Western domination over them they could find in all the theories one common factor, the simple message that 'imperialism' was the name for most of the evils and troubles of the world.

In the countries actually responsible for the peace, order, and good government of tropical territories, there was a general feeling that 'possessing' them was simply a disgrace, if they were unprofitable, and doubly disgraceful if they were profitable. This attitude was of no help towards the investment in them of the energy, manpower, capital, imagination, and wisdom which were needed for their good government and development.

What was provided from British resources for Nigeria—in a manner symptomatic of the general apathy—was a guarantee for loan funds (at 6 per cent interest in 1919) and a trickle of men to bring the ratio of administrators to administered up from the lowest level of about 1 : 250,000 to something like 1 : 60,000. Public interest was so slight that the recruitment of handfuls of men to govern Africa was quietly left in a pre-Northcote–Trevelyan limbo. It was a little regarded function of one or two young men, employed in the private office of the Secretary of State as Assistant Private Secretaries. Their position was uncertain—they were not even established civil servants themselves. Their job was to select, for the formal approval of the Secretary of State, candidates to fill administrative and other vacancies notified by Governors. It was left to one of these men, later Sir Ralph Furse, by his enthusiasm and persistence to build up, from this insecure place as an Assistant Private Secretary (Patronage), a more formal and defensible system for recruiting men to administer dozens of governments responsible for seventy million people. He sought always to make them into a *corps d'élite*, admission being decided not by the kind of qualities which could be tested by written examination, but by careful personal interviewing of candidates and careful collection and examination of candidates' school and university records, academic, athletic, and personal. In the early twenties, however, the process of formalizing and legitimizing the offspring of the 'Father of the Colonial Service' had not made much progress. Sir Ralph Furse has himself described how, in February 1919, he returned to the Colonial Office from the war in France, and, still in the uniform of a cavalry major, resumed the work of colonial service recruitment of which he had had a few years' experience before the war, as a young graduate. He accepted an invitation to return as Assistant Secretary (Appointments) to the newly appointed Secretary of State (Lord Milner) because deafness disqualified him from a permanent army commission.[1] His account makes it plain that the Colonial Office (responsible, in those days, for both the dominions and the colonies or 'dependent territories') was faithfully reflecting the public preoccupation with matters other than the new countries shown red in the world atlas. Furse found that 'no plans or preparation for the obviously urgent task of reinforcing a tired and short-handed Colonial Service' had been made, and that he was expected to tackle it single-handed, 'with the half-time help of one registry clerk—that is to say, half the staff considered necessary in the comparatively quiet

[1] Sir Ralph Furse's memoirs (*Aucuparius, Recollections of a Recruiting Officer*, Oxford University Press, 1962) show that throughout his long career as 'a highly irregular civil servant' and unashamed 'amateur' he remained at heart a cavalry officer and English country gentleman, and an innocent imperialist, with the outlook on the world and on society of one who was also an Etonian and an Oxford classics graduate. His long tenure of responsibility for the selection of men for the administrative and some of the professional services of the colonies (from 1910 to 1948, with a break during the first World War) earned him the title of 'Father of the Colonial Service'. But, as Sir John Macpherson (Governor of Nigeria and later Permanent Under-Secretary at the Colonial Office) pointed out in his foreword to Professor Heussler's *Yesterday's Rulers* (Oxford University Press, London, 1963) there is a tendency to over-emphasize the idea that Furse's personal character and tastes were rigidly reflected in the men selected. In practice, very few men of Furse's own social background offered themselves after the first World War for the colonial service; like Furse himself the Eton and Oxford 'establishment' could find more attractive careers outside it. It is also a fact that all Nigeria's Governors, and many of those in the other senior posts, entered the service by methods other than Sir Ralph Furse's selection—either by competitive examination (like Sir John Macpherson himself, Lord Milverton, and others) or by transfer from other services, or by promotion from the clerical ranks (like Cameron).

period before the war'. There were mounting piles of applications for appointment on the floor of his office. These had been acknowledged (but not examined) by a colleague who died, 'of overwork', shortly afterwards. 'A long list of vacancies had come in from colonial governments.'[1] Not surprisingly, it was eight months before the colonial service received any reinforcement; perhaps, if conditions in Nigeria had been matters of wide public knowledge, it would have been impossible to find reinforcements at all. One is left with a strong impression, from Furse's memoirs, and from accounts by Sir Charles Jeffries, Sir George Fiddes, and Sir Cosmo Parkinson, that the Office's view was that economic progress should soon make it possible for any well-run territory to afford an orthodox civil service, recruited by Civil Service Commission competition—like the Home, Indian, and Far Eastern civil services—underpinned by increasingly competent local civil services. And meanwhile, until the 'pioneering' stage was over, the old system of patronage, indefensible in theory, had practical advantages. One of them was its amateur, makeshift character, which offered an easy line of withdrawal if it was seriously challenged and its defence proved inexpedient. Meanwhile, the Colonial Office professionals could maintain, through the Colonial Regulations, the degree of control over salaries, pensions, discipline, and general conditions which was necessary if the available talent and manpower were to be spread sufficiently to avoid breakdowns in the administrations of territories too poor or too small to develop self-contained career services. By this control, used with skill, a bad climate and poor conditions could be balanced against better leave, or shorter tours, and a good climate could be set against low salary; the permutations and combinations were endless.

Since Nigeria was by far the largest of the dependent territories, in population and in demands for staff, the salaries and conditions of service adopted there were of crucial importance to the whole system of staffing the dependent territories. They must somehow fall into line with the other West African territories, and be compatible, if possible, with conditions elsewhere. This was a tall order, and what emerged from Cameron's work was a compromise dictated by the amount of money available in 1920. Because it worked, and because money became no more plentiful, the compromise lasted for more than twenty years. The administrative service itself was the basis of the system, particularly in the early years, and the salary and conditions fixed for

[1] Sir Ralph Furse, *Aucuparius, Recollections of a Recruiting Officer*, p. 57.

administrators decided the rest, except for the medical service.[1] The subsequent tendency, wherever funds permitted, was to enlarge the existing specialist departments and create new ones, rather than to increase the numbers of administrators in the provinces.

Poverty meant first the thinnest possible spread of administrative officers in the provinces—the 1921 provincial cadre was 159 in the North, and 159 in the South, less than 200 on duty on any one date. To get recruits, salaries had to be fixed £50 higher than East Africa, which meant paying £450 per annum to new men. The complaint about promotion was met by introducing 'the long grade' permitting officers to advance in eighteen years to about £1,000—the limit of the normal expectation of advancement, without promotion to the grade of Resident, but no higher than the standard pension of the I.C.S. officer. Since each officer was responsible for the administration of some fifty thousand his salary over twenty years would therefore average at less than 4*d.* per head per annum. But even this was as much as the revenues could stand, once provision was made for a few modestly paid subordinates, for roads, for a few hospitals, for a few departments, for Secretariats, for the completion of the railway system from the socialized mines at Enugu, where a new capital was to be built, to the junction of the railways at Kaduna, through largely empty country. The thin spread of administrators, the consequent overwork and the strain of constant touring, the continuance of bad housing, health, and general living and working conditions—all these combined to make it impracticable to reduce the period of leave or to increase the length of officers' tours of duty beyond eighteen months. It was only the short tour and the seven days' vacation leave per month of service which made the life tolerable for serving officers, and offered a possibility of getting new recruits. Had the tour of duty been made longer, or leave shorter, it would have been necessary to raise salaries, and to provide housing and health facilities suitable for families. And, of course, there was no money for such things. So a series of forced economies, some of them false economies in the long run, dictated a strange evolutionary pattern. Palliatives were found for the 'makeshift, picnic fashion of living': 'bush allowance' for living in particularly uncomfortable conditions; travelling allowances for journeying with cook and servants from one ramshackle rest-house to

[1] The medical service, thanks to the existence of the influential British Medical Association, had received special treatment in salaries and conditions (including limited rights to private practice) since the early years of the century.

another; free warrants for the transportation of provisions by rail from Lagos, to offset the exorbitant costs of transportation. These things cost less than the payment of higher salaries, or the capital expenditure to make permanent improvement, and they made discomfort a means of solvency for some officers. Since discomfort and constant travelling were unavoidable, it was just as well to create a vested interest in them. They survived, despite constant criticism by legislators of the 'multifarious allowances' which were making Nigeria 'a paradise' for officials. Some of these 1920 'improvements' still survive: the obvious examples are the bicycle, motor-cycle, and motor-car advances, and allowances for their upkeep and running, originally intended only for the 'bush-whacking' officer, but later extended to become a universal status symbol and 'entitlement', with a car advance and allowance the final proof of 'senior service' status. A less obvious example is the institution known as the 'catering rest house'—originally proposed by the Salaries Committee as an answer to the problem of accommodation and refreshment for Europeans passing through Lagos and other main centres. In the bad old days, there being no hotels, officials returning from leave were reduced to walking the streets of Lagos for the night, if they were too shy to ask an acquaintance or a stranger for a place to sleep on his verandah. So the Government was forced into a new field of 'socialist' enterprise, the running of makeshift hotels to ease the discomforts of officers in transit and the burden of enforced hospitality on hosts who had neither room nor money to spare. As Sir Alan Burns pointed out, this was a familiar vicious circle in Nigeria. No private hotels, so the Government ran hotels: so no private hotels; no contractors, so the P.W.D. undertook works directly: so no private contractors.

It was of course the collapse of the system of international trade, and its accompanying financial stringency, beginning not long after Cameron and Clifford had set the pattern of administocracy, which made it impossible for their successors to alter its shape very radically. Cameron left Nigeria in 1924, Clifford in 1925. Between them, they had pulled Nigeria out of the quagmire. Cameron had become, by the time he left, Clifford's faithful disciple, and wrote in 1939 what must be regarded, in view of Clifford's sad condition at that time, as a considered judgement on his work, written in the knowledge that its subject would never read it:

> If I may venture to express an opinion, a man of great human understanding, who identified himself always with the interests of his officers;

intolerant of any suspicion of slackness in the discharge of public duties but ever ready with his generous meed of recognition where work was well done. I write of him as I knew him intimately and in close personal association for more than five years. His was the task to open the windows and the doors in the public service of Nigeria in those years, admitting light and air, where, here and there, some mildew, some dry rot, was to be discerned . . . He came from the Malayan service, as did the Governor to whom Nigeria owes more in the field of economic development than any other Governor . . . Sir Walter Egerton.

Of the Nigerian Secretariat which Clifford had created, and Cameron himself had been the first head, he wrote, contrasting it with the previous disorder:[1] 'It was a good and efficient department . . . it all came from Hugh Clifford'; and, as if to underline the point that he himself took Clifford and not Lugard as his guide and model, Cameron compared 'the two schools' in colonial administration. The first (clearly the Lugard school, although Cameron was almost as cryptic as Temple had been) meant 'administering from an office in comparative seclusion, with but little contact with the outside world and that little of one's own seeking'. The second school he called 'administration in the field'—'discussing affairs frankly and openly, merging oneself with the general community as far as that can be possible . . . examining the administrative machine with the driver and seeing the engine revolve "with the bonnet off" '. He preferred the second: 'I honestly shrink from the first method . . . I have never aspired to such Olympian heights.'[2]

Sir Alan Burns, despite his admiration for Lugard as 'a delightful chief to work for', shows clearly enough which of the 'two schools' gave better results, saying that close co-operation between 'two brilliant men', Clifford and Cameron, 'brought the administration of Nigeria to a high level of efficiency'. In his memoirs, Burns wrote of his years in the Nigerian Secretariat under Cameron:

We had to work very hard, and for very long hours, and our work was measured by the very high standard set by our chief himself. He suffered no fool gladly, and quickly got rid of those who failed to reach the standard. With Sir Hugh Clifford as Governor (from 1918 to 1925) and Sir Donald Cameron as Chief Secretary, the staff of the Nigerian Secretariat received such a training as is seldom given to younger officers.[3]

Of Clifford himself, Burns wrote:

He was a good office man, and he reorganised the machinery of govern-

[1] See Cameron, *My Tanganyika Service and Some Nigeria*, pp. 16 ff.
[2] Cameron, op. cit., p. 30. [3] A. C. Burns, *Colonial Civil Servant*, p. 47.

ment so that it worked more efficiently. He worked hard and played hard, and his tremendous energy allowed him to do both . . . we all appreciated the personality and powers of the new Governor.[1]

So far, so good: good enough, even, for Clifford to defer his departure from Nigeria, after the announcement of his appointment as Governor of Ceylon, to act as host to the Prince of Wales on a visit to Nigeria. This would have been unthinkable a few years before. As luck would have it, simultaneous outbreaks of plague and of yellow fever restricted the Prince's movements and foiled one of the main purposes of the visit, which was to demonstrate that Nigeria's evil health reputation was undeserved.

But Nigeria's administrative health had improved. The country had recognizable institutions of government—an efficient Secretariat, a Legislative Council to replace the useless Nigerian Council. Some stability had been given to the public service. The railway was working again. The Lieutenant-Governors had been given clear executive responsibilities, instead of being mere secretaries to an autocratic Governor. Central departments had been set up. At Clifford's insistence, reinforced by ordinary financial prudence, heads of departments had repeatedly examined their cadres with a view to the substitution of Africans for Europeans. And despite the misgivings of many, the level at which the filling of posts by Europeans was regarded as essential had been set a little higher—particularly in the Railway, the Marine and the other departments in which industrial training could be arranged. This was a highly significant development; the first wave of 'Nigerianization', although not so called, had begun. With the revenues almost doubled since 1918 (from £4 million to £8 million in 1925) it must have looked as if the pre-war process of carefully calculated annual expansion of 'services alike in *personnel* and *matériel*' was again in full swing. And the choice, to succeed Clifford, of 'the greatest transport officer since Noah'[2], showed where the Colonial

[1] Burns, op. cit., p. 55.

[2] Clifford's successor was Sir Graeme Thomson, who did not join the colonial service until after the first World War, during which, as an Admiralty civil servant and Director of Shipping, he had earned a great reputation for efficient management of the complex problems of organizing British shipping during years of submarine warfare, of convoys, and of large-scale movements of troops, munitions, and food supplies to and from the beleaguered British Isles. Ill-health dating from soon after his arrival in an appointment requiring good health and a strong constitution steadily worsened. After six years of ill-success and ill-health Thomson was transferred to Ceylon as Governor, but died at Aden on his way home for an operation. Under the peculiar arrangements for Governors' pensions

Office, pressed by mercantile interests at home, as well as by obvious necessity, thought the emphasis in economic development should lie. Indeed, the Colonial Office, separated from the Dominions Office in 1925, was now becoming, gradually, a more effective instrument for the development of the dependent Empire, and beginning to equip itself with specialist advisers—a commercial adviser in 1921, a chief medical adviser in 1926, an agricultural adviser in 1929. Very soon, even the old patronage system of recruitment for the colonial service was to be superseded by a more elaborate and formal method of selection to what were called the Unified Services. In practice, Furse, as director of recruitment, selected men for jobs notified from the colonies on much the same basis as before, and the question whether 'H.M. Colonial Service' or the so-called Unified Services ever really existed was one to which different answers could be given for different purposes—yes, for purposes of recruitment, and no, if the purpose was to avoid contingent liabilities, particularly financial ones.[1]

The best hopes of continued progress and growth remained unfulfilled after the departure of Cameron and Clifford. By 1931, when Cameron was harnessed once more to the task of pulling the Administration out of the quagmire, there had been four consecutive years of budget deficits as international trade conditions worsened. Meanwhile, though the structure and numbers of the public service had not changed much, there had been other changes—many of them for the worse—in the whole complex environment of which the public service

at that time a Governor who did not complete ten years as a Governor was paid pension on his previous civil service salary before promotion to Governor. This was presumably the explanation for Thomson's transfer from Nigeria to another colony, despite his failing health.

[1] The official recruitment pamphlet C.S.R.I. *Appointments in His Majesty's Colonial Service* issued annually—gave guidance on this point, in wording which did not vary significantly from year to year until 1954, when the term 'H.M. Overseas Civil Service' was introduced. The 1950 version is quoted below:

'The term "The Colonial Service" is a wide one. It embraces all the public services of all those British Colonies for the administration of which the Secretary of State for the Colonies is responsible . . . Each of these Colonial Governments is a separate administrative entity. Members of the Colonial Service serving in any Colony are public servants of that Colony and their salaries are paid from local revenue. The Colonial Service thus differs from other British public services in that it is not a single service for purposes of administration and discipline. Opportunities occur however, for members of each Colony's public service to be considered for promotion or transfer to the public service of other Colonies. This fact, and the fact that all officers serve under a single basic code of regulations laid down by the Secretary of State for the Colonies, give reality to the idea of a comprehensive Service covering the Colonial territories as a whole.'

was a dominant and to outward appearances a fairly simple part. There were at least three kinds of economy: the export economy, the 'native' internal cash economy, and a subsistence economy—not neatly separated, but mingling and changing, with societies to match, whose members seemed to many observers to be living in different centuries (some indeed seemed to be living in several different centuries at once).

It was the export economy, on which the whole structure of officialdom rested, which had brought into being the old, prosperous class of Nigerian traders in Lagos and the South, and the beginnings of a comfortable middle class of lawyers, doctors, and officials. The wealthy traders were the first victims of the collapse in international trade—their numbers dwindled until they left little trace, other than a few opulent family residences in Lagos. The next victims were the smaller European merchants and firms, who had formed a distinctive, critical, and energetic element in the country's commercial and political life. They too disappeared, their businesses usually absorbed in one of the great trading combines whose vast resources enabled them to survive lean times. But the new men on the coast were now merely managers, not principals, unable to speak out and influence officialdom in Lagos (either in the new Legislative Council or outside it) or in London.[1] With the decline of cotton, and the drift of industry and commerce to London, the old, personal links between Liverpool and Manchester and Lagos were snapping, one by one. Despite the increasing population of Lagos, there was an impoverishment and depersonalization of the capital's life—no one to take the lead in public munificence, in founding libraries, in patronage of deserving social causes, or in vigorous political life. There was a similar depersonalization and impoverishment in the official world. As the Colonial Office slowly organized itself to deal with the problems of the dependent territories, acquiring advisers on policy one by one, mind and management drifted from Lagos to London, especially in the field of

[1] The African Society *Journal* from 1901 to the thirties shows the gradual draining away of non-official interest; the society was originally founded in memory of Mary Kingsley, and was a forum of discussion to which merchants (European and African), officials (mostly 'Coast' officials), missionaries, and politicians all contributed. With the disappearance of the old traders, it became increasingly an 'official' business. In 1932 a member, regretting this development, mentioned that he could not recollect any occasion on which the great Unilever enterprise (90 companies, and capital of £200 million) had been represented by one of its heads at the society's functions, in the way in which men like Sir Alfred Jones and John Holt had represented the interests of commerce.

commercial and trade policy. Cameron's 'good and efficient' Nigerian Secretariat was too good to last, under the Colonial Office arrangements for world-wide spreading of exceptional talents. Cameron and Burns mention in their memoirs that within a few years no less than six members of the Lagos Secretariat of the early twenties (presumably the ablest of the small team trained by Clifford and Cameron) were serving simultaneously elsewhere as Governors, and another filled a senior post in the Colonial Office. Despite the size, population, and potential of the country, Nigeria was beginning to take on the look of a mere branch, inconveniently large and inconveniently poor, of a vast estate which could thrive only if international trade thrived.

The depressing effect of adverse trading conditions was of course felt most in those parts of the country which had known the beginnings of prosperity and modernization through trade. The societies which had continued to rely wholly on subsistence agriculture were not so vulnerable as those which had come to depend on cash crops—such as the cotton farmers who produced in 1925 34,500 bales of cotton priced at 3*d.* per lb., and five years later could get only ½*d.* per lb. for a much smaller crop (14,000 bales).

The developments during the period of Sir Graeme Thomson's administration must therefore be seen against a very gloomy background of commercial decay, declining production, and growing discontent with British rule amongst those who had had most cause to welcome it in the earlier days.[1] A Governor in robust health, who had himself been 'right through the mill' of administration, might have had a better chance of holding things together; but the new Governor's health was bad, and rapidly worsened. Outside the field of transportation, in which he had great experience (and in which progress was made), Sir Graeme Thomson was by no means so

[1] These were the peoples of the coast, and their dissatisfaction reached a climax in the Aba market-women's riots of 1929 attributed by commissioners of inquiry to a fear of direct taxation and to Sir Graeme Thomson's decision (on Lugard's advice, and despite Clifford's warnings about 'building on quicksand') to resume the process of modelling native administration in the South-East on the pattern of the North, and to introduce direct taxation. The riots were directed against the warrant chiefs and native officials, but the women made it clear that they had been protesting too about the hardships of trade, and believed that white man's rule had 'spoiled' everything, bringing no tangible benefits in return. Margery Perham's *Native Administration in Nigeria* contains an account of these riots; this seems to be the fullest account easily available, but see also Legislative Council Sessional Papers, nos. 12 and 28 of 1930.

well-equipped as men like Clifford and Cameron for the colonial administrator's speciality—making bricks without straw, achieving adequate progress with inadequate means. Even in the field of transportation, the failure of international trade coincided with the completion of the railway system and the improvement of trunk roads to take motor traffic, so the immediate results were heavy interest charges and heavy railway running deficits (£1 million in the years 1930 to 1935) at a time of decreasing rail traffic and increasing road competition in the profitable sectors near the coast. Outside the field of transportation the Governor's lack of experience led him into acceptance, apparently without question, of the myth of the Lugard achievement, while his worsening health made it impossible to give effective leadership to a public service dividing into two factions.

This was one of the most significant developments in the rather obscure interregnum between Clifford's departure and Cameron's return as Governor. There was a growing schism between 'Lagos' (the Chief Secretary and his Secretariat, and the senior professional officers in the departments) and the provincial administration, particularly the Lieutenant-Governor of the North and the Northern administrators. Basically, this was a necessary controversy, and a healthy one, and those concerned in it would undoubtedly have thought themselves to be failing in their duty if they had not prosecuted it with energy and conviction. Sir Alan Burns (from the uneasy vantage point of one who had just returned to Nigeria to sit at the centre, as Deputy Chief Secretary, and had to act as Chief Secretary for long periods during which the Chief Secretary acted for the ailing Governor) saw the dispute as both a personal one between the substantive Chief Secretary and the Lieutenant-Governors and also as something deeper than the usual run of 'staff' versus 'line' controversies:

> . . . it was a struggle, accentuated by the personal antipathies of the combatants, which could quickly have been settled by a firm decision from the Governor. Closely connected with this struggle was another far more far-reaching. This was the struggle of the technical departments to escape from the control of the Administrative Service, exercised by the Lieutenant-Governors through Residents and District Officers, more especially in the Northern Provinces.[1]

Personal antipathies and poor communications clearly played a part, but this seems to have been the beginning—in the absence of

[1] Burns, *Colonial Civil Servant*, p. 103.

decisive leadership, vigorous political life, and economic progress—of what was to become a complex, almost theological dispute between the believers in indirect rule and the sceptics. Cameron's practical common sense made him impervious to the philosophical and mystical charms of the theory of indirect rule. He deliberately simplified the issue to one of local government based on the traditions of the people—the 'people', not 'the chiefs'. This effectively limited the field of dispute, but as Lord Hailey observed in his *African Survey* (1938), the controversy at its height had reflected basically different political philosophies. It is doubtful whether the controversy would have become acute if the cornucopia of world trade had been showering forth abundant material benefits. There would then have been a general eagerness for modernization and development, and less talk about the other half of *The Dual Mandate*—the aspects of 'conservation', 'preservation', and 'non-interference with native ways' which were near to the heart of the advocates of indirect rule.

As we have seen, Lugard's actual practice, as opposed to his more pretentious explanations, had been to use 'native' institutions as part of a system of authoritarian rule, separated from the process of commercial development—for which he looked to British capital and commercial enterprise to supply the driving force 'on parallel lines' to the official efforts to maintain authority. It was Temple and his friends, less keen on domination, who had developed the more far-reaching philosophical ideas, in revulsion from narrow regimentation through a system of command and control from above; it was they who set themselves the aim of greater freedom and independence for the states they had helped to evolve. But the Lugards' unwearying propaganda had so confused the issues that it was never generally realized how narrow and yet how disingenuous his actual practice had been, with talk of 'progress' disguising the reality of action designed to prevent it. Brisk economic development in the twenties and thirties would have forced attention on adaptation of institutions to modern life, rather than upon their preservation. As things were, the provincial administration, particularly in the North, selected in the main by a conservative director of recruitment from a class of men tending to be conservative and rural in outlook, had what appeared to them excellent reasons for following the proud traditions of Northern administration and opposing the apparently destructive and unprofitable innovations pressed on them by bureaucratic 'outsiders' in Lagos.

Lagos, for the Northern officer, living among a people still conservative and wedded to traditional ways, came to represent, in adverse economic conditions, the evils of modernization, of 'bureaucracy', of slummy urbanization, of indiscipline, discontent, and insolence, where the British officialdom lived as if in Whitehall, ignorant of the country, showing no deep sympathy and understanding of the long-term interests of the country and its peoples, brusquely rejecting their requests for finance, but spending comparatively large sums of money on a central 'bureaucracy', on new Secretariat posts, often filled by imported men suspected of being 'careerists', better housed and better paid than the men in the 'bush'. They did not want agricultural officers, for instance, to be let loose in their provinces to advise farmers to grow cash crops which would afterwards rot unsaleable, after great efforts in sowing and harvesting them. They did not want a wholesale influx of subordinate departmental officials from the South to come upsetting everybody by enforcing health regulations or forestry regulations, demanding privileges, liquor permits, quarters, and legal rights, or extorting money from the locals by threats. They felt sure that the native authorities, with the help of a few sympathetic white men who understood their ways and spoke their language, could make a better, more economical job of meeting the basic needs—simple roads, bridges and water-works, simple schools and dispensaries—than any centrally organized bureaucracy of professional specialists whose schemes were always too expensive.

The central bureaucracy itself (often filled, in the senior ranks, by officers promoted, in their last years of service, from other territories) found it difficult to be patient with the inefficiency, the delays, and the 'indirectness' of rule which made it impossible for them to act without first securing the co-operation of Residents, district officers, Emirs, district heads, and others. Sometimes heads of departments were asked to remove from the North their best and most energetic men because their impatience with forms of protocol and time-wasting courtesy visits had aroused suspicion and resentment.

These were honest differences in approach between the professional 'modernizers'—the engineers, the agricultural specialists, the doctors, and the rest—and the provincial administrators, whose training and experience in essentially conservative societies had imbued them with scepticism about the value of innovations made without the consent and co-operation of those they were designed to benefit but sometimes harmed. It was not until the economic climate changed and the advantages of modernization became more clear that the balance between 'development' and 'conservation' shifted.

Cameron's return in 1931 (described by Burns as 'a fortunate event for Nigeria') meant that for the first time Nigeria had a Governor whose experience had mostly been gained in Africa—mostly in Southern Nigeria, and mostly in Secretariat posts, although he had acted as a Provincial Commissioner in the South in Egerton's day. The priority tasks were to restore order to Nigeria's finances and to decide the general issues of policy which were in dispute. He had the necessary qualities:

Cameron had a remarkable capacity for work, a quick grasp of essentials, an astounding memory for details, and a facility for lucid expression in writing and speech. His manner was often forbidding and his mordant humour made many enemies. In his official life he was ruthlessly efficient and he never learned to suffer fools gladly; his dislikes were often too obvious and sometimes cruel in their results. He was, however, a man of deep sympathies and humanity, and he delighted in secret kindnesses to those in need. Never popular with the crowd, he was greatly liked and respected by his intimate friends and by those who worked in close contact with him. He had a genuine sympathy for the people of Africa.[1]

Cameron's struggles with the financial deficit took the grim forms of retrenchment of officers—the Governor making himself responsible for the choice of men to go—and of reduction in salaries for those who stayed. There was a virtual cessation of new recruitment, and stringent control over every form of expenditure in the estimates. These were days in which the auditor and the accountant had to question every expense; the touring officer must explain at length even such minutiae as the payment to canoe-pullers or porters of 1*d*. per day more than the local authorized rate, at which, as often as not, no labour could be obtained. Administrators and professional officers without the funds to carry out schemes laboriously planned, costed, and proposed each year had to spend an increasing proportion of their time in squeezing often pitifully small amounts of revenue out of the often unenthusiastic public, in taxes, licences, and fees, and in fines for failure to pay the other dues. Living in houses with leaky roofs, responsible (there being few banks) for the custody of revenues in 'strong rooms' so flimsy that they leaked money, constantly checking and re-checking accounts kept by ill-paid, ill-educated Government and native administration subordinates, trying

[1] *Dictionary of National Biography* (contribution by Sir Alan Burns).

constantly to make each penny do the work of two or three, the average administrator and departmental official became preoccupied with financial detail—not from choice, but from necessity.

This preoccupation certainly led to a narrowing of vision, but it achieved its main object. By 1934, with practically no outside help, Nigeria achieved a small budget surplus, although no provision could be made for railway renewals. This broke a seven-year succession of deficits. It was the turn of the tide. By the time Cameron left in 1935—yet another Governor with health damaged permanently—financial equilibrium had been restored, and the Government was contriving to spend 30 per cent of the scanty revenues on economic development and social services (£1.3 million, or about 1*s*. 3*d*. per head of population). Nearly £1 million had to be set aside annually for interest charges on loans other than railway loans, £½ million for pensions, £1.3 million for administration as a whole, nearly £300,000 for defence.[1]

Something like 8*d*. per head per annum does not seem to offer scope for social services like health and education, even when supplemented by a few pence per head from the native administrations. It was quite insufficient to meet the rising flood of demand in the South; and where, as in most of the North, demand had not arisen, it would have been pointless to spend money in attempts to stimulate it. In the South demand for education and for certain kinds of medical attention had been building up for many years. The combined effect of amalgamation and of economic depression was to make it impossible for the Government to meet the educational demand by setting up schools of its own, or by grants-in-aid large enough to provide efficient, inspected, well-staffed schools managed by other agencies. The result was hundreds of unassisted schools, mostly mission schools, stretching the resources of those who ran them well beyond any possibility of supplying adequate buildings or anything but ill-paid, untrained teachers in quite inadequate numbers. Instead of using grants to raise standards, the penniless Government made unpopular attempts to control and even to prevent the proliferation of substandard 'hedge-schools', as Clifford had called them. As the depression deepened and mission resources dwindled, the standard of

[1] Figures for 1936–7 estimates analysed in *African Survey* (1938 edition), p. 1433. The 'administration' costs include, as well as 'provincial administration', such heads of expenditure as judicial, legal, audit, Treasury, Customs, Secretariats, police, etc.

the schools they had been led by popular demand to open dropped, the products of the schools became even less well prepared for life and employment than before, ill-paid teachers left in increasing numbers to take up clerical and other subordinate posts in Government and commerce. So there was an acceleration in the downward spiral of educational standards, a deepening mistrust of the Administration's intentions, a growing belief that the whole scheme of things was a wicked conspiracy to restrict the black man permanently to 'hewing wood and drawing water'. In 1929, when a central Department of Education was formed by combining the separate Northern and Southern departments, its annual budget of little more than a quarter of a million pounds was mostly swallowed up in the cost of maintaining a mixed bag of institutions founded in more optimistic days. Most were in the South, and ranged from teacher-training institutions to a few secondary schools like King's College, Lagos, and the Government primary schools set up in the days of Moor and Egerton. The Northern legacy of institutions was much smaller[1]—a miscellany of small schools originally opened for the education of chiefs' sons, a small complex of institutions at Kano founded on Sir Alfred Jones's bequest of £10,000 for education in Nigeria—in all, in 1929, 116 schools conducted by the Government, with financial assistance from the native administrations, and an average attendance of some three and a half thousand pupils. The Christian missions, mostly in the non-Moslem areas, were running 152 schools in the North, of which only 5 were assisted by the Government. In contrast to the South, there was not only no demand for education on Western lines, there was actual opposition to it, especially education for girls.

The problem of the medical services was not dissimilar; in the South, there was a brisk demand for injection treatment, stimulated by the Medical Department's success in curing yaws. Private practitioners and mission doctors were few, so demand was partly met by permitting private practice to Government medical officers. This gave rise to some abuses, and to exaggerated talk of abuses. The growing confidence in Western medicine led to demands for hospitals and dispensaries. These, once built, could be kept going, on the funds available, only by such expedients as the use of intelligent lads as 'dispensers' and daily-rated labourers as 'nurses'—their training being

[1] Smaller, but not less significant for the future; the Katsina College, for instance, was to provide most of the North's small but very prominent élite in later years.

what they managed to pick up as they went along from individual doctors and nursing sisters. It was the only way to meet the demand, without the necessary funds. And it worked, somehow. In 1920, there were 16 dispensaries in Nigeria. In 1940, there were 350, treating 2,288,000 out-patients. In 1920, there were 18 hospitals with 569 beds; by 1940 there were 85, with 4,135 beds.[1] These were nearly all in the South, where the demand existed, and where there were missions to help.

As in education, the efforts of the Government and of the missions were judged inadequate and inefficient. But when one considers that there was no real increase in the Government's revenues between 1920 and 1939, and that everything, from medical skill to drugs, bottles, and distilled water, was an expensive import, it is difficult to understand how it was possible to do all that was done; neither effort nor efficiency was lacking, but simply money.

Efficient and ruthless economy in the management of money was undoubtedly Cameron's chief contribution to Nigerian progress, but he did not allow financial stringency to prevent the resumption of administrative 'remodelling' where Clifford and he had been forced to leave it. Thomson's following of Lugard's advice and attempts to re-establish authoritarian 'indirect rule' and 'direct taxation' in the South had reached their culmination in a series of riots from 1927 to the Aba riots of 1929. Although direct taxation, a very hardy perennial plant when once introduced, was to survive, it was at least clear that 'rule' from above, direct or indirect, was not what worked in the South-East. Since authoritarian rule in the North was breaking into separate quasi-independent medieval states, and was also being undermined in the West by the growth of education, the time was ripe for a re-examination of 'indirect rule'. Cameron seems quite deliberately to have rejected the 'philosophy' of 'indirect rule' as 'a rather mysterious business', and to have insisted that, henceforward, it was simply 'local native administration' or local government. By introducing a new Native Administration Ordinance, and introducing protectorate courts presided over by officers who had no political functions, he broke the old notion of the administrator administering people, indirectly or directly, and made him responsible, under a fairly elaborate law, for the development of indigenous forms of local government which had to satisfy two requirements: first, they must be based on traditional ways, and second, they must be adaptable to

[1] *Nigeria Handbook* (1951 edition), pp. 122–3.

new, modern needs. This was a deliberate reversal of what he called 'the unhallowed policy insidiously introduced in the later twenties of this century (but not at the insistence of the Emirs) to claim eventually sovereign rights for the Moslem Emirates';[1] it was also a deliberate reversal of the tendency to make chiefs where none existed and to 'rule' through them. Cameron was thus intent upon trimming both the provincial administration and the native authorities down to manageable size. The Residents were to be agents of the central Government, no longer judges and indirect rulers, but functionaries whose duty in the field of local government was the fostering of 'development from below' in the interests not of the chiefs but of the people, according to law. And the native authorities themselves were to develop, not into independent states, but into effective forms of local government.

The next logical step, in view of the perennial difficulty of deciding how the apparatus of central government should dovetail with that of local government, would have been a review of the functions of the provincial administration as co-ordinators of both. Cameron was aware of the danger of a situation where the Residents were 'little more than deputies under a head Resident' (the Lieutenant-Governor, later Chief Commissioner, being 'head Resident'). Cameron found it impossible for him 'to tackle yet another delicate problem' within his 'abbreviated term of office'.[2] Had he found time—and of course money—it seems very likely that his reorganization would have been on the lines of what Cameron described as Egerton's 'efficient' system of Provincial Commissioners, each with a small Secretariat and a team of administrators and specialist officers assigned to him. Clearly, this process would have involved making the provinces effective units of government, responsible directly to the central Government, with their own legislature and budget, and they might then have formed the unit states in a future federation.

But Cameron did not complete 'the remodelling of the administrative machine' which Clifford and he had begun in 1919. His successor, Sir Bernard Bourdillon, made only one major change in the structure of the Administration, in 1939, when he divided the old Southern Nigeria into two, with the Niger as the dividing line. This

[1] Cameron, *My Tanganyika Service and Some Nigeria*, p. 75. See also A. H. M. Kirk-Greene, *The Principles of Native Administration in Nigeria* (Oxford University Press, London, 1965), pp. 193–225.

[2] Cameron, op. cit., p. 151.

step had the advantage of administrative convenience, as well as being a recognition of the social differences between the peoples who formed the majority in the West, the Yoruba, and those who formed the majority in the East, the Ibo. It is not clear whether the possibility of reverting to Egerton's three provinces (plus the Southern Cameroons) was ever contemplated, after Cameron's day; the Lugard myth had consigned all that to limbo. And later, when Bourdillon's successor Sir Arthur Richards (Lord Milverton) came to make his constitutional proposals for the post-war era, he decided to take the existing framework of three regions outside the colony of Lagos as a 'natural' division of the country and a firm basis for decentralization and constitutional advance.[1] Ironically, in the dispatch containing these proposals—the last major proposals for the political future of Nigeria to be put forward without prior discussion with Nigerian politicians —Lord Milverton gave pride of place, among the writings and the ideas he had studied, to Lugard himself; so the author of the original confusion was succeeding still in bedevilling the issues.[2]

Before this final act, however, which was to bring the period of what Dr Azikiwe called 'untrammelled bureaucracy' to an end, there had been a period of gradual recovery from depression, and the upheaval of a second World War, during which, once again, the overstretched administrative machinery came very near to collapse. There was the same process, as in the first World War, of extra war-time chores, of controls, shortages, depletion of staff, overwork, length-

[1] 'Nigeria falls naturally into three regions, the North, the West, and the East, and the peoples of those regions differ widely in race, in customs, in outlook and in their traditional systems of government. This natural division of the country is reflected in the machinery of administration, the three sets of provinces being grouped together each under a Chief Commissioner; but this purely administrative arrangement, besides being incomplete in itself through the lack of an adequate regional organisation at each Chief Commissioner's headquarters, has no counterpart in the constitutional sphere. Dispatch, dated 6 Dec. 1944, Governor of Nigeria to Secretary of State, published as Cmd. Paper 6599 (H.M.S.O., 1945).

[2] In his dispatch, having also mentioned that Lord Hailey's writings had been the foundation of his study of the subject, the Governor went on: 'I have also steeped myself in the writings and thought of Lord Lugard, who has had no equal in knowledge of the people and in grasp of the principles and practice of colonial administration. . . . If I may be permitted the observation, Lord Lugard never allowed principles to become divorced from practice and he held always before him the ideal of natural growth' (ibid., Cmd. 6599). Lugard was also a prominent and active member of the committee guiding Hailey's African research survey; his influence as an 'elder statesman' in African affairs was remarkably pervasive, and almost unchallenged in these years.

ened tours, constant inflation, and all the rest. But there were significant differences, too, the most significant being the stirring of political consciousness in both the well-educated few and the ill-educated many who were the products of the thousands of 'hedge schools'. In the last few years before the outbreak of war some of the ablest Nigerians had fought their way, without benefit of scholarships and official assistance, to and through universities in the United States and the United Kingdom, and were returning to Nigeria full of political and nationalist fervour,[1] finding eager and impressionable followers among the new literate generation—teachers, artisans, clerks, and junior civil servants, who became avid readers of a new and lively daily press ten times more scurrilous, more seditious, and more extreme than the sober and more dignified weeklies which had aroused Lugard's wrath during the first World War. The British official took pride of place in the demonology of this press, as a vicious oppressor, a racialist, living a life of ease and luxury, an enemy of freedom, a ruthless imperialist exploiter, and worse. The very excess of the spate of vituperation defeated its own ends, and for the most part libels and accusations went unchallenged and uncontradicted; a mistake, perhaps, since a few well-chosen libel suits would have done much to raise press standards—a vital consideration in any country, but especially so in a country where rival newspaper-owning political parties were soon to become rival newspaper-owning governments fighting acrimonious campaigns against each other in the columns they controlled.

As after the first World War, although this time without the same element of confusion through 'one-man rule', there was what Clifford had called 'a certain sourness of temper' and a 'disgruntled spirit' throughout the public service. History had practically repeated itself—establishments depleted, mounting pyramids of groundnuts at buying stations in the North which an overworked railway could not move, impoverishment of individual officers through inflation in the war years, strikes on a large scale by junior officials, open discontent among the weary veterans of the service. It was the mixture as before, except that the basis of magic on which the whole system had rested

[1] It was in 1938 that, with the help of Azikiwe and the newspaper he had just founded, the *West African Pilot*, the Nigerian Youth Movement won the Lagos Town Council elections and supplied the three elected members of the Legislative Council, supplanting the old-style politicians who had represented the older 'Lagosian' interests. There are several recent studies of the growth of political parties in Nigeria—see bibliography.

was disintegrating. It was only 'the white man's prestige' which had made it possible for a few hundred white officials to regulate the affairs of many millions. So long as the white man was regarded with some awe, his advice, judgements, and decisions were on the whole accepted and things got done. In 1946 Obafemi Awolowo wrote '... this myth about the omniscience and omnipotence of the Administrative Officer is fast disappearing (thanks to the agency of lawyers and public letter-writers)'.[1] In the remoter areas, this had not happened, and it was still possible for administrators to feel that they were doing useful work. It was by no means so easy to feel that in the areas where neither the old ways nor the new were working properly, and the district officer had to control the staff and the finances of the native administration, preparing the estimates, ensuring that the tax was collected, and taking decisions which ought to have been taken by councils and committees composed of suspicious old traditionalists and angry young literates who were unable to reach agreement. But for the district officer to step in at last and do what was necessary was an offence in nationalist eyes:

> Each Native Authority functions, or is supposed to function under the advice and guidance of one or more Administrative Officers. But in practice the Native Authority is a mere smoke screen for the petty autocracy of an Administrative Officer.[2]

As at the end of the first World War, the personnel and the *matériel* of the public service had reached breaking point at the very time when the need for a concerted effort of post-war reconstruction was greatest. For years both administrators and specialist officers had been diverting their efforts to the needs of war. The Public Works Department had constructed some thirty military airfields, and military camps and barracks. The Forest Department had turned its attention to the production of rubber and timber, the Veterinary Department had turned to dairy farming and meat production, a Labour Department had been brought into existence to supply and control the use of labour for a rapid expansion of tin and agricultural production, after war in the Far East had cut off supplies of tin, rubber, and oils. War at sea had brought losses of ships and men, shortages of essential imports, and a mass of paper-work, controls, rationing, licensing, and their attendant regulations and restrictions. Once

[1] O. Awolowo, *The Path to Nigerian Freedom*, p. 92.
[2] Awolowo, op. cit., p. 43.

again, long years of drudgery, discomfort, and increasing penury had left their mark on the European members of the service:

> If the vast majority of officers of between fifteen and twenty years' service are asked about their plans for the future, they reply without hesitation: (a) they wish to get out as soon as possible, (b) they will do all in their power to dissuade their sons from following in their footsteps, (c) they will not recommend young men of their acquaintance who may soon be on the look-out for jobs to accept a Colonial career.[1]

Sir Alan Burns has recorded in his memoirs some of his bitter impressions of this period, when 'overwork and overstrain, and a belief that their financial and other difficulties were not receiving sympathetic consideration, led to much discontent among the European members of the Civil Service, who nevertheless continued to perform their duties with their usual loyalty and efficiency.'[2] These remarks applied to the civil service in all the West African territories. Sir Alan Burns himself, as Governor of the Gold Coast, made repeated representations for a complete overhaul of conditions for over two years without result. Although the Colonial Office agreed that an inquiry was necessary, they professed themselves unable to find a suitable officer to undertake it. Finally, after all four West African Governors (in October 1945) had sought an interview with the Secretary of State ('we achieved nothing from our interview, except, speaking for myself, a deep sense of frustration'[3]), an inquiry into the public service discontents which were endangering the future was authorized, and made possible only by the release of the Chief Justice of the Gold Coast, Sir Walter Harragin, to undertake a review of conditions for all the public services of British West Africa simultaneously.

The principal structural change which emerged from the Harragin Commission was the replacement of the old pattern of 'African' and 'European' posts by a new concept of 'senior' and 'junior' services, with the same basic salary for both Europeans and Africans, and pensionable 'expatriation pay' for Europeans. The differential of expatriation pay, while insufficient to satisfy Europeans, was a bone of political contention, while the distinction between the senior service privileges (car allowances, first-class travel, European style quarters, etc.) and junior service conditions (shorter leave, bicycles and motorcycle allowances, etc.) was seen as a sinister and hypocritical move to

[1] From a 1945 report of a sub-committee, at Aba, of the Association of European Civil Servants (*Nigerian Journal*, vol. xxv, no. 4, Mar. 1945).

[2] Burns, *Colonial Civil Servant*, p. 207.

[3] Burns, op. cit., p. 209.

perpetuate racial discrimination. Actual increases in pay were not large enough, on the whole, to give satisfaction. And some of the 'improvements' had the effect of inducing the weary veterans to go rather than serve on. One of these changes was voluntary retirement at the age of 45; another was the abolition of rent-free quarters, and the introduction of rent payments at 10 per cent of salary—with a corresponding 10 per cent in increase in pensionable salary. This served to increase pensions by the same approximate percentage and helped those contemplating departure to make up their minds.

So the age of administocracy was ending more or less as it had started, in the aftermath of a World War, and in an atmosphere of general dissatisfaction, within the public service and outside it. But there were two significant differences. At last there was an élite of several thousands of Nigerians clamouring for constitutional advance, for career opportunities, for economic development, for 'democracy', 'freedom', 'independence', 'self government', 'socialism', and 'progress'. At last, there was a slight change in the external climate of opinion; in Britain, although 'imperialism' was no more to the public taste than it had been in the twenties, there was sufficient consciousness of past neglect and sufficient vague goodwill towards the overseas dependencies to permit the supply of some funds for their development, and no disposition at all to stand in the way of their independence. The ardent nationalists did not believe it, but they were beginning to beat noisily upon a door which was not locked, just a little stiff through lack of use.

# CHAPTER IX

# Transition to Ministerial Rule, 1948–1960

We are fed up with being governed as a Crown Colony, which we are not, nauseated by the existence of an untrammelled bureaucracy which makes, administers and interprets our laws without our consent.

Nnamdi Azikiwe.

THERE are several justifications for the somewhat arbitrary choice of the year 1948 as the starting point of the process of transforming alien 'administocracy' into the apparatus of modern, federal, parliamentary government, complete with Nigerian Ministers and 'Nigerianized' career public services. It was in 1948 that a newly-arrived Governor (Sir John Macpherson) and a very recently arrived Chief Secretary (Sir Hugh Foot, later Lord Caradon) set in motion the two simultaneous processes which were to lead to political independence in little more than one hectic decade. These two processes were the planned 'Nigerianization' of the public service, and the revision, through country-wide consultation, of the recently introduced 'Richards' Constitution. It was thus in 1948 that the celebrated 'wind of change' began to blow strongly in Nigeria, although it was not until 1960, the year of Nigerian independence, that the phrase was coined by the British Prime Minister during a tour of Africa. It was an on-shore wind from the Atlantic and the coast—the kind of storm-laden wind which annually contends with the dry harmattan and brings moisture and life even to the furthest parts of Nigeria, right to the edge of the Sahara.

It was also in 1948 that the financial provisions of the Richards Constitution came into effect. These gave reality to the idea of unofficial majority control of expenditure, through the Standing Committee on Finance of the Legislative Council. Divorced from executive responsibility, this was merely a power to oppose, delay, and obstruct official proposals, and to deny officials the men, money, and materials needed for the officially prepared ten-year programme of development. The element in the legislature hostile as a matter of course and of principle to officialdom was the N.C.N.C. party—the first recognizably nationalist and militant party, formed by Dr.

Azikiwe from one faction of the divided Nigerian Youth Movement. Zik's own 'nationalism' had in it ideological elements of something wider than 'nationalism'—pan-Africanism, international socialism, and the old 'West African Nationalism' of the Lagos intelligentsia of the twenties which Clifford had castigated a quarter of a century before, when saying 'some straight and hard things' to the old Nigerian Council.[1] Indeed, like most revolutionary movements, the new 'nationalist' spirit claimed a kind of world-wide relevance, an affiliation with the oppressed everywhere. The party could back the trade unions in the general strike of 1945, and at the same time it could reconcile this socialist emphasis with backing for the narrower commercial interests of the Nigerian businessman and small capitalist. But the movement's chief appeal within Nigeria was by no means nation-wide; it was to Zik's own people, the Ibo, prepared for 'charismatic' leadership by all the ferments of mission teaching, of land hunger, of population pressure, of emigration in search of wealth and employment in the towns of North and West as well as East, of disruption of traditional ways through changes in administrative policy—a whole series of upheavals affecting a social structure always less stratified and more egalitarian than the societies in North and West to which 'indirect rule' had been applied more easily.

Thus a 'nationalist' movement which was a conscious part of an 'international' movement for freedom came to be identified in the eyes of many other politically conscious Nigerians as a predominantly 'tribal' or at best as a 'regional' force in politics.[2] It was not long before this internationally inspired 'nationalism' gave rise to rival

[1] According to Clifford, a 'West African nation' was 'as manifest an absurdity as that there is, or can be an "European Nation"—at all events until the arrival of the Millenium, when we may perhaps hope to see a Sicilian Brigand falling into the arms of a Wee Free Scots trader of Glasgow, claiming him as his European brother, and a Burra highlander, of Biu, disembarrassing himself of his poisoned arrows the more cordially to embrace a Fanti barrister from Cape Coast' (*Address to Nigerian Council*, Dec. 1920). Clifford's words have been taken as evidence of official 'anti-nationalism'; but what Clifford wished to do was to get the educated element to pay more attention to Nigerian rather than 'West African' political institutions—both in the proposed Legislative Council and in the indigenous political institutions of Southern Nigeria, whose development he thought in danger of being 'stayed or stunted' as the result of amalgamation with the North.

[2] The international flavour of N.C.N.C. politics can be seen clearly in the title as well as in the content of the party newspaper the *West African Pilot* and in the books and speeches of Dr. Azikiwe himself—e.g. *Liberia in World Politics*. There are many recent accounts of the development of political parties in Nigeria; one of the clearest summaries is James O'Connell's chapter in *The Politics and Administration of Nigerian Government*, edited L. F. Blitz (1965).

'nationalisms' based on the main regional, linguistic, and ethnic groups in North-East and West. A catalyst was the introduction, at the beginning of 1948, of the financial arrangements of the Richards Constitution. The problem of allocating fair shares of revenue between the three regions became, suddenly, the most serious and intractable political issue. The regional Houses (with unofficial majorities nominated by provincial electoral colleges) had no power to appropriate revenue. They were themselves electoral colleges for the central Legislative Council, which made available, by its votes, an allocation of revenue based on the principles of derivation and the assignment of specific revenues to the regions or groups of provinces. At this time the actual needs of each region to maintain existing services did not coincide with the derivation of funds, but with the intensity of past demand for education and other services. So it was necessary to give the Eastern Region an 'extra' allocation. It was this necessity which brought out the latent possibility of inter-regional strife over the division of centrally collected revenues.

At the same time, the second intractable problem which was to dominate public administration in the next few years was being formulated—like the first—in the financial arena where officials and unofficials collided. The new unofficial majority, reproduced in the Finance Committee, contained 'nationalists' whose hostility to alien officialdom took the form of demands for Nigerianization and rejection of official proposals designed to make it possible to recruit and retain the expatriates needed for the execution of the development programme. There was a good deal of exasperation and frustration on both sides. For the officials, with memories of the days before the war when progress had been limited chiefly by lack of money rather than by lack of men to fill the establishment or by lack of authority to decide how available funds should be spent, it was a strange turn of events, now that more money was available, to find the progress of development held up by shortage of men and of materials, and by unofficials' disagreement with them over their proposed allocation of funds, or over improvements in conditions designed to recruit and retain the 'expatriates' whose services were needed if development was to make quick progress. For the unofficials, with bitter feelings about the inadequacy of services by officialdom in the past, and with deeply ingrained suspicions that Nigeria was being run by officials for their own benefit, it was anathema to be associated with measures to increase the numbers and to improve the conditions of British officials.

These two problems—the sharing of revenues between the regions and the question of salaries and conditions for expatriate officials—were the twin poles around which controversy sparked for several years, tending to distract political attention from the actual work of planned development of resources. The initiatives of 1948 in constitutional and public service reform can therefore be seen as radical ways out of current difficulties. The alternatives were either to slog on painfully through the proposed nine-year period of the Richards Constitution, with an official executive at the centre and in the regions, obstructed at almost every turn by an indirectly elected central legislature; or to throw everything into the melting-pot again, in the knowledge that constitutional change would certainly be in a centrifugal, fissiparous direction. The choice of the second course was a momentous one; it involved unleashing party political forces in the South and deliberate stimulation of political parties in the North before, rather than after, the laying of a firm foundation of economic development and of a Nigerian public service. To have deferred constitutional reform would have increased the tension of discontents in the South, and would have required a degree of direct moral and financial support for official rule which the British Government had never been able to provide—even in the days of Chamberlain and of expansion. As Sir Hugh Foot makes plain in his autobiography, the big step forward was taken without much sounding of local official or unofficial opinion, but with one eye on the disorders in the Gold Coast:

I arrived in Nigeria as Chief Secretary late in 1947, Sir John Macpherson came to take up his post as Governor in 1948. Not long after his arrival we had a vital conference in Government House. The Richards constitution had then been in full effect for little more than a year, and it had been stipulated that it must remain in force unchanged for nine years. We reviewed the whole political situation: we took into account the disorders and the changes which had recently taken place in what was then the Gold Coast. We came to the conclusion that we must at once take a new initiative. The Legislative Council was to meet in August. That seemed to be the best time to make an announcement. A recommendation was made by telegram to the Colonial Office. There was a quick reply.[1]

[1] Hugh Foot, *A Start in Freedom* (London, 1964), p. 103. This autobiography reveals that 'taking and holding the initiative' had become in him, by the time of his Nigerian appointment, almost a conditioned reflex. Of this episode in Nigeria he wrote: 'I tell the story to illustrate one principle only—and it is the essence of my experience whether in Asia or Africa or the West Indies or anywhere else. The most important thing is to take and hold the initiative. That is another way of

Although the writer adds: 'we were off . . . We had the people with us', he is perhaps nearer the mark in suggesting that the political initiative taken in 1948 was 'not in response to public pressure but in advance of it' and that 'its purpose was of course not only consultation but also the awakening of political awareness in every corner of the country'. In this, of course, it succeeded, but this awareness, in the West and in the North, was primarily an awareness of the danger of their regions and their peoples being first left behind and then dominated by the Ibo. It was no longer simply the division of money that was in question, it was the central issue of political power in an independent Nigeria.

The parallel initiative in the field of public service reform, or Nigerianization, included the appointment of a commission, of which Sir Hugh Foot was chairman and of which Dr. Azikiwe was a prominent member, 'to make recommendations as to the steps to be taken for the execution of the declared policy of the Government of Nigeria to appoint Nigerians to posts in the Government senior service as fast as suitable candidates with necessary qualifications come forward with special reference to scholarships and training schemes'. Appointed in June 1948, the commission reported on 10 August 1948,[1] in time for the meeting of the Legislative Council at which the preparation of further constitutional changes was announced by the Governor. The speed with which the commission's unanimous report was prepared and presented was a remarkable demonstration of its chairman's love of the initiative and of speedy action—and of his powers of oral persuasion. The proposals, which were accepted, amounted, in essence, to establishing the principle that Nigerians should be appointed (in the words of the terms of reference) 'as fast as suitable candidates with the necessary qualifications came forward'; that new Public Service Boards with unofficial majorities should judge 'suitability'; that a special effort should be made in scholarships, training courses, and survey of material within the service to ensure that 'the necessary qualifications' were obtained, and

saying that timing is all important. Not to allow frustration to set in. Not to allow opposition to bank up. The people must be given a lead, a hope, an assurance that orderly and constructive effort will be worthwhile. . . . Everything depends on clear lead and a sense of urgency in pursuing it' (op. cit., p. 106).

[1] *Report of the Commission Appointed by his Excellency the Governor to Make Recommendations about the Recruitment and Training of Nigerians for Senior Posts in the Government Service of Nigeria* (Lagos, 1948)—usually called 'the Foot Report'.

that candidates did 'come forward'. There was no overt suggestion that 'Nigerianization' might come to mean 'Northernization' for the North, 'Westernization' for the West, and 'Easternization' for the East, but there was a significant recognition of the difficulties of the Northern provinces, in a recommendation that 'special consideration should be given to applicants for scholarships and training courses from the Northern Provinces'. Four hundred and fifteen new scholarship and training awards were proposed for the next three years, including thirty reserved for women. There was also a recommendation that 'Nigerians should continue to be recruited to the Administrative Service'. This meant that Nigerians should be recruited into the provincial administration, as well as into administrative posts in central and regional government. But the commission still entertained the notion that provincial administration (which they called 'the administrative service', disregarding that service's role in central and regional government) was a temporary 'scaffolding' which would not always be needed.[1]

In the same year, 1948, there were two other initiatives in reform of public service which deserve mention. One was the introduction of the Whitley Council system of negotiation between Government 'official sides' and staff sides. The Harragin Commission sitting in 1946 had suggested separate 'advisory' Whitley Councils for senior and junior services. A report by Mr. T. M. Cowan of the United Kingdom Ministry of Labour in May 1948 went further, recommending that Councils should be empowered to agree changes in conditions, subject to the Governor's authority—the idea being that the official chairman of the Council (as in the United Kingdom) would be a senior officer able to negotiate within the limits of what would find favour with the Government—but, because of the Finance Committee's dogged hostility, there was in practice no room for negotiation, so far as the senior Whitley Council was concerned. So far as the two junior Whitley Councils were concerned—one for the clerical and supervisory grades and for technical personnel, and one for the immense variety of industrial employees, including Railway and Marine grades—the differences between official and staff sides were even

[1] 'The Commission recognises that the eventual aim must be for Native Authorities and other local government bodies to be developed to a stage when the need for an administrative service as we know it today will disappear.' But Nigerians should be recruited: 'the experience which they gain in the administrative service will be invaluable to them in whatever form of public service they may subsequently undertake' (Foot Commission Report).

more profound. Most of the 'staff sides' were at that time poorly paid and untrained trade-union officials, militant nationalists rather than sober negotiators. When the 'nationalist' movement began to separate into 'regionally' based parties it was a difficult time for the trade unions; they could no longer hope to organize themselves on a 'national' basis as the industrial wing of a 'nationalist' movement. The oldest of them, the Civil Service Union, succeeded in maintaining its organization and influence in the clerical grades, but as Nigerianization progressed the union lost most of its most energetic and able members, when they were promoted to the senior service. A spate of disagreement over matters such as the deliberate differential between the entry point to the standard clerical grade and the slightly higher technical grade, and the rigidity of the distinction between senior and junior service, led to demands for arbitration after disagreement in Whitley Council, on the pattern of the United Kingdom system. This the Government refused to concede, chiefly on the ground that there would be little attempt in council to reach agreement if disagreement were automatically followed by arbitration—and that if this kind of automatic arbitration developed the Government would have abdicated its duty of deciding salaries and conditions.

The other innovation in public service machinery in 1948 was made in recognition of the increasing complexities of personnel management in a growing and changing civil service. It was the appointment of a senior officer, with the rather misleading title of Civil Service Commissioner, in the Nigerian Secretariat, responsible to the Chief Secretary and the Financial Secretary, and in some matters directly to the Governor, for the whole personnel management function of the civil service in its process of expansion and transformation. This was a centralization of management in Lagos, taking place at a time when the tide of political 'regionalization' was beginning to run strongly, and for most of its six years of formal existence the Civil Service Commission's staff were struggling against the tide of devolution, the hardest pressed of all branches of the Secretariat, the most nearly submerged in a flood of papers of complaint, protest, query, and criticism.

Any outline of the structure and the personnel of the still unitary Nigerian public service in the year 1948 runs the risk of making the situation appear rather less confused and complex than in fact it was, when measures designed to reconstruct a unitary system of official government and to adapt it to the needs of the Richards Constitution and of the new development programme had to be quickly accommodated to a change of pace and direction. Rapid devolution to the regions and complex federal arrangements at the centre were to reverse the immediate post-war efforts to elaborate the old unitary structure and to strengthen administrative and specialist cadres in the provinces in order to carry out the ten-year official programme of development. This programme, as originally framed in 1945, was designed to spend £55 million in ten years (£23 million in grants under the Colonial Development and Welfare vote, £16 million in loan funds, and £16 million from Nigerian revenues). There were separate grants by the United Kingdom Government, amounting to £3½ million, for the new University College at Ibadan, for the Nigerian College of Arts, Science, and Technology, for broadcasting, for geological survey, and for roads in the Cameroons.[1]

In 1945, when the plan was made, the permanent 'senior service' in Nigeria numbered less than 1,400 men (1,300 expatriates and 75 Africans), although the authorized establishment in the 1945–6 estimates gave a total of 2,225. There were 227 temporary staff, mostly men on contract in the industrial departments (Railway, Public Works, and Marine). So, including temporary staff, there were about 1,600 men and women in 'European posts'. Of these, not more than 1,200 were on duty in Nigeria at any one time—a number much less in total than, for instance, the number of driving-test examiners in the U.K. civil service in 1965. There were 309 Europeans, 4 Africans, and 12 temporary staff in the largest division, the 461 posts making up the Administration; the next largest body was the Public Works Department, responsible for the construction and maintenance of trunk roads, bridges, airfields, public buildings of all kinds, and for several electricity undertakings, with 353 posts, 155 permanent European staff, 60 temporary staff, and one African officer in a 'European' post.

[1] The authors of the 1962–8 National Development Plan described this 1945 plan and its revision in 1951, in error, as 'the first attempt at any form of planning in Nigeria', but went on to describe them as 'not plans in the true sense of the word' but as 'a series of projects which had not been co-ordinated or related to any overall economic target'. But the 1945 planners had said clearly enough that their blend of economic and social programmes was a plan to put right 'certain fundamentals' and to ensure that, simultaneously, the people were put in a position to participate in the later consideration of a later 'properly balanced plan of development and welfare'. Their success in hitting this target should not be regarded as a failure to hit a different target not within range and so not chosen by them. (See Sessional Paper 24 of 1945 and National Development Plan, 1962–8.)

The third largest department, the Railway, had 318 posts, 19 senior Africans, 219 European permanent staff, 57 temporary staff. The fourth department, in size of establishment, was Education, with 137 posts, with 4 Africans, 86 Europeans, and more than 40 vacant posts. Other departments with more than 100 posts were Marine (129 posts), Agriculture (118), and Police (114). The Medical Department had 83 posts, Posts and Telegraphs 74, Forestry 51, Veterinary 47, Judicial 42 (with a significantly high proportion of Africans—16), Land and Survey 38, the Accountant-General's Department 36, the Colliery 30, Geological Survey 26, Customs 22, Audit 21, Mines 19 (with 9 vacancies), Legal 10 (1 African), Printing 9 (4 vacancies), Inland Revenue 9 (5 vacancies). One or two small departments scraped along with one caretaking officer—for example, the Government Chemist's Department and the Administrator-General. Even if there had been another Clifford to describe the scene at this time, it is doubtful whether even he would have had time to do so—the makeshift, picnic fashion of living had persisted; once again there were pyramids of groundnuts piling up in the Northern provinces which the exhausted railway could not shift quickly enough. In each department it was the same dismal story of shortages, 'bottlenecks', arrears, makeshifts in staff, in housing, in accommodation, in transport, stores, and equipment.[1]

By 1948 the grossly overburdened machinery of 'white man's rule' had been strengthened, or rather saved from collapse, chiefly by the foresight, based on long experience, of Sir Ralph Furse, who had sworn in 1919 to avoid chaos in recruitment next time there was a war, if he still had any responsibility for it.[2] As a result, the colonial service was one of the first major employers of manpower to tap the rich vein of men being demobilized. There was an unprecedented flow, in both quality and numbers, into the colonial service, of men slightly older and more experienced than the pre-war entry, coming from a wider social background.[3] They had spent their formative

[1] When in 1946 a Surveyor of Antiquities, Mr. K. C. Murray, was appointed (from the Education Department) his house was office and museum, and he remarked in his first annual report that he had not recruited a clerk because it had been impossible to acquire a typewriter!

[2] Sir Ralph Furse, *Aucuparius*, p. 268.

[3] Practically the only serious criticism before the war of the personnel of the colonial administrative service (and of the other professional services) was that they were being drawn too much from one class of men (public school and Oxbridge), and that this class tended towards more aloofness, less imagination, and less natural sympathy with the aspirations of colonial peoples than other classes

years in conditions of danger, hardship, and privation in deserts, jungles, Arctic convoys, or combat in the air, after which the tribulations of a colonial service life of constant improvization and makeshifts and changes of posting and of policy were merely irritating rather than intolerable. They were a generation whose expectations of comfort and security were little higher than those of the surviving 'old coasters'. By the end of 1948 this 'War Group' was the largest distinct group in the administrative service and in other services, and members of it were already in charge of divisions and doing responsible work in the Secretariats and departments. Without overseas recruitment of many hundreds of men in these immediate post-war years (before the inception of the welfare state and full employment in the United Kingdom) it is certain that the concurrent processes of post-war reconstruction and planned expansion of services, of 'Nigerianization', of 'regionalization', and political development generally, would have been gravely hampered. But the first effect of large-scale expatriate recruitment, as converted troopships and bomber aircraft arrived carrying dozens of new officials, was to stimulate fear and suspicion of a new era of alien official rule stretching into the distant future, with Nigerians relegated again to the role of 'hewers of wood and drawers of water'. There was no general appreciation that an increase in overseas recruitment was a condition precedent to an increase in Nigerian participation in government.

By the middle of 1948, there were in the 'senior service' or higher public service of Nigeria 3,786 posts (including 380 Railway posts)—an increase of 1,561 over the 1945 figure. But nearly one-third of the total number of posts was vacant—1,245. Only 245 posts were occupied by Africans[1] (36 in the Railway, 9 in the Administration). There were 148 vacancies in the total administrative establishment of 582

in British society from whom recruits might have been drawn in greater numbers. There was certainly a preponderance of Oxbridge recruits in the late twenties and thirties, when jobs were hard to find, but the post-war selection, mostly from those who had served as officers in the armed services, produced a wide variety of social and educational background difficult to classify but easy to distinguish from scrutiny of Colonial Office Lists: public school and Oxbridge, public school only, grammar school or state secondary school with and without Oxbridge or Redbrick degree. The 'ruling class' idea of the colonial administrator can easily be overdone; the majority, at any rate after the second World War, were 'officer material' from a very wide variety of backgrounds, rather than a single 'officer class'.

[1] i.e. 'non-expatriates'—Nigerians and 'West African officers' from Sierra Leone and the Gold Coast. None of these was a Northern Nigerian.

posts. The nine Nigerians were all men who had earned promotion 'the hard way' through the clerical ranks, through being given opportunities in the war years to hold down senior jobs in the Secretariats at Lagos, Kaduna, Ibadan, and Enugu. The best showing of Nigerians was made by the Medical Department, with 75 African officers, compared with 303 expatriates. Not all of these were doctors—the figure of 622 posts in the Medical Department included, as well as medical officers, senior posts in nursing, health inspection, leprosy control, and other miscellaneous posts. No less than 244 of the 622 posts were vacant. In the Education Department the shortage was even worse, with 288 vacancies out of 384 posts—and only 12 Africans in senior posts. Agriculture had 63 vacancies and 3 African officers in a total establishment of 131 posts.

The supply of overseas candidates from demobilized services was already dwindling;[1] already East African salaries were higher than West African salaries (they had been lower before the war), while Far Eastern salaries were much higher. Inflation was eating away the gains of the 'Harragin' salary settlement of 1946, the lack of security for a permanent career in West Africa was already apparent, the evil reputation of the Nigerian climate persisted, the official information supplied to candidates revealed the awkward fact that living costs could barely be met from the ordinary starting salary, and not infrequently candidates referred to serving officers for advice and information would be given enough of both to make them think again. In short, there was no practical prospect of filling the establishment by overseas recruitment from the United Kingdom, despite all the efforts made by greatly enlarged appointments branches of the Colonial Office and the Crown Agents. Everything pointed to fuller use of Nigerian talent.

Little has been said in previous chapters about the failure, since the early days of the century, to make full use of Nigerians in the civil service. Dr. Henry Carr, the first Nigerian to reach the rank of Resident, retired in 1924, and died in 1945. Between his retirement and his death no Nigerian reached comparable rank in the service—either in the Administration or in departmental work. One African, Joseph McEwen, rose in the Secretariat in Lagos to the position of

[1] Nigerian ex-servicemen were enabled to enter the civil service in large numbers by an ordinance reserving messengerial and similar jobs for ex-servicemen, and by the fact that English had been made the official army language. But no Nigerian had reached commissioned rank, and the level of entry was very low.

Principal Assistant Secretary (Establishments), a post graded equally with that of Resident, but one not requiring the 'white man's prestige' for its execution—merely hard work, specialized knowledge, ability to write clearly and quickly, and the 'embalmed wisdom' necessary in any senior civil servant.

There must have been many Nigerians of similar potential in the service; why so few reached senior rank is something of a mystery. It does not seem to have been the result of any overt, identifiable act of policy, but the outcome of the gradual estrangement between the educated class of Nigerians and the alien Administration. This began with Chamberlain's planned expansion into the interior, and the building up of a pioneering civil service based on the military model of officers and other ranks—the officers relying on the white man's prestige and on the mutual confidence between like-minded men. The first Nigerian casualties were the doctors taken on military patrols in the South; there was no confidence established between them and their white officer patients, and they were written off as failures. In the technical departments some of the first Nigerian engineers, qualified but lacking the technical background and experience, had been judged to have failed, and as unable to earn the respect of their subordinates—particularly that of their often very rugged, practical, experienced European foreman. There are examples of such cases, in the Colonial Office archives, of Africans tried out in senior posts, turning out unsatisfactory work, being warned and reprimanded, reacting in despair with lengthy protests and petitions alleging victimization because of race, and finally, having thus added breaches of decorum to errors of judgement, being demoted or asked to resign, amid official head-shakings of disappointment that yet another promising Nigerian should have failed to make the grade. It is easy to put these cases down to colour prejudice and a harsh, draconian system of discipline acting in combination, but doubts remain; in some of these instances the psychological strain of an isolated, senior position as a black man in an alien officialdom composed of white 'supermen' seems to have brought about a kind of nervous prostration in all but the toughest of Nigerians. And any educated Nigerian posted to the North had a further obstacle to surmount, in the antipathy of the Northerner educated in a different tradition. Whereas the white man had the help of 'prestige', the black official was likely to suffer slights and indignities on all sides. In these circumstances, it was easy, for a long time, for British and Nigerians alike to agree tacitly that 'administocracy' was 'white man's work' and that no ordinary black man, made conscious at every turn of the inadequacy of his own education and the inferior status of his people, could really be expected 'to sweat in the service of the white man'. The exceptional men who did, and were rising to the top when Nigerianization became a practical proposition, were exceptional in several ways:[1] in innate ability, in the educational opportunities they had enjoyed, or in an assured status in their own society, and in strength of physique and character. There was nothing of 'the brittle intellectual' or of the insecure upstart or sycophant in the Nigerians who forced their way to the front before Nigerianization was more actively encouraged. They were a new kind of Nigerian—neither 'black Englishmen' nor impassioned, revolutionary 'nationalists', but solid citizens and careful civil servants, well able to form conclusions of their own as to their country's future—a new 'estate' in the state, whose standpoint was significantly different from that of British officials and that of Nigerian politicans. But they were few, and some of them already nearing the age of retirement—fifty-five; like most of the other conditions of service in the 'senior service', the age of retirement was determined for purposes of recruitment from overseas to a service in which physical fitness was a prerequisite. Even in the sedentary posts in Secretariats and departmental headquarters a strong constitution was needed to withstand the pressures of the work itself, and—for Nigerians—the social and family pressures to which any senior civil servant was constantly subjected.

The direct pressure of the work itself may be judged from the fact that, at any one date in 1948, there were only some 1,500 'expatriates' and 200 'non-expatriate' senior service officers on duty 'governing' a country of some thirty million. And the 'governing' of the country was by no means the aloof, detached supervision which is erroneously supposed to have been one of the outstanding characteristics of British colonial administration. Nor was it simply a question of presiding effortlessly over the activities of a fully trained and competent

[1] Examples are invidious, but those whose names come most readily to the writer's recollection from these years were all men of exceptional physical and mental toughness and strength of character—in the Lagos Secretariat, S. O. Adebo, S. Ade Ojo, B. A. Manuwa; in the Medical Department, Dr. Manuwa; in the Judicial Department, A. Ademola—all of whom later reached the top of their professions, and, as it happened, all Yoruba, an indication of the greater progress in education and longer history of administration in Lagos and its protectorate.

subordinate caste of trained 'junior service' officials.[1] The most junior clerk was often more haughty and aloof in demeanour to the illiterate farmer than the Resident; the senior administrator was often more willing than the junior Nigerian graduate to take off his shirt and help in community road building and other manual work, fearing no loss of prestige thereby. There was in fact a good deal less 'aloofness' possible for the British administrator or medical officer, working without competent and numerous subordinates, than their counterparts in Whitehall or in a London teaching hospital would have considered necessary to maintain their dignity. The Nigerian civil service was typically a workaday, active service of youngish men in shorts and open-necked shirts, from the Marine pilot climbing the ship's side by rope-ladder to the touring judge in a kit-car, from the development officer improving cattle-tracks in the Cameroons to the bush doctor and leprosy control officer living their allegedly 'aloof' lives in the Government leper settlements. The white official did not consider it beneath his dignity to sweat and to dirty his hands if necessary, wearing much the same clothing as the daily-rated labourer. It was the educated black man whose literacy was an avenue of escape from manual toil who was more concerned about the outward trappings of dignity and more consciously 'aloof' in many ways.

Most of the 1,500 expatriates, in 1948, were directly engaged, not in maintaining 'law and order', but in the work of economic and social development—in efforts to stimulate the economy of the country. The old, model-T Ford machinery had been elaborated just before, during, and just after the second World War by the addition of new refinements—the setting up, just before the war, of the new office of the Financial Secretary, and, just after the war, of the new office of the Development Secretary, both of them contained, with the new office of the Civil Service Commissioner, in the old Nigerian Secretariat, in the building begun by Egerton as ample accommodation for the Secretariat of the Southern Nigeria of half a century before. There were also new departments crammed into the original

[1] 'Another Public School-imbued characteristic of colonial civil servants was their aloofness from the people they ruled.' This is an American view (Robert Heussler, *Yesterday's Rulers*, p. 97) which seems not to take into account the fact that nearly all colonial civil servants were in close, daily contact with Nigerians of all kinds in their daily duties—from the Governor to the most junior European; some preferred privacy and seclusion in their leisure, but the majority had at least one leisure activity—usually sport—which involved contact with Nigerians on more nearly equal terms.

building and the temporary war-time huts in the Secretariat grounds —the new Department of Commerce and Industry and the new Department of Marketing and Exports. The first was the offspring of the development plan, set up 'to assist, to advise, and where necessary, to participate in such economic improvements and developments as may be decided upon'. The second, the Department of Marketing and Exports, was formed from the first, in 1948, when the functions of marketing export produce were transferred, leaving to the Department of Commerce and Industry as its main responsibility the development of local trade and of local industries, accelerating industrial development, the control of goods in short supply, and the preparation of commercial reports and surveys.

Of all the departments of the unitary, official Government as it approached the era of 'regionalization', of 'Nigerianization', and of ministerial government, only the Nigeria Police, the Prisons Department, and of course the Judicial Department could properly be said to be exclusively concerned with that maintenance of law and order erroneously regarded as the main preoccupation of British colonial administration.

And these three departments of the central Government directly concerned with the 'tough' functions of government were basically Southern departments—both in the origin of their Nigerian staff and in the actual field of their operations. In the North, outside the new urban centres or townships, the enforcement of law and the maintenance of order remained the business of native courts and native authorities under the system of indirect rule, supervised by the British provincial administrator.

In normal times the peace was undisturbed, and the administrator could relegate the 'tough' functions of fighting and quelling disorder to the background, and concentrate his attention on the 'tender' functions of government—the various kinds of progress which post-war revenues were at last making possible: economic development (under the stimulus of Colonial Development and Welfare Funds), political development (under the stimulus of the Colonial Office's new zeal for democracy in local government[1] and the decision to revise the

[1] See R. E. Wraith's chapter v, '*Local Government*', in J. P. Mackintosh's *Nigerian Government and Politics* (London, 1966) for a description of the efforts made by British administrators in Nigeria in this period to democratize local government, in response to the dispatch from the Secretary of State dated 25 Feb. 1947 which 'laid upon African Governors the duty of developing, as a

Richards Constitution), and the development of social and welfare services. To the new generation of British administrators this work of development on a wide front made a strong appeal, and was a satisfying outlet for high ideals of altruistic service. Compared with this 'constructive' work, the basic task of keeping the peace was rarely a main preoccupation. Older Residents and district officers knew well enough the times, the seasons, and the occasions when minor disorders might flare up—chieftaincy disputes, boundary disputes, disputes over tax-collection—and prided themselves on their ability to detect the signs in good time and take tactful action to end the trouble before it grew and spread into the kind of conflagration which led to loss of life, police or military action, judicial inquiry, and possible censure and damage to official careers and reputations. In this kind of work, however, it was not the innumerable successes which became publicly known; it was the infrequent failures.

Failures by administration and police to settle public disturbance without loss of life were so infrequent, in the years before independence, that little political attention was directed to the structure and the role of the military forces in aid of the civil power in an independent Nigeria, or to means of ensuring civil control over the armed forces. The small army, commanded by a series of seconded British officers with the rank of major-general, and officered until independence almost exclusively by British officers seconded for two tours from their parent regiments, was not regarded as an integral part of the machinery of government. In a Nigeria at peace, the army, paid and serviced by the War Office in London, was publicly seen only as a ceremonial and musical adjunct on important occasions and as a source of ceremonial guards for Government House. The army was rarely called out for duties in aid of the civil power; its British officers on loan were divorced almost completely from the social and political life of the country. It was not until after Nigerian independence that political and popular attention came to be focused on the fact that the ultimate force in the newly independent country remained under the command of a white, British general, aided by senior British advisers. Only then was it realized that nothing like the same attention had been given to this crucial form of power as had been given over the years to the civil service and to civil politics. Until then, the army had remained quite aloof from politics, in a world of its own. There was

matter of urgent priority, an "efficient and democratic system of local government" '.

no 'service' lobby among the politicians; hardly any parliamentarians had a service background; the Nigerian Ex-servicemen's Welfare Association wielded little influence; there was as yet no Nigerian 'officer class' waiting on the side-lines to seize power from politicians whom they regarded as corrupt and inefficient.

Lack of thought, or perhaps lack of fear for political control of the armed forces, turned out to be a principal deficiency in the planning of independence, as the military *coup d'état* of January 1966 was to demonstrate so clearly.[1] Apart from this omission, which appears in retrospect so startling and fateful, there was a rough kind of balance being maintained, throughout the decade before independence, between economic development, constitutional development, the development of Nigerian public services, the development of local government on the model of the United Kingdom, and the development of social services.

Great effort was put into all these forms of development, but the results were unevenly spread; they showed only in patches where the various demands were strongest. Thus, for the services of the Medical Department, the Education Department, the Co-operative Department, the Land Department, and such exotic novelties as the Public Relations Department, the Broadcasting Department, and the Social Welfare Department,[2] the chief demand was in the South. It was only in the work of the Veterinary Department, the Mines Department, and, to a less extent, the Geological Survey Department that the predominant activity was in the North rather than the South. Each of these three departments had its headquarters in the North—Geological Survey at Kaduna Junction, in old railway buildings, the Veterinary and Mines departments at Vom and Jos, respectively, on the plateau. The Agriculture and Forest departments had remained based on Ibadan, where the early history of development of the old Lagos colony had placed them. Their strongest representation in staff was still in the South, with their training schools; they had relatively few men serving in the North or recruited from the North.

Similarly, the main installations of the major industrial departments, or 'socialized industries' of the unitary Nigerian Government

[1] See pp. 307–8.

[2] The last three, dating from the second World War, were still in their infancy, and not readily accepted into the British colonial hierarchy; most administrators were suspicious of the first two; the third was virtually confined to activities in Lagos.

—the Railway, the Posts and Telegraphs, the Marine, and the Public Works Department—were still in the South, with only a few minor installations and workshops in the few Northern centres of developing communications. These departments too recruited most of their staff, and trained them, in the South. Each of these departments had a large number of trade unions representing different grades of workers. The unions also were almost entirely Southern both in their cadre of paid officials and in their membership. One or two of these officials of Government trade unions were attracted into Government service, as trainee labour officers, in the immediate post-war years when the official Colonial Office policy was the rapid development of democracy in industry, as in national and local government. The Labour Department, originally staffed by seconded administrative officers, was one of the first departments to make really effective use of Nigerian talent in 'senior service' posts, and to train young Nigerians (once again, mostly Southerners) in the skills of conciliation and arbitration in industrial disputes. This kind of training, and subsequent experience, was perhaps as good a preparation as any for senior administrative work in a developing country. The work of a labour officer gave some insight into both the public and the private sector of the Nigerian economy, brought civil servants into direct, face-to-face contact with both sides of industry, on their own ground, usually at times when passion and prejudice were at their height, and developed the ability to see more than one side of any given problem, and the ability to devise and to negotiate tactfully workable solutions, with careful attention to the law and to accurate drafting and interpretation. It is therefore no accident that so many of the first Nigerian permanent secretaries had a Labour Department background.[1]

[1] At least four of a small group of young Nigerians trained by E. A. Miller, the first Commissioner of Labour (and known as 'Miller boys'), were among the first Nigerians to reach the level of Permanent Secretary. One was the first Nigerianization Officer appointed by the Federal Government (F. C. Nwokedi) and later Permanent Secretary, Ministry of Foreign Affairs; another was the first Permanent Secretary to the Federal Ministry of Establishments (M. O. Ani); another was the first Nigerian Secretary for Establishments and Organization in the Western Region (P. Odumosu); another (a former railway union official) became Permanent Secretary to the Federal Ministry of Labour (M. A. Tokunboh). None of these men had a university or legal education; they were personally selected and trained by an able and experienced administrator building up a single new department. Ali Akilu, first Northerner to become head of the region's public service, was also a product of the Labour Department.

In 1948, as the wind of change began to blow towards 'regionalization', 'Nigerianization', and an eventual independent federation, the general picture was therefore one of the old 'Model-T' administrative machine more than fully stretched in the attempt to adapt itself to enormous economic, political, and social demands. Lack of money was no longer the chief difficulty—revenues were buoyant throughout the whole decade before independence; it was the shortage of trained staff which was the most persistent problem. Repeated collision between official and non-official opinion on how best to spend the funds available made it impracticable fully to overcome the immediate post-war shortages of staff, of quarters for staff, and of equipment and plant needed for staff to use. Conditions of service and salaries fell short of what was necessary to avoid a high rate of wastage of those recruited from overseas. Even with Nigerianization on an increasing scale and considerable effort by the recruitment branches of the Colonial Office and of the Crown Agents, the overall 'senior service' shortage remained about a quarter of the total establishment. There was constant inflation; salary adjustments were conceded only when discontent had reached danger-point, or when political developments were about to demand a special effort on the part of the public service. This became the recurrent pattern in the years between 1945 and independence in 1960.[1]

[1] The cyclical pattern was one of 4–5 years. The first post-war revision of 1945–6 (the Harragin Commission) set the pattern of senior and junior services, introduced voluntary retirement at the age of 45, and the concept of 'basic' salary common to Nigerians and overseas officers, with pensionable 'expatriation pay' for the latter; an internal inquiry by two senior officers of the Civil Service Commission in 1951–2 (the Milne–Levy Report) led to the consolidation in new salary scales of temporary additions granted the previous year, reintroduced overlapping between 'senior' and 'junior' salaries, and began the trend towards a new 'executive' class in the civil service. In 1954–5 the Gorsuch Commission, appointed by the Secretary of State on the original initiative of the leader of government business in the Western Region (Obafemi Awolowo), led to a revision of the structure of the public service in each of the new public services which came into being in October 1954, the federal service, and the three regional services. The 'Gorsuch' recommendations on structure sought to abolish the 'senior' and 'junior' service distinction, and to replace it by the U.K. pattern of administrative, executive, and clerical classes, with corresponding equivalents in the professional branches. Expatriation pay for overseas officers was replaced by 'inducement addition' for overseas officers below the superscale level, and by giving superscale officers, Nigerians as well as overseas officers, a 'consolidated' salary which included the old 'expatriation pay' element. Children's passage concessions and children's allowances proposed by the Gorsuch Commission to benefit overseas officers with families were unacceptable to the Nigerian governments, which introduced measures of their own which they thought might be more acceptable

After each delayed review civil servants and Government labour would receive several months' arrears of pay at new rates. This would be followed or accompanied by revised salaries for teachers, local government and commercial employees, Ministers, and legislators, and would set a new trend in price inflation which briskly obliterated any advantage gained. Then would follow years of growing discontent, not curable without another all-round increase in pay to the whole of the Nigerian salariat and organized labour force, all being linked to and based upon the wage and salary rates adopted by the Government. The increases granted were thus normally cancelled out by further increases in the cost of living as soon as they came into effect.

In the public service, each of the major revisions of salary thus became something of an inducement to British officials to leave the service. The Harragin Salaries Commission of 1945–6, for instance (introducing voluntary retirement at the age of forty-five at a time when 'anti-colonialist' national feeling was strong and political initiatives were being taken which many of the older officers considered unwise), convinced many of the British officers recruited in the twenties—before the depression which halted recruitment for several years—that it was time for them to go. Many were convinced that political 'concessions' to nationalist politicians and 'agitators' with dubious records were 'selling-out' the whole idea of developing a harmonious polity founded on more effective, more responsible, and more representative local government. And those who had always been sceptical of the orthodox doctrines had equally good reasons for deciding to go. The arithmetic was simple: some of these officers, both in the Administration and in the departments, might have served for twenty or even twenty-five years on 'the long grade' without a single promotion other than the routine crossing of a promotion or efficiency bar; those abler or luckier might have been promoted to senior district officer, or its professional equivalent, and have no further prospect of promotion. The provisions of the pensions legislation were such that, if they retired, they would be paid at least half their salary for sitting quietly at home. For many, particularly the married men with young families who had to maintain two establish-

to public opinion. In 1959–60, at the suggestion of the Secretary of State, the Mbanefo Commission was appointed to revise salaries again (but not structure) by the federal, Northern, and Eastern governments: the West had already appointed the Morgan Commission to undertake its own review.

ments, continued service in the new post-war Nigeria at something like £1,600 a year, constantly eroded by uncompensated inflation, with poor or uncertain prospects, in difficult and still uncomfortable conditions, seemed too foolish as an alternative to peaceful retirement and family life at home on a pension of £800 a year. Supplemented perhaps by a pleasant and less demanding job, or by a small private income, life on pension was an idyllic prospect compared with life in the pillory in Nigeria as 'a wicked imperialist' accused of standing in the way of that progress which would not have been possible without them. So, in the immediate post-war years, many of the pre-depression vintage of British officers quietly left the field. Those who stayed the full course until the age of fifty-five were usually the bachelors or childless married men on whom the homeward pull was not so strong. By 1954 most of this generation had gone, and with them such diehard opposition in principle as had ever existed to the unplanned, party-political form which Nigerian nationalism was now taking.

After the wide gap in recruitment during the lean years of the early thirties the next clearly identifiable group of British officials was formed by those appointed in the five or six years before the second World War. For these men—mostly able men recruited from the universities in years of keen competition for scarce opportunities of a career—the Staff List took on a more interesting appearance as their seniors departed and 'regionalization' and expansion of services developed. Quite apart from any reasons of greater sympathy with the aspirations of Nigerian nationalist politicians,[1] it was clearly in these men's interests to adapt themselves as cheerfully as possible to the wind of change; public duty and private interest coincided, more or less. This group of men, who in about 1950 were in their forties, had better short-term prospects of promotion (and so of higher pensions) than the generally low level of remuneration in the service would suggest. A promotion worth £200 per annum in salary for a few years before retirement could mean an increase in pension for the rest of the officer's life of rather more than that sum, if only he waited long enough to take advantage of the possibility of retirement under the *interim* constitutional arrangements

[1] For those educated at school and university, after the first World War, the general intellectual background in the United Kingdom was that of the post-war revulsion from imperialism, and of guilt feelings about empire. Volumes from Victor Gollancz's Left Book Club were on most officers' bookshelves, when they had bookshelves.

providing for an addition to pension of approximately one-quarter.[1]

For some of this generation, and for all of the large 'war group' who entered the service in the forties, it might be best to hang on until regional self-government (long heralded in the East and West) or Nigerian independence brought with it the promised scheme of lump-sum compensation for loss of career. As the maximum compensation under this scheme was fixed at forty-one (except for the judiciary) its prospects were less alluring for the very young and for those well over forty. It is hardly possible in a summary to do justice to the complexities of individual cases, but in general the financial and other difficulties of continuing to serve in Nigeria in the years before independence contrasted sharply with the benefits which each stage of constitutional advance offered to those who chose to go. And each salary revision, usually coinciding with another constitutional change, seemed to one category or another a suitable point of departure.

The large 'war group' of overseas officers were increasingly the work-horses of the service as they gained experience. Probably no officer in this category in Nigeria was simple enough to believe, once he was in the service, that there was a prospect of a full, normal career before him—whatever impression he might have gained from the recruitment authorities. It was these men, joining at varying ages, but mostly in their twenties, after war service, who had most to gain by seeing Nigeria through to independence. Under the schemes for compensation for loss of career eventually introduced, officers with a minimum of ten years' service and aged forty-one qualified for the

[1] The scheme for retirement on pension with additional allowance came into force in the East and West in 1954, and in the federation and the North in 1957; i.e. when the senior officials who had been members of the Council of Ministers (Chief Secretary and Financial Secretary) and of the regional Executive Councils (Civil Secretary, Financial Secretary, Development Secretary, and Legal Secretary) left those councils, their offices being abolished and their places taken by Ministers; in practice, with the Governor-General or regional Governor continuing to preside, and with an official appointed as Attorney-General in each case, and with each Minister advised by an overseas officer as Permanent Secretary, there was no sharp, sudden change from official/political dyarchy in council to purely political cabinet government at this stage. But the officer with, say, 25 years' service in 1952 who postponed his retirement until he qualified for additional allowance found it profitable. E.g. a Western officer on £1,800 p.a. aged 47 in 1952 would qualify for a pension of £900 on retirement in 1952 after 25 years. If instead, he secured a promotion in 1952 to £2,000 p.a. and retired in 1955 his pension would be approximately £1,400 p.a., *discounting* the salaries revision which took effect in 1954. *With* the benefit of salaries revision, his pension could be of the order of £1,600 p.a., almost twice the hypothetical pension on retirement in 1952.

maximum lump sum compensation (about four years' salary, up to a maximum of £9,000) in addition to earned pension. It so happened in Nigeria, therefore, that the largest single group of officers, those recruited just after the second World War, could count on completing ten or more years' service and reaching the age of forty-one fairly near the time when the various compensation schemes came into force in the regional and federal services (1956 in East and West, 1959 in the North, 1960 in the federal service). Thus these men, like those who entered the service immediately before the war, tended to have their eyes fixed, for the last few eventful years before independence, not so much on full career prospects and unlikely ameliorations in service conditions as upon securing promotion to superscale posts before independence and then departing at the point in time when the factors affecting both compensation and pension gave the most favourable result. A handful of older men in the administrative and professional services preferred to remain in the provinces, away from the political turmoil and ferment of Lagos and the regional capitals, continuing the work of paternal administration so long as that pattern continued to make sense. But from the rest, the majority, brought more and more into the growing central and regional ministries as the years went by, Nigerian politicians obtained a degree of cheerful co-operation in destroying the old pattern and building ministerial rule in its place which was a source of frequent surprise to them. Misled by the popular, stereotyped preconception of the British administrator as a stiff, unadaptable authoritarian, and themselves eager for power, they found it difficult to believe that the average British officer was just as eager to see Nigeria successfully independent as they were themselves;[1] for both, independence meant liberty. The attitude of British officials in the North was on the whole rather less valetudinarian than the general attitude in the South, in the earlier stages, for the good reason that career prospects there seemed to be longer, by a few years; but to set against this, living conditions for families were not so good, and promotion, when the new regional services were created, was noticeably slower.[2]

[1] As one Western region adminstrator said to an overseas visitor who asked what British officials thought of the prospects of independence: 'Independence? Why, our wives and children demand it!'

[2] In *Nigerian Government and Politics* (p. 32) J. P. Mackintosh noted the much greater attachment to the people and nostalgia for the country among retired Northern Region officers whom he visited at home than could be detected in officers retired from the Southern regions.

If British officials in Nigeria had been more numerous, more powerful, more entrenched in lucrative office (if, in fact, they had resembled the Indian Civil Service rather more closely), Nigerian nationalists would have had a harder struggle for power; but neither in Nigeria nor in London was there any vested official interest in maintaining official rule a day longer than necessary to complete the complicated process of withdrawal. From 1948 onwards, there was no dispute between British officials and Nigerian politicians about the objective—an intact, independent Nigeria with a 'viable' economy, under 'majority rule'. But, from the point of view of the Secretary of State and of the Colonial Office, there was an obvious need, until Nigeria became fully self-governing, to ensure that the public services, the machinery of government, should remain under the effective control of the Governor, and capable of governing the country, no matter what political and constitutional developments took place. This immediate practical need led to constant emphasis, throughout the series of constitutional conferences in the fifties, on the importance of maintaining the 'independence' of the civil service, and of the judiciary. Control of the machinery of government, the public service itself, was, therefore, the ground over which nearly all the minor skirmishes and major battles between the politicians and the officials were fought, in the years of constitutional change. Although the professed ideal on both sides was a politically 'neutral' civil service, protected from party political interference, such processes as Nigerianization, regionalization, and the assertion of political authority over British officials by Ministers were issues of the first political importance, exacerbated by emotional nationalism and hunger for power on the one hand, and by scepticism, conservatism, and distrust on the other. When a direct collision occurred, it was usually resolved by some compromise with the principle of insulating the public service from political interference, often accompanied by the voluntary transfer or retirement from the service of the senior official concerned, making way for another, usually one more prepared, for whatever reason, to give way gracefully.[1]

As to the three main processes mentioned above—'Nigerianization', 'regionalization', and the assertion of political authority over officials in the newly organized ministries (which came to be known as 'integration of ministries')—it was the order in which they occurred

[1] There were many such instances, widely known in the service, but no good purpose would be served by giving names and details.

which can now be seen to have had more significant and lasting results than the mechanics of each of the processes.

In particular, the big move forward in Nigerianization in 1948 took place before, and not after, the pattern of a loosely knit federation with separate federal and regional public services began to emerge. For the first few years, Nigerianization was regarded as a process of finding and training the best qualified Nigerians available and appointing them to posts in the unitary officialdom. With education in the North so far behind the South, this meant 'Southernizing' the senior branch of a civil service already almost wholly 'Southern' in its junior branch. The new Nigerians were fitted into the colonial service pattern of an administrative service under the leadership of Governor and Chief Secretary and of Lieutenant-Governors and Residents, and of separate professional departments under senior British professional directors. But as soon as serious Nigerianization of this alien administocracy began, there was a stiff price to be paid for the lack of uniformity of policy in North and South in the previous half-century. Educated Southerners pressed their demands for admission of Nigerians to the 'senior service', and both educated and uneducated Northerners who had been happy to accept white men in positions of authority were not prepared to see Southerners in dominant positions.

It was not long before the salient fact emerged that 'Nigerianization' could mean very different things in different parts of the country, and that the 'tribal' or 'racial' or ethnic origin of the new 'non-political' public services was to be kept right in the forefront of politics.

The process of constitutional reform begun simultaneously in 1948 in a sense militated against the progress of both Nigerianization and economic development, by concentrating attention and interest on political development. One of the unintended results was that political independence was reached (unlike the position in India, in Ceylon, and in Ghana) when two of the governments which emerged (the Federal Government and the Northern Region Government) were still uncomfortably dependent upon the services of overseas officials in crucial senior posts.

An alternative course in the planning of the new machinery of government would have been to use the period of the Richards Constitution to the full, building up a career service of Nigerians—including a special effort in the field of training and education in the

North—and a firmer economic base, and rearranging the provincial administration, the Secretariats and the departments into a form nearer to the ministerial pattern, before Ministers were appointed. This done, Ministers would have come into a pattern of administration already adapted to receive them.

To have embarked on ambitious administrative engineering of this kind would have been very 'un-British'. It would have run counter to both the old idea of the development of indigenous institutions from below which characterized indirect rule at its best and the new idea of constitutional development from below. Under both the old and the new doctrines answers to the question how Nigeria should be governed were to be given by Nigerians themselves, not by British officials. The process of throwing this question out for public discussion at all levels led, through the Regional and General Conferences in 1949 and 1950, to the 'Macpherson Constitution' of 1951. Thus Ministers arrived on the scene before there were ministries to receive them; they represented the new 'regional' party-political forces (N.P.C., N.C.N.C., A.G.) committed to the task of consolidating their power in the regions as they existed; for the largest region, the North, remaining large was fundamental.[1] For British officialdom to have sought to impose a new pattern of states and public service machinery before admitting Nigerians to participation in the Government would certainly have been bitterly resented; but appointing Ministers first, without ministries in working order, and then telling them they should not attempt to interfere with the civil service were also measures bitterly resented. To have deferred the date of participation in the executive Government by party politicians might have endangered peace and embittered the political atmosphere further; but from the narrower point of view of building up an effective Nigerian non-political career service there would certainly have been advantage in building first a stronger cadre of indigenous officials, Northern and Southern, before superimposing mixed ministerial and official rule.

When Ministers were appointed at the centre and in the regions, at the end of 1951, they made 'Nigerianization' one of their first concerns.[2] The Nigerian service was still a unitary public service, with

[1] The crux of the matter, of course, was the distribution of seats in the central legislature on the basis of population (see Mackintosh, op. cit., pp. 25–6).

[2] The regional scholarship schemes begun in 1952 by each region's Ministry of Education were intended primarily, although not exclusively, for the training of regional talent to fill 'senior service' posts in the civil service.

some powers delegated by the Governor to regional Lieutenant-Governors and to heads of departments, with an Assistant Civil Service Commissioner posted to each region acting as a link between the central Civil Service Commission and the regional authorities. Regional Ministers had no power and no authority over the public service; they were given an administrative officer as a Secretary, whose thankless duties ranged from attempts on the Minister's behalf to persuade heads of departments to accept some of the Minister's policy suggestions (and putting officials' rejection of these suggestions into tactful language) to accompanying the Minister on tour as baggage-master and general factotum. Some officers brought in from running their own districts to the regional capitals and to Lagos in order to play this role of Figaro to a newly appointed Minister found all their adaptability and sympathy for nationalist aspirations fully stretched. The Ministers were sensitive of their dignity, inexperienced, and felt that they were being deliberately kept as useless extra wheels on the coach; regional Ministers in particular resented the fact that the public service was a unitary service directed from Lagos, over which even their own official colleagues in the regional Executive Councils had little influence in matters of policy.

One of the first things to become clear, in the early days of the Macpherson Constitution, was the intensity of the apprehension felt by the Northern Region Ministers lest the progress made as a result of the Foot Commission should have the effect of 'Southernizing' public service posts in the Northern Region. If Southerners entered the 'senior service' in great numbers, quickly, before Northerners were trained, Northern politicians feared that these men would be senior and dominant, and would gain a permanent hold. In May 1952 the Northern Region Executive Council, soon after taking office, reached the conclusion that suitable and qualified Northerners should be given preference over other claimants for office; and that no appointments of Southerners should be made to posts in the Northern Region without prior consultation with the Northern Region Executive Council. Simultaneously, the Executive Council of the Western Region was digging in its toes over the appointment of new expatriates, and adopting the so-called 'frigidaire' policy: this used the legislature's powers of supply to provide that no 'expatriation pay' should be paid to new expatriates unless the Executive Council had first specifically authorized payment. Ministers in the West also expressed misgivings about the appointment of Easterners

—particularly in the Police—to posts in the West. Meanwhile, in the Eastern Region, the first region to attempt a reorganization of local government on the United Kingdom model,[1] the main political thrust against officialdom was directed at the post of Resident, the personification of official authority in the system of 'indirect rule'.

These were the chief tensions and dissatisfactions which led to the appointment, in April 1952, of Sir Sydney Phillipson, and Mr. S. O. Adebo 'to review the policy of Nigerianization of the Civil Service and the machinery for its implementation and to make recommendations'. Their report,[2] a lucid analysis of the problems, in their historic setting, was submitted a year later, in April 1953—just at the time when inter-regional tensions were at their height, showing themselves in the bitter opposition by the North to the Western motion for 'self government in 1956' debated in the central legislature in March, in the Kano communal riots in May 1953, and in the resignation of Action Group members from the Council of Ministers, which made it impossible to keep the Macpherson Constitution in being. After the Kano riots the Secretary of State openly abandoned the attempt to operate a closely-knit Nigerian federation, and decided to summon the Constitutional Conference in London in July 1953, resumed at Lagos in January 1954, expressly designed to provide for greater regional autonomy.[3]

Thus, it was not until after the conference ended, in January 1954, and after it had been decided to split up the unitary Nigerian public service, that it was found 'practicable' to have the Phillipson–Adebo Report examined by the Council of Ministers.[4] It was then possible

[1] The Eastern Region Local Government Ordinance of 1950 established three tiers of councils (local councils, district councils, and county councils) consisting of elected members. The district officer suddenly became merely an adviser, powerless to control the new councils, which soon became corrupt and inefficient. The Eastern Regional Local Government Law of 1955 restored some of the provincial administration's lost powers of control by making them an Inspectorate of Local Government. It was in the first flush of enthusiasm for democratic local government, between 1950 and 1955, that the abolition of posts of Resident and district officer was a major issue. (See R. E. Wraith's chapter 'Local Government' in Mackintosh, *Nigerian Government and Politics*.)

[2] *The Nigerianization of the Civil Service, a Review of Policy and Machinery*, by Sydney Phillipson, Kt., C.M.G. and Mr. S. O. Adebo (Government Printer, Nigeria, 1954).

[3] See J. P. Mackintosh, op. cit., pp. 26–8 and Lord Chandos, *Memoirs*, p. 419.

[4] The 'Statement by the Council of Ministers' which introduces the Phillipson–Adebo Report in its published form contains the following reference to the year's delay between submission of the report and its publication: 'When it was sub-

for the Council of Ministers, with evident relief, to declare that the report, although 'of great interest and value', had been overtaken by political developments, and that 'the machinery recommended for implementing this Government's policy of Nigerianization would not now be appropriate to the new constitutional structure'. 'The method of furthering the policy of Nigerianization must, therefore, be left to the Federal and Regional Governments when they are set up.' This said, however, the official statement went on to declare that two of the recommendations made by the reviewers would 'conflict with the vital principle of promotion on merit by introducing a form of racial discrimination', would 'seriously impair the morale and efficiency of the Service', would 'make it impossible to retain expatriate officers now on contract', and would make it 'almost impossible to recruit new expatriate officers on contract, or indeed on any terms'. The proposed modifications from which these dire consequences were feared were: first, that non-Nigerians on contract, or on secondment, or in temporary posts should not be eligible for promotion; and secondly, that new posts, other than those in a recognized promotion pyramid, and all posts in new departments, should not be regarded as promotion posts for which non-Nigerians were eligible. These two recommendations the statement also declared to be in conflict with the statement of the political leaders at the Lagos Conference of January 1954 which was designed to reassure overseas officers about their future prospects:

We are determined to press forward with the Nigerianization of the Civil Service, but we are aware that the efficient administrative machinery which the country must have cannot, as yet, be provided unless a sufficient number of experienced and qualified officers continue to be available . . .

We also declare our intention to ensure that the interests of overseas officers who continue in the future to serve in the public services of Nigeria will be fully safeguarded . . .

We assure them that future terms and conditions of service will be fair and reasonable, and no less favourable than those obtaining today . . .

We hope that the traditional principle of promotion according to qualifications, experience and merit, without regard to race will be maintained . . .

We hope that these assurances will help to allay the feeling of

mitted at the end of April, 1953, full examination by the Council of Ministers was impracticable for political reasons, and it was decided to defer examination of it until after the London Conference, and, subsequently, until after the Resumed Conference in Lagos.'

uncertainty at present existing among overseas officers and will be acceptable by them as an expression of our genuine goodwill . . .[1]

Whether this statement, wrung from the Nigerian politicians by the Colonial Office as a part of the bargain for constitutional advance and for stronger party-political control, did in fact give much reassurance to overseas officers at the time is highly doubtful. Any reassurance it may have given was soon dissipated by evidence in each of the new services that the political imperatives of Nigerianization were far too strong for considerations of equitable treatment of both Nigerians and overseas officers to stand in their way. None of the Nigerian governments was capable of honouring its pledges, and the British Government was unable and unwilling to enforce them.

From 1954, when the overburdened Civil Service Commission performed its last task of splitting the unitary service into one federal public service and three regional public services, 'Nigerianization' ceased to be a single process under the control of the civil service itself. The initiative had passed to the politicians. The horse had bolted.

On 1 October 1954 regional public services came into being, composed of the civil servants occupying the posts provided in the estimates of each region. The regional legislatures became competent to discuss and decide provision for new posts, salaries, allowances, and conditions of service for the new public services—subject to the proviso that alterations should not adversely affect serving officers. Recruitment, transfer, and discipline were to be in the exclusive control of regional Governors, advised by a Public Service Commission, but not bound to accept the Commission's advice. At the Constitutional Conference in London in 1953 the declaration had been made by the Secretary of State for the Colonies that in 1956 those regions which desired it would be granted self-government in respect of all matters within regional competence—and that provision must be made at that point for 'certain categories' of officers to retire with compensation for loss of career and proportionate pension.

This 'regionalization' of the public services, in 1954, a step dictated by the desire of the political parties in each of the regions to be masters of their own regional machine, in preparation for the forthcoming struggle for power in an independent Nigeria, was generally welcomed by the public service itself. The Phillipson–Adebo Report had not been 'based on the assumption that the Service ought to re-

[1] Cmd. 9059.

main unitary'[1] but on the argument that all that was needed in the way of devolution to the regions could be achieved by the delegation of authority from the centre, rather than by the formal establishment of regional civil services. The authors of the report stressed the significance of the unitary character of the civil service, despite the existing modification of that unity by delegations to Lieutenant-Governors and to heads of departments, in the following passage:

> Nevertheless in spite of these practical modifications, the unitary character of the service remains a fact of great significance. The general position reflects the political history of Nigeria, which is a political entity originally created by the administrative and stage-by-stage amalgamation of a British Colony and several Protectorates and later welded into a centrally administered territory, though with some persistence of the regional pattern, and, later still, developed into a State with advanced political institutions of federal design. This reverses the normal history of federal States which in all other cases within our knowledge owe their origin to the coming together of political units hitherto separate. It follows from this circumstance that a picture is presented very different from the normal federal picture. Normally a political unit joining with others to make a federal State brings with it and retains its own public services and though with federation federal officials will be appointed for federal purposes within the confines of that unit, these federal officials will be working jointly with the State public service which will remain under State control for the staffing of State services. The difference of the present Nigerian picture from this is clear, for in Nigeria, in theory at any rate, even the humblest Civil Servant is a federal officer. This would be an odd position even in the most centripetal of federal States, but we do not for that reason advocate at this stage the formal establishment of Regional Civil Services. All that is necessary for practical purposes at present can be achieved by delegation. Whether the present situation will lead ultimately to separate Regional Civil Services with a distinctive Federal Civil Service is scarcely for us to say, but a development of that kind would merely make *de jure* what is already tending to be the *de facto* position.[2]

In practice, the 'regionalization' of government in 1954, with the old unitary service bursting apart into regional fragments, had the effect of speeding up 'Nigerianization' in the East and West and making it more difficult in the North and at the centre. The old unitary service died unregretted. There were protests from the unions forming the staff sides of the two 'junior' central Whitley Councils,

[1] The official statement accompanying the report asserted this as the main justification for the conclusion that 'political developments' had 'overtaken' the report.

[2] Phillipson and Adebo, *The Nigerianization of the Civil Service*, p. 42.

who feared the effects of regionalization on their own organization, but these were so contrary to current political sentiment that they were expressed without much conviction. The senior civil servants' anxieties were assuaged by the proliferation of new promotion posts in regional ministries and departments, and by the new definite prospect of lump-sum compensation in a few years for overseas officers, with consequential promotions to take the places of those who would depart. There was the prospect of ending the over-strained and cumbersome system of centralized control by the Civil Service Commission in Lagos. For Southern Nigerians, including those serving at the centre, there was a prospect of rapid advancement to fill posts in their home regions. Buoyant revenues and the progress made under the post-war development programme were beginning to show results in better material conditions.[1] The new governments in the regions all had ambitious plans and were prepared to spend money at a rate which the old official Government of thrifty and puritanical administrators would never have contemplated. Often money was wasted, or swallowed up in expensive cars, houses, and foreign tours for Ministers, but a good deal rubbed off on the public service itself in the form either of better equipment and tools for their work or of better salaries and conditions. One of the apparently favourable omens, for the civil service, was the appointment of a salaries commission[2] to report to all the governments on the 'structure and remuneration' of the new civil services formed on 1 October 1954. The initiative for this had come from the Action Group Government of the Western Region, which as soon as it could introduced a 5*s.* per day minimum wage for daily-rated labour in the Government's direct employment.[3] This decision, taken without consultation with the

[1] Government revenues, 1947 £14 million, 1953 £51 million, 1958 £81 million (*Economic Survey of Nigeria*, 1959, Federal Government Printer, Lagos, p. 11).

[2] The Gorsuch Commission.

[3] The previous minimum rate for Government labour in the Western Region (fixed in 1952) was 2*s.* 3*d.* per day—except for Lagos and Ikeja, which had rates of 3*s.* 5*d.* and 3*s.* respectively, and Burutu and Forcados (2*s.* 7*d.*). The basis of the previous system—known as 'the Miller structure'—was a provincial wage committee in each province, consisting of officials, employers, and workers' representatives, whose task was to study local changes in living costs and by negotiation agree which of the varying wage levels in the Miller structure was applicable within the province. In the West, committees did not meet between 1952 and 1954; Western rates were already higher than Eastern and Northern rates. Eastern rates varied from 1*s.* 6*d.* to 2*s.* 7*d.*, Northern rates from 1*s.* 6*d.* to 2*s.* 3*d.* (*Report of the Fact Finding Committee on the Minimum Wage Question*, Federal Survey Dept., Lagos, 14 Mar. 1955.)

governments dominated by rival parties, by a Government then more prosperous than its rivals, immediately ahead of the forthcoming federal elections, was widely regarded as an open bid for workers' support at the polls. Its effect on the actual poll was uncertain, but its immediate effect on the rival parties then seeking to establish a firm base of power in their respective regions, against the forthcoming struggle for power on a national scale, was to strengthen their animosity against the Action Group and make it easier for them eventually to ally themselves against it, in 1959. The decision to 'regionalize' the machinery of the public service in 1954 (instead of maintaining a unitary service with some powers devolved regionally, as proposed in the Phillipson–Adebo Report) enabled each of the regional governments immediately to mould the constitutional forms common to all three into very distinctive shapes to suit each party's urgent political priorities and ambitions. In the very confused power structures which were emerging in 1954, it was the new regional structures which presented the least confused appearance. At a lower level, the accretions of local government and of native administration on top of traditional and customary authority and law were extremely complex, in each of the regions; at the higher level, the truncated centre was a mixture of colonial government (with Governor-General, Chief Secretary, Financial Secretary, and official Attorney-General, still in the Council of Ministers), of ministerial federal government with Ministers representing rival parties, and of territorial government, with new responsibilities for the administration of the Southern Cameroons and of Lagos as federal territories. The regional governments alone had a fresh start.

Thus, the 'regionalization' of government in 1954 had the effect of releasing, under strong party government in each region, a pent-up reserve of energy, while at the centre, under an uneasy dyarchy of officials and Ministers from rival parties, there was instead an increase in the complexity of government, taking place at the same time as a drying up of the normal, regional sources of administrative staff and a loss, to the new regional services of East and West, of some of the most competent Nigerians.

By contrast, each of the new regional governments had a clear field in which to work, a new freedom from overburdened central machinery, a sufficiency of men in the reservoir of provincial administration to be brought into new ministries, and more money to spend than ever before. It was primarily the success of each of the regional governments in the years between 1954 and 1960 which gave credibility to the myth of Nigeria as a 'stable democracy'. Much of the 'stability' was due to the fact that the open struggle for federal power between the regionally based parties had not yet been joined[1]—and to the fact that the British officials occupying posts in the new public services naturally found co-operation and co-ordination between each other easier than did their later, Nigerian successors. For a British Permanent Secretary in Lagos to telephone a British Permanent Secretary in Ibadan to inquire his views on a matter of common concern was a more hopeful undertaking, usually, than it was for his Northern Nigerian successor to approach his Yoruba or Ibo opposite number. And because successful administrative co-operation depends upon hundreds of daily, minor acts of mutual trust and co-operation of this kind, the snapping of these fragile, personal links between Government and Government as expatriate officials left had a cumulative effect, in later years, with suspicion and distrust spreading down from the political level to the public services.

For the first few years after 1954, however, each of the regions was able to make good progress. Between October 1954, when each of the three regions had received its share of the old unitary service, and October 1960, when independence was achieved, each region's civil service had managed to transform and adapt itself to ministerial rule.

In the West, which made most of the running in the earlier years, the share-out of the unitary 'senior service' in 1954 came to about 500 overseas officers (both pensionable and contract officers) and a little less than 300 Nigerians.[2] Within six years, on the sixth anniversary of the founding of the regional public service, and on the first day of Nigerian independence, the Western Region Government was able to celebrate the event and embarrass its rivals by declaring that 'the retention of overseas officers in key posts in the Public Services' would be 'inconsistent with the dignity and interests of an independent Nigeria', and by immediately replacing the nine overseas Permanent Secretaries then in office by Nigerians. The West thus won the race for Nigerianization, but a more scrupulous regard for the pledges

[1] The struggle became open in the 1959 elections, after which the Northern party and the Eastern party (N.P.C. and N.C.N.C.) shared federal power and the Western party (A.G.), athough still in power in the West, formed the parliamentary opposition in the federal Parliament.

[2] *Nigerianization of the Public Service of Western Nigeria* (Government Printer, Ibadan, 1960), p. 2.

given to overseas officers[1] and a little less haste in discarding the overseas element in the team which had made such progress, under the leadership of a Nigerian head of the public service, would have been more, not less, 'dignified'. The removal from office of the overseas Permanent Secretaries, and the simultaneous removal of overseas professional heads of divisions, were party-political decisions, running counter to the whole concept of an independent, 'non-political' career public service; these actions showed how easy it was to circumvent the constitutional and other provisions intended to safeguard the public service from political interference. In the West particularly, every effort had been made, before 1960, to establish the conventions and traditions of a 'non-political' career service. The machinery of control was modelled on the proposals of the Phillipson–Adebo Report, itself modelled partly on the precedents of Ceylon and of the Gold Coast, and partly on the United Kingdom pattern of Treasury control. The regional Public Service Commission had been housed in a new purpose-built block of offices, standing separate from the buildings of the legislature and of the ministries, in order to emphasize its constitutional separation. The Permanent Secretary to the Ministry of Finance (Chief S. O. Adebo) was formally appointed as head of the public service in August 1957, when the West, with the East, became self-governing. In 1959 a Public Administration Law[2] was passed, establishing a Treasury Board, defining the functions of the Minister of Finance and of the Treasury, and making legal provision in relation to audit of accounts, financial regulations, and general orders for the public service, for custody of public funds, and for investigation and punishment of corruption by public officers. This law, together with the Public Service Commission Regulations, made the legal and constitutional basis of the Western Region Public Service Commission more complete than that of any other service in Nigeria. The principle of 'Treasury control' of establishments was fully worked out, with a competent Establishments Division of increasing size in the Ministry of Finance (later the Treasury) under the immediate control of an officer of Permanent Secretary rank, responsible

[1] Apart from statements of policy assuring overseas officers of 'equal treatment' with Nigerians for promotion, etc., the Western Region Government entered in 1957 into a formal Special List Agreement to this effect, except for certain 'reserved posts' listed in a schedule to the agreement. The later addition of all the important posts in the service to this list, by unilateral decision, made nonsense of this agreement.

[2] Western Region law no. 29 of 1959.

to the head of the public service (the Permanent Secretary to the Treasury) not only for financial control of posts, salaries, allowances, conditions of service, etc., but for the reorganization of the service into the 'Gorsuch' structural pattern,[1] for the control of the general executive class posted to the various ministries, departments, and provinces, and for the work of an Organization and Methods Branch and (from 1958) of a Training Branch. All overseas recruitment on pensionable terms had ceased at the end of 1955, but by the time the exodus of overseas officers taking their compensation began in 1957, the flood of young, qualified Nigerians returning from universities and training courses made it possible not only to maintain but actually to increase very considerably the number of senior posts arising from expanding services and from the more elaborate organization of 'integrated' ministries. The expansion of headquarters staff was made possible only by decreasing the numbers of administrators posted for provincial work under the control of the Ministry of Local Government. (This was not a forced expedient; it was part of the planned reorganization of local government begun in 1955—a policy of 'disengagement' from direct control over local government, and of division amongst officials of other ministries of the former district officer's many miscellaneous functions.)[2] It was on the initiative of the Western Region that, in 1957, a National Council on Establishments was set up to enable the various governments to consider together, under the chairmanship of the Prime Ministers, such public service problems of common concern as lay outside the Public Service Commission field of appointments, promotion, and discipline. All that seemed necessary, at the end of 1960, even after the precipitate displacement of the senior expatriate officers in the service, was a period of quiet consolidation and development. What happened instead was

[1] The 'Gorsuch' structure divided the service into five main grades, seeking to end the old 'senior service—junior service' distinction: superscale, administrative, executive, clerical, and sub-clerical, with corresponding classes in the specialist professional services. A Colonial Office training mission in the same year had produced a report (the Imrie–Lee Report) criticizing the shape of the public service as an 'hour glass' rather than a 'pyramid'. It was left to specialist advisers from the U.K. civil service to work out with each Government how to introduce the new 'executive' grade. The result of their labours, at a time of rapid expansion and combing of each service for 'officer material', was more like a reclassification as 'executive' of a large mass of clerical work, and an obstinate persistence of the old concept of 'senior' and 'junior' status, with the 'senior' Nigerians inheriting the status, quarters, motor cars, and privileges of departing Europeans.

[2] *The Duties and Functions of Administrative Officers in the Western Region of Nigeria*, W.R. Sessional Paper no. 1 of 1955.

the destruction of the Action Group Government in battle with its rivals who had come to power at the centre; in this struggle the career civil servant was a mere spectator, unable to influence events.[1]

By contrast, the Eastern Region public service began its existence in 1954 in somewhat less auspicious circumstances, but in subsequent years had better fortune, the region not yet being torn apart by political dissension. The shortage of funds in the first few years after 1954 restricted expansion in numbers, and made the regional Government hesitate before deciding to participate with the other governments in the improvements in senior salaries recommended in the Gorsuch Report. Providence lent a hand, with the development of the oilfields in the Eastern Region, and with the outcome of the 1959 federal elections—which made the governing party in the Eastern Region the ally rather than the enemy of the federal Government. But the years of stringent economy until about 1958 had some effect in concentrating the attention of both Ministers and officials on the bare, immediate essentials.

Otherwise, the problems of organizing the new public service in the East and of Nigerianization were not unlike those of the West—indeed in many matters the Eastern Region was not too proud to copy what had been done in the West where it seemed sensible to do so. There was the same kind of influx of trained Nigerians returning from scholarships and training courses, together with men from the Northern Region being displaced by the policy of Northernization. There was a mutual exchange of officers between East and West, the gains of the East including the first Nigerian head of the public service, Oputa Udoji, who had served in the West as one of the first Nigerian district officers.

There was, however, one remarkable difference in the apparatus of civil service control, as between East and West, which was largely dictated by financial necessity. Instead of immediately setting up expensive new ministries in new office blocks, the Eastern Region simply turned the old Secretariat under a Civil Secretary into the Office of the Premier. Thus the Chief Secretary to the Premier inherited directly the basic Secretariat responsibilities, including the

[1] *Report of the Coker Commission of Inquiry into the affairs of certain corporations in Western Nigeria*, 1962. The report contains a tribute to 'some bold and courageous Civil Servants who stuck to their guns with remarkable fortitude in the face of circumstances of a trying order'. But, while the civil service itself had not become corrupt, it had been powerless to stop the plundering of the revenues and reserves by politicians.

responsibility for co-ordinating the activities of the departments—now become ministries. The Office of the Premier was also the Treasury, and the Premier himself remained firmly head of the Treasury, leaving only 'day to day matters' to the Minister of Finance. The Premier's Office was also the office for the Executive Council, the legislature, the Security and Intelligence Service, the Administration (i.e. the provincial administration), and Establishments. From the beginning, therefore, the Chief Secretary to the Premier was the lynch-pin of the public service. On the attainment of regional self-government he naturally became head of the public service, having meanwhile also served as Secretary to the Executive Council. When, in 1960, Dr. Kingsley of the Ford Foundation came to write a report on staff development in the Eastern Region it was a result of a request by the Chief Secretary to the Premier to analyse the manpower situation in the Eastern Nigeria public service, with particular attention to 'the need for training Nigerians for higher posts of responsibility'.[1] In his report, Dr. Kingsley wrote: 'The key figure in staff development in the Region is the Chief Secretary. He alone has at his disposal most of the instruments essential to the task and he alone is in a position to exercise the degree of staff leadership required.'

In the preface to the report, by the Chief Secretary to the Premier, there was a short statement of the role of the civil servant, in terms far less ambiguous than those found in the usual accounts of the civil servant's role in the United Kingdom:

> Just as the role of Government has changed, so too has the role of the Civil Servant. Not only must he be capable of giving sound advice to the political Leaders and of controlling the traditional aspects of governmental activity, he must also be an efficient executive who manages and directs all the complex operations of the modern state.

This concept of the senior civil servant as a manager and director of complex operations is in refreshing contrast to the subtleties of the Whitehall model, and more in keeping with the realities of the public service in developing countries. It contrasts also with the instruction which was being conveyed at the same time to the new entrant to the

[1] *Staff Development in the Public Service of Eastern Nigeria*, by J. D. Kingsley (Enugu, Government Printer, 1961). This was Dr. Kingsley's second report on staff development for a regional government. The first, for the West, was not published, the third, for the North, written with Sir A. N. Rucker, was published under the title *Staffing and Development of the Public Service of Northern Nigeria* in January 1961.

Western Region public service, which sought to impress upon him the constitutional subservience of the civil servant to the will of the elected representatives of the people:[1]

As a civil servant you must never forget that however well qualified and expert you may become in your job, you have not been elected to it by any vote; and in a democratic country it is the elected representatives—in our case, the Regional Legislature—who must settle the lines on which the government of the community is to work . . . You must do what the Regional Legislature wants you to do . . . Your loyalty is to the Minister of the day.

Dr. Kingsley's report for the Eastern Region emphasized the 'notable success' already achieved in Nigerianization, and the necessity for consolidating the achievements by improvements in efficiency and performance. Staff development should be a top priority:

An army cannot move constantly forward without opportunity to consolidate its position. Neither can a Civil Service . . . There are limits, even if difficult to define, to human or institutional adaptability. In this instance, they may have been nearly reached.

On the whole, the danger seems to have been recognized. The Eastern Region did not follow the West's example by precipitately displacing overseas Permanent Secretaries and professional heads, or by dismantling the provincial administration, the load-carrying 'scaffolding', but used the time the presence of expatriates gave to intensify the training of Nigerian staff. There was not quite so marked a tendency to withdraw men from the provinces. Instead, under the guidance of a head of the public service who had spent several years as a district administrator, young Nigerian administrative officers were generally sent for training and experience 'in the field' before being brought into the ministries in Enugu. This was a revival of the old colonial service tradition; it seems to have reflected more the long history in the Eastern Region of fluidity, experiment, and innovation in local government, and the more diffuse and scattered pattern of human settlement in the Eastern Region, compared with the large

[1] *A Handbook for Officers Joining the Western Region Public Service* (Ibadan, Government Printer, 1959). Neither this extreme concept of the 'nonentity' and subservience of the civil servant nor the confident assertion of inherent authority as executive, manager, and director contained in the preceding Eastern Region quotation had any express warrant in the Constitution itself. There the only guidance—vague enough—was for Permanent Secretaries; they were made responsible for the 'supervision' of such departments as were placed under the 'general direction and control' of a Minister.

Yoruba towns and cities. The Eastern Region, the first of the Nigerian governments to begin dismantling the administrative 'scaffolding' around local government, in the early fifties, was also the first to introduce the new pattern of provincial administration (when it became clear that the 'scaffolding' was all that held the structure together) and to appoint political Provincial Commissioners served by career service administrators (provincial Secretaries and local government Commissioners).[1] There was thus a tendency—as there had been in the old days of the Southern Nigeria Protectorate under Sir Ralph Moor—for the Eastern pattern of administration to be less centralized than the Western Nigerian pattern; the West had built up, in the regional capital, a larger and more sophisticated central administration, but had less to show in the way of provincial administration. But the similarities between the services in East and West were greater than their differences; in particular, each service had hundreds of returning graduates from universities at home and in the U.K. and the U.S.A. from whom their Public Service Commissions could begin to reject some of the weaker candidates. It was no longer a case of taking all who reached the minimum standard. In the cadre of administrators being built up in both East and West there were two distinct groups discernible—the older men, often without a background of university education, but with long 'junior service' experience, and the young, university-trained entry (of whom a high proportion had degrees in economics). There was naturally some tension between these two groups, representing different generations, but the sharp edges of distinction were blurred by the fact that most of the older men had received some education and training overseas, by means of colonial service courses of instruction and 'study leave', while many of the younger men had been 'birds of passage' in the junior service for a year or two before going overseas for university education.[2] There had been no need, in either East or West, to recruit administrators by denuding the teaching or other professions, although, in both, one or two university scholars were brought into the civil service in senior positions,[3] and specialist officers (e.g. education

[1] See, for a fuller discussion of these developments, R. E. Wraith's chapter 'Local Government' in Mackintosh, *Nigerian Government and Politics*.

[2] The staff lists of the Eastern and Western Region show the wide age-range of new appointments, the academic qualifications of each, and in many cases the length and type of 'junior service' experience in each case.

[3] e.g. Dr. Biobaku in the West and Dr. Okigbo in the East, both from the University College, Ibadan.

officers and labour officers) were promoted into the 'generalist' administrative cadre. Compared with the backward North, and with East and central African territories already on the move to independence, the East and West were amply supplied with educated men for the higher public service.

The problems of 'regionalization' of the public service of the vast Northern Region were fundamentally different, and more difficult. In 1948, when Northerners began to realize their unpreparedness for the wind of change and to fear domination by Southern politicans and civil servants, Northern Nigeria was still set in the unique pattern of oligarchy which had taken shape in Lugard's day. In it there was a basic stratum of traditional and tribal societies, overlaid by the oligarchy of the Fulani, part 'colonial', part 'religious', part 'racial',[1] overlaid again by British 'indirect' officialdom, which relied in part on the pre-existing patterns, in part on the introduction into the region of Southern Nigerian subordinates in most of the modernizing work of administration which required the skills of literacy in English and of industry. The North had been left behind, and there was an immense amount of leeway to be made up. First, the Fulani, the 'born rulers' who had adapted themselves to Lugard's conquest and had continued to rule, had now to adapt themselves quickly again and assume the form of a political party, the N.P.C., deriving its strength from the system of native administration, from religion, from conservatism, from patronage, and from the sympathy and encouragement of the British administration.[2] This first feat of emulation of the more modern South once begun, the first political imperative was 'Northernization' of the machinery of government, beginning at the level at which 'Northernization' was practicable and 'Southernization' had gone furthest—the junior ranks—and proceeding from that level upwards right to the top, relying meanwhile on the British to keep the machinery moving and to help in the training of Northerners. The second imperative was to secure adequate representation of the North in the new central system of power—in the legislature, in

[1] Categories of 'oligarchy' used in *The Politics of the Developing Areas* (Almond and Coleman, Princeton, 1960). Although Aristotle's categories of the ancient Greek city-state (oligarchy, democracy, tyranny) help in the understanding of individual communities (e.g. the Yoruba city, the Northern Emirate), it is difficult to apply them meaningfully to the complexity of regional and federal government in modern Nigeria.

[2] There is a full account of the formation and growth of the N.P.C. by B. J. Dudley in Mackintosh, *Nigerian Government and Politics.*

ministerial ranks, in membership of statutory corporations, and in the federal public service. This required an immense effort of mobilization and penetration. As early as 1949 the Northern Region had been the first of the governments to establish a scholarship fund, which virtually assured a university scholarship for the few candidates with the necessary minimum qualification for university entry,[1] and at the same time made it inevitable that standards of entry into junior posts should be forced downwards if there was to be any prospect of immediate Northernization. The backwardness of education in the North made pre-service and in-service training an even more obvious necessity than it was in the South. Without intensive training of under-educated Northerners at each level, there could be no effective Northernization for a generation.

All the major decisions of policy which shaped the new Northern public service were influenced by fears of Southern domination and hopes of Northern domination. Thus in 'Northernization' replacement of Southerners in all posts took higher priority than the replacement of expatriates in the higher posts. Expatriates were accepted as a transient phenomenon, and, quite correctly for the most part, as harmless and disinterested workers—for the time being. Nigerians from the South, on the other hand, were regarded with fear and suspicion as the advance guard of an invasion of Southerners; in evidence to the Phillipson–Adebo review body, the Northern spokesmen alleged that, unlike the British officer, Southern Nigerians appointed to the civil service in the North tended to bring wives, children, and relations and settle there, taking leases of land, exploiting the services of Northern peasants in its cultivation, and using their official influence to infiltrate their brothers and cousins into jobs previously held by Northerners.[2]

This kind of fear was so strong that from the first the Northern Region Public Service Commission made itself responsible for the recruitment and appointment of even the lowest grades of public servant, heavily overburdening its own office in the process. There was no delegation to heads of departments or Permanent Secretaries or Residents of provinces of power to appoint civil servants. For pro-

[1] In March 1949, at the first session of the Northern legislature following the meeting of the central legislature at which the Foot Commission's Nigerianization proposals were put forward and accepted.

[2] *The Nigerianization of the Civil Service: A Review of Policy and Machinery*, by Sir Sydney Phillipson and Mr. S. O. Adebo (Lagos, Government Printer, 1954), p. 64.

vincial recruitment Appointments Advisory Committees were established in 1955, under the chairmanship of the Resident or his representative, to interview candidates and make recommendations to the Public Service Commission at Kaduna, which thus became closely involved in a mass of executive and clerical work which would ordinarily be the responsibility of departmental establishment branches, rather than that of an advisory, quasi-judicial body. In 1959, after the Public Service Commission had become an 'executive' body rather than an 'advisory' one, a committee of the Executive Council called the Northernization Implementation Committee was established, with broad terms of reference including many of the tasks normally left to internal civil service establishments branches—evidence again of the strength of the political drive behind 'Northernization' and of reluctance to leave the implementation of policy to the civil service.

In the North, with its meagre resources of educated men and its inheritance of decentralized provincial administration on the indirect rule pattern, there was no question of attempting to build up a Whitehall pattern of central ministries, or of removing the 'scaffolding'. 'The Administration' was still the backbone of a system of authority; when, in 1957, the Institute of Administration at Zaria began to train Northerners for 'the Administration', it was the Ministry of Local Government to which the Principal was responsible, not the Ministry of Finance.[1] The training given—by British administrative officers seconded for the purpose—was designed simply to turn out assistant district officers as quickly as possible, from the material available. There was no question of training these men for the 'staff' work of central administration in the ministerial headquarters: but they could be given preparation for routine in a province. There were a few Northerners returning with university degrees, but the Zaria administrative officer trainees had a basis of academic qualifications which would scarcely have qualified them for the clerical service in the East and West. The best that could be done, by the British administrators responsible for teaching, was to 'pass on accumulated experience', although aware of the danger that this might look like 'turning out replicas of the expatriate district officer of an earlier decade'.[2] It was a matter of initiation into the 'mysteries' of rule by

[1] At that time, the central Establishments staff were placed in the Ministry of Finance, as in the West; later, they were placed directly under the Secretary to the Premier, in the Premier's Office.

[2] 'Administrative Techniques' by A. H. M. Kirk-Greene and J. H. Smith in *Journal of Local Administration Overseas*, vol. 1, no. 3 (July 1962).

a small élite. One of the three groups of subjects in the course was entitled 'Social *savoir-faire* and "senior service" *etiquette* and *mores*'. The concentration on matters of form went to the length of 'a handbook on ceremonial, including photographs of how to wear uniform'. The course included attendance at functions such as 'school sports days, agricultural shows, polo matches, plays and military parades, where they observe the social traditions as well as the organisational techniques':

Careful attention is given to the formal side of an administrative officer's responsibilities (which so far show no sign of decreasing) such as official entertaining—and to the semi-official hospitality still expected from him in his position as an agent of Government.

This emphasis on decorum, in an emergency training course for the young administrators of a region with serious, practical problems of development and of maintaining law and order, may seem surprising; but given the need for 'prestige' in the administrator they were as serious and practical a part of the work as anything else. The North was, significantly, the only region to introduce a ceremonial uniform for its administrative officers, replacing the while helmet (a legacy from the days of General Wolseley) and altering the cut of the white drill suit, but retaining the sword and the brass buttons and badges of rank. The other services felt able to dispense with this kind of visual aid to prestige.[1]

Just before Nigerian independence in October 1960 the Ford Foundation was invited by the Government of the Northern Region to undertake a survey of the staffing and staff development problems of the regional public service, in terms which made it clear that effective methods of further implementing the Northernization policy 'while maintaining efficiency' were in contemplation. The survey was conducted by Dr. J. D. Kingsley of the Ford Foundation (who had thus conducted an investigation into the training and staff development problems of all three regions) and by Sir Arthur Rucker. They described the training problems confronting the Government as

[1] The *Administrative Instructions to Provincial Commissioners and Provincial Secretaries* published by the Northern Government after independence, in 1962, were to show the same careful attention as Lugard's *Political Memoranda* to status, precedence, and dignity, to the need 'not to derogate from the prestige' of the (political) Provincial Commissioner, and the need for them to maintain 'the dignity and status' of their office. There are full instructions on the flying of the flag, on precedence and etiquette, but there is no reference to development or to social services.

'staggering'; the figures presented in the report show that even this was an understatement. The general short-fall in staff, as compared with the approved establishment, was over 25 per cent, with 'an adverse effect on governmental operations and hindering the development of desirable Government programmes'. Northerners occupied only 28 per cent of administrative posts, 25 per cent of executive posts, under 20 per cent of the technical supervisory establishment, and 5 per cent of professional posts.[1] Assuming no change in existing training plans and programmes and no change in establishment, they estimated that the short-fall in the Administration would be greater in 1970 than it was in 1960, and almost as great in professional officers. By 1970, the Administration might be expected, on the same assumptions, to be 60 per cent Northern. But even the degree of Northernization already achieved had been 'accompanied by some lowering of standards and a decline in efficiency'. The 'chronic shortage of experienced staff' particularly in the Administration had led to 'an extreme instability in postings'. 'The handful of experienced officers is shunted hither and yon in response to crises and pressures. There is, consequently, little sustained leadership of staff and considerable weakness in following through projects once initiated.' Only the clerical class was over-staffed—and that was because the attempt was being made 'to redress by an excess of numbers a lack of competence'.[2]

The remedial measures proposed were, in essence, a strengthening and co-ordination of all the functions of training, establishments, staff development, recruitment and organization and methods under the direction of the Secretary to the Premier, who was already the head of the public service, but had not previously had direct responsibility for them all. At the time of independence, therefore, the Northern Region public service was a long way from the political objective of Northernization, and there was no possibility of dispensing with overseas recruitment. What had been achieved, at some cost in efficiency, was Northern political control of the civil service,

[1] Administration, establishment 293, Northerners 83, expatriates 145, Southerners 1, vacancies 64; education officers, establishment 437, Northerners 33, expatriates 297 (156 on contract, 141 pensionable), Southerners 2, vacancies 105; agricultural officers, establishment 86, Northerners 4, expatriates 56, vacancies 26. In the whole higher public service establishment of 3,318 posts, there were 911 vacancies and only 534 Northerners in posts—a 'Northernization gap' of 2,784 men.

[2] *Staffing and Development of the Public Service of Northern Nigeria* (Kaduna, Jan. 1961).

and the almost complete exclusion of Southerners from posts of authority and prestige. And it was authority and prestige, rather than the performance of social services, on which the whole structure rested still, as in Lugard's heyday. The North, with its huge area and population of more than 20 million people,[1] had only 8 dentists (all expatriates) and 116 medical officers (6 of them Northerners, and 27 posts vacant). The Northern administration was still a system of authority, not an instrument of modernization.

Each of the regional public services, therefore, despite their common constitutional forms, had taken on a distinct style and personality, between 1954 and 1960. The federal public service, however, the rump of the old unitary service, presents a far more complex and bewildering picture. Its history in the years from 1954 to 1960—and in particular, in the years after the disappearance of the office of Chief Secretary—is one full of complexities and schizophrenic, irrational contradictions. In each of the regions the dominance of one main party had produced a consistent and reasonably coherent public service policy; each regional service had had to learn how to live with the party in power. The new services, though not so free from political interference as they might have been, were ruled 'indirectly' through their own acknowledged 'chief'—in East and North the Premier's Secretary, in the West, until 1962, the chief Treasury official.[2] The picture in the federal service, especially after the disappearance of the post of Chief Secretary in 1957, was one of a crew without a captain, in a ship riven by a series of explosions, each more disconcerting than the last. Under uneasy coalition government there was insufficient agreement at the political level to permit the framing of rational civil service policies; the politicians were unable either to leave the civil service to govern itself or to agree on a consistent method of control.

In 1955, after the regional services were amputated from the old unitary service, there were 2,450 senior posts in the federal public service, 550 of them filled by Nigerians (all Southerners). Quite apart from the responsibilities of federal government in the ordinary sense, the federal Government had to provide a miniature public service machine of administrators and departments for the Southern

[1] The 1962 census gave the North 22·5 million, its 'verification' 31 million, and the 1963–4 census gave a figure of 29·8 million.

[2] Headship of the public service was not conferred 'ex-officio' on the holder of the post of Permanent Secretary to the Treasury; during the political upheavals of 1962 it seems that the post was deliberately left unfilled for a long period.

Cameroons, and a few to administer the federal territory of Lagos, split away from the Western Region. By 1960, there were 864 pensionable overseas officers in the federal service (compared with 1,350 in 1955), while the total establishment had increased to approximately 4,000 senior posts, and the number of Nigerians in senior posts to 2,308. A year later, the establishment was 5,000, Nigerians numbered more than 3,000, and many expatriates had left. In six years, therefore, the establishment had been doubled, and the number of Nigerians in senior posts had been increased almost tenfold. Some of this increase was due to planned expansion of the police, and to the planned improvement of social services, communications, and public works programmes. But much of it was haphazard growth due to the weakness of financial control over establishments. A part of the increase was due to panic measures to create scores of supernumerary superscale posts for Nigerians, and to the lack of order in the building up of the new executive class. This kind of organizational upheaval, together with the 'integration' of ministries, the creation of new ministries, acute discontinuity in postings, and complete uncertainty about the Government's policies (particularly in regard to Nigerianization and the treatment of overseas officers) combined to press the organization beyond the practical limits of organizational adaptability. It became impossible for any officer, Nigerian or overseas, to place confidence in conflicting policy statements. So far as overseas officers were concerned, there was always the solution of departure with compensation and pension if things became intolerable, but for the average Nigerian officer who could not afford to retire voluntarily at or after the age of forty-five there was no way out.

The most striking example of the confusion brought about by political interference in the civil service, made easier by the lack of effective internal leadership within it, is presented by the federal approach to Nigerianization in the years 1955–60. In 1955, the House of Representatives called on the Council of Ministers 'to make a comprehensive statement and present specific proposals' to speed up Nigerianization. The Council of Ministers (composed of British officials still responsible for civil service matters, Southern Ministers eager to press on with Nigerianization by Southerners, and Northern Ministers anxious to hold back until Northerners could be considered) produced in 1956 a compromise policy statement. This touched on the need to honour the pledges given to overseas officers, and on the need 'in the interests of the Federation' to make the federal public service 'a good cross-section of the population',[1] and went on to propose both an increase in scholarships and training awards and the appointment of a Nigerianization Officer and a Standing Committee on Training. It was not until 1957 that the first Nigerianization Officer took up his duties of 'co-ordination' of the work of the scholarship-awarding Ministry of Social Services, the Establishments Branch of the Chief Secretary's office, and the Public Service Commission. But this officer had no executive authority; federal Nigerianization did not have the dynamic drive behind it which was speeding up the similar process in the regions. In the same year an Adviser on Training was appointed, and the Standing Committee on Training met for the first time. But meanwhile, in August 1957 the Chief Secretary and the Financial Secretary, the two key posts in the service, were abolished, a Nigerian Prime Minister and Minister of Finance were appointed, and, although the Governor-General remained titular head of the federal civil service, that service in practice simply 'lost its head'.

From then on, all the major issues of civil service policy were no longer the responsibility of any one person, but were parcelled out incomprehensibly between a large number of ministries and organizations. In London, the Colonial Office sought by increasingly sophisticated schemes and formal agreements to safeguard overseas officers' rights and conditions in order to achieve a smooth and gradual withdrawal.[2] In 1959 the Secretary of State personally intervened, as a result of representations by the Association of Senior Civil Servants, to suggest that a revision of salaries (unchanged since 1954) was essential. The Governor-General remained responsible in the last resort for the civil service, until independence, but the management of the service was dissipated between several offices. The central establishments machinery moved in 1957 from the Chief Secretary's office to the Ministry of Finance, rested there for a matter of weeks, was then transferred to the Prime Minister's Office, and later made into a separate ministry—first entitled 'Ministry of Pensions' and later Ministry of Establishments. The Adviser on Training was made responsible to the (Southern) Nigerianization Officer, who was now responsible (through the (expatriate) Secretary to the Prime Minister)

[1] *Statement of Policy of the Government of the Federation on the Nigerianization of the Federal Public Service and the Higher Training of Nigerians*, 1956–60. Sessional Paper no. 4 of 1956.

[2] There is a description of the complicated schemes for the overseas civil service in these years in K. Younger, *The Public Service in New States* (1960).

to the (Northern) Prime Minister. Scholarships were the business of the Ministry of Education. In the following year, 1958, back-bench political pressure for faster Nigerianization led to the appointment of a parliamentary committee on Nigerianization, which was to produce lengthy and only partially informed reports clamouring for immediate Nigerianization of all the top posts in the service, and bitterly attacking the good faith of many senior officials.[1] The tone of this committee's reports was sufficient to increase the speed of the exodus of overseas officers; the Government's reply, although sub-titled 'A Statement of Policy', confined itself largely to piecemeal comment on individual recommendations, supplemented by detailed commentary by individual ministries and by the Nigerianization Officer. One paragraph, however, was a significant revelation of the abandonment of any idea of internal leadership over the civil service as a whole:

> The Permanent Secretaries and other Heads of Divisions are directly responsible for the proper conduct of their own systems of in-service training, and they must so remain. The evolving of such systems, their application to the needs of a professional or technical unit and the absorption of the trained or semi-trained officers into the working machinery are matters which depend to a large extent upon professional knowledge and experience. Staff training in any large concern, whether a Ministry or a business, is an integral part of the duty of the management and it is a responsibility which cannot be devolved upon some remote central authority.[2]

In practice, the lack of internal leadership affected most adversely the centrally controlled 'profession of Government', the administrative class and the executive classes subject to posting from one ministry or department to another as new ministries were created, other officers retired, or quarrelled with ministers over political interference. Least affected were those departments, such as the Police and Prisons Department, which remained as disciplined forces under a single commander, with prescribed legal powers and duties. Nor did the overall lack of direction and civil service authority directly affect the Judicial Department or the Audit Department, which had very specific constitutional protection. The damage was not too great in

[1] The first report (Sessional Paper no. 7 of 1958) recommended displacement of senior British administrative officers before independence; it led to the creation by the Government of 'supernumerary' posts for Nigerians, as an 'emergency operation'.

[2] *Matters arising from the Final Report of the Parliamentary Committee on the Nigerianization of the Federal Public Service. Statement of Policy by the Government of the Federation*. Sessional Paper no. 2 of 1960, paragraph 20, page 10.

those branches which were fully 'professionalized', in the sense that their members (doctors, lawyers, engineers) felt themselves to be part of a wider profession, an international society with its own standards and code of conduct and professional practice.

It was in the once powerful and coherent 'Administration' that the cumulative effects of weak central control were already showing themselves at the time of Nigerian independence. Political divisions at the ministerial level had made it impossible for authority to be firmly delegated to officials; the lack of official leadership led to a loss of confidence and of initiative in the official ranks. The Prime Minister himself, in the absence of a head of the public service to whom both he and the senior officials could look for advice and guidance, was brought more and more into detailed questions of civil service management, as if he were the direct heir of Governor and Chief Secretary. The federal public service had in fact become as faithful a reflection of divided and confused political direction as the regional services had become reflections of strong party government.

With the federal Government responsible for raising the bulk of the country's revenues, and for apportioning them, and responsible through the police and in the last resort through the armed forces for the maintenance of order throughout the federation, and responsible for maintaining the continuous official dialogue between the governments on which the preparation and progress of constructive development depended, confusion and weakness in the federal public service were bound to have ever-widening and more serious cumulative results. Confidence, leadership, decision, and initiative were steadily drained out of the higher civil service. But in the same years, although quite separate from the civil service processes, another new élite body of young Nigerians—nearly all Southerners—was being trained for the army officer corps at Sandhurst and other officer training schools in Britain. Their training was expressly designed to bring out those qualities of leadership, confidence, initiative, and prompt decision which were being lost in the administrative service—the same qualities which Lugard had sought and found in his young 'soldier administrators' of a previous age.

# CHAPTER X

# The Problems of the Present

A purely contemporary view of any problem is necessarily a limited and even distorted view. Every situation has its roots in the past . . . The past survives into the present; the present is indeed the past undergoing modification.[1]

NIGERIA'S experience, since independence at the beginning of the United Nations Development Decade, has been one of 'undevelopment'. First came the collapse of the structure of federal parliamentary democracy; then a military regime which sought to establish a unitary government; then a new military regime overthrowing the first and seeking to create a looser federation, with more and smaller regions; and then a bitter civil war. Earlier optimism about political stability in Nigeria has been replaced by pessimism. There is no sign, in 1968, of any equilibrium save that of exhaustion and near-bankruptcy.

Admittedly, some of the administrative apparatus has continued to function, with difficulty; in the civil profession of government and in the judiciary who have seen and survived so much in the last ten years or so, and had to play so many unexpected roles, there are men whose wisdom and experience are great assets. But they cannot put Humpty-Dumpty together again; nothing constructive can be done without some accepted central authority.

The past in which this tragic situation has its main roots is not so much the immediate past of evanescent political movements and leaders, nor the more remote past of the period before British intervention, before Nigeria was brought into existence. The main root system of Nigeria's present is to be found in the first half of the twentieth century, and particularly in the earlier years of that period, studied in detail in the previous chapters. In the growing literature on Nigerian government and politics it is usually this period which has attracted least scholarly attention. Political commentators have tended to concentrate on political developments after, rather than on

[1] Phillipson and Adebo, *The Nigerianization of the Civil Service* (Govt. Printer, Lagos, 1954), p. 49.

administrative developments before, the Second World War. Historians have tended to probe into the more remote past, the period before the birth of Nigeria in 1900. And inquirers into British administration have tended to look at local rather than central government.

The consequent partial vacuum left by this *trahison des clercs*, by the scarcity of hard fact and harder thought about how Nigeria was administered before independence, has not been left conceptually empty, however. It has been filled by preconceived ideas of British administration and administrators. To some extent these are mere stereotypes, to some extent they are the products of deliberately hostile or deliberately favourable propaganda. When these are superimposed rather vaguely one upon the other, a strange kind of composite portrait takes shape in the imagination; a portrait of the British colonial administration as an élite (in the dirty senses of the word) of not very imaginative, not very intellectual, not very sympathetic middle to upper-class Englishmen—honest, maybe, but limited in outlook, aloof, 'racist', more concerned with maintaining tradition, law and order, and some variant of what has been called 'the Whipsnade policy', than with economic and political development; or, in so far as they were concerned with economic development, concerned mostly for their own benefit, to exploit the people, as 'wicked imperialists' or 'colonialists'.

In the unquestioning acceptance of this unflattering picture there are of course elements of hostile prejudice, the perfectly understandable prejudice of liberal American and British writers and publics, and of nationalists of all kinds, against the unpleasing idea of alien, undemocratic, authoritarian rule. The more overtly hostile school of caricature, founded by Lenin on 'Hobson's choice', needs no explanation. In the circumstances, it is doubly regrettable that the most effective propagandist in defence of British colonial administration in the period, Lugard himself, bore so close a resemblance to the hostile caricature, and yet succeeded in conveying the impression that he was more imaginative and creative than the rest, a man whose great work was spoiled by smaller-minded men, before him, over him, under him and after him.

This picture, of course, will never do. It impedes understanding of the real difficulties of the Nigerian situation. In particular, the idea of one great administrator, Lugard, with the rest inferior, is absurd, and has to be turned on its head to make sense. Men like MacGregor,

Moor, Egerton, Temple, Girouard, Clifford, and Cameron—to mention only the earlier names—were men of great intelligence, character, and energy, fully aware that whatever decisions they took and whatever they did there would be (in Mary Kingsley's words) Africans in a thousand years to thrive or suffer for it. They were men of very varied social provenance and professional background. In no sense were they uniform white pawns moved across the board in a game played against the black man by unseen hands. Their decisions and actions can be understood only by studying the evidence, and by an effort of empathy, an effort to understand the men, their problems, and their decisions.

Men and problems were unique, inexplicable in terms of conspiratorial theories of imperialism. MacGregor, the Scottish Presbyterian doctor, was the son of a poor cottar. Moor, the Irish Constabulary officer, was the son of a doctor. Clifford, the aristocrat, novelist, and highly professional administrator, was the grandson of an English Catholic peer. Egerton came from the English middle class, with a public school education, followed by administrative and judicial experience; but his great talent was for businesslike economic development. Girouard, military officer and railway engineer, was a French Canadian. Temple, from the consular service, was the son of a very eminent Indian civil servant. Cameron, who began his career as a clerical officer in British Guiana, was the Irish, orphaned son of a sugar planter in that colony. In so far as the administrative behaviour and the administrative decisions of these diverse men form a pattern, it is one of able and dedicated men conducting public business in the public interest—that is, in the interest of the governed. Given this common and pretty firm administrative ethos, their problems were those of means, rather than ends, and their decisions can be rationally followed. One problem common to them all was the classic problem of colonial administration—the making of bricks without straw. But for these particular men another serious and common problem was the deviant behaviour of Lugard. To Moor, MacGregor, Egerton, and Temple the problem of Lugard was how to stop him wrecking the work by lack of co-operation. For Girouard, Clifford, and Cameron it was the problem of tidying up after him.

These were difficult problems: in administration neither piety nor wit will serve wholly to undo harm done.

Mary Kingsley was right: the actions of British administrators in the early years will leave a thousand-year legacy as important as the Norman conquest of England. Of the major, ineluctable decisions of the first importance taken at the start, the most fateful of all was Chamberlain's choice of Lugard for the North. Given the practical necessity for separate administrations at the beginning, the rational course would have been the choice of an experienced, utilitarian civil administrator who could have run comfortably in harness with his colleagues. Instead, a frontier soldier was chosen with a history of mental imbalance, of political intrigue, and of bloodshed, a man whose footsteps 'had never been dogged by peace', and one who had always found it difficult to run in harness with others. This was a political decision, not an administrative one. It was almost a guarantee that there would be a widening and deepening of existing differences in the new country. It would have been far better for the Secretary of State to follow Colonial Regulations, and to choose on the basis of 'official qualifications, experience and merit'. The second decision, to appoint the same man more than a decade later as amalgamator, seems the direct outcome of the Lugards' talent for political intrigue and assiduous cultivation of the arts of rising. It was to result in confusion and disorder.

Many of the endemic present problems of Nigerian government seem now to flow directly from Lugard's own characteristic decisions. The proof of this contention would be long, since it involves the imaginary construction of a world in which Lugard never existed, or, as a minimum, of a Nigeria unaffected by his decisions. A computer could conceivably be programmed to do something of this kind, but such elaboration is not needed to show that Lugard's most crucial and characteristic decisions in the North worked against future amalgamation, and that his later decisions as amalgamator were aimed at the destruction of his predecessors' achievements in establishing a rational and modern system of administration. In the North, there was his choice of conquest rather than peaceful penetration, followed by the decision to keep the institution of Fulani rule, while replacing each ruler by a creature of his own; there was the decision to impose direct taxation; the decision to keep out of the North the influence of missionaries, lawyers, traders, and civil administrators from other territories; the decision not to establish a capital in a commercial centre; there was a whole series of decisions to avoid contact and co-operation with the South, and to concentrate all power in one pair of hands. All this was not so much civil administrative behaviour as the kind of military behaviour in civil situations to which the term 'militarism' can fairly be applied.

The decisions made by the other early administrators, more mindful of their professional business, were hardly of the same kind. MacGregor's tact, wisdom, good works, and more genuine indirect rule, Moor's energetic and systematic 'elevation' of the people, Girouard's brisk railway-building, Egerton's economic development, all these were the basic stuff of decent administration, working towards unity, prosperity, and modernity, when these were clearly desirable goals and ones within human reach. These were obliterated, partly by Lugard's own actions in the period 1912–18, partly by the destructive effects of the first World War itself. So too, the work of his successors, particularly Cameron and Clifford, devoted to repairing what could be repaired, and restoring peace, order, confidence, and good government, was good administration, but gravely prejudiced by what Lugard had done and by what he and his wife continued tirelessly to do from their carefully contrived eminence as internationally recognized authorities on the administration of dependent territories.

So, according to this thesis, Lugard was not so much an administrator as a militarist unfortunately chosen for tasks which required men and skills of a very different kind; the joker in the pack, if not the villain of the piece. Had his place in history been taken by one of the 'good rulers' available, British colonial administration in Nigeria would have gone more smoothly, on the basis of a more genuine indirect rule in the provinces, and more modern, more orthodox administration from the centre, nurturing communications, development, and the institutions and apparatus of the modern state, a process which might even have succeeded in the nation-building needed to keep together many disparate peoples in a viable new federation.

There is a sense in which a naïve interpretation in terms of one individual's personality is true enough, so far as it goes. But there are much deeper issues. In any bold enterprise of the kind which the British Government undertook in Nigeria, in 1900, mistakes in the selection of men to carry out the task were certain to occur. Lugard was the most serious of these mistakes; not only was the first mistake not fully or openly corrected, it was committed again, in 1912. There was enough, in both of his periods of rule, to have brought about—in another and different world—public scandal and inquiry on the scale of the trial of Warren Hastings, if there had been a public in Britain interested enough or 'imperialist' enough to have organized it. But Clifford's words come to mind. The British public was never 'shaken out of apathy', and colonial officials continued to find that few people in Britain 'cared a fig for them or the work they were doing'. Such interest as developed in the final years was an interest in getting rid of the white man's burden. With little understanding of how that burden had been carried in the past, or by what kind of men, wishful thinking about the bright prospect of its being borne onwards more happily without their help was easier. Doubt was taken as evidence of, at best, paternalism; at worst, of racism and reactionary imperialism.

It is now recognized that the Nigeria of the 1950s into which a system of federal representative government was introduced had not developed the social conditions in which institutions of this kind could succeed. Then, it was thought that the new institutions would themselves induce appropriate changes. So long as the new men remained under the tutelage of the old, and the tutors remained reticent in public about the difficulties and dangers of the situation, optimism remained, and Nigeria, not yet a nation, marched towards independence, not at a pace well suited to the slowly moving main body, but at a pace better suited to those most anxious to make an end of colonial dependence. Prominent among these, of course, were the Southern political leaders; but British political leaders and the leaders of practically every member country of the United Nations were pressing in the same direction.

At such a time little hearing could have been gained for homilies and warnings about the requisites and desiderata for institutions of federal representative government, although there is nothing novel about these. John Stuart Mill, surveying the wreckage of European experiments in parliamentary government a century ago, set them out clearly enough.[1]

For a 'nation' Mill prescribed 'common sympathies' uniting 'a portion of mankind' which made them 'co-operate with each other more willingly than with other people, desire to be under the same government, and desire that it should be government by themselves or a portion of themselves exclusively'. By this criterion, there was in 1960 no one Nigerian nation, but the possibility of one or of many. In mid 1968 there was one 'nation', the Ibo nation, struggling, under strong internal leadership, against a strongly hostile external environ-

[1] J. S. Mill, *Considerations on Representative Government*, chapter iv.

ment, to become a nation-state. The hostility looks too strong for either separation or peaceful reconciliation.

For free institutions, in a country made up of different nationalities, Mill saw little prospect:

> Free institutions are next to impossible in a country made up of different nationalities. Among a people without fellow-feeling, especially if they read and speak different languages, the united public opinion, necessary to the working of representative government, cannot exist. The influences which form opinions and decide political acts, are different in the different sections of the country. An altogether different set of leaders have the confidence of one part of the country and of another. The same books, newspapers, pamphlets, speeches, do not reach them. One section does not know what opinions, or what instigations are circulating in another. The same incidents, the same acts, the same system of government, affects them in different ways; and each fears more injury to itself from the other nationalities than from the common arbiter, the state.[1]

For a federation of 'nationalities' in the circumstances of this kind (very close to those of Nigeria in the 1950s when federation was being considered) Mill prescribed three conditions: first 'a certain amount of mutual sympathy among the populations'; second, an inability of each of the constituent parts to rely on its own unaided strength; and a third condition 'not less important than the two others':

> The essential is, that there should not be any one State so much more powerful than the rest as to be capable of vying in strength with many of them combined. If there be such a one, and only one, it will insist on being master of the joint deliberations: if there be two, they will be irresistible when they agree: and whenever they differ everything will be decided by a struggle for ascendancy between the rivals.[2]

The Nigeria of the 1950s could not have passed Mill's first test. Mutual sympathy between the regional peoples was not strong; in particular, antipathy to the Ibo-speaking peoples was strong in North and West. Nor could Nigeria have passed the third test. It was not a case of the North being so big that it could insist on being master of the joint deliberations prior to independence, but it was a case where the balance of electoral strength between the North and the rest was so poised, during the brief years of experiment with federal representative government, as to bring about just the kind of struggle for ascendancy between two rivals which Mill predicted. First, after the 1959 elections, while the leaders of North and East agreed on the

[1] Mill, op. cit., chapter xvi. [2] Mill, op. cit., chapter xvii.

sharing of power at the centre, they were irresistible; their chief item of agreement was on the destruction of the opposition government of the West, and on the dismembering of that region. Later, when the Eastern leaders realized that these developments had greatly strengthened the North, with its disciplined electorate, and when in consequence the leaders of North and East began seriously to differ, their struggle for ascendancy brought the whole system into discredit and finally into general contempt. The first military coup in January 1966 which swept aside the discredited system of representative government was soon identified as a new and more deadly kind of struggle between North and East, a struggle between Easterners seeking to establish unitary government and the North determined to resist Eastern dominance. Civil war between rival military factions, between the East and the rest, was thus a logical if not the inevitable outcome of mutual antipathies exacerbated by much bloodshed; first individual assassination, then civil massacre, then military war.

As to Mill's second condition for a federation, that no one of the constituent parts should be able to rely on its own unaided strength, there were some grounds for believing, in the years immediately before independence, that this requirement had been more or less fulfilled. Earlier, before Lagos was excised from the Western Region to become federal territory, the West might have decided to rely on its own strength. But it could not do so in 1960, or afterwards, when Lagos was in the hands of a federal Government composed of its regional rivals. Later, when the extent of the East's oil resources became known, and the strength of antipathy to Easterners was proved by massacre, the East could and did decide to secede and to rely on its own strength. The men in power in the East could hardly have done anything else. For North, and West, and hapless new Mid-West, such disentanglement remained impracticable.

For the good government of countries in such a plight Mill the great utilitarian could offer no perfect prescription. The 'ideally best polity' of representative government being inapplicable, the alternatives offering the best hopes seemed to him either (in 'a country not dominated by foreigners') the 'rare accident of a monarch of genius'; or (in 'the dependency of a civilized nation'), the choice of 'good rulers'—men selected on merit and trained up from youth to administer the country in the interests of the governed.[1] Lugard excepted (and perhaps Sir Graeme Thomson, who came to colonial administra-

[1] Mill, op. cit., chapter xviii.

tion in middle life after a meritorious Whitehall administrative career), Nigeria as a dependency was governed by men of this kind.[1] The phase of dependency is over; it ended, before there was a sound basis either for representative government or for federation, on the reckoning that alien official rule was necessarily an evil, and that any more respectable and democratic system which could be negotiated with elected representatives of Nigeria's peoples would be better. This was faulty reasoning; alien official rule was not necessarily good or evil; much depended, as in any other system, on the men chosen as rulers.

With the ending of British authority before the establishment of the conditions necessary for the survival of representative government, the hope of even reasonably good government depended, if Mill was right, on the 'happy accident' of the emergence of a leader of genius. And, as he wrote, it would be absurd to construct institutions 'for the mere purpose of taking advantage of such possibilities'.[2]

Institutions have to be constructed, though, if government is to continue, in countries where representative government does not work. Here Mill goes on to contemplate rule by a 'constitutionally unlimited, or at least a practically preponderant authority in the chief ruler of the dominant class' as 'the best prospect of improvement for a people thus composed'. In modern terms, this would mean authoritarian rule by the dominant member of a power élite. Even this prospect seems denied to the peoples of Nigeria and Biafra. The situation is hideously complicated by the wreckage of the federal system, with imperfect government being carried on not by any one élite, but by several élites, civil and military, traditional and modern, each claiming some allegiance, authority, and legitimacy, either from past custom or from present emergency. The clearest focus of authority visible in what was Nigeria, during the period of civil war in 1967 and 1968, was in the person of the Ibo war leader, Colonel Ojukwu, former administrative officer, then professional soldier, but Oxford graduate, and son of probably the wealthiest and most successful of Nigerian entrepreneurs; from such sources no doubt a man might derive sufficient 'preponderant authority' to administer Biafra acceptably, as a separate state, until some better polity could be devised. But to bring about a confederation between Biafra and the rest of

[1] Except that most of them received their professional formation in other countries—notably in Malaya.

[2] Mill, op. cit., chapter iv.

what was Nigeria, or even to bring about co-operation and willing subordination to one central authority in the rest of Nigeria—however loosely devised—would now require statesmanship and leadership of genius in several places at once—not one happy accident, but several, simultaneously. Is it not too much to expect?

As social engineering and nation-building, then, the sixty years of British colonial administration in Nigeria must be judged a failure. Colonial administration did produce, in countries like Nigeria which were not nations, a workable system of estate management in which oppression, corruption, and the curtailment of basic human rights were exceptional, and less prevalent than they were to become after independence. The chief indictment now levelled against colonial administrations is that they did not do enough to prepare their peoples for independence. To the labour of love which such a task represents most colonial administrators in Nigeria, throughout the sixty years of British rule, did in fact devote themselves, with a good deal of skill, courage, and altruism.

This may be incredible; it is, however, true. But if it is true, how did these efforts end in failure? Much of the answer can be found in the fact that during the sixty years of British colonial administration in Nigeria the world was one of mutually hostile national political systems, each professing its own version of nationalism and of democracy. Within each of these systems, including the domestic British system, a growing distaste for 'colonialism' was an inevitable and domestically eufunctional accompaniment of the current complex of ideas about national self-determination, liberty, democracy, and the dangers of uncontrolled bureaucracy. Colonial administrators shared these ideas, and some of the universal distaste for the colonial situation; it was thus possible for them to work as hard as they did to end it. But where the distaste for colonialism was not helpful was in depriving colonial administrations of most of the support, the funds, the encouragement, the understanding, and the time which were required for a first-class job—including time to make good if possible any work botched by bad workmanship.

On this subject too, John Stuart Mill had something to say, nearly a century ago: that there were few more important problems in the world than how to organize foreign rule, so as to make it a good rather than an evil, providing the subject peoples with the best attainable government, and conditions favourable to improvement; that how to do this was 'not well understood'; that government by foreigners was always difficult, and very imperfect, 'a work of much labour, requiring a very superior degree of capacity in the chief administrators, and a high average among the subordinates'. So the utmost that could be done was to give some of the best men 'a commission to look after it; to whom the opinion of their own country can neither be much of a guide in the performance of their duty, nor a competent judge of the mode in which it has been performed'. And even with the best men commissioned for a lifetime of learning and doing the work, 'Real good work is not compatible with the conditions of the case. There is but a choice of imperfections'.[1]

Mill's observations on nineteenth-century Europe and India are not irrelevant to twentieth-century Africa. In Nigeria, any conceivable form of institutionalized government must involve government, by some Nigerians, of other Nigerians alien to them. The best that can be hoped is that, since there must be rule by some kind of élite alien to some of the ruled, for some time to come (if there is to be recognizable government at all), it will include activities worthy of the names of 'public service' and of 'administration', involving sensible choices, made in the public interest, between unsatisfactory alternatives.

In several Nigerian languages, there is a proverb, to the effect that in Nigeria nothing good ever turns out as good as men hope, and nothing bad turns out as ill as men fear. Whether or not this could be expressed as a general law, it has certainly been so. It has something to do with the variety of peoples, and with the relative absence, in the past, of great natural disasters, of great pressure of population on natural resources, of great wealth and of great poverty. It was certainly so with the high hopes of the early British administrators, and with the fears of those about to be administered. It was so with the hopes pinned to independence, to federation, to parliaments, to political parties, to economic planning, to laws and constitutions. It was so with the best hopes and the worst fears following the overthrow of civil government in 1966. It was so with the hopes of both sides embarking on civil war. It is not so with the worst fears of that war, which have not fallen short of fulfilment in horror.

Now much but not all is to do again, without clear authority anywhere, without any confident tutelage; both the establishment of authority, as in 1900, and the further development of the estate. With the pressures of growing population and of urbanization the restoration of order and economic development are more urgent and

[1] Mill, op. cit., chapter xviii.

imperative than ever before. If the central puzzle, the finding of a minimum of acceptable authority, were once solved, the Nigerian educated élite of civil, public services would have a chance to prove themselves, not as rightful heirs to the estate, but as its new administrators. Even if military leadership is for the time being the only acceptable authority to be found, it is not militarism which is required, but civil administrative skills, ingenuity, compassion for the governed, and honesty.

These can be found in plenty, and nurtured, in all societies, given even brief consensus. Even in the imperfect colonial past they prevailed, on the whole. Until a more ideal polity becomes possible—and of course beyond that point as well—there is nothing better to be had, anywhere, for the relief of man's estate, than good administrators and good administration. Rejection of this fact can take many atavistic forms; a provisional but customary working acceptance of it, on the other hand, with a few grains of scepticism and no loss of vigilance, is in itself the only authority or force needed for reasonably good and improving government.

# Bibliographical Notes

1. *Primary Sources*

During the years 1962–5 when access to archives in the United Kingdom and in Nigeria was possible for the author, the fifty-year rule was still in force. It was thus only for the period up to 1915 that the Public Record Office and the Nigerian National Archives could provide much of the material needed to supplement knowledge derived from other sources; these 'other' sources included the author's own service as an administrative officer in Nigeria between 1947 and 1962, leaving the background of the period between the World Wars to be filled, as far as possible, from published sources mainly, but partly from the 'oral traditions' of the service. Of the Colonial Office records studied, the following were the most useful for this study:

C.O.147: vols. 130–79, C.O.149—Lagos
C.O.520: vols. 1, 2, 3, 6, 25, 29, 30, 37—Southern Nigeria
C.O.446: vols. 3, 7, 15, 24, 25, 30, 31, 32, 38, 40, 52, 53—Northern Nigeria
C.O.583: vols. 1, 3, 4, 5, 10, 12, 22—Nigeria

The H.M.S.O. *Guide to the contents of the Public Record Office*, vol. ii (London, 1963) is useful.

Of the documents available in the Nigerian National Archives, the chief value for this study of what had been preserved and recovered (despite the ravages of time, climate, insects, and administrative poverty and change) was the material dealing with departmental and provincial business, and relations between the various levels of government. For the larger questions of policy which required reference to London, even the most important of the Nigerian sources are unfortunately so incomplete as to defeat efforts to bridge gaps by interpolation. In the field of internal business too—a large one—there are big gaps in the 'memory-bank' which can never be satisfactorily filled; nevertheless, Group I of the papers at the National Archives at Ibadan contains material of great interest, of which, as Professor Anene mentions in the bibliography to his *Southern Nigeria in transition 1895–1906* (Cambridge, 1966), the C.S.O. and Calprof series are the most useful, as sources supplementary to the Public Record Office archives.

2. *Published Official Sources*

The most useful, on the whole, are the Governors' and High Commissioners' annual reports, the departmental, provincial, and divisional annual reports, the *Blue Books*, the *Gazettes*, *Staff Lists*, *Civil Lists*, the annual *Estimates* and the *Memoranda* on the estimates, the *Nigeria Handbooks*, and the *Colonial Office Lists*. For the years after 1945, the rapidly increasing use of commissions and committees of inquiry as problem-solving instruments has left a useful legacy of valuable material. Here the chief difficulty is to find reasonably complete holdings of the materials. The best guides to official publications known to the author are:

CONOVER, HELEN J., *Nigerian official publications, 1869–1959: a guide* (Library of Congress, Washington, 1959).

COLONIAL OFFICE, *Monthly list of official publications* (London, 1948–60).

UNIVERSITY OF IBADAN, *Nigerian publications* (Ibadan, annually from 1950).

HEWITT, A. R. *Guide to resources for Commonwealth studies in London, Oxford and Cambridge* (Athlone Press, University of London, 1957).

### 3. *Other Published Sources*

#### A. BOOKS

Difficulties of access to primary sources make the yield from other sources more crucial. Here, too, there are difficulties, with copies of out-of-print books hard to find—a gap being filled to some extent by the reprint series published by Frank Cass, London, in recent years.

Books directly relevant to a study of twentieth-century Nigerian officialdom can be roughly divided into three classes. Writings by officials and former officials possessed by what Temple called *furor scribendi* form the first category, inevitably suspect (as this book itself must be) for partiality and for the amateur's approach to history and to political and social analysis. Writings by non-academic, non-official observers, from the outside looking in (or in some cases, not looking at all), form a second, rather thin and sparse category. The third category is formed by academic works, by Nigerians and others, in recently growing numbers.

Predictably, the author has found the first category, on the whole, more directly valuable as material. In none of the three categories is it easy to distinguish fact from fiction, truth from error; there is pure fiction in all three, as well as pure fact, with a wide range of indeterminate mixtures in between. It is often safer to rely on the accounts of the 'insiders' for insights into what administrators were trying to do, and on the writings of the others for an understanding of the background of attitudes against which (in more senses than one) their work was done.

The reliance on officials' writings arises partly from necessity, partly from deliberate choice, in the belief that the apparently barren wastes of officialese and of cryptic and reticent personal commentary and reminiscence by officials are potentially fertile ground; and that they can be made to yield a richer harvest than the relatively few and often sour acres of commentary from the outside—important though these are as evidence of the external environment of the administrators.

Of the first category—books by officials and former officials, of one kind or another, on matters within their experience—the following seem indispensable for an understanding of what the administrators of Nigeria were trying to do. Included are books by men with official backgrounds far from Nigeria—Colonial Office civil servants, men with official experience in India and in other colonial territories; and books by officers of the armed services. There is no uniformity about these writings, or the men who wrote them. They range from the complacent and the conformist to the most trenchantly critical. Indeed, it is in books by former administrators (Woolf, Cary, Barnes) that the most vigorous criticism of British colonial administration can be found.

ADAMU (E. C. ADAMS), *Lyra Nigeriae* (1911). Ironic verse, of interest.

AKPAN, N. U., *Epitaph to indirect rule* (1956). By the Nigerian administrator who later became head of the Eastern Region public service.

BARNES, LEONARD, *Empire or democracy?* (1939). Trenchant criticism by a Colonial Office rebel.

BELL, SIR HESKETH, *Glimpses of a Governor's life* (1946).

BERTRAM, SIR ANTON, *The colonial service* (Cambridge, 1930). By a former Chief Justice of Ceylon—covers wider ground than the title might suggest, and is excellent on the constitutional basis and the machinery of colonial administration, and on the Nigerian court system.

BURDON, J. A., *Historical notes on certain Emirates and tribes* (1909).

BURNS, A. C., *History of Nigeria* (1st ed. 1929); *Colonial civil servant* (1949).

CAMERON, SIR DONALD, *My Tanganyika service and Some Nigeria* (1939). Indispensable, but, like the title, cryptic; Cameron chose not to write about his earlier service in Nigeria.

CARY, JOYCE, *Mister Johnson* (1939). Much of Joyce Cary's fiction is intensely factual on Nigerian conditions. This is the classic work on the Southern 'stranger' civil servant in the North. The best guide is MAHOOD, MOLLY M., *Joyce Cary's Africa* (1964).

COHEN, SIR ANDREW, *British policy in changing Africa* (1959). Clear, but reticent, by a man who was in turn Colonial Office civil servant, Colonial Governor, diplomat at the United Nations, and Permanent Secretary to a Whitehall ministry.

CROCKER, W. R., *Nigeria: a critique of British colonial administration* (1936); *On governing colonies* (1947).

CROZIER, F. P., *Five years hard* (1932).

DENNETT, R. E., *At the back of the black man's mind* (1906); *Nigerian studies* (1910).

DOUGLAS, A. C., *Niger memories* (1927).

ELGEE, C. H., *Evolution of Ibadan* (Lagos, 1914).

FALCONER, J. D., *Geology and geography of Northern Nigeria* (1911).

FIDDES, SIR GEORGE, *The Dominions and Colonial Offices* (1926).

FOWLER, W., *Harama* (1963). A novel by a former (Western Region) Resident which captures the atmosphere of change from administocracy to ministerial rule.

FURSE, SIR RALPH, *Aucuparius* (1962).

GEARY, SIR W. N. M., *Nigeria under British rule* (1927). (Although 'unofficial' in Nigeria, Geary had served as Attorney-General, Sierra Leone.)

GUGGISBERG, F. F., *Handbook of the Southern Nigeria Survey* (Edinburgh, 1911). By the officer later Governor of the Gold Coast—see also pp. 46–54 in WRAITH, R., E., *Guggisberg* (1957): fell foul of Lugard.

HAIG, E. F. G., *Nigerian sketches* (1931). By 'Alphabetical' Haig, administrator and founder of the Co-operative Department.

HAILEY, LORD, *An African survey* (1938, revised 1956); *Native administration in the British African territories* (1950–3). (Not an African 'official', Hailey wrote from a wealth of official experience in India; the two editions of *An African survey* are of very great importance, and of particular value if comparison of Nigeria with other territories is undertaken.)

HALL, H. C., *Barrack and bush in Northern Nigeria* (1931). 'Johnny' Hall's plain tale of an administrative officer's life; excellent as an unvarnished account.

HARRIS, P. J., *Local government in Southern Nigeria* (Cambridge, 1957).

HASTINGS, A. C. G., *Nigerian days* (1925). Very readable; Northern administrator's reminiscences.

HIVES, F., *Juju and justice in Nigeria* (1933); *Momo and I* (1934). An Australian administrative officer's reminiscences of early Southern Nigeria.

JEFFRIES, SIR CHARLES, *The colonial empire and its civil service* (Cambridge, 1938); *The Colonial Office* (1956).

JOHNSTON, SIR HARRY H., *The colonization of Africa* (1899); *The story of my life* (1923).

JONES, G. I., *The trading states of the Oil Rivers* (1963).

KIRK-GREENE, A. H. M., *The principles of native administration in Nigeria: selected documents, 1900–1947* (1965). By a former Northern administrator, now an academic; contains important documents, and very useful explanatory and bibliographical notes.

KISCH, M. S., *Letters and sketches from Northern Nigeria* (1910). Girouard's time in the North, with an introduction by Girouard.

'LANGA-LANGA', *Up against it in Nigeria* (1922). Pseudonym of Northern administrative officer (Hermon-Hodge) and, like Hall, Hastings, and Crozier, a corrective to more inflated accounts of administrative achievement.

LEONARD, A. G., *The lower Niger and its tribes* (1906).

LUCAS, C. P., *Historical geography of West Africa* (1913); *The partition and colonization of Africa* (1922).

LUGARD, F. D., *The dual mandate in British tropical Africa* (Edinburgh, 1922).

MEEK, C. K., *The Northern tribes of Nigeria* (1925); *Tribal studies in Northern Nigeria* (1931); *Law and authority in a Nigerian tribe* (1937).

MIGEOD, F. W. H., *Through Nigeria to Lake Chad* (1924). A former Gold Coast administrator: useful 'impressions'.

MOCKLER-FERRYMAN, A. F., *Up the Niger* (1892); *British Nigeria* (1902).

MUFFETT, D. J., *Concerning brave captains* (1964). Valuable for an understanding of Lugard. A former Northern Nigeria administrative officer argues that Lugard's measures of armed force against the Fulani Emirates were not in fact provoked by 'defiance' on the Emirs' part: the thesis is a persuasive one, and carries conviction.

OKIGBO, PIUS, *Nigerian national accounts, 1950–57* (Enugu, 1962).

ORR, C. W. J., *The making of Northern Nigeria* (1911).

PARKINSON, SIR COSMO, *The Colonial Office from within* (1947).

PEDRAZA, HOWARD J., *Borrioboola—Gha; the story of Lokoja, the first British settlement in Nigeria* (1960). Very readable short account, by a former (Northern) administrative officer, of the town that was Baikie's, Goldie's, and Lugard's headquarters.

SHIRLEY, W. R., *History of the Nigerian police* (Lagos, 1950).

TALBOT, P. A., *Life in Southern Nigeria* (1923); *The peoples of Southern Nigeria* (1926); *In the shadow of the bush* (1912).

TEMPLE, C. L., *Native races and their rulers* (Capetown, 1918). A most important but cryptic book. New edition by Cass (London, 1968). See also KIRK-GREENE, A. H. M., *The principles of native administration in Nigeria* (1965) for extracts and discussion.

THOMAS, N. W., *Anthropological report on the Edo-speaking peoples of Nigeria* (1910); *Anthropological report on the Ibo-speaking peoples of Nigeria* (1913–14).

WOOLF, LEONARD, *Imperialism and civilization* (1928); *Economic imperialism* (1921); *Empire and commerce in Africa* (1920); *Sowing* (1960); *Growing* (1961). An articulate former colonial administrator (Ceylon) who became one of the severest critics of British imperialism, and of Lugard.

In the second category (non-official, non-academic) there are not many books of significance, but some are important; trading, missionary, and humanitarian interests provided some incisive public commentary on administration until the age of party politics began, but little during the last years; the politicians' own contributions are more useful for an understanding of the political environment than for any real insight into administrative machinery and administrators.

AWOLOWO, O., *Path to Nigerian freedom* (1947): Shrewd but not very well-informed criticism of British administrators. *Awo* (Cambridge, 1960): autobiographical.

AZIKIWE, NNAMDI, *Zik* (Cambridge, 1961). Speeches.

BASDEN, G. T., *Among the Ibos of Nigeria* (1922); *Niger Ibos* (1938).

BELLO, SIR AHMADU, *My life* (Cambridge, 1962).

CALVERT, A. F., *Nigeria and its tin fields* (1910). One of the first 'industrial' appreciations.

DELANO, ISAAC, *The soul of Nigeria* (1937). Interesting as an earlier expression of the strains of change as felt by an educated Nigerian of the time.

EGHAREVBA, J. U., *A short history of Benin* (Lagos, 1936).

HUXLEY, ELSPETH, *The walled city* (1948): a strangely percipient novel based on the colonial service in the twenties. *Four guineas* (1954).

JOHNSON, SAMUEL, *History of the Yorubas* (1921).

KINGSLEY, MARY, *West African studies* (1899); *The story of West Africa* (1899); *Travels in West Africa* (1900). See, in particular, GWYNN, S., *Life of Mary Kingsley* (1933), and HOWARD, C., *Mary Kingsley* (1957), also the new introduction by J. E. FLINT to the Cass 1964 edition of *West African studies*.

LETHBRIDGE, ALAN, *West Africa the elusive* (1921). One of the last books in the tradition of commercially influenced criticism of bureaucracy in West Africa.

LUGARD, FLORA, LADY, *A tropical dependency* (1905). Journalist, wife of an official. (New edition by Cass, 1964.)

MILLER, W. R., *Reflections of a pioneer* (1936); *Yesterday, today and tomorrow in Northern Nigeria* (1938); *Have we failed in Nigeria?* (1947); *Success in Nigeria?* (1948), Indispensable for an understanding of Northern Nigerian administration; by a distinguished missionary.

MOREL, E. D., *Affairs of West Africa* (1902); *Nigeria: its peoples and problems* (1912). By the Radical publicist who from being the spokesman, after Mary Kingsley, of commercial humanitarian interests, moved towards socialism and pacifism, was imprisoned during the First World War, became am M.P. after the war, and almost became the first Labour Colonial Secretary. See COCKS, F. S., *E. D. Morel, the man and his work* (1920) and ADAMS, W. S., *Edwardian portraits* (1957).

MURRAY, A. V., *The school in the bush* (1929). Good on education and indirect rule.

ROBINSON, C. H., *Hausaland* (1896); *Nigeria, our latest protectorate* (1900). Vigorous books by Canon Robinson, a 'muscular Christian'.

TEMPLE, MRS. C. L., *Notes on the tribes, provinces, Emirates and states of the Northern provinces of Nigeria* (Lagos, 1922). By the wife of an official (Charles Temple).

THORPE, ELLEN, *Ladder of bones* (1956). By the wife of an official; a short book of great interest.

As to the third category—academic books—this author has to confess, with diffidence, a sense of disappointment with most of the books which have appeared in recent years, particularly in the field of politics and administration in Nigeria. There has been a marked tendency not to question, soon enough, assumptions and preconceptions about colonial rule in general, about bureaucracy, about political systems, parties, the press, the various Nigerian élites, and so on; and, in particular, to regard the machinery of central, alien rule in Nigeria as a transient phenomenon of no great complexity or intrinsic interest. This said, the author hastens to give a list of the purely academic books which seem to him to have been the most helpful contribution towards an understanding of administration in Nigeria:

ANENE, J. C., *Southern Nigeria in transition 1885–1906* (Cambridge, 1966).

BLITZ, L. F., ed., *The politics and administration of Nigerian government* (1965). Good chapters on constitutional development, political parties, the courts, and the police and penal system in 1964.

BRETTON, H. L., *Power and stability in Nigeria* (1962).

BUCHANAN, K. M., and PUGH, J. C., *Land and people in Nigeria* (1955).

BUELL, R., *The native problem in Africa* (1928).

CHURCH, R. J. HARRISON, *West Africa: a study of the environment and man's use of it* (Cambridge, 1955).

COLE, R. TAYLOR and TILMAN, R. O., *The Nigerian political scene* (1962).

COLEMAN, J. S., *Nigeria: background to nationalism* (1958). Authoritative, and very useful indeed; but falls into error about the motives, methods, manners, and standards of British administration by over-reliance on hostile political and press comment.

COOK, A. N., *British enterprise in Nigeria* (1943). The first full American study, written under considerable difficulties, in war-time, without visiting Nigeria, but after interviews with many of the older administrators—including Lugard, 'who was most helpful'. Does not seriously question the Lugard version, but otherwise invaluable, with an excellent bibliography. New edition, Frank Cass, 1964.

FAGE, J. D., *An introduction to the history of West Africa* (Cambridge, 1955).

FLINT, J. E., *Sir George Goldie and the making of Nigeria* (1960).

HEUSSLER, R., *Yesterday's rulers* (1963).

LLOYD, P. C., *The new élites of tropical Africa* (1966); *Africa in social change* (1967). Particularly good on Nigeria.

MACKENZIE, W. J. M., and ROBINSON, K., *Five elections in Africa* (1960).

MACKINTOSH, J. P., *Nigerian government and politics* (1966).

McPhee, Alan, *The economic revolution in West Africa* (1926).
Nadel, S. F., *A black Byzantium* (1942).
Oliver, R., and Fage, J. D., *A short history of Africa* (1962).
Perham, M., ed., *The economics of a tropical dependency*, 2 vols. (1946, 1948).
Prest, A. R., and Stewart, I. G., *The national income of Nigeria* (1953).
Smith, M. G., *Government in Zazzau* (1960).

B. SERIALS

It is only fitting that the best single non-official source of published information about administration in West Africa should be the journal of the society founded in 1901 in memory of Mary Kingsley. This is the journal of the African Society, later Royal African Society, published from 1901 to 1946 as the *Journal*, since 1946 as *African Affairs*. For events, developments, literature, and personalities, particularly before the First World War, the contents of the *Journal* seem to give an excellent balance of official and non-official, European and African, Lancashire and London points of view, with informed articles and reviews of literature published throughout the period. Any student of the West Africa of the period (there is a bias towards West Africa) would save himself much waste of time and effort if he took this *Journal* as a principal guide. Later, to some extent, the *Journal* became more an 'official' and a 'London' affair, and lost its earlier range and balance. Its place was taken, increasingly, by the weekly *West Africa* (1917 +). This, particularly in recent years, under the editorship of Mr. David Williams, is an indispensable record of events and review of literature.

Unfortunately, there is little to be said about the press in general—British, Nigerian, or other—as a consistent and reliable source of information.

The learned journals of the period from 1900, having their special fields of interest, do not throw much light on current problems of Nigerian government. Even the *Journal of African Administration* (London, H.M.S.O., 1949 +) is not much concerned with issues of central government.

Of Nigerian publications, *Nigeria*, which in 1960 became *Nigeria Magazine* (1934 +), *The Nigerian Field* (1931 +), *The Nigerian Journal* (the organ of the senior civil servants' association), and *The Quarterly Review* of the Department of Labour (from 1959 Ministry of Labour and Welfare) contain articles of interest—particularly the special independence issue of *Nigeria Magazine* (October 1960).

Guidance to other publications can be found in:

Conover, Helen J., *Serials for African studies* (Washington, 1961); *Africa south of the Sahara: a selected, annotated list of writings* (Washington, 1963).

HARRIS, JOHN, *Books about Nigeria* (Ibadan, 1962).
JONES, RUTH, *Africa bibliography series: West Africa* (International African Institute, 1958).
LEWIN, EVANS, *Subject catalogue of the library of the Royal Empire Society*, vol. i (London, 1930).
RYDINGS, H. A., *The bibliographies of West Africa* (Ibadan University Press, 1961).
There is also the excellent fifteen-volume *Catalogue of the Colonial Office library* (G. K. Hall & Co., Boston, 1964).

4. *Dame Margery Perham's Writings on Nigeria*

For the author, as for many of his former colleagues in Nigeria, and for many Nigerians, Margery Perham's books, articles, lectures, forewords, and broadcasts have always been in a category of their own for careful and authoritative scholarship—in particular the two-volume biography of Lugard. If the author has dared to differ with her fundamentally in his judgement of Lugard, without himself undertaking the labour of research into the Lugard papers, it is only because of the thoroughness and meticulous care with which she has treated Lugard's work. Indeed, the author's case, in this book, is that the work on Lugard's achievements has been so well done, compared with the work done on other men, that some loss of balance both in the literature on Nigeria and in the actual outcome of British administration in Nigeria was bound to occur. In the circumstances, it seemed to the author both more fair and more important to base an examination of Lugard's public life and public acts on publications and on public records rather than on an examination of his private papers. In this, Dame Margery Perham's works, particularly her *Native administration in Nigeria* (1937) and *Lugard*, vols. i and ii (1956 and 1960), have been indispensable.

# Index